Constraint on Trial

Gerrit Voogt

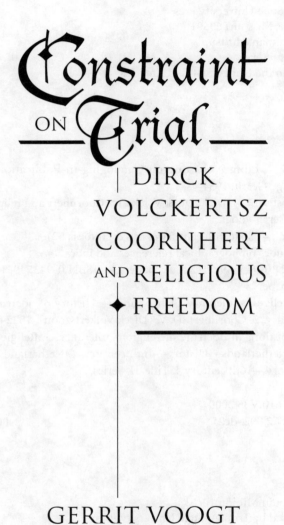

Constraint on Trial

DIRCK VOLCKERTSZ COORNHERT AND RELIGIOUS FREEDOM

GERRIT VOOGT

SIXTEENTH CENTURY ESSAYS & STUDIES
VOLUME LII

Library of Congress Cataloging-in-Publication Data
Voogt, Gerrit, 1954–
Constraint on trial : Dirck Volckertsz Coornhert and religious freedom /
    Gerrit Voogt.
    p. cm. – (Sixteenth century essays & studies ; 52)
Includes bibliographical references and index.
ISBN 0-943549-71-X (alk. paper) — ISBN 0-943549-84-1 (pbk. : alk.
    paper)
1. Religious tolerance—Christianity—History of doctrines—16th cen-
    tury. 2. Coornhert, D. V. (Dirck Volkertszoon), 1522–1590—Contri-
    butions in doctrine of religious tolerance. 3. Religious tolerance—
    Netherlands—History—16th century. 4. Netherlands—Church his-
    tory—16th century. I. Title. II. Series.

BR1610.V86 2000
261.7'2'092–dc21   00-036454

Text is set in Minion 10/12
Composed by Truman State University Press
Cover Art and Title Page by Teresa Wheeler

Contents

Portrait of Dirck Volckertsz Coornhert, Hendrick Goltzius, 1592 (Prentenkabinet, University of Leiden).

A Sixteenth-Century
Defense of Toleration

D IRCK VOLKERTSZ COORNHERT (1522–90) was a Dutch notary, artist, poet, playwright, translator, and controversialist who defended the freedom of conscience and toleration. This study examines Coornhert's contribution to the sixteenth-century debate on toleration through an exploration of his words and deeds.

The first two chapters of this biography discuss Coornhert's life in public service and exile, a period which ended in 1577, when he returned to Haarlem. By that time, Coornhert was well into his fifties and no longer served in an official capacity, but spent his time pursuing his literary and intellectual work and, above all, his polemics and disputations, which he regarded as an integral part of his struggle for religious freedom. I regard this period(1577–90) as the time when Coornhert truly came into his own. Since this is also when he produced some of his finest works on toleration, I chose to interrupt the chronological narrative of his life here, and set forth, in the following five chapters, an examination of the position taken by Coornhert on the issue of toleration. The final chapter picks up the remaining threads of Coornhert's life in relation to toleration, through the final dénouement of his clash with Justus Lipsius.

For convenience, the appendix provides a survey of the main events in Coornhert's life. Readers who want to assess Coornhert's essential contribution to the debate on toleration in the sixteenth century without the distractions of disputes and controversies in which his life abounded, will do well to go straight to chapters 5, 6, and 7.

.   .   .

Introduction

Next it is helpful to have an understanding of the concepts and terms used in this study. The verb "to tolerate" was used in the sixteenth century in the sense of "to endure" or of religious concessions made by the stronger to the weaker. It was already used in this way during the Middle Ages by Thomas Aquinas.[1]

When the authorities of the province of Holland decided to put an end to a debate between Coornhert and some Delft ministers (February 1578), they explained their action by stating that they "could not tolerate (from the verb *tolereren*) such public disputations without prior consent."[2] This use of the Latin-derived verb "to tolerate" is exceptional in sixteenth-century Dutch and belongs in the realm of bureaucratic jargon.

The noun "toleration" (*verdraagzaamheid*) rarely was used—it does not occur in Coornhert's writings. Instead, words such as "love" and "forbearance" are found.[3] More common is the usage of the verb "to suffer" (*lijden*), as in the exclamation by Gamaliel in the *Synod on the Freedom of Conscience:* "Oh, if only we could suffer one another."[4]

Toleration is an attitude evinced by an individual or a government or other institution. Based on such an attitude, religious freedom or freedom of conscience can be established, although we should realize that when we use the words "freedom of conscience," they are understood to imply the freedom to give expression to that conscience in word or deed. In a state that allows such freedom, religious pluralism will ensue.[5]

To be tolerant always seems to imply a hierarchical relationship and a condescending attitude: one "puts up" with something disagreeable.[6] But a more positive definition is possible. Johannes Kühn gave the brief description of toleration

[1]Thomas Aquinas, "Utrum ritus infidelium sint tolerandi?" in the *Summa*; see Joseph Lecler, *Toleration and the Reformation*, 2 vols, trans. T. L. Westow (New York: Association Press, 1960), 1:x.
[2]"*soedaanige disputatiën ... niet en behoeren getollereert te werden sonder voorgaende consent...*" *Bronnen tot de kennis van het leven en de werken van D. V. Coornhert*, ed. Bruno Becker. Rijks geschiedkundige publicaties, Kleine Serie, 25. (The Hague: Nijhoff, 1928), 70–71, no.106, 25 February 1578. For the context of this quotation, see chap. 8, p. 180.
[3]Hans R. Guggisberg, "The Defence of Religious Toleration and Religious Liberty in Early Modern Europe: Arguments, Pressures, and Some Consequences," *History of European Ideas* 4, no. 1 (1983): 36, notes that in Latin also, mostly terms such as *caritas* or *mansuetudo* are employed.
[4]Dirck Volkertz Coornhert, *Wercken*, 3 folio vols. (Amsterdam: Colom, 1633), vol. 2, fol. xiC: "*Och of wy malcanderen conden lijden.*"
[5]This sequence of toleration, religious liberty, and religious pluralism is based on Guggisberg, "The Defence," 36; on freedom of conscience as the freedom to express such freedom: see Henk Bonger, *De motivering van de godsdienstvrijheid bij Dirck Volckertszoon Coornhert* (Arnhem: Van Loghum Slaterus, 1954), xiv–xv.
[6]Cf. Jay Newman, *Foundations of Religious Tolerance* (Toronto: University of Toronto Press, 1982), 5.

as a positive attitude towards the "other," in which the "other" represents the deviant, alien, dissident, exotic—elements that, it is feared, threaten a core of beliefs that a person, group, or society holds. Besides "suffering" the presence of the deviant, toleration is, in Kühn's words, *"das Geltenlassen des Andern"* (allowing the "other" the space to be and express himself).[7] This does not necessarily imply that, in the case of religious toleration, one accepts or judges the content of the other person's beliefs. One simply accepts that the other person holds and manifests such beliefs, within certain bounds set by the demands of social interaction—the Golden Rule. Defined in such a manner, toleration is a *virtue* when it finds the right mean between the extremes of not accepting any deviance from a norm, and accepting all forms of deviance. This virtue then opens the way for religious freedom and the freedom of conscience.[8] Aristotle made the point against indiscriminate toleration by stating that "to endure the greatest indignities for no noble end or for a trifling end is the mark of an inferior person."[9]

It goes without saying that during the period with which we will be concerned in this study, the virtue of toleration was not practiced widely. Indeed, most people did not regard it as a virtue at all, and most states operated from the notion that the polity represented the seamless robe of Christ, which led to an automatic predisposition to regard religious deviance as political disobedience.

• • • •

In a historiographical survey, E. O. G. Haitsma Mulier makes the general remark that Coornhert's actual historical person and circumstances are less important than historical evaluation of and reflections on his place in sixteenth-century society.[10] Often such reflections do not obey Tacitus's call

[7]Johannes Kühn, "Das Geschichtsproblem der Toleranz," in *Autour de Michel Servet et de Sebastien Castellion,* ed. B. Becker (Haarlem: H. D. Tjeenk Willink, 1953), 3.

[8]Hans R. Guggisberg, "Allgemeine Einleitung," *Religiöse Toleranz: Dokumente zur Geschichte einer Forderung,* ed. Guggisberg. Neuzeit im Aufbau: Darstellung und Dokumentation, vol. 4 (Stuttgart-Bad Cannstatt, 1984), 9, 11.

[9]Newman, *Foundations,* 20 (from Aristotle's *Nichomachean Ethics*). Newman, "Tolerance Without Relativism" and passim, *Foundations,* makes the point that toleration does not imply relativism. See also Etienne Gilson, *Dogmatism and Tolerance,* address to students and faculty at Rutgers University (New Brunswick, N.J.: Rutgers University Press, 1952), 1–14.

[10]E. O. G. Haitsma Mulier, "Coornhert in de geschiedschrijving," in *Dirck Volckertszoon Coornhert: Dwars maar recht,* ed. H. Bonger et al. (Zutphen: De Walburg Pers, 1989), 155; full historiographical survey at 154–70. An earlier historiography can be found in Henk Bonger, *Leven en werk van D. V. Coornhert* (Amsterdam: G. A. van Oorschot, 1978), pt. 2, chap. 8, pp. 390–415.

for a reconstruction *sine ira et studio*, for Coornhert continues to stir up controversy long after his passing.

Specific consideration of Coornhert's activities and ideas in connection with freedom of conscience came relatively late. Today one sees an upsurge of interest in the topic of toleration, which coincides with growing deconfessionalization as well as with concern about the thought control exercised in certain twentieth-century totalitarian states.[11] In the early eighteenth century, men like Gottfried Arnold, Pierre Bayle, and later Wilhelm Dilthey, pointed out Coornhert's significance for the promotion of freedom of conscience, but their examination of the topic was brief or peripheral to their main concerns (such as placing him in the framework of the history of ideas).[12]

The first thorough investigation of Coornhert's position on toleration did not appear until after World War II, in the form of a thesis by Henk Bonger whose title and content reveal the influence of Johannes Kühn's important study, *Toleranz und Offenbarung* (1923).[13] After a general introduction about the notion of tolerance and its defenders in the sixteenth century, Bonger separates the different strands that can be detected in Coornhert's position. He distinguishes three main clusters of motives that support his idea of toleration: rationalist, spiritualist, and mystical.

In more recent years we have seen an increased awareness of the important place that Coornhert's polemics and debates take in the early history of the Dutch Republic. Gerhard Güldner contributed a well-researched and perspicacious analysis of the problem of toleration in the Netherlands of the late sixteenth century, which includes an excellent account of the confrontation

---

[11] See e.g. the wide-ranging, well-documented study of the progress of toleration during the Reformation by Joseph Lecler, *Toleration and the Reformation*, 2 vols.; Coornhert is discussed in 2: 5, 271–86.

[12] Gottfried Arnold, *Unpartheyische Kirchen- und Ketzerhistorie vom Anfang des Neuen Testaments bis auf das Jahr Christi 1688*, 2 vols. (1729; reprint, Hildesheim: Georg Olm Verlagsbuchhandlung, 1967), Coornhert in 2:60–66; Pierre Bayle, *Dictionnaire historique et critique*, Nouvelle Edition (1820–24, Geneva: Slatkine Reprints, 1969), 8:579–88 (the first time Coornhert was incorporated in the *Dictionnaire* was in the 2d ed., 1702); W. Dilthey, Weltanschauung und Analyse des Menschen seit Renaissance und Reformation, vol. 2 of Dilthey, Gesammelte Schriften, 5th ed. (Stuttgart: B. G. Teubner/ Göttingen: Vandenhoeck & Ruprecht, 1957), 95–100.

[13] Johannes Kühn, *Toleranz und Offenbarung: Eine Untersuchung der Motive und Motivformen der Toleranz im offenbarungsgläubigen Protestantismus: Zugleich ein Versuch zur neueren Religion- und Geistesgeschichte* (Leipzig: Meiner, 1923): Kühn only mentions Coornhert in passing; Bonger, *Motivering*, states specifically, in his preface, vii, that he aims to fill the gap left by Kühn, who stated in *Toleranz und Offenbarung*, 141 n. 3, that he had omitted a chapter on Coornhert because of "lack of space."

between Coornhert and Lipsius.[14] Martin van Gelderen, in his book on the political theories of the Dutch Revolt, also examines, in a chapter on "politics and religion," how the debates of Coornhert functioned in this context.[15]

In this study, I opt for frequent, and at times substantial, quotations from and paraphrases of Coornhert's writings as well as those of some of his opponents.[16] This serves two purposes. First, it does not muffle the sixteenth-century voice. Secondly, it makes these primary sources available in English for the first time. This better understanding of Coornhert outside the confines of the restricted Dutch-speaking world helps shed light on the conditions in the early Dutch Republic and on the backgrounds of the Arminian-Gomarist religious disputes that took place in the Republic in the early 1600s. The knowledge of Coornhert and his writings outside the Netherlands has been limited, mainly because Coornhert was a promoter of the vernacular and a defender of a pure Dutch language, and therefore consistently wrote in Dutch.

[14]Gerhard Güldner, *Das Toleranz-Problem in den Niederlanden im Ausgang des 16. Jahrhunderts,* Historische Studien, 403 (Lübeck and Hamburg: Matthiesen, 1968), chap. 4: "Coornhert und Lipsius," 65–158; appendix 6.1: "Coornhert und Castellio,"159–69.

[15]Martin van Gelderen, *The Political Thought of the Dutch Revolt 1555–1590,* Ideas in Context (Cambridge: Cambridge University Press, 1992), chap. 6.4: "The debates of Dirck Volckertsz Coornhert," 243–56. We can also deduce this greater general awareness of Coornhert's contributions from the fact that there are numerous passages on Coornhert in the recent, much acclaimed, general history of the Netherlands by Jonathan I. Israel, *The Dutch Republic: Its Rise, Greatness, and Fall 1477–1806,* Oxford History of Early Modern Europe (Oxford: Clarendon Press, 1995): esp. 371–73, 500–3, 566–68.

[16]Unless otherwise indicated, all quotations are my own translations.

1

BEFORE ENTERING
PUBLIC SERVICE

1522–1561

THE FIRST FIFTY-FIVE YEARS of Dirck Volkertsz Coornhert's life were set against the background of the momentous and tumultuous developments taking place in the Low Countries in the early to mid-1500s. These were the formative years of Coornhert's life, during his career as a self-made humanist in Haarlem, in the province of Holland.[1] Years later, he wrote his *Weltanschauung*, which was anchored in this rich life experience of literary, intellectual, and artistic endeavors, as well as service to a town government and to the cause of the revolt against Spain.

POLITICO-CULTURAL DEVELOPMENTS IN THE NETHERLANDS

The area of the Low Countries, in the northwest of Europe, eventually produced two modern sovereign states, the kingdoms of Belgium and the Netherlands. This outcome is mostly a result of the vicissitudes of geography and

---

[1]Holland is the name for the northwestern part of the Low Countries, located north of the big rivers (Maas, Waal, and Rhine) and bordering the North Sea. Because of Holland's prosperity and dominance within the later Dutch Republic, foreigners tended to use "Holland" as a *pars pro toto* for the entire republic (much like "England" is often used when the United Kingdom is intended).

politics, which then hardened into a distinct cultural and national awareness and self-image.[2]

In medieval times the Low Countries fell mostly under the Holy Roman Empire, but ties to the empire were loose and of limited significance. The lords of the feudal entities within the Low Countries—such as *Flanders, Brabant, Holland, Friesland,* and *Gelre*—acted independently despite their status as vassals. The economic preponderance within this region of Flanders and Brabant during the High Middle Ages was based chiefly on their textile industry.[3] To the north, Holland's prosperity increased through the development of trade and fishing.

The *Burgundian-Habsburg* period saw a gradual ending of the fragmented existence of the Netherlands. Charles the Bold dreamed of resurrecting an independent middle kingdom between France and Germany. His premature attempts to centralize his holdings, which stretched from the duchy of Burgundy in the south, through Lorraine, Luxembourg, Flanders, and Brabant to Holland in the north, provoked resistance, and ended when he died at the battle of Nancy (1477).[4] After his death, his successor, Mary of Burgundy, undid a number of Charles's measures and restored some of the provincial privileges. Soon, however, through their fortunate marriage policy, the Habsburgs added the Netherlands to their possessions and continued the drive for centralization.

The Burgundian period merits further consideration. New institutions were created, such as the States General, intended to facilitate the taxation of the dukes' lands, and the *Grote Raad,* the supreme judicial body of the Netherlands, seated in Mechelen. As the Burgundian Kreits, the Netherlands were recognized as a separate entity, and protonational feelings developed, which were tied to the ruling dynasty. The Low Countries often were referred to as the *pays par deça* (*landen van herwaarts over*), and the name *Belgians*, harking back to a glorious past, was employed to indicate all their inhabitants. The dynasty also brought in a distinct French element that dominated the administration (and

---

[2]See Hugo de Schepper, *"Belgium Nostrum" 1500–1650: Over Integratie en Desintegratie van het Nederland* (Antwerp: De Orde van den Prince, 1987). This accidental nature of the eventual political division is also the chief theme of Pieter Geyl, *The Revolt of the Netherlands (1555–1609)* (New York: Barnes & Noble, 1958).

[3]By 1477 almost half the population of the Low Countries lived in Flanders and Brabant; see table in Israel, *Dutch Republic,* 15.

[4]H. P. H. Jansen, *Middeleeuwse geschiedenis der Nederlanden,* 4th ed. (Utrecht/Antwerp: Uitgeverij Het Spectrum, 1974), 226–27.

would continue to do so under the Habsburgs) and that exerted influence through the late flowering of chivalric culture at the Burgundian court.[5] Johan Huizinga sees in the establishment of Burgundian power the origin of the twin nations of Belgium and the Netherlands.

The Burgundians realized that the provinces of the Netherlands with a "German" character—above the linguistic divide that separates the "Flemish"- or "Dutch"-speaking Netherlands in the north from the French-speaking provinces in the south[6]—were their most prosperous holdings. Interprovincial contacts among the Germanic inhabitants of the Kreits led to a measure of cultural and historical unity.

From the sixteenth century on, and in the person of Charles V, the House of Habsburg held under its unified control the Holy Roman Empire, Bohemia, Hungary, Spain, Portugal, and the Netherlands. Thus, the Habsburgs dominated Europe and held extensive territories in the New World. The interests of the Netherlands often were sacrificed in favor of the Habsburgs' global interests. The Habsburg monarchs tried to rationalize and centralize their government of the Netherlands. They were represented in Brussels by a regent, and preferred university-trained jurists for the provincial administration.

The Habsburg drive for a modern centralized state ultimately would shatter in the Netherlands, due to the forces of particularism, combined with resistance to the government's ecclesiastical and antiheretical policies.

In the elective Holy Roman Empire, Charles V was hampered in his efforts to stifle heresy and finally had to concede the territorial *cuius regio, eius religio* principle to the princes in the Peace of Augsburg. In the Netherlands, where his hands were not so tied, he pursued a much tougher antiheresy policy. The government equated heresy with high treason. Therefore, the regular judicial procedures through local authorities did not apply, and this "implicit abrogation of their privileges" irked the towns.[7]

---

[5]See the famous cultural history of this epoch: J. Huizinga, *Herfsttij der Middeleeuwen: Studie over levens- en gedachtenvormen der veertiende en vijftiende eeuw in Frankrijk en de Nederlanden*, 13th ed. (Groningen: H. D. Tjeenk Willink, 1975). Translated as *The Waning of the Middle Ages: A Study of the Forms of Life, Thought, and Art in France and the Netherlands in the Fourteenth and Fifteenth Centuries*, trans. F. Hopman (Harmondsworth: Penguin, 1990).

[6]Today this linguistic divide (the so-called *taalgrens*) runs roughly through the middle of Belgium.

[7]James D. Tracy, *Holland under Habsburg Rule, 1506–1566: The Formation of a Body Politic* (Berkeley: University of California Press, 1990), 151.

The movement of religious renewal had made early inroads into the Netherlands with the *Devotio Moderna* and Erasmus's Christian humanism. The situation in the Netherlands was essentially different from that in England, Scandinavia, or Germany, since, because of repression, religious change could only come as a movement that worked from the bottom up instead of from the top down.[8]

In 1525 Jan de Bakker (also known as Joannes Pistorius) was burned in The Hague and became the first Protestant martyr in the northern Netherlands.[9] Around that time, Antwerp, the main capitalist and commercial hub of Europe, was also the main center and conduit for the spreading of Luther's influence. The authorities countered with the Netherlands Inquisition.[10] Repression aimed especially at paralyzing the budding heretical movements by targeting an intellectual elite. As a result, in these circles Nicodemism, or simulation, became rife.[11]

Anabaptism spread to the Netherlands with the arrival of Melchior Hoffman in Emden (1530).[12] It mostly attracted laymen of artisan and lower-class background and absorbed the Sacramentarian movement that had preceded it. The Anabaptist emphasis on the direct working of the Spirit on the individual bred contempt for established churches and their ceremonies, and a rejection of infant baptism. Membership in this sectarian type of church organization revolved around the practice of regenerative adult baptism. From the start, the movement had a strong chiliastic component, represented in Trijpmaker, Hoffman, and others. This culminated in attacks on Amsterdam and other places, and led to the well-known excesses in Münster, where violent efforts were made to establish the heavenly Jerusalem. These excesses of the few were visited on all Anabaptists, who through these years provided the vast majority of the victims of repression. As Henry Kamen states in his history of toleration, throughout the sixteenth century the attitude of authorities and individuals toward the Anabaptists was a litmus test: "The universal detestation in which

---

[8]Israel, *Dutch Republic*, 74.

[9]L. J. Rogier, *Eenheid en scheiding: Geschiedenis der Nederlanden 1477–1813*, 5th ed. (Utrecht/ Antwerp: Uitgeverij Het Spectrum, 1976), 53.

[10]See A. F. Mellink, "Prereformatie en vroege reformatie 1517–1568," in *Algemene Geschiedenis der Nederlanden* 6 (Bussum: Unieboek, 1980): 148.

[11]Israel, *Dutch Republic*, 83.

[12]Andrew Pettegree, *Emden and the Dutch Revolt: Exile and the Development of Reformed Protestantism* (Oxford: Clarendon Press, 1992), 12–13.

these sectarians, or *Schwärmer* (enthusiasts), were held in the sixteenth century make them the touchstone for any proponents of religious toleration."[13]

Menno Simons, the priest at Witmarsum (Friesland) who became an Anabaptist leader, abhorred the violent outbursts he witnessed, and from the onset advocated pacifism.[14] Mennonites rejected state control of the church, and would not swear oaths, nor involve themselves with the government, although they did accept its authority. A firm belief in the dichotomy between the secular world and the world of the spirit permeated the movement.[15] Within the Mennonite community, however, strict enforcement of church discipline was the norm.

Anabaptist church discipline impressed the Reformed, who may have been incited to a greater stress on consistorial discipline in their churches because of the Anabaptist example (expressed in the Anabaptist practice of the exclusionary ban against offenders in their midst). On the other hand, the fragmentation of the Anabaptist movement demonstrated, to the budding Reform, the importance of establishing and upholding within the Reformed church a measure of doctrinal uniformity.[16] The Reformed church organization in the Netherlands adopted a presbyterian church order.[17] In this order, the classes—gatherings of ministers and elders that had jurisdiction of the Reformed churches in a certain district—were crucial for the maintenance of church discipline.[18]

John Calvin paid close attention to developments in the southern Netherlands, which bordered on his province of origin, Picardy. In 1545 Martin Bucer's emissary in the Walloon Netherlands, Pierre Brully, became the first martyr of what would become Netherlandish Calvinism. Intense persecution led to the flight of many. In the exiled communities, the Reformed wing of religious dissidence began to take a distinct shape. Refugees went to England

---

[13]Henry Kamen, *The Rise of Toleration* (New York: McGraw-Hill, 1967), 62.

[14]See e.g. Cornelius Krahn, *Dutch Anabaptism: Origin, Spread, Life, and Thought* (Scottdale, Pa.: Herald Press, 1981), 152.

[15]Expressed, for example, in Balthasar Hubmaier's slogan, "die göttliche Wahrheit ist untödlich"; see Kamen, *Rise of Toleration*, 61.

[16]Alastair Duke, "The Ambivalent Face of Calvinism in the Netherlands, 1561–1618," in *International Calvinism: 1541–1715*, ed. Menna Prestwich (Oxford: Clarendon Press, 1985), 115–16. Cf. Mellink, "Prereformatie," 156. The first Dutch translation of the *Institutes* appeared in 1560: Mellink, "Prereformatie," 160.

[17]Duke, "Ambivalent Face," 122.

[18]A. Th. van Deursen, *Bavianen en Slijkgeuzen: Kerk en kerkvolk ten tijde van Maurits en Old-enbarnevelt* (Assen: Van Gorcum & Comp., 1974; repr., Franeker: Van Wijnen, 1991), 5, 7–8.

(during Edward's reign) or to Germany, where especially Emden (in East Friesland) played an important role as the cradle of the Dutch Reformed movement.[19] After the Treaty of Cateau-Cambrésis (1559) between France and Spain, there were increased contacts between the Dutch religious refugees and the French communities "under the cross." Guy de Bray's Reformed confession of faith (1561) was modeled after the French confession.[20]

Since the early 1540s, besides the Anabaptists, Calvin had confronted other radicals and free spirits as well. Thus, toward the end of his life, he was asked to respond to a Dutch heterodox tract translated into Latin for his convenience. The tract was written by Coornhert, and is a good example of the radical Spiritualist tendencies within the Reformation. In his book, *War against the Idols*, Carlos Eire relates that of the Nicodemite tracts to which the Genevan Reformer responded, Coornhert's—which was itself a refutation of Calvin's anti-Nicodemite *Petit traicté*—is the only extant one. In all of Calvin's other anti-Nicodemite writings we have to derive the Nicodemite position from Calvin's responses.[21] Therefore Coornhert's tract—not thoroughly analyzed by Eire, who for Coornhert relies entirely on secondary sources—is of special interest and merits closer analysis.[22]

Rejection of the use of religious images in worship and of other forms of "idolatry" was the unwavering position of Calvin, who in this regard agreed with Bullinger and Zwingli against Luther and the Catholic theologian John Eck.[23] To Calvin, purity of worship was essential, and with regard to Catholics he asserted that "the seriousness of their corruption … is evident in their

---

[19]See Pettegree, *Emden and the Dutch Revolt*; W. Nijenhuis, *Ecclesia Reformata: Studies on the Reformation*, vol. 2. Kerkhistorische Bijdragen, vol. 16 (Leiden: E.J. Brill, 1994), chap. 5: "The Synod of Emden 1571," 101–24.

[20]Mellink, "Prereformatie," 161.

[21]Carlos M. N. Eire, *War against the Idols: The Reformation of Worship from Erasmus to Calvin* (Cambridge: Cambridge University Press, 1986), 239; see also Eire's earlier articles: idem, "Calvin and Nicodemism: A Reappraisal," *Sixteenth Century Journal* 10, no. 1 (1979): 45–69; and idem, "Prelude to Sedition? Calvin's Attack on Nicodemism and Religious Compromise," *Archiv für Reformationsgeschichte* 76 (1985): 120–45.

[22]The most extensive, but flawed discussion of this topic in Olga Rinck-Wagner, *D. V. Coornhert 1522–1572 mit besonderer Berücksichtigung seiner politischen Tätigkeit*, ed. E. Ebering. *Historische Studien* 138 (Berlin: Matthiesen Verlag, 1919; repr., Vaduz: Kraus Reprint, 1965), 29–42; see also Henk Bonger, *Leven en werk van D. V. Coornhert* (Amsterdam: G.A. van Oorschot, 1978), 28.

[23]See David Steinmetz, *Calvin in Context* (New York: Oxford University Press, 1995), 58. For Calvin's categorical rejection of all forms of idolatry, see John Calvin, *Institutes of the Christian Religion*, 2 vols., ed. John T. McNeill, Library of Christian Classics, 20 and 21 (Philadelphia: Westminster Press, 1960), esp. vol. 1, bk. 1, chaps. 11 and 12.

failure to see that worship is the soul of the Christian life."[24] He firmly closed the door to those who might conclude that, since they knew that Catholic idolatry was false and meaningless, it was no grave matter if they participated in it while inwardly they kept their faith pure. With some hesitation,[25] Calvin labeled such simulation "Nicodemism," after the Pharisee Nicodemus who came to Jesus in secret, by night (John 3:1–2). In France as well as in the Habsburg Netherlands, accommodation to Catholic worship and concealment of one's religious sentiments were tempting ways out of the predicament posed by severe persecution. Calvin's rejection of simulation and compromise, based on a clearly and repeatedly stated theological position, helped maintain the purity of distinct Reformed communities "under the Cross."[26]

The *Petit Traicté* (to which Coornhert would respond) was one of several strong denouncements of Nicodemism written by Calvin.[27] In his rejection of the Nicodemites, Calvin often uses scatological language and pollution imagery, repeatedly referring to Catholic images and practices as *ordure*.[28] This comparison reflects Calvin's fear of mixture and contagion through contact with the ungodly: he warns that "the utmost zeal and caution must be employed, lest the impious with whom we come in contact should infect us by their vicious behavior, especially where there is danger of idolatry, towards which each of us is inclined."[29] The central objection against the use of certain physical objects and other impurities in worship is, that this transfers the honor that is rightfully God's alone to his creatures,[30] and God is a jealous God. In even stronger terms, Calvin asserts, in the *Petit traicté,* that service in a

[24]Cited in Eire, *War against the Idols*, 200.

[25]See Eire, "Calvin and Nicodemism," 47; the biblical Nicodemus is not a good example of a dissembler.

[26]Eire, *War against the Idols*, 3.

[27]The full title is: *Petit traicté monstrant que c'est que doit faire un homme fidele congnoissant la verité de l'Evangile, quand il est entre les Papistes* (1543), in *Corpus Reformatorum, Ioannis Calvini opera quae supersunt omnia*, G. Baum, E. Cunitz, and E. Reuss, 59 vols. (Braunschweig, 1893–1900), 6:540–88 (hereafter cited as CR with the *Opera Calvini* volume and page numbers). The other chief anti-Nicodemite tracts are: *Epistolae duae de rebus hoc saeculo cognitu necessariis* (1537), CR 5:239–78; *Excuse de Iehan Calvin a messieurs les Nicodemites sur la complaincte qu'ilz font de sa trop grand' rigueur* (1544), CR 6:591–614; *Quatre sermons de M. Iehan Calvin, traictans des matieres fort utiles pour nostre temps* (1552), CR 8:374–440; and finally the *Response a un certain Holandois lequel sous ombre de faire les chrestiens tout spirituels, leur permet de polluer leur corps en toutes idolatries* (1562), CR 9:584–628.

[28]E.g. , Calvin, *Petit traicté*, CR 6:547, 553, 558, 561, 570, 572, 576, 578.

[29]Cited in William J. Bouwsma, *John Calvin: A Sixteenth-Century Portrait* (New York: Oxford University Press, 1988), 36.

[30]Cf. Steinmetz, *Calvin in Context*, 61.

manner forbidden by God is service to the devil.[31] In his discussion of Nicode-mism, Calvin distinguishes between dissimulation, which is acceptable, and simulation, which is always inexcusable. Dissimulation means that one hides what is in one's heart. Simulation means actually to engage in acts of worship that one knows to be idolatrous, in other words: to lie in deed.[32] All objections by Nicodemites—their use of biblical examples of purportedly excused Nico-demite behavior, their contention that some sins are much worse than this one, and that we must not be like the Pharisees—founder upon God's unmis-takable commandment. Idolatry is not a trivial matter, as some contend, for we have to measure the offense against God's grandeur.[33] If simulation or flight is impossible, then the only Christian option left is constancy and trust in God's protection and concern for his flock. And if sincere Christians fail in the face of persecution and oppression, they should daily beg God for forgive-ness instead of attempting to justify or rationalize behavior that is impermissi-ble.[34] To the objection that it is easy for Calvin to counsel constancy from the safety of Geneva, the Reformer counters that he only counsels according to what his conscience presses him to say. He prays that, if faced with such a situ-ation, he would be able to stand firm. But if he did not, and if he should sin and act contrary to what he professes, then that would not excuse others who sin similarly.[35]

It is mostly assumed that opponents provided Coornhert's treatise with its provocative title, "Apology for Roman Idolatry" ("Verschooninghe van de Roomsche Afgoderye").[36] The request by these Dutch Protestants for an authoritative rebuttal by Calvin of Coornhert's 1558 tract illustrates the grow-ing importance of the connection between the Dutch Reformers and Geneva. The tract's stated objective was "to prove that no one should feel obliged to risk death for the use and abuse of ceremonies."[37] In Spiritualist fashion Coornhert claims that ceremonies or rituals cannot pollute or stain a clear conscience.

[31]Calvin, *Petit traicté*, CR 6:549.

[32]Ibid., CR 6:546: "Dissimulation se commet en cachant ce qu'on a dedans le cueur. Simula-tion est plus, c'est de faire semblant et feindre ce qui n'est point. En somme, ce qui seroit mentir de bouche, est simuler de faict."

[33]Calvin, *Petit traicté*, 6:566: "C'est donc de sa grandeur [viz. God's] qu'il faut estimer l'offense: et en ce faisant elle ne nous semblera jamais petite."

[34]Ibid., 6:576.

[35]Ibid., 6:573.

[36]See Bonger, *Leven en werk*, 28; Coornhert, *Verschooninghe van de Roomsche afgoderye*, in *Wercken*, vol. 3, fols. xviii–xxiii.

[37]Coornhert, *Verschooninghe*, vol. 3, fol. xviiiAB.

Therefore, he asserts, it is better to be prudent, and not let yourself be killed over such external matters. The fact that Calvin counseled his followers to prefer martyrdom over participation in "false" ceremonies is proof that ceremonies still play a crucial role for him. What to Calvin was a praiseworthy outcome of constancy and faith, Coornhert simply regarded as senseless loss of life. He blames Calvin and other church leaders for imposing unnecessary burdens on their flock.

The treatise shows that in 1558 Coornhert's theological views were already fully developed. The Jews, so the argument runs, lived under the Law, in a visible kingdom and under a visible priesthood, but Christ ushered in a spiritual kingdom and priesthood. This latter kingdom is not bound to any particular place, but is established in the hearts of Christ's subjects. Jesus summarized the entire Law and the prophets in the commandment to love God and to love your neighbor. He broke the law of the Sabbath, which God gave to Moses. The Pharisees attacked Jesus for this in the same way that the current leaders of visible churches—he mentions Calvin and Menno Simonsz in one breath—vilify the unrestrained followers of the spirit of Christ. By analogy, Coornhert asserts, Christ's spiritual subjects should not be punished for not upholding Moses' law forbidding the worship of idols, prescribed in the Old Testament, since they are now only subject to Christ's spiritual laws (that is, to love God and neighbor).[38] Ceremonies were originally given as a way to shield people from a greater evil: to keep them from turning to false gods and idols. God gave these ceremonies, writes Coornhert, as a father will give his children dolls, so that they will not be tempted to play with knives or fire instead. Once the child reaches maturity it can be sensible without those dolls. Reformers like Calvin, however, insist on putting these dolls back into their hands. In this context Coornhert refers explicitly and with approval to Sebastian Franck, from whom he borrowed the doll-simile.[39] Man sees the "pious" outside, but God sees only what is within. "What good is it," Coornhert asks rhetorically, "to worship him (God) through ceremonies such as the Supper, baptism, and similar worldly things (which are no more than shadows of the other) ... ?"[40] Externals are irrelevant, and therefore may not be used as a gauge for one's

---

[38]Ibid., fol. xviiiCD.

[39]Ibid., fol. xixB. Cf. Sebastian Franck, who writes that "God permitted, indeed gave, the outward signs to the church in its infancy, just like a doll to a child ..."; see Franck, "A Letter to John Campanus," in *Spiritual and Anabaptist Writers: Documents Illustrative of the Radical Reformation*, ed. George Huntston Williams. Library of Christian Classics, 25 (Philadelphia: Westminster Press, 1957):155.

[40]Coornhert, *Verschooninghe*, vol. 3, fol. xxiA.

piety: in claiming that one can be led to perdition by following improper rituals, Calvin makes the devil more powerful than Christ.[41]

In his response to Coornhert, which Eire calls "one of the clearest expositions of Calvin's theological opposition to simulation,"[42] Calvin expresses himself with the vehemence he reserved for opinions he considered to be dangerous and unorthodox. Not knowing the identity of the Dutch author, he addresses his *Response* "to a certain Dutchman, who, under the guise of wanting to make Christians entirely spiritual, allows them to pollute their bodies by engaging in all sorts of idolatries." The *Response* is elaborate and clear: Calvin restates his position and systematically refutes his unidentified opponent's arguments. But despite its lucidity, the tract is by no means dispassionate, for nearly every page of the *Response* contains some invective against the "obtuse Dutchman," with some of Calvin's terms of choice for Coornhert: "yokel," "drunkard," "scatterbrain," "mad dog," "pig," "wild beast," "baboon," and "ass."[43] Later, in his dispute with Lambert Danaeus, theologian at the University of Leiden, who had referred to Calvin's refutation of the "Apology," Coornhert would give an anthology of Calvin's vituperations against him, and make a point of showing the irrationality of such epithets. In one place, for example, Calvin calls Coornhert an "old fox," but elsewhere he is described as obtuse.[44] Clearly, since Calvin regards Catholic idolatry and worship as a pigsty, he cannot be cool and detached about a man who advises his readers that they can wallow in it with impunity.

Coornhert's principal mistake, as the title of Calvin's tract indicates, is that he wants to spiritualize everything without discrimination and without regard for the divinely ordained boundaries. The *moqueur de Dieu* does not discern between faith and everything that pertains to it, and the commandments that teach us how to live the right life while here on earth. Thus, in his effort to show that under Christ ceremonies no longer matter, Coornhert asserts, based on John 4:23, that we can pray in whatever manner we see fit. Calvin in response cites passages (1 Tim. 2:8 and Acts 20:36) that state unequivocally that we need to *bend our knees* and *bare our heads:* these are clear rules, laid down in the New Testament. The Dutchman does not distinguish between essential and nonessential, as when he concludes from Christ's lesson on the

---

[41] Ibid., fol. xxiB.

[42] Eire, *War against the Idols*, 250.

[43] Calvin, *Response a un certain Holandois, lequel sous ombre de faire les Chrestiens tout spirituels, leur permet de polluer leurs corps en toutes idolatries*, passim.

[44] Coornhert, *Levende Kalck*, in *Wercken*, vol. 3, fol. ccclviiiA.

keeping of the Sabbath that this also implies that we have a license to bend our knees for idols. Among the Jews, writes Calvin, the Sabbath had turned into an artificial straitjacket; Jesus broke the Sabbath in order to do heavenly work. Idolatry, however, belongs to an altogether different category: it concerns the honor of God, which is no trifling matter. To separate the spiritual from the physical, and to allow for total human freedom in the latter, means in fact to "deny God sovereignty over the physical world, and that is the heresy of the Manicheans."[45]

The Scriptures contain guidelines which help distinguish God's people from the world at large: the practice of circumcision, Calvin grants, is indeed abandoned in Christ and replaced by "spiritual circumcision." However, with a reference to Col. 2:11–12, Calvin shows that the passage on circumcision is immediately followed by the mention of the "ceremony" of baptism, a ceremony that finds clear sanction in the New Testament. Likewise was the Lord's Supper instituted by Christ himself (1 Cor. 11:24), and when Jesus rejects Satan's temptations, he states unequivocally that we should not kneel for anyone but God (Matt. 4:10). Such "ceremonies," he contends, are not mere child's play. They belong to the worship of God according to his unmistakable commandments.[46] Calvin refuses to accept what he sees as an artificial separation of interior belief from external worship in the individual believer. The Dutchman draws false conclusions based on erroneous analogies: baptism is indeed worthless if it is devoid of its spiritual truth, but this does not mean that it is useless. Temporal things can be the vessels of God's eternal Word. Calvin vehemently denies the assertion that a Christian cannot sin through outward acts. It is indeed sinful to feed the host to dogs, or to set up idols for worship. The fact is, Calvin explains, that humans possess a body, an exterior, and this exterior should manifest the heart's faith in ways that are appropriate and prescribed. If Coornhert counters, writes Calvin, that true worship of God is found in the heart, he is right with regard to the essence. "But what he says comes down to stating that you can easily cut somebody's throat without taking his life, because life resides in the soul."[47] Since man has body and soul, he must worship God externally and internally. The final conclusion of this "wild beast" [i.e. Coornhert] can only be, Calvin contends, that there is no visible church, in which case there can be no church organization and no order in the

---

[45]Eire, "Prelude to Sedition?" 129. Cf. Calvin, *Institutes*, 1.3.19, on "Christian Freedom."

[46]Calvin, *Response*, 591–92, 595.

[47]Ibid., 611: "c'est autant comme s'il disoit qu'on peut bien coupper la gorge à un homme sans luy oster la vie, d'autant que la vie gist en l'ame."

Christian commonwealth, a notion that Calvin abhorred in his fear of the "void."[48]

Whereas Coornhert appears to manifest concern for the senseless slaughter of people merely because of attachment to ceremony, Calvin naturally attacks the Dutchman as a hypocrite, a traitor, and an apostate for advocating accommodation in external matters. Simulation is a slap in the face of all those martyrs who had preferred to lose their lives rather than pollute themselves. Instead, men like Coornhert are cowardly, choosing to flee from persecution and valuing their life more than the honor of God.[49]

We see in this altercation a meeting, at least in spirit, of two very different men, and yet both in their ways products of humanism: one a Reformer, advanced in years and weighed down with the responsibilities of leading his flock and vindicating the Genevan community's raison d'être; the other a Haarlem printer and engraver in his late thirties, about to embark on a checkered career in the fledgling Dutch Republic as a civil servant and as a debater of almost national dimensions. Overall, Coornhert's chief concern appears to be the safeguarding of the freedom received in Christ—freedom from human restrictions and laws, but within the bounds set by the Golden Rule: "Why," he asks, "should I have somebody else's conscience pass judgment on my freedom?"[50] Thus, in what appears to be a theological dispute over Nicodemism, the issue of toleration plays an important role for Coornhert. Calvin rejected toleration: he rejected the toleration of impure ceremony by his followers living "under the cross," and encouraged them to take a stand on this matter. In the Christian polity which he envisaged, he also rejected toleration of the religious dissident, "which he equated with permissiveness toward pollution."[51] On the other hand, the writer of the *Apology* rejected any artificial shackles placed on Christ's followers, and eulogized the freedom of the spiritual realm that had been opened up by Christ's new dispensation. It is apparent that in a way, Coornhert's defense of the freedom of conscience is a logical extension of this freedom, and he is quick to label Reformers who are setting up a new church order as "new Pharisees." His ideas were by the time that he penned his tract, fully developed, and he proved himself willing to leap into the fray and cross swords with anyone whom he saw as endangering principles that he held

[48]Cf. Bouwsma, *John Calvin*, chap. 2, "Calvin's Anxiety."
[49]Calvin, *Response*, 618.
[50]Coornhert, *Verschooninghe*, fol. xxiC.
[51]Bouwsma, *John Calvin*, 211.

dear. Thus, this seems an opportune moment to take a backward look and to describe Coornhert's life up to this point.

Coornhert's Early Life

Dirck Volckertszoon was born between 21 May and 2 October 1522 in Amsterdam, the fourth of five children.[52] His parents were prominent and respected burghers, well established in the drapery business. After his father had retired, this business was continued by his mother, Truy Clements, together with his older brother Clement who was listed, around 1543, as one of the five richest merchants of Amsterdam.[53]

Since the struggle against any form of religious constraint formed such a pivotal part of Coornhert's life, one looks for clues in his early years that might explain his preoccupation with this topic. His thoughts on toleration, as expressed in his writings, seem already to be fully developed when he starts to publish. When he was in his early teens, one experience that may have imprinted itself on the young Coornhert's mind was the millenarian Anabaptist uprising in Amsterdam and the subsequent executions, which took place in 1534 and 1535.[54] Whereas, during the previous period, the towns had generally resisted efforts by the Habsburg government to bypass their privileges in the persecution of heresy, their attitude underwent a temporary change as a result of the eruption of revolutionary Anabaptism in the 1530s. The Anabaptist threat temporarily swayed the towns in Holland to the government's view, which saw heresy as sedition. In 1534, fifteen male Anabaptists were executed in Amsterdam, and the next year there were sixty-two executions, forty-six of them after the Anabaptist attack on city hall on 10 May.[55] Yet, after the threat of Melchiorite uprisings diminished, and after a few years of a stricter antiheresy policy, the zeal for severe prosecution subsided and the municipal government returned to its policy of only lukewarm enforcement of the "placards"

---

[52] Bruno Becker, ed., *Bronnen tot de kennis van het leven en de werken van D. V. Coornhert.* Rijks geschiedkundige publicaties, Kleine Serie, 25. (The Hague: Nijhoff, 1928), 98 n. 2, and 108; *Het Leven van D. V. Coornhart,* in *Wercken,* vol. 1, fol. 1A, gives details about each of his siblings.

[53] *Het leven van D. V. Coornhart,* fol. 1A (probably written by C. Boomgaert), states that D. V. Coornhert was "from an old, good, bourgeois lineage" ("van ouden goeden Borgherlijcken gheslachte"). Further details are in Bonger, *Leven en werk,* 21.

[54] Bonger, *Leven en werk,* 22, states that these events left an "indelible impression." It is not clear, however, what evidence this statement is based on.

[55] Tracy, *Holland under Habsburg Rule,* 163–65; see also George H. Williams, *Radical Reformation,* 3d ed., rev., Sixteenth Century Essays & Studies, 15 (1992: reprinted Kirksville, Mo.: Truman State University Press, 2000), 543–46.

(that is, the posted punishments for heresy).[56] The Coornherts lived so close to city hall that it is hard to imagine that all this commotion passed them by.[57]

When he was just seventeen, Coornhert married Cornelia ("Neeltje") Symons, a woman of comparatively modest means and twelve years his senior. The marriage was against the wishes of his parents. Within the class of the wealthy and prominent burghers, endogamy was the norm, and to marry someone with barely any means meant that the family would miss out on the dowry that a girl of his own class would have contributed. Part of the safe-guarding of the family's capital was that the amount provided for marrying daughters to pay as dowry would be offset by what the marrying sons would receive. By 1539 Dirck's father had passed away, so it was his mother who par-tially disowned him in punishment of his violation of parental stipulations. That he went through with the marriage anyway is testimony to his indepen-dent spirit and the attraction he must have felt. Neeltje and Dirck remained together until Neeltje's death in 1584.[58]

Neeltje's sister, Anna Symons, was for a time the mistress of Count Reinoud III of Brederode, whose family owned the most land of anyone in Holland. This connection was undoubtedly instrumental in getting Neeltje's young husband a position at castle Batestein in Vianen, situated between the provinces of Holland and Utrecht, where he worked for a time as steward.[59] Coornhert's connection with the Brederodes through his wife would later become important: During the "miracle year" of 1566, he had to negotiate with Hendrick of Brederode, active in the cause of the revolt, on behalf of the town government of Haarlem.[60]

With regard to education, Coornhert was chiefly a self-made man. His biographer in the *Wercken* mentions the many fields in which he excelled— music, poetry, etching, engraving, sparring, and so forth. What *Wercken* does not explain is how and where Coornhert acquired these skills. He was

---

[56]Tracy, *Holland under Habsburg Rule*, 170–71.

[57]F. D. J. Moorrees, *Dirck Volckertszoon Coornhert: Notaris te Haarlem, de Libertijn, bestrijder der Gereformeerde predikanten ten tijde van Prins Willem I: Levens- en karakterschets* (Schoonho-ven: S. & W.N. van Nooten, 1887), 6, gives an evocative but imagined account of this episode.

[58]See H. F. K. van Nierop, "Coornherts huwelijk: Een bijdrage tot zijn biografie," in *Bijdragen en Mededelingen van het Historisch Genootschap* 106/1 (1991): 33–44.

[59]Bonger, *Leven en werk*, 22–23; cf. Van Nierop, "Coornherts huwelijk," 39–41, who presents a different interpretation of this episode in Coornhert's life.

[60]Bonger, *Leven en werk*, 23–24.

obviously intelligent and a fast learner,[61] but for unknown reasons he never attended the Latin school in Amsterdam.[62]

Coornhert's stay at Batestein was also important for his spiritual development. The extensive library at the castle included many heretical books, which reflected the anti-Catholic atmosphere at Vianen. Around 1560, Reinoud's oldest son, Hendrick, started some printing establishments specializing in forbidden books. While staying at the castle in his early twenties, Coornhert was able to peruse a number of heterodox works, including books of Luther, Calvin, Menno Simons, and Sebastian Franck. These writings made him aware of the existence of controversial religious issues. He had been studying the Bible intensely since he was fifteen years old and discovered what he saw as discrepancies between the teachings of the Roman Catholic Church and what he found in Scripture.[63] Confronted with the various sects into which Christianity had split, he was determined to find out for himself what the patristic sources really said about such pivotal dogmas as original sin and predestination.[64] Therefore, when he was in his thirties, he took up the study of Latin and became so proficient that soon he was producing translations of classical texts.

By 1546, Coornhert had settled in Haarlem, where he made his living by etching and engraving. He worked mostly in conjunction with the Renaissance painter Maarten van Heemskerck, who was his senior by twenty-four years, and who had returned to Haarlem from Rome in 1537.[65] Coornhert executed more than three hundred designs by artists from the northern and southern Netherlands.[66] He did this simply to make a living, but he also found in this art an avenue for the expression of his theologico-philosophical ideas. He left an unmistakable imprint on the themes that were expressed and the form in which they were expressed.[67] For example, with regard to the print series

[61] *Het leven van D. V. Coornhart*, fol. 1B.

[62] Bonger, *Leven en werk*, 22.

[63] His parents owned a Dutch Bible; see Bonger, *Leven en werk*, 26.

[64] See Coornhert, *Wercken*, vol. 2, fol. dliiR.

[65] See Ilja M. Veldman, *Maarten van Heemskerck and Dutch Humanism in the Sixteenth Century*, trans. Michael Hoyle (Maarssen: Gary Schwartz, 1977), esp. chap. 4: "Dirck Volkertsz. Coornhert and Heemskerck's Allegories" (54–93). Coornhert is first mentioned as an engraver in Haarlem's treasury accounts of 1547; ibid., 55.

[66] Ilja M. Veldman, ed., *Dirck Volkertsz. Coornhert*, The Illustrated Bartsch, 55, supplement (n.p.: Abaris Books, 1991) contains all of Coornhert's graphic work.

[67] See Ilja M. Veldman, "Coornhert en de prentkunst," in Bonger et al., eds., *Dirck Volckertszoon Coornhert*, 115. Veldman, *Maarten van Heemskerck*, 92, also notes that the genre of the "didactic-moralistic allegory," Coornhert's trademark, vanished from Heemskerck's work after the collaboration between the two artists had ceased.

known as *Jacob's Ladder* or *Allegory of the Road to Eternal Bliss*, Ilja M. Veldman, in her analysis, concludes that the combination of the ideas presented and the form "together lead us straight to Coornhert's own concept of salvation."[68] In Carel van Mander's *Schilder-boeck (Book on Painting)*, Coornhert is described as someone "whose spirit, intellect, and hands were skillful and adept at understanding and executing anything that man could possibly understand and do." Most of the prints that Coornhert produced were moralistic: they assailed arrogance and vainglory, excessive ambition, cupidity and avarice. These moral lessons closely resemble those presented in Coornhert's later book of ethics, or in the *Lied-Boeck*.[69]

In 1560, Haarlem's municipal government granted Coornhert and three partners an interest-free loan[70] so that they could start a printing business that lasted four years. At least five of the ten books printed by this establishment were a direct result of Coornhert's initiative, starting with his translation of Cicero's *De Officiis*. Coornhert's prints and his translations helped turn Haarlem into a center for Renaissance activities.[71]

Coornhert was about to embark on his public career at a time when politico-religious tensions were rising within the *Habsburg* Netherlands. His 1558 tract, the *Apology* to which Calvin had taken such exception, was only one of several publications which demonstrated that Coornhert's perfectibilist[72] theological ideas were fully developed. These ideas were already recognizable in his first play, the *Comedy of the Rich Man (Comedie vande Rijcke man)* (1550). Throughout his writings, Coornhert's primary theological and moral concerns are much in evidence. Coornhert himself considered the collection of biblical *loci communes*, which he started in 1558 but was not destined to finish, as his most important intellectual undertaking.[73]

[68]Veldman, *Maarten van Heemskerck*, 60.

[69]Quoted in Veldman, "Coornhert en de prentkunst," 116, 124–25.

[70]See Becker, *Bronnen*, 9 (no. 15).

[71]Bonger, *Leven en werk*, 31.

[72]Perfectibilism—the belief that man can come to full obedience of God here on earth—is discussed below, in chapter 4.

[73]See his letter to Agge van Albada, c. 1583, in *Brieven-boeck*, in *Wercken*, vol. 3, letter 44, fol. cviiiiCD.

2

REVOLT AND EXILE

1561–1576

BY 1560, COORNHERT HAD BECOME a rather well known figure among the Haarlem burghers through his translations, his printing activities, and his etchings. The mayors solicited his services for the town government of Haarlem. He was groomed for his public career by Quirinus Talesius,[1] a renowned lawyer who had served for about seven years (ca. 1524–31) as Erasmus's secretary.

In November of 1561, while he still was involved in the printing business, Coornhert took the oath as notary.[2] Early the following year, he also added the position of secretary for the municipal government, and as of 11 March 1564, he served as first secretary to Haarlem's mayors.[3] In the Habsburg Netherlands, the town secretary could act as the town's mouthpiece: In the States of Holland which represented the entire province,[4] for example, he would be sent on missions to other cities and give political advice to the mayors. It was not necessary for this functionary to belong to the regent class, as indeed

---

[1]Becker, *Bronnen*, 13 (no.19, 13 November 1561): "Dirck Volckertsz. Coornhert, als notaris bij Quirinum Talesium gecreert...."

[2]Ibid.

[3]Ibid., 14, 21.

[4]See Tracy, *Holland under Habsburg Rule*, 15, 43. In the States of Holland, only seven votes counted: one for the nobles, six for the major cities of Haarlem, Amsterdam, Delft, Leiden, Dordrecht, and Gouda. The Stadtholder formed the main liaison between the Netherlandish burghers and the Burgundian, later Habsburg, court.

Coornhert did not, but he had to be versatile and trained in legal matters.[5] Some of Coornhert's feverish activities and frequent travels during the following years served Haarlem's commercial relations with other towns or provinces and other practical matters. But the chief concern of the town officials was with the turbulent political and religious developments that had engulfed the Netherlands towards the end of 1565 and later.

Charles's long reign ended with his abdication in 1555, which was followed by a period of some confusion and uncertainty, marked by a "temporary lack of a clear focus of power,"[6] until Philip II, the new king of Spain and the Americas, left the Low Countries after the peace of Cateau-Cambrésis, which concluded the Valois-Habsburg wars (1559). Effective control in the Netherlands now passed to Granvelle and Viglius, dominant members of the *Geheime Raad* (Secret Council).

The opposition to these men and the centralizing tendencies and infringements of age-old privileges coalesced in a rejection of the government's antiheretical policies. Before sailing to Spain in 1559, Philip instructed his governess to make sure that "the courts enforce the placards without mitigation."[7] Lutheranism, Anabaptism, and lately Calvinism were all spreading through the Netherlands. Many saw the creation of new bishoprics, presented as a reform aimed at restructuring and improving church organization, as an attempt to perfect the government's repression of heresy. This new diocesan structure became the focus of dissent, led by noblemen.[8]

An anti-Granvelle League, consisting of great nobles, formed within the "Council of State." The grandees boycotted the Council's sessions as long as Granvelle took part, and their actions were crowned with success when Granvelle departed in 1564. Consequently, the League's influence within the Council increased significantly, a fact which was underscored in William of Orange's forceful pro-toleration speech in the Council on new year's eve of 1564.[9] Through his inheritance of the principality of Orange (in southeastern

[5]See A. Th. van Deursen, "Staatsinstellingen in de Noordelijke Nederlanden 1579–1780," in *Algemene Geschiedenis der Nederlanden*, 5:380 ff.; also Israel, *Dutch Republic*, 126.

[6]Israel, *Dutch Republic*, 135.

[7]Tracy, *Holland under Habsburg Rule*, 177.

[8]See J. J. Woltjer, *Tussen vrijheidsstrijd en burgeroorlog: Over de Nederlandse Opstand 1555–1580* (n.p.: Uitgeverij Balans, 1994), 24–25.

[9]See M. E. H. N. Mout, "Van arm vaderland tot eendrachtige republiek: De rol van politieke theorieën in de Nederlandse Opstand" *Bijdragen en mededelingen betreffende de geschiedenis der Nederlanden* 101, no. 3 (1986): 351.

France), his titles, his riches, his marriage first to Anna van Buren, then to Anne of Saxony, Orange ranked as one of the most prominent noblemen in the Netherlands. Now, in his speech to the Council (of which only a summary survives), besides insisting on more input for the Council in the government of the Netherlands, Orange pleaded against religious constraint and persecution. At issue were the written instructions which Count Egmont should take with him on his mission to Spain, where he was to inform Philip of the concerns of the Council. After Orange's presentation, the Council decided to ignore the instructions proposed by Viglius and to accept instead the substance of Orange's address.[10] This plea for toleration by the Low Countries' principal nobleman and its acceptance by the majority of the Council members constitute something of a turning point.[11] Egmont's mission, however, turned out to be a failure, and in his letters of late 1565, Philip II ordered that the enforcement of antiheretical placards must be sharpened instead of mitigated. As a result of this intransigence and this clear casting of the die by Philip, Orange started to lose some support within the Council. By this time, however, resistance was also stirring outside the Council chambers.[12] A group consisting chiefly of minor noblemen, mostly Protestant or crypto-Protestant, and led by Hendrik of Brederode, formed a League of Compromise. In April 1565, Brederode rode at the head of a procession of three hundred of these confederates, who solemnly presented a petition to Margaret of Parma, asking for the dismantling of the Inquisition, an end to religious persecution, and the convocation of the States General for the purpose of developing a solution for this and other matters.[13] The governess made a tactical retreat by sending out orders to mitigate the application of the placards temporarily. She would await her sovereign's reaction to the petition.

During the spring and summer of 1565 clandestine Reformed mass gatherings were held outside city walls, encouraged no doubt by the regime's softening of persecution. These open air meetings, known as *hagepreken* (hedge-preachings), spread rapidly from Flanders northward. Then, in August 1566,

---

[10]See A. Th. van Deursen, "Willem van Oranje," in A.Th. van Deursen and H. de Schepper, *Willem van Oranje: Een strijd voor vrijheid en verdraagzaamheid* (Weesp: Fibula-Van Dishoeck, Tielt: Lannoo, 1984), 116–17.

[11]Ibid., 116.

[12]See Geoffrey Parker, *The Dutch Revolt* (Harmondsworth: Penguin, 1977), 76.

[13]The text of this petition together with Margaret's response is printed in E. H. Kossman and A. F. Mellink, eds., *Texts concerning the Revolt of the Netherlands* (London: Cambridge University Press, 1974), no. 4, pp. 62–64.

stimulated by these gatherings, and by the apparent inability of the central government to prevent or stop them, Protestant groups began to sack monasteries and churches. This *beeldenstorm* (literally "storm against images") spread quickly, again moving from the southern to the northern provinces of the Habsburg Netherlands. During these confused and troubled times, town governments had to determine their policy as the storm approached.

In the weeks following the 5 April presentation of the petition to the governess, Hendrik of Brederode, leader of the "Beggars" (*Gueux*), traveled through Holland to persuade towns to ratify the petition. Ratification was, of course, risky for these towns, as the sovereign's reaction to the petition was not yet known. One of the towns on his list was Haarlem.[14]

On behalf of the mayors, Coornhert was sent to Brederode in order to persuade the "grand Gueux" to desist from pressuring the Haarlem *vroedschap* (town government) to ratify the petition. His kinship with Brederode, through his wife Neeltje and his years of serving as steward at Batestein, must have facilitated Coornhert's mission.[15] His efforts ultimately were crowned with success,[16] and during Coornhert's visit to Brussels, together with Mayor Van Duvenvoirde, Orange expressed his approval of the way Haarlem had handled the situation.[17]

Hedge-preaching reached the vicinity of Haarlem in the summer: on 21 July, Pieter Gabriël (who, earlier, had preached near Delft) preached near Overveen.[18] The crowd could be seen from the tower of Haarlem's city hall by Coornhert and some others who had climbed it.[19] Orange, Holland's *stadholder*, had instructed the mayors to put a stop to such illegal gatherings, but the Haarlem authorities found themselves powerless since the services were held on land that belonged to Brederode. The only thing they could do was to try to persuade the latter to stop the preaching, and it was to this end that, on 30 July, Coornhert journeyed to Vianen, where he stayed until 3 August. A week later, an iconoclastic fury was unleashed in Steenvoorde, in the

[14]A. C. Duke and D. H. A. Kolff, "The Time of Troubles in the County of Holland, 1566–1567," *Tijdschrift voor Geschiedenis* 82 (1969): 318; Bonger, *Leven en werk*, 39.

[15]Rinck-Wagner, *Dirck Volckertszoon Coornhert*, 20.

[16]Bonger, *Leven en werk*, 39–40; Becker, *Bronnen*, 36–38 (nos. 54–56, 60); Duke and Kolff, "Time of Troubles," 318.

[17]Becker, *Bronnen*, 36–37 (nos. 55–56).

[18]Joke Spaans, *Haarlem na de Reformatie: Stedelijke cultuur en kerkelijk leven, 1577–1620.* Hollandse Historische Reeks, 11 (The Hague: Stichting Hollandse Historische Reeks, 1989), 34.

[19]Becker, *Bronnen*, 110.

south of Flanders. By 22 July it had reached Breda, two days later Utrecht, and the next day it hit Leiden, at a distance of about ten miles from Haarlem.[20]

Upon the approach of iconoclastic activity, the city fathers of Haarlem decided to take action to prevent its entry into their city. They closed the St. Bavo church on 23 August, and took other measures, such as the registration of any stranger wishing to stay in a Haarlem inn, since they expected the fury to be spread by out-of-town *provocateurs*.[21] For other churches protective measures were taken, in which Coornhert was actively involved. Some nuns of the convent of St. Cecil testified during Coornhert's later trial that he had held the statues and other items from the convent in safekeeping until the danger had passed. Coornhert had promised these scared nuns that they could always call on him in case of trouble.[22]

Coornhert and Alckemade, the town pensionary,[23] visited people suspected of wanting to incite iconoclastic trouble in the town, and pressured them to leave Haarlem.[24] For a while, the situation remained volatile. In Haarlem, as elsewhere in the towns of Holland, support from the *schutterij* (civic militia) in the suppression of possible attacks on churches was doubtful.[25] In the end, however, the storm passed by Haarlem. The St. Bavo church was not reopened until 7 December.[26]

In August 1566, during these disturbances that had engulfed many towns throughout the Netherlands, the regent, Margaret of Parma, attempted to restore order by granting freedom of Protestant worship in places where it was already taking place. Elsewhere, it would continue to be prohibited. This attempt at preserving the status quo soon proved unworkable; in many places, new concessions were made to the Reformed Protestants, for example in Antwerp, where, as of 4 September, Orange allowed full-fledged Protestant worship (for Reformed Protestants and Lutherans, though not for Anabaptists) in and outside the city.[27] In arduously striving for a compromise and the

[20]See Parker, *Dutch Revolt*, 77.

[21]Spaans, *Haarlem na de Reformatie*, 34.

[22]Becker, *Bronnen*, 171.

[23]In the northern Netherlands, the pensionary was the town's legal adviser and first assistant to the mayor; see Van Deursen, "Staatsinstellingen," 381.

[24]Becker, *Bronnen*, 39 (no. 61).

[25]Spaans, *Haarlem na de Reformatie*, 34; the explosiveness of the situation in Haarlem further appears from a letter that Brederode sent to Louis of Nassau on 27 August: see Duke and Kolff, "Time of Troubles," 323.

[26]Spaans, *Haarlem na de Reformatie*, 35.

[27]Parker, *Dutch Revolt*, 81–84.

establishment of a religious peace, Orange attempted to tread middle ground by simultaneously assuaging the Protestants and protagonists of armed rebellion, and trying to pacify and allay the fears of the nobles in the south who saw with alarm the concessions made to the followers of Calvin.

As in Antwerp, efforts also were made in Haarlem toward the implementation of a *religievrede*. This proposed "religious peace," or rather coexistence, was similar to what the prince earlier had introduced into his own principality of Orange. Coornhert appears to have played an important role in this policy. Towards the end of October, he was sent to Antwerp to ask Orange if Haarlem could permit the Protestants to erect a temporary shelter outside Haarlem's walls. This was a politically sensitive issue, since allowing Protestant structures went well beyond what was permitted under the 23 August accord with Margaret of Parma. The city fathers and Orange, however, were well aware that the need for shelter against the approaching inclement winter weather was a powerful incentive for the iconoclastic attacks.[28] Therefore, Orange granted permission, arguing that Egmont had permitted the same for Flanders.[29] Construction of what was to be not much more than a wooden shed was turned over to four prominent members of the nascent Protestant community, and by 1 November the structure was ready.[30] Coornhert traveled to Amsterdam in late December to receive a written injunction from the prince, that Protestants and Catholics were not to harm or harass each other or call each other names because of their religion. Thus, we see the town secretary play an active role in the establishment of a *religievrede* in Haarlem, as an intermediary between Orange, Haarlem's town government, and Hendrik van Brederode.[31] Within the *vroedschap*, Mayor Nicolaes van der Laen proved to be the staunchest supporter of Coornhert and Orange's policies.[32]

This policy of coexistence was not destined to stay in place for very long. It would soon become evident that a middling position such as Orange's was no longer tenable, as the only alternative to revolt was submission.[33] By September, rumors already were heard of the imminent dispatch, by Philip II, of a large army to the Netherlands. Mayor van Duvenvoirde and Coornhert traveled to Vianen (September 23–25) at the request of Brederode, who wanted to

[28]See Duke and Kolff, "Time of Troubles" 326.
[29]Becker, *Bronnen*, 42–44 (nos. 64–65)
[30]Spaans, *Haarlem na de Reformatie*, 35.
[31]Spaans, *Haarlem na de Reformatie*, 36; Becker, *Bronnen,* 49 (no. 75).
[32]Spaans, *Haarlem na de Reformatie.*
[33]Israel, *Dutch Republic*, 152.

inform them about these threatening developments and asked that Haarlem's mayors remonstrate with the *stadholder* in an effort to avert the coming of these troops into the Low Countries.[34] By January, the manifest signs of an imminent crackdown by the governess, as well as the approach of royal troops, now openly announced by Margaret, induced the Haarlem mayors to close the Protestant "church" and to engage in hasty efforts to hide the traces of an overly indulgent past policy toward the Protestants.

During the second half of 1566 there were several indications that the disaffected noblemen and Calvinists were preparing to arm themselves. One device used to raise money was the initiative known as the "Three Million Guilders Request." The plan called for the Calvinist consistories and their sympathizers to raise said amount, with which they would purchase religious freedom from their sovereign. The formal petition was drawn up (in French) by the Ghent consistory and presented to the government on 27 October. Should the Request be rejected, its provisions called for the money to be utilized "for the country's defense."[35] Thus the Request was a barely veiled attempt at raising troops for the Calvinist cause, to be placed under Brederode's command.[36]

The day after the petition was presented to the authorities, François van Haeften (Orange's agent) showed Coornhert a printed copy of the Request, translated into Dutch, and asked him to review it. This happened in Schoonhoven, where Van Duvenvoirde and Coornhert took part, as representatives of Haarlem, in a meeting with other Holland towns to discuss the current situation.[37] After this meeting, Van Duvenvoirde returned to Haarlem, but Coornhert traveled to Vianen and Utrecht, together with Orange and his brother, Louis of Nassau.[38] Louis asked Coornhert to translate the Request anew. Although Coornhert did not find much wrong with the existing translation, he took the Request home and made some minor modifications of a tactical nature, and then sent the amended version to Orange. During his trial of 1567, Coornhert would claim that he had merely, and literally, translated the French original.[39] This involvement of Coornhert with the seditious Request, as well as his frequent and seemingly rather intimate contact with Brederode

[34]Becker, *Bronnen*, 39–42; Bonger, *Leven en werk*, 41–42.
[35]Quoted in Parker, *Dutch Revolt*, 93.
[36]Van Gelderen, *Political Thought*, 86, calls the Request "part of an attempt to create a unified protestant movement."
[37]Bonger, *Leven en werk*, 42.
[38]Becker, *Bronnen*, 45 (no. 67).
[39]Ibid., 120–23.

(ringleader of the rebellion) Orange, and Louis of Nassau (the key figure between the confederated noblemen and the Calvinist consistories) go a long way towards explaining his arrest in 1567 and his later failure to obtain a pardon allowing him to return to the Netherlands.

During late 1566 and early 1567, the tide was turning and the central government gained in strength, and managed to mop up all remaining pockets of resistance. The siege of Valenciennes, a Calvinist stronghold, began on 17 December. The assembled Calvinist forces of west Flanders were crushed, and resistance at Tournai ended 2 January. This left only Brederode, formally elected as leader of the Beggars in January, and perhaps the French Huguenots, to offer any possible relief to Valenciennes. During this same month of January, Coornhert visited the Grand Gueux twice, in order to help him prepare his written defense during a visitation by two commissioners. The latter had been sent to Brederode by the governess with critical questions about the concentration of troops at Vianen, about the presence there of a clandestine printing press, and about the dissemination of a pamphlet entitled "Concordance of Vianen," illegally printed there and aimed at a reconciliation between Calvinists and the adherents of the Augsburg Confession.[40] The government's increased clout and self-confidence can also be seen in its obstruction of a January session of the States of Holland. The delegations, assembled in The Hague (26–29 January)—including a rather large Haarlem delegation—had to be sent home by Orange because of a missive from the governess, which notified them that Philip II had forbidden any meetings by the States for the time being.[41] The States sent representatives to Brussels to insist that they be allowed to hold a meeting. Coornhert and council member Zybrant van Berckenrode were sent on behalf of Haarlem.[42] The governess, Margaret of Parma, apparently kept them waiting a long time, for they stayed in Brussels for twenty-eight days (11 February through 10 March). She could afford such tactics, since the government forces were gaining strength daily. She required that all knights of the Golden Fleece—the high nobility—as well as soldiers and all officials sign a new oath of loyalty to the king. Most of the grandees complied: Egmont, Aerschot, Berlaymont, Hoorne, and Hoogstraten as of 24 May. Orange and Brederode were among those who refused, eventually preferring exile over compliance.

[40]Bonger, *Leven en werk*, 44; Rinck-Wagner, *Dirck Volckertszoon Coornhert*, 65–66.
[41]Becker, *Bronnen*, 51–53 (no. 80).
[42]Ibid., 54–55 (no. 82).

Chapter 2

By January, Brederode could no longer count on open support from Orange or other grandees. His 2 February request for a safe conduct to Brussels, so he could present the government with a third petition for freedom of worship, was turned down peremptorily by the governess. Brederode continued to raise troops, gathering some three thousand men at Oosterweel, just outside Antwerp, meant for the relief of Valenciennes. After his departure, on 13 March, the Calvinist forces at Oosterweel were routed in a surprise attack by eight hundred royalist troops. Orange, in his capacity as governor of Antwerp, demonstrated his loyalty to the government by preventing an attempted sortie by Antwerp Calvinists who wanted to come to the rescue of their coreligionists in Oosterweel.[43] On 24 March, Valenciennes finally surrendered, and a little more than a week later, with the fall of Vianen, "the rebellion was over."[44] Orange resigned all his offices on 10 April, and fled to Germany. On 7 April, Coornhert sold his house, in preparation for his flight.[45] Brederode made a last-ditch, desperate effort to win over Amsterdam to his cause. He concentrated his troops around Ouderkerk, close to Amsterdam, intending to enter the city by ruse in the early morning of 27 April, through the Haarlemmer gate. The plan failed, and Brederode himself fled that very day to Emden.[46]

The next day, Coornhert tried to enter Amsterdam, purportedly having been sent by the Haarlem mayors "to get some firm information from the mayors [of Amsterdam] about the soldiers who had assembled in considerable number at Ouderkerk."[47] It seems more likely that Coornhert possessed inside information on Brederode's plan, and that he went on a reconnaissance mission, to see if the plan had met with success.[48] An Amsterdam gatekeeper testified later that he had witnessed how, when the alarm sounded (with Coornhert outside the gate), the latter had tried to hide and seemed to be in a panic.[49] However, apparently Brederode's soldiers surrounding the city prevented Coornhert from entering it, so he returned home. A document, submitted by the Amsterdam *vroedschap* for the trial against Coornhert, states that on 28 April Frans Coornhert, a resident of Amsterdam, had failed to obtain

[43]Parker, *Dutch Revolt*, 97.
[44]Ibid., 99.
[45]Becker, *Bronnen*, 55–56 (no. 83).
[46]Rinck-Wagner, *Dirck Volckertszoon Coornhert*, 66–67.
[47]Becker, *Bronnen*, 57 (no. 87).
[48]See Rinck-Wagner, *Dirck Volckertszoon Coornhert*, 66–67.
[49]Becker, *Bronnen*, 175.

permission for his brother to enter the city. Their statement, in the same document, that the three brothers, Frans, Clement, and Dirck, frequently had visited Brederode when the latter was staying in Amsterdam, seems only to confirm the suspicion of complicity.[50]

A couple of days later Coornhert's resignation as secretary was accepted, and in May he fled the country.[51] He stayed in Deventer, Cologne, and Emmerich. While Coornhert was in Emmerich, he received a letter from Orange asking the prince to come to see him at Dillenburg. It is certain that Coornhert met with the prince in May in Siegen (near the prince's castle at Dillenburg).[52]

Around 20 July, Coornhert returned to Haarlem and resumed his old duties, as if nothing had happened.[53] His return was probably prompted by the withdrawal of Count Meghen's troops from Haarlem, and by pleas from his wife and friends in Haarlem. It would soon become manifest that he had grossly misjudged the situation.

The arrival of the duke of Alva, always the proponent of a hard line, with a Spanish army, meant a turning point. Alva's objectives were simple: to safeguard orthodoxy and to model the regime in the Netherlands after the situation back in Castile, where the Cortes had little clout vis-à-vis the king.[54] Alva arrived in Brussels on 22 August and immediately set to work. He created the Council of Troubles, nicknamed the Council of Blood, a supreme tribunal for the prosecution of those implicated in heresy or rebellion, which in the following months tried more than twelve thousand people. Margaret of Parma left in December, whereupon Alva had the monopoly of executive power in the Netherlands.

Coornhert was arrested on 14 September and transported to the Hague the next day, like a common criminal.[55] Most of those in Haarlem who were at risk because of their involvement in the events of 1566 had been forewarned by the town authorities, managed to escape on time, and were tried in absentia. The fact that Coornhert was not saved from the Blood Council's clutches may have been a result of his naïveté—during the trial he would claim that he had been confident that he had nothing to fear from the authorities. But this

---

[50]Becker, *Bronnen,* 140 (statement dated 9 October 1567).

[51]Ibid., 175–79.

[52]Bonger, *Leven en werk,* 46–47.

[53]Becker, *Bronnen,* 129 (Coornhert's interrogation during trial).

[54]Woltjer, *Tussen vrijheidsstrijd en burgeroorlog,* 40.

[55]Rinck-Wagner, *Dirck Volckertszoon Coornhert,* 73.

argument seems contradictory, for if he had nothing to fear, then why his initial flight? During the trial, he explained his flight by saying that in a war situation one could not count on fair treatment by the law, and added that he had wanted to study law in Cologne.[56] These explanations come across as rather transparent subterfuges, since his flight was certainly motivated by his contacts with Brederode, Orange, Louis of Nassau, and the others. He returned because he thought the coast was clear. The arrest caught him by surprise—the *schout* (bailiff) and his men came for him when he was in bed, asleep. It, therefore, may be seen as plausible that at least part of the town government had been willing to sacrifice the secretary, perhaps because he had alienated them by his actions or personality.[57]

Coornhert remained in custody for more than six months—from mid-September 1567 to mid-April 1568—as his case dragged on. After about three months he succeeded in obtaining release from strict confinement and was allowed to "have The Hague for a prison" during the day, as long as he spent the nights in his cell.[58] Earlier, he had already been granted permission to have paper, pen, and ink at his disposal, of which he made good use, writing a comedy, poems, and the rough draft of the tract that would much later see the light as *Boeventucht (On the Disciplining of Criminals)*. It contained proposals for a thorough reform of prisons and the penal system.[59] His wife, Neeltje, at one point was so desperate that during one of her visits she informed her husband of her intention to go visit sufferers from the plague until she herself was infected, and then to pass the plague on to Coornhert so that they could die together.[60] Coornhert reprimanded her for placing him before God, who forbade suicide, but he would later commemorate and laud her faithfulness and devotion in one of his songs.[61]

The trial consisted of two main phases: the first one conducted by the prosecutor-general of the Hof van Holland (the high court of the province of Holland), the second starting after 7 January when interrogations were taken over by commissioners from Alva's Council of Troubles. It is hardly surprising

[56]Becker, *Bronnen*, 125.

[57]Spaans, *Haarlem na de Reformatie*, 37.

[58]Becker, *Bronnen*, 141–42 (dated 22 December 1567).

[59]Bonger, *Leven en werk*, 54–55; see Coornhert, *Boeventucht*, ed. Arie-Jan Gelderblom et al. (Muiderberg: Dick Coutinho, 1985).

[60]See *Het Leven van D. V. Coornhart*, in *Wercken*, vol. 1, fol. 1C.

[61]Song no. 30 of the *Lied-Boeck* (*Book of Songs*), in *Wercken*, vol. 1, fols. 503D–504A. This is a moving and skillful acrostic, the first letters of each stanza together forming his wife's name.

that after that date Coornhert's case seemed to take a quick turn for the worse, and that more hostile witnesses stepped forward.

During the first two interrogations (2 and 7 October 1567), Coornhert refuted the allegations, which had been laid down in seventeen questions, without accusing or implicating anybody. Charges mainly revolved around his contacts with Brederode, his involvement with the Three Million Guilders Request, his flight, his communications with Willem Bardes (the former *schout* of Amsterdam) and his presence at a religious disputation.[62] In his reply, Coornhert emphasized his crucial role in averting iconoclasm in Haarlem as well as the fact that he had initially been on very poor terms with Brederode, even having to fear for his life. He claimed that he and Mayor Van der Laen had successfully temporized with regard to the ratification of the petition, and other visits to the Huys te Cleef and to Vianen (both Brederode residences) were explained away by referring to personal issues between Brederode and Anna, Coornhert's sister-in-law (payment of her alimony, which was in arrears), and between Brederode and one of Coornhert's brothers, in which Coornhert had served as mediator. Coornhert spoke "frankly" of an incident that had occurred during a drunken party at Vianen at a time when he and Mayor Van Duvenvoirde were visiting.[63] On that occasion, an intoxicated Brederode had hung a Beggars' chain, symbol of allegiance to the Beggars, around the necks of Van Duvenvoirde and Coornhert. The mayor felt at a loss about what to do, but Coornhert, who knew the Big Beggar and how alcohol affected him, counseled Van Duvenvoirde to play along for the moment. Later, they unobtrusively returned the chains, and the next morning, a more sober Brederode accepted Coornhert's objections and no longer insisted that he and the mayor wear the insignia. With regard to the Three Million Guilders Request, he claimed that he had merely followed Count Louis's orders, and had no idea what had happened to the Request after he had translated it. He tried to put the best face on his flight to Cologne by pointing out that his ill wishers had been apt to misrepresent his contacts with Brederode, that the presence of soldiers and war conditions had made him fearful that the law would not be respected, and that his wife had urged him to flee. In support of his innocence, Coornhert submitted documents clarifying his relations and contacts with Brederode, and statements by Haarlem's ex-mayors, confirming

[62]Becker, *Bronnen*, 107–8.
[63]23 September 1566.

history of why he had decided to flee. But the court also received incriminating statements, sent in by the Amsterdam *vroedschap*.[64]

In February, Alva's commissioners were in Haarlem on a fact-finding mission. They recorded several statements that were damaging to Coornhert. Former mayor Van Roosvelt (whom Coornhert called "my public enemy") gave a deposition in which he mentioned the secretary's frequent and intimate contacts with Orange, and complained that Coornhert always communicated with other mayors—especially Van der Laen—and excluded him, Van Roosvelt.[65] Another witness declared that Coornhert embraced sectarians of all stripes, and was "the principal initiator and perpetrator" of religious innovation.[66] But the most damaging accusations came from Jacob Foppesz, whose daughter had married the son of one of Coornhert's sisters.[67] Because Foppesz seemed to know the Coornherts more intimately, having been a frequent guest at their home, his accusations may have had the ring of truth. Foppesz presented himself as a staunch Catholic, and several people attested in writing to his respectability. Coornhert tried to undermine Foppesz's stature by producing a witness, a physician from Amsterdam, who had treated Foppesz for the "Spanish pox" (syphilis), and inferred that Foppesz cheated on his wife. Foppesz seems to have assumed that Coornhert was Protestant, and started his deposition by stating that it had been common knowledge, among the burghers of Haarlem, "that most of the sectarians found support and refuge with the Prince of Orange, with Count Louis of Nassau, his brother, and with Lord Brederode, and [that] this chiefly [happened] through the aid and intercession of Dierick Volckaertsz., secretary...."[68] Much of his testimony is based on hearsay; he relates, for example, how Talesius had told him that Coornhert always conferred with the chief Beggars directly following the meetings of the Haarlem *vroedschap* (which Coornhert, as secretary, naturally attended). The confrontation between the two men, which took place on 11 February, only resulted in Foppesz's maintaining his assertions and Coornhert's either refuting or categorically denying them. In the following

[64]Becker, *Bronnen*, 115–18, 121, 123–25, 133–41.

[65]Ibid., 145. Van Roosvelt would be hanged in 1573, during the siege of Haarlem, together with Talesius, for his pro-Spanish sympathies.

[66]Becker, *Bronnen*, 146–47.

[67]For court documents relating to Foppesz and his confrontation with Coornhert, see Becker, *Bronnen*, 147–57, 164–68. Some of Foppesz's zeal may be explained by his ambition for an official position; he would later become bailiff in Haarlem.

[68]Ibid., 147.

month, Coornhert submitted a number of documents disproving and discrediting Foppesz's incriminations: attestations to Coornhert's good and Foppesz's despicable character, the testimony by the nuns lauding the secretary's kind services to them during a perilous time, a statement by two former mayors of Haarlem affirming that Coornhert's trip to Amsterdam on 28 April 1567 had been an official reconnaissance mission.[69]

The court documents on Coornhert's case close with a rather lengthy précis written by the accused, in which he once again, and methodically, refutes all the charges. It contains nothing new, except for the secretary's complaint about the long wait, and about the fact that he is forced to prove his innocence, whereas it is his accusers who should prove his guilt.[70]

The entire dossier on Coornhert was sent to Brussels for a verdict. When word reached Coornhert that a letter had arrived from Brussels ordering his reimprisonment, he decided to flee.[71] First he stayed in Leiden for a few weeks, hiding with his friend Van Montfoort. Next, he was in Haarlem for about a month, and then went to Germany, where his wife soon joined him. His possessions were confiscated after Alva had banished him in perpetuity from the king's lands.

During the following period, until his brief return to the Netherlands in 1572, Coornhert lived in exile in the Cleves and Berg area which was known for its tolerance, again in Cologne, and briefly in Emden, where his two brothers, fellow exiles, were staying.[72] While in Cologne, Coornhert became friends with the Schwenckfeldian lawyer Aggaeus van Albada, and he also associated with Hendrick Niclaes, founder of the Family of Love, who earlier had stayed with him in Haarlem on several occasions, and who lived in Cologne from 1570 till 1580.[73]

These were years of feverish activity on behalf of the nascent Revolt. At Dillenburg, William of Orange, having lost his possessions and position in the Netherlands, placed himself at the head of the armed struggle. Brederode had died in 1567. Now the only real candidate for leadership of the Revolt was Orange.[74] He sold off much of the Nassaus's remaining possessions to finance the planned invasion. In Germany, Coornhert was actively engaged in the

[69]Ibid., 173; the documents submitted by Coornhert at this point: pp. 167–74.
[70]Ibid., 179–96. See article 59, pp. 195–96, for a "summary of the summary."
[71]Bonger, *Leven en werk*, 60; *Het Leven van D. V. Coornhart*, fol. 1CD.
[72]Bonger, *Leven en werk*, 60.
[73]Becker, *Bronnen*, 62–63.
[74]Israel, *Dutch Republic*, 161.

collection of funds in support of the armed struggle from exiles who were not affiliated with the Reformed communities "under the cross." To this end, he had to travel extensively.[75]

Orange's 1568 invasion of the Netherlands failed miserably, and by 1569 Alva considered the job of pacification all but finished, allowing him to concentrate his efforts on the construction of a more centralized state that would provide him with enough revenue to support his troops. His tax plans—especially the so-called Tenth Penny—encountered widespread resistance and obstructionism in the towns. Social discontent, combined with the loss of credibility by many town governments due to their apparent collaboration with Alva's hated tax schemes, laid the foundations for the events of 1572.[76] Orange planned a synchronized fivefold invasion for the summer of that year. The Sea Beggars, however, with no port to fall back on after Elizabeth had expelled them from the English coast, were induced to start early and took Brielle in the south of Holland (1 April). By the end of July, twenty-six towns had declared for the Revolt. The rebellious towns of Holland and Zeeland convened at Dordrecht, where they proceeded to acknowledge Orange as their *stadholder*.

Once the massacre of Huguenots in France on St. Bartholomew's Day (23/24 August 1572) had diminished greatly the threat of a Huguenot invasion into the Netherlands from the south, Alva went on a highly successful northward campaign of reconquest and of devastation and cruelty, meant as a deterrent. By the end of the year, Mechelen, Zutphen, and Naarden had been destroyed and their inhabitants put to the sword. The area in revolt had shrunk to Holland and Zeeland, with Alva's forces closing in, and the prince headquartered in Delft, in Holland which, he wrote, he had determined to make his grave.

Coornhert returned to Haarlem in September 1572, on the eve of Alva's campaign. On an earlier occasion he had conferred with the prince in Gelderland. Orange wanted Coornhert to serve him in some capacity, but the latter had stalled, saying that he still had business to attend to in Germany and would not be able to achieve much in Holland "because of the Calvinists' hatred toward me."[77] When he returned, however, he was appointed secretary to the free States Assembly of Holland.[78] Earlier, the Assembly formally had accepted Orange's *religievrede* between Catholics and Protestants, and for

---

[75]Bonger, *Leven en werk*, 64–66.
[76]See Parker, *Dutch Revolt*, chap. 3, "The Second Revolt (1569–76)."
[77]*Het Leven van D. V. Coornhart*, in *Wercken*, fol. 2B.
[78]Becker, *Bronnen*, 64–65 (no. 98).

Coornhert this was an essential precondition for accepting the job.[79] The practical value, however, of this freedom of worship promised to Catholics seemed slight in Holland and Zeeland, where the Beggars' victories had left churches denuded and firmly in Calvinist hands, and where the maintenance of the religious peace was entrusted to the lieutenant-governor, Lumey—the same Lumey who, somewhat earlier, had perpetrated acts of unspeakable cruelty against priests in Gorkum.[80] After 1572, in Holland, the *religievrede* soon became a casualty of war hysteria. Typically, anti-Catholic measures or attacks would intensify when the Revolt experienced military setbacks.[81]

Coornhert's tenure as secretary of the States and his stay in Holland were rather short-lived. In October, the States' Assembly determined that there should be an investigation into the "exactions" which had been imposed by the Beggar troops in the various towns and into the "costs" that had been incurred. Coornhert was put in charge of the investigation in the district of Kennemerland (stretching roughly from Hillegom up to Petten in the west of Holland). He proceeded with his usual thoroughness and gathered ample evidence of the pillaging and cruelties by Lumey's Beggars against priests and monks in the area.[82] When Lumey was apprised of the tenor of this impending report, he marked the "papist" Coornhert for death. The secretary, who had been in office for a mere three months, felt compelled to go into hiding with his friend Van Montfoort in Leiden, and then fled to Germany once again. He had left the report in Haarlem, to be sent to the States, but the document never reached that body because of the siege of Haarlem, which began shortly after Coornhert's departure in early December 1572, and was to last until 12 July of the following year.[83] This flight began four more years of exile, and it also meant the end of Coornhert's political career as a public official.[84]

---

[79]See Bonger, *Leven en werk*, 68.

[80]Rogier, *Eenheid en scheiding*, 83. G. Janssens, "Van de komst van Alva tot de Unies 1567–1579" in *Algemene Geschiedenis der Nederlanden*, 6: 220–22.

[81]Alastair Duke and Rosemary L. Jones, "Towards a Reformed Polity in Holland, 1572–78," in Alastair Duke, *Reformation and Revolt in the Low Countries* (London: Hambledon Press, 1990), 206–7. Rosemary Jones, "Reformed Church and Civil Authorities in the United Provinces in the Late 16th and early 17th Centuries, As Reflected in Dutch State and Municipal Archives," *Journal of the Society of Archivists* 4 (1970–73): 116, emphasizes the magistrates' concern over the maintenance of order as an important reason for the suppression of Catholic worship.

[82]Orange was highly troubled by Lumey's unruly behavior; he would dismiss him in 1573: see K. W. Swart, *Willem van Oranje en de Nederlandse Opstand 1572–1584*, ed. R. P. Fagel et al., (The Hague: Sdu Uitgeverij, 1994), 52–53.

[83]Bonger, *Leven en werk*, 68; Parker, *Dutch Revolt*, 159. Coornhert comments on his motives for flight in *Vande Leydtsche Disputatie* in *Wercken*, vol.3, fols. cclxviA and clviD–clviiA.

[84]Rinck-Wagner, *Dirck Volckertszoon Coornhert*, 107.

The four years spent in Xanten (in Cleves), where he made a living with his engraving and became the master of Hendrick Goltzius, were rather uneventful. Coornhert was far from the action, for the prince was in Holland, and these were climactic and crisis-filled years for the Dutch Revolt. Coornhert tried to stay abreast of the events and in his writings would react to some of them.

The long siege of Haarlem sapped the strength of the Spanish, and the massacre that followed Haarlem's surrender—despite promises that no harm would befall the defenders upon surrender—only strengthened the resolve of the other towns. From this point on, none of them would yield without a struggle. Don Fadrique had to give up the siege of Alkmaar, *Stadholder* Bossu was captured by the Beggars, and at the end of 1573 Alva departed for good, having failed in his mission. Still in that year, a crucial episode began with the epic siege of Leiden.[85]

It was at this stage that the States of Holland forbade public worship by Catholics and that Orange openly chose the side of the Calvinists. It seems a paradox that at a time when Orange's influence in Holland and Zeeland was at its peak, he was unable to use this influence to implement his ideal of religious toleration. In these provinces, a minority was engaged in a life-and-death struggle, and it did not feel it could afford itself the luxury of being lenient toward the Catholic majority. The prince had no alternative: he expected nothing from the king and did not trust royalist promises.[86] Two of his brothers died that year in a battle near Mook, which thwarted their intention of bringing relief to the besieged town of Leiden.

In a poem that he sent to a friend in Holland, Coornhert eulogized the heroic defense by the Leidenaars, who were finally liberated in October 1574 and rewarded the following year with the establishment of a university.[87] In that same year, however, he also wrote a *First Draft of a Discourse* (*Discours onder verbeteringhe*), which his enemies labeled "defeatist" and "treasonous" because Coornhert admits therein that the Netherlands would not be able to defeat Spain decisively, and proposes negotiations, with the Holy Roman Emperor as an arbiter.[88]

[85]Israel, *Dutch Republic*, 180–81; Parker, *Dutch Revolt*, 160.

[86]Swart, *Willem van Oranje*, 42–46, shows that, to a certain extent, Orange himself was to blame; e.g. already in 1570, he had promised his financial backers that they would be amply compensated from Catholic ecclesiastical properties.

[87]Quoted in Bonger, *Leven en werk*, 74.

[88]The *Discours onder verbeteringhe* was incorporated into the Coornhert's biography in *Wercken*, vol. 1, fols. 2B–3B; criticism by the Delft ministers in *Theriakel*, in *Wercken*, vol. 2, fol. 264B.

In the meantime Requesens, who had succeeded Alva as governor-general, made peace overtures that were doomed to fail because of the religious question. In June of 1574 he announced a general pardon, from which Coornhert was excluded.[89]

The financial crisis brought on by the second Spanish state bankruptcy of September 1575, and the widespread mutinies by unpaid troops that ensued, opened the door to a more general revolt: an illusory phase that was to last three years (1576–79). The anarchy of mutineering troops forced the provinces to unite, and the States General proceeded to fill the power vacuum left after the sudden death of Requesens in March 1576.[90] The Pacification of Ghent between representatives of the States General and delegates from Holland and Zeeland suspended antiheretical placards, and stipulated that a new governor-general would be accepted only if he agreed to work with and through the States General and would send home all foreign troops. The terror of the "Spanish Fury" that raged through Antwerp in November and left some eight thousand citizens dead underscored the urgency of unified action.[91] However, despite some successes in this collaboration, differences soon surfaced and would, in 1579, lead to rupture.[92]

In September 1577, when Orange was hailed almost as a messiah as he rode triumphantly into Brussels, royal power in the Netherlands reached an all-time low. The new governor-general, Don Juan, had very little authority. A growing number of towns sided with the prince, usually after a pact (*satisfactie*) guaranteeing their privileges. But then the tide started to turn again, as Don Juan's troops inflicted a crushing blow on the States' forces at Gembloux in early 1578. Southern nobles, dismayed by the radical nature of the Revolt and the excesses of Calvinist domination in towns such as Ghent, increasingly turned away from the Revolt and back toward Spain. Orange tried as long as possible to appease both sides by touting his "religious peace,"[93] proposing that wherever more than one hundred families requested it, religious freedom should be granted: to the Reformed (outside Holland and Zeeland), and to the Roman Catholics (in Holland and Zeeland). "This,"

[89]Bonger, *Leven en werk*, 73. Coornhert asked the Haarlem mayors why he had been excluded, but they professed their ignorance: see Becker, *Bronnen*, 100, p. 66.

[90]Janssens, "Van de komst," 230.

[91]Parker, *Dutch Revolt*, 178.

[92]See De Schepper, "*Belgium Nostrum*," 6–10, 17–18.

[93]Eloquently and movingly defended by Philip du Plessis Mornay in a discourse published in 1579: see Kossman and Mellink, eds., *Texts concerning the Revolt*, no. 36, pp. 163–64.

concludes Van Deursen in his brief biography of the prince, "was a very logical and reasonable plan, and hence doomed to failure. Neither side was inspired by common sense and reason, but by militancy and mistrust."[94] In many cases, the introduction of the *religievrede* simply meant the first step toward the establishment of a Calvinist monopoly.[95] That this religious peace was an illusion became painfully clear when Orange's brother, Jan de Oude, upon becoming governor of Gelderland in May of 1578, immediately started to push through Calvinist domination there, much to his brother's chagrin. In Haarlem, on 29 May1578, rowdy soldiers violently disrupted a Catholic service in the St. Bavo church and robbed the churchgoers; the church was closed and in the fall it was handed over to the Reformed.[96] Under such circumstances, no agreement on war objectives between the "Flemish" and southern Walloon provinces was feasible, and this impasse demonstrated the weak basis of the Pacification of Ghent. Things started to fall apart once again, and the result would be a formalization of the fissure that had already been a reality for some time. At the start of 1579, the Walloon provinces began to coalesce around the Union of Arras, which pledged its Catholicism and its loyalty to the king. A powerful incentive to obedience had appeared in the person of the duke of Parma, Don Juan's successor, who scored spectacular military successes. In the north, representatives of Holland, Zeeland, Flanders, Gelderland, Utrecht, and the Ommelanden (the area surrounding Groningen) signed the Union of Utrecht, a treaty which, although few realized it at the time, signalled the birth of the new independent northern state of the Dutch Republic.[97]

The favorable turn of events that had found expression in the Pacification of Ghent led to the return to the Netherlands of great numbers of exiles. Coornhert was one of them. He first consulted with the prince in Veere (Zeeland); then he stayed in Delft for a while, and as of March 1577, he was back in Haarlem, which had declared itself for the prince on 22 January of that year.

That Coornhert had become rather desperate during the final stage of his exile in Xanten can be deduced from the request that he sent to Philip II in 1576. The request—which was rejected or, more likely, ignored—remained

[94]Van Deursen, "Willem van Oranje," 140.

[95]Israel, *Dutch Republic*, 192; see Van Gelderen, *Political Thought*, chap. 6.2: "The debate on Religious Peace"; and Duke and Jones, "Towards a Reformed Polity," 203.

[96]See Spaans, *Haarlem na de Reformatie*, 57–59.

[97]De Schepper, *Belgium Nostrum*, 18–19.

undetected until 1931, and it does not seem likely that any of his contemporaries in the Dutch Republic were cognizant of its existence, or else Coornhert's enemies would gladly have availed themselves of this golden opportunity for attack. In this petition, which Bonger calls a "black page in his [i.e. Coornhert's] …book of life," Coornhert presented himself as a faithful supporter of the king and as a loyal Roman Catholic, and spoke of the "so-called States of Holland." [98] The first two statements were simply untrue, and the last one was a denial of the Revolt which he had served so assiduously. Coornhert apparently felt the pinch of his many years in exile, badly wanted his confiscated goods returned to him, and was simply homesick.

During the period under review in this chapter, Coornhert served Haarlem in an important and politically sensitive position. A storm was gathering over the Habsburg Netherlands and it was unleashed during the "miracle year" of 1566, when politico-religious tensions led to the petition and the iconoclastic outrage. As Haarlem's secretary, Coornhert found himself in the eye of the storm, and his kinship with Brederode, the lead figure in the incipient revolt, made his role all the more pivotal. Traveling frequently in 1566, he tried to rein in the ebullient and impulsive Big Beggar, and he also kept in touch with Orange. He was instrumental in averting the spread of iconoclasm to Haarlem and in implementing Orange's policy of "religious peace" between the conservative and predominantly Catholic town government and the Protestant minority. Coornhert's involvement with the Three Million Guilders Request is further evidence that at this time he was in the thick of the anti-Spanish resistance. Consequently, he was swept up in the wave of repression brought on by the coming of the duke of Alva and escaped to Germany in the nick of time. With the exception of a brief stay in Holland in 1572 as secretary of the States of Holland, after which he was forced to flee again, this time to escape Lumey's ire, he spent some eight years, over half the period covered in this chapter, in exile. The first half of this exile was shared with the prince and marked by feverish activity in behalf of the Revolt. His 1572 flight, however, led to a less eventful exile, even as the Revolt passed through a grueling and heroic phase and his adopted town lived and died through a long siege. Perhaps this long exile and his absence from the climactic life-and-death struggle explain to a degree Coornhert's lack of awareness of how in Holland and Zeeland relations, in the thick of the struggle, had become polarized between the two sides (Protestant and Catholic), and how much more difficult and indeed, some would

[98]Bonger, *Leven en werk*, 80; 166 n. 177.

argue, more unrealistic, it had become after 1572 and 1573 to strive for an open and peaceful coexistence between the two sides.

Coornhert's flight, toward the end of 1572, had in effect ended his political career. When he returned to Haarlem in 1577, he resumed his notarial work. He no longer served in any public capacity, neither did he fight on the anti-Spanish front. Nevertheless, in the last thirteen years of his life that follow, he gained wide recognition (and notoriety) as an intrepid and relentless fighter, in debates and in numerous writings, for his ideas on religious toleration and theology.

The following chapters will address Coornhert's motivations and arguments for religious toleration, as expressed in his most important writings that appeared after 1577. The final chapter will then resume the narrative of Coornhert's life."

3

"ONLY GOD IS MASTER OVER MAN'S CONSCIENCE"

ADVOCATES OF RELIGIOUS FREEDOM IN THE SIXTEENTH CENTURY

TWO YEARS AFTER COORNHERT'S BIRTH, Erasmus penned his defense of the freedom of the will, against Luther, to which the Wittenberg Reformer responded with a vehement defense of the bondage of the will and the freedom of God's grace.[1] With this exchange a Rubicon was crossed and a rift made apparent between humanism and the Reformation.[2] This rupture was by no means complete, and we can see the influence of humanism in men like Philip Melanchthon or Huldreich Zwingli (who admired Erasmus). But up to Coornhert's death, this divide was an important determinant in the attitude taken towards religious deviance, with the humanist element generally advocating concord and reconciliation.

Somewhat later (1531), Sebastian Franck, another admirer of Erasmus and initially a follower of Luther, published a heterodox "bible of history" that manifested an aversion to institutionalized religion and ceremony as well as a

---

[1]Disiderius Erasmus, *De libero arbitrio diatribe* (1524); Martin Luther, *De servo arbitrio* (1525).

[2]Roland H. Bainton, *The Reformation of the Sixteenth Century*, 14th ed. (Boston: Beacon Press, 1966), 68–69.

conviction that the true church had fallen when the original disciples died.[3] Franck and the mystical-spiritualist strain in the Reformation that he represents constitute another important groundswell of opposition against the omnipresent practice and animus of constraint and enforcement of uniformity in religion.

The last centuries of the Middle Ages were marked by societal change and religious ferment. Evangelical movements emerged (such as the Bohemian Hussites and the English Wycliffites) that focused on the Bible and manifested a strong antisacerdotalism. Renewed religious sensibilities were increasingly expressed outside the bounds of the established church. In the Low Countries, the *Devotio moderna* of Geert Groote (1340–84), although still sanctioned by the papacy, reflected an aversion to the religious "establishment," and its followers strove for an internalized, practical, and personal piety.[4]

At the same time, the Renaissance acted as a catalyst on the intellectual development in parts of Europe, especially urbanized regions such as the Italian city-states and the Low Countries. The term "Renaissance" itself of course indicates a program and a historical self-awareness: it tends to negate and bypass the "nonperiod" of the Dark Ages and reach back to a putative golden age of Classic Antiquity when pure unadulterated Latin was written. This Burckhardian understanding of the Renaissance as a clear break with the medieval past[5] has given way to an increased awareness of the continuity in this movement. The Renaissance functioned more as an accelerator in several areas. In many ways the Renaissance also created the "context" and atmosphere contributing to the ferment that brought about epochal developments in science and in other fields.

Within the Renaissance, humanism was a literary and educational movement that provided the motivational and instrumental nexus from which the Reformation would spring. Humanists never embraced a unified ideology, never formed a uniform group, but they did share a common "program" centered on the *studia humanitatis* and the value of *bonae litterae*.[6] They strove for a new golden age and clung to an almost chiliastic expectation that such an age might be at hand, thanks in large part to the emancipation of humankind

[3]Sebastian Franck, *Chronica, Zeytbuch und Geschychtbibel* (1531).

[4]J. van Rompaey, "De Bourgondische Periode," in *De Lage Landen van prehistorie tot 1500*, ed. R.C. van Caenegem and H. P. H. Jansen (Amsterdam: Elsevier, 1978), 420–21.

[5]Jacob Burckhardt, *Die Kultur der Renaissance in Italien* (1860).

[6]See Paul Oskar Kristeller, *Renaissance Thought II: Papers on Humanism and the Arts* (New York: Harper Torchbooks, 1961), chap. 1: "Humanist Learning in the Italian Renaissance," 1–19.

through the liberating forces of rationalism and by way of the *imitatio* and *emulatio* of the classics.

Central to the humanist endeavor were the philological efforts and the urge to go *ad fontes*. In their exegetical efforts humanists like Jacques Lefèvre d'Etaples sought to bypass the cumbersome accretions of mechanical medieval exegesis and penetrate to the core of the sacred texts, interpreted in a strongly Christological sense. Lorenzo Valla's discovery of the forgery of the *Donation of Constantine* had the double effect of demonstrating the superiority and useful-ness of the critical philological method and of undermining complacent asser-tions of papal supremacy. A good example of how dear this "fountain" of crystal-clear waters from antiquity was to the humanists is Erasmus (1469–1536),[7] who once reportedly admitted that the most moving episode in his life was when he chanced upon an original fragment of Cicero's writings in Lou-vain's university library. His great passion and life's aim was the pursuit of optimally pure texts, as when he edited the classical and patristic authors and taught linguistic skills in his *Colloquies*. There was a genuine sense here that content could not be conveyed without proper form, or that the sword of high moral principles could only be effective when it had at its disposal the whet-stone of pure Latin, the perfect mode of human expression. Furthermore, the study of the classics became the avenue for the acquisition of many virtues thought to be essential: rhetoric taught how to use language to influence oth-ers, and the vicissitudes in the fortunes of the Greek city-states and the Roman Republic provided numerous persuasive analogies with current situations and events. This same set of mental preoccupations and priorities would still be very much in evidence in the late-sixteenth-century humanist scholar Justus Lipsius.

The period between 1510 and 1525 was the high point of humanism in Europe, a period when hopes of restoring an age of purity and lauded virtues were peaking. It produced a great number of important texts, such as Eras-mus's *Enchiridion* and the Polyglot Bible, and contributed to changes in the philosophy and practices of monarchical government. But when the Reforma-tion began to spread, many humanists found themselves between the Scylla of theologizing and dogmatizing, which they firmly rejected, and the Charybdis of tradition, superstition, and fetishism that they loathed. Erasmus is an

---

[7]For Erasmus see Johan Huizinga, *Erasmus and the Age of Reformation*, trans. G. N. Clark (Princeton, N.J.: Princeton University Press, 1984); C. Augustijn, *Erasmus van Rotterdam* (To-ronto: University of Toronto Press, 1991).

excellent case in point: he was inclined, caught between a rock and a hard place, to take refuge under the rock. He never tired of criticizing sterile Roman Catholic theology; indeed this scoffing came naturally to him. His most popular works, highly critical of Church practices—the *Encomium Moriae*, the content of his *Colloquies*—were more or less the gratuitous by-products of his philological exploits that were far more important to him. But despite early pro-Reform sympathies, he could not break with the Catholic Church, and although he tried to avoid conflict, ultimately he could not avoid it.

Erasmus regarded Christianity primarily as a way of life and sought to honor his motto: *Vita magis quam disputatio* (life rather than disputations). He lacked the inclination to theologize since he believed that it was an excess of theologizing that had perverted true faith. His insistence on living the Christian life—perhaps manifesting the influence of his exposure to the *Devotio moderna* during his youth—and his efforts to find the doctrinal common ground that he regarded as a prerequisite for the restoration of Christian unity were to have a great impact. The central goal for Erasmus was the restoration of concord in Christendom, and he felt that his philological endeavors—allowing learned men to return to the documents that stood at Christianity's cradle —would provide the tool that would help rejuvenate Christ's faith.[8] When Luther's movement spread, Erasmus advocated it be tolerated temporarily until unity was restored through a departure from theological hairsplitting and a return "to scriptural and patristic sources, the careful study of the sacred text in its original language, and reference to the Fathers, whose interpretation was closest to the *philosophia Christi.*"[9]

Erasmus's advocacy of a simple creed and a common ground of fundamental verities found practical if unsuccessful application at the interreligious colloquies that were held in Germany (1530–50) and in France, culminating in the Colloquy of Poissy, 1561.[10] Erasmus saw man as a rational creature, fundamentally able, when informed, to make a wise choice. This rationalism, as well as his moral imperative (expressed through ethical rationalism, for example, in his ridiculing of superstitions or of rich pompousness), greatly influenced critics across the theological spectrum. His insistence on free will and on living

[8]G. H. M. Posthumus Meyjes, "Protestants irenisme in de 16e en eerste helft van de 17e eeuw," *Nederlands Theologisch Tijdschrift* 36 (1982): 210.

[9]Lecler, *Toleration and the Reformation*, 1:125.

[10]See Lecler, *Toleration and the Reformation*, 1:18 ff.; on the Colloquy of Poissy, see Donald Nugent, *Ecumenism in the Age of the Reformation: The Colloquy of Poissy.* Harvard Historical Studies, 89 (Cambridge: Harvard University Press, 1974).

the Christian life put him in the spiritual company of the Anabaptists. All these factors led G. H. Williams to conclude that "Erasmus was, more than he would himself acknowledge, the source and sanction for much in Anabaptism, Spiritualism, and Evangelical Rationalism."[11]

Using distinct labels such as in the passage just quoted could be misleading. It is now known that the sixteenth century was an age of beginning confessionalism and growing plurality of faiths, more or less coinciding with the breaking up into sovereign political units of the medieval *christianitas*. Scholars today must not project back onto this age a relatively modern notion such as denominationalism, because virtually all participants in the sixteenth-century disintegration of the one church were either convinced that they represented the entire *corpus christianum* in its pristine form, or that division was a sad, temporary situation that would be resolved.[12] This corpus naturally extended to the polity as well, for Catholic and Protestant churches "shared a belief in the unity of the body social and political…."[13] For most of the sixteenth century, a majority of the historical participants still saw religious concord as the supreme goal and coveted outcome of their endeavors, whether bloody or peaceful. Only in the final decades did an increasing number of people abandon this hope for reunion. This reality is reflected in Jean Bodin's *Colloquium Heptaplomeres* (1593), whose participants unanimously decide to live in harmony but never to discuss religion again.[14]

In spite of Erasmus's insistence on his cosmopolitanism, his nondogmatic approach and irenic appeal especially affected the Low Countries. In fact, the link between the humanist and the early Reformation in the Habsburg Netherlands actually was strengthened after the final break between Erasmus and Luther in 1524: because of the extreme persecution of heterodoxy in the

---

[11]Williams, *Radical Reformation*, 42. See also Kamen, *Rise of Toleration*, 24–28, who remarks that Erasmus's actual achievements for toleration were "minimal," but that he found many supporters in the next generation. One blot on Erasmus's legacy of toleration is, of course, his negative attitude towards the Jews, based on their ceremonialism and their nonacceptance of Christ: see C. P. van Andel, *Jodenhaat & Jodenangst over meer dan twintig eeuwen antisemitisme*, 2d ed. (Amersfoort: De Horstink, 1984), 72–73.

[12]See Posthumus Meyjes, "Protestants irenisme," 207.

[13]James D. Tracy, "Magistracy: Germany and the Low Countries," in *Oxford Encyclopedia of the Reformation*, ed. Hans J. Hillerbrand.

[14]On Jean Bodin's *Colloquium Heptaplomeres*, which was not published during his lifetime, see Lecler, *Toleration and the Reformation*, 2:178–84, and M. L. D. Kuntz, "Introduction" to Jean Bodin, *Colloquium of the Seven about the Secrets of the Sublime*, trans. and ed. Kuntz (Princeton, N.J.: Princeton University Press, 1975).

Habsburg Low Countries, "the main Netherlands Reformation could, for some decades, develop only as a nondogmatic pluriform crypto-Protestantism..."[15]

Many humanists eventually would take sides in the religious conflicts that wracked and polarized Europe.[16] The spirit of humanism was like a dynamo, helping to set in motion several reform movements across Europe. Because of its very nature, humanism never coalesced into a well-defined party or ideology. Since most men, however, cannot live in a state of fluidity or spiritual anarchy for very long without a feeling of anxiety and discomfort, the Reformation—be it Protestant or Catholic—answered a fundamental need in man to make (philosophical) sense of reality. Those who held positions of responsibility keenly felt the need for institutions. Pedagogues desired more than just debunking, and to many humanist pedagogues, the Reformed explanation of things made supreme sense. Some believed they had found the harmony cherished by the humanists in the new all-embracing view. Thus, new orthodoxies were established that failed to convince an Erasmus that they were of a higher moral standard—the essential criterion for him—than the one that they purportedly replaced.

Rejection of the institutionalized Reform movements on the basis of their new dogmatism and formalism, and because of their failure to give evidence of moral regeneration, also motivated the believers in a more "inward," spiritualized faith. Like the Reformers, Spiritualists advocated free Bible research, but as a result of the notion of a direct and personal relationship with God—an individual approach to salvation that we also find in Erasmus—they attach great importance to an unimpeded access of the Spirit to the individual. At the same time they tend to minimize the importance of "externals": ceremonies, sacraments, the church, often also the supreme authority of the Bible, for they consider the Spirit of prior significance; the Bible without that Spirit becomes a "paper pope," as Franck put it.[17]

Beyond the influence of Erasmus, men like Thomas Müntzer, Caspar Schwenckfeld, and Franck were influenced by late-medieval mystical traditions found in Eckhart and Tauler. Although these thinkers themselves were often

---

[15]Israel, *Dutch Republic*, 53.

[16]Thus one of Lefèvre's pupils (Netherlander Josse Clichtove) in the end fell in with Roman Catholic orthodoxy, another (Guillaume Farel) became a Protestant leader, and yet another (Vatable) just like his teacher and Erasmus, sought the golden mean.

[17]J. N. Bakhuizen van den Brink and W. F. Dankbaar, *Handboek der kerkgeschiedenis*, vol. 3: *Reformatie en Contra-reformatie* (Leeuwarden: De Tille B. V., 1980), 97–98; the characterization of the Bible as "papieren Papst" is from Lecler, *Toleration and the Reformation*, 1:168.

too "inwardly directed" to be involved in daily life, some sixteenth-century radical thinkers took the raw material of transrationalism and transinstitutionalism found with them, and turned them into anti-intellectual and anti-institutional arguments.[18]

A highly influential text, often employed or referred to by the sixteenth-century exponents of radical dissent, is the anonymous fourteenth-century tract known as the *Theologia Deutsch* (German Theology).[19] Henry Niclaes, founder of the Family of Love, was profoundly influenced by this work (and by Thomas à Kempis' *Imitation of Christ*). He, and his main disciple (and later rival) Barrefelt, felt attracted to the *Theologia*'s theme of the return to a Platonic oneness and of the freedom of the will. They embraced the notion, found in this booklet, that incarnation continued after the Ascension of Christ. This incarnation—known among Familists as *Vergottung* (godding)—takes place, they believed, whenever the Spirit enters the individual. Calvin execrated the *Theologia Deutsch*, calling it filth and devil's poison because it taught the "degenerate doctrine" that perfection can be attained on earth.[20] Franck paraphrased the tract in his *Paradoxa*, and Castellio translated it into Latin and French. For Franck it confirmed his belief that in his day and age there was no identifiable place or person with authority in religious matters. The locus becomes internalized, for God dwells in "the heart," or in "conscience," and does not have a preference for the learned or powerful, but speaks to the humble and lowly.[21] The *Theologia* confirms the subjectivization of faith that takes place with the mystical-Spiritualist thinkers.[22] The more "down-to-earth" Protestant dissenter, Sebastian Castellio, also defended the *Theologia*'s insistence on the basic incommunicability of the experience of regeneration. He stressed the conversion of the will to God—that is, the abandonment of one's own will—is a prerequisite to following God's will in a living faith, expressed in moral acts. "True believers," he affirmed, "receive the 'force and courage' to fulfill the commandments."[23]

[18]Steven E. Ozment, *Mysticism and Dissent: Religious Ideology and Social Protest in the Sixteenth Century* (New Haven: Yale University Press, 1973), 8, 12.

[19]Ibid., 14–60.

[20]Alastair Hamilton, *The Family of Love* (Cambridge: James Clarke & Co, 1981), 8–10.

[21]Ozment, *Mysticism and Dissent*, 15. Pope Paul V placed it on the Index; see 15, 35, 37–38.

[22]Cf. Samme Zijlstra, "'Tgeloove is vrij': De tolerantiediscussie in de Noordelijke Nederlanden tussen 1520 en 1795," in Marijke Gijswijt-Hofstra, ed., *Een Schijn van Verdraagzaamheid: Afwijking en tolerantie in Nederland van de zestiende eeuw tot heden* (Hilversum: Verloren, 1989), 44.

[23]Ozment, *Mysticism and Dissent*, 45. Here again is the notion of perfectibilism, of which Coornhert also was an adherent; see also chap. 4 of this work.

Around 1556, Coornhert read the *Theologia* for the first time, and after that he read it at least once a year. In his *Paradoxa* (1558), he praises it, writing that "it is a small book, but contains only pearls, gold, and gems."[24] The purely mystical aspects, however, the loss of self in an *unio mystica,* withdrawal from the world, and quietistic resignation, are alien to Coornhert's activist, practical attitude towards life.[25] One element of the *Theologia* that does leave a strong imprint on Coornhert, as we will see—but mostly through the mediation of Sebastian Franck, and, to a lesser degree, Caspar Schwenckfeld—was the idea of the invisible church, vested in the hearts of true Christians wherever they may be found.

Franck (1499–1542) joined the Reformation after he had been ordained as a Catholic priest, but as a Lutheran preacher he was soon disappointed at what he saw as the deplorable morals prevalent within that church as well. He left the priesthood and worked as a translator and author, translating an account of the Ottoman Turks in which he makes reference to the rise of spiritual religion as a new, fourth force besides Lutheranism, Zwinglianism, and Anabaptism.[26]

In a letter to his friend, John Campanus (a radical Lutheran who became an Anabaptist), probably written in 1531, Franck gave full expression to his feelings about religious institutions and the invisible spiritual Church.[27] In the letter he indicts all who claim to be religious teachers in his day, and asserts that the fall of the pure, original church of Christ already took place c. 130 A.D. The church fathers who came after that, Franck wrote, were generally wolves and representatives of the Antichrist.[28] These false, external teachers confuse the Old with the New Testament: when the New Testament does not provide the needed or desired ammunition to support war, the swearing of oaths, or the power of the magistrate, they resort to the "empty quiver" of the Old Testament. But Christ's outward church was, in reality, taken up into heaven and concealed "in the Spirit and in truth,"[29] and for the last fourteen hundred years, Franck writes, there has been no gathered church or real sacraments. The

---

[24]Coornhert, *Paradoxa: T'samensprake vande volmaeckte Onvolmaecktheyt, tusschen Opinie ende Experientie,* in *Wercken,* vol. 1, fol. 418C. (This passage is also quoted in part by Bonger, *Leven en werk,* 27.)

[25]Cf. Bonger, *Motivering,* 123–28.

[26]Ozment, *Mysticism and Dissent,* 140 n.18.

[27]Franck, "A Letter to John Campanus"; also Williams's introduction to the letter, ibid., 145–46.

[28]Ibid., 148, 151. He mentions, among others, Clement, Irenaeus, Tertullian, and on p. 151 "foolish Ambrose, Augustine, Jerome, Gregory" of whom "not one knew the Lord."

[29]Ibid., 149, 151.

Spirit, however, still imparts the essence of these sacraments to the faithful, while the external sacraments—which Franck compares with dolls (playthings for the immature)—have become tools in the hands of Satan. Those who listen to the Inner Word of the Spirit thus have access to the essence, or reality, of which the sacraments and ceremonies were merely the symbol. Franck claims, therefore (this claim was refuted by Anabaptist leaders,[30] since it also negated their church organization) that any effort spent on existing churches is wasted. The church is entirely spiritual, he claims, and exists wherever people are baptized by the Inner Word, be they Christians, "Turks," or pagans.[31] Christ's church can be gathered only by someone who bears a distinct sign of his divinely ordained mission. In the absence of such a verifiable sign, all those who make claims are false teachers who act of their own accord.[32]

In Franck's highly subjective conception of faith, nothing can claim precedence over the inner working of the Spirit. He tells Campanus that if he finds that Scripture appears to contradict what his "conscience" tells him, he should obey his conscience.[33] It is this subjectivization of faith, this belief in an invisible church, that we also find in Coornhert, together with a rejection of "ceremonialism." Important differences, however, existed between the two. Coornhert is less extreme in his treatment of the church fathers than Franck, and less relativizing in his understanding of the status of Scripture.[34]

Franck was an advocate of universal tolerance also for the non-Christian, and regarded persecution as an unmistakable mark of heresy. God is impartial (*unparteiisch*), and so should we be.[35] Franck was the first to stipulate that only God knows the true believers and that human beings are unable to identify heretics.[36] Furthermore, Franck believed that the true followers of the Spirit were scarce. This caused him to give his own, original interpretation of

[30]See e.g. Dirk Philips' defense of the Anabaptist church as the restored church of the apostles: Dirk (here called Dietrich) Philips, "The Church of God," in Williams, ed., *Spiritual and Anabaptist Writers*, 228–60, esp. 240–55.

[31]Franck, "Letter to Campanus," 150; cf. Ozment, *Mysticism and Dissent*, 163.

[32]Franck, "A Letter to John Campanus," 153–54. This notion of the "uncalled teachers" can be found in Sebastian Franck, *280 Paradoxes or Wondrous Sayings*, trans. and introd. by E. J. Furcha. Texts and Studies in Religion, 26 (Lewiston: Edwin Mellen Press, 1986): 305–13 (paradoxes 171–74).

[33]Franck, "Letter to John Campanus," 159–60.

[34]For a clear survey of similarities and differences between the two men, see H. Bonger and A. J. Gelderblom, "Coornhert en Sebastian Franck," *De zeventiende eeuw* 12, no. 2 (1996): 321–39.

[35]Lecler, *Toleration and the Reformation*, 1:174.

[36]Guggisberg, ed., *Religiöse Toleranz*, introd. to chap. 2, p. 63.

the famous "proof text" of toleration, the parable of the wheat and the tares (Matt. 13:30)—he deemed it most likely that Christ had forbidden his disciples to weed out the tares, because he foresaw that the religious leaders themselves would soon constitute these tares and be only too eager to get rid of the wheat (calling it tares), so they could have the field to themselves![37]

Pessimism about the state of the world and especially about religious leaders in his day contributes to Franck's often displayed anti-intellectualism. In the Bible, he reminds his readers, we see that God even spoke through a donkey (namely Balaam's ass), and Christ's disciples usually were unlearned men. In a selection from Agrippa's *Praise of the Donkey*, published by Franck, Agrippa observes that "often a wretched, coarse idiot ... sees what the great schoolteachers and doctors, ruined and corrupted by human arts, cannot see."[38] In Franck's *Paradoxes* we find a pithy statement that sums up this anti-intellectual sentiment: "the more learned, the more perverted."[39] The self-made Coornhert did not share Franck's pessimism,[40] but he did employ the anti-intellectual theme, often referring to himself as an unlearned idiot.[41]

By 1562, Franck's ideas were quite influential in the Netherlands, and many editions of his works appeared in Dutch translation.[42] These elicited reactions from defenders of "orthodoxy." Becker found that one of Franck's detractors paraphrases not Franck but rather Coornhert, namely his (1558) *Verschooninghe* (*Apology*). From this and other evidence—the writings of Coornhert's inveterate Reformed opponent, Reinier Donteclock, for example—it is clear that perceptive contemporaries were well aware of the close affinity of Coornhert's ideas with those of Franck.[43] It is mainly through

---

[37]Roland H. Bainton, "The Parable of the Ta res as the Proof Text for Religious Liberty to the End of the Sixteenth Century," *Church History* 1 (1932): 85.

[38]Quoted in Ozment, *Mysticism and Dissent*, 147.

[39]Franck, *Paradoxes*, 306 (paradox 171).

[40]This is seen, by Bonger and Gelderblom, "Coornhert en Sebastian Franck," 329, as an essential difference between the two.

[41]See, e.g. *Aertzenij der zielen* in *Wercken*, vol. 1, fol. 472B; *Schijndeught der secten* in ibid., vol. 3, fol. ccccxliiiD; *Hemel-werck*, ibid., vol. 2, fol. cccxlv, where he uses the above-mentioned motto in Dutch: *Hoe geleerder hoe verkeerder.*

[42]Bruno Becker, "Nicolai's Inlassching over de Franckisten," *Nederlands Archief voor de Kerkgeschiedenis*, 18 (1925): 286–96. See also Cornelis Augustijn and Theo Parmentier, "Sebastian Franck in den nördlichen Niederlanden 1550 bis 1600," in Müller, ed., *Sebastian Franck (1499–1542). Wolfenbütteler Forschungen*, 56 (Wiesbaden: Harrassowitz Verlag, 1993), 303–18.

[43]Becker, "Nicolai's Inlassching," 288–91; 294. Augustijn and Parmentier, "Sebastian Franck," 308–9, point out several passages in Coornhert's *Verschooninghe*, in *Wercken*, vol. 3, fol. xviii–xxiiii, and in his (1574) *Schijndeught der secten*, in ibid., fols. cccxlii–cccl, where Coornhert either

Coornhert that Arminius and his followers would become informed of Franck's ideas.[44]

A close relationship existed between Sebastian Franck and Caspar Schwenckfeld (1499–1542)—in their analogous peregrinations and in the perception of their contemporaries, who often mentioned both in one breath.[45] Schwenckfeld also started out (1518–26) as a follower of Luther, only to become "the chief exponent of an irenic and evangelical Spiritualism...."[46] In 1526, Schwenckfeld had a spiritual experience, which he describes as the *Heimsuchung Gottes* ("God's finding of a home"). After this regeneration, he writes, "I could not join with any party or church in the observance of the sacraments and in other respects, nor could I allow men to rule over my faith." He was no systematic theologian, nor did he have a university degree, yet Schwenckfeld started out believing he could reconcile the old (the Catholic Church) with the new. No sudden rupture occurred between Schwenckfeld and Luther, but Schwenckfeld gradually drifted away from the Reformer by charting the heterodox waters of Spiritualism. He maintained his belief in justification through faith, but with a synergistic emphasis that safeguarded the freedom of the will: "Justification," he wrote, "derives from the knowledge (*Erkenntnis*) of Christ through faith." He regarded this "knowledge" as a living knowledge, expressed in a moral life. It was based on a spiritual understanding of the Eucharist as "the inward feeding upon the divine nutriment, the bread from heaven," which freed the will that, up to that regenerative point, had been bound, enabling the reborn person to keep God's commandments.[47]

Despite affinity and similarities between Franck and Schwenckfeld on several aspects of religion, some fundamental differences can be detected in their respective attitudes and ideas. Franck was the more radical of the two. Although Schwenckfeld believed in Spirit over flesh and Inner Word over Outer Word, he did not regard the external church as entirely useless. Because of the abuses in the ceremonial and other practices in the churches, however,

refers directly to Franck, or gives specific signs of the latter's influence. Cf. Hans Weigelt, "Sebastian Franck und die lutherische Reformation: Die Reformation im Spiegel des Werkes Sebastian Francks," in Müller, ed., *Sebastian Franck*, 50.

[44]Weigelt, "Sebastian Franck," 51.

[45]See Robert Emmet McLaughlin, *Caspar Schwenckfeld, Reluctant Radical: His Life to 1540* (New Haven: Yale University Press, 1986).

[46]Williams, *Radical Reformation*, 199,

[47]See ibid., 203–4, 207; see also Lecler, *Toleration and the Reformation*, 1:178.

he called for a suspension *(Stillstand)* of the Lord's Supper.[48] In the meantime, until the day when God would reestablish his church, Christians should gather in conventicles for prayer. This was Schwenckfeld's so-called *Stillstands-kirche*,[49] and it shows, despite his rejection of current divisions and practices, that he did believe that in the end the pure sacraments and a true, apostolic church could and would be restituted.[50]

The two men also differed on Scripture, which played a more central role for Schwenckfeld. Franck tended to regard Scripture as historically dated and of more secondary importance. Schwenckfeld saw the Bible as "a mirror in which the Inner Word could find its reflection, and as an arena in which the believer could exercise his knowledge and faith."[51] For Franck, the Incarnation, the Fall, the Crucifixion, were timeless and reoccurred in each believer,[52] and Christ's importance mostly resides in his work as a teacher or guide. But for Schwenckfeld, Christ is much more central.[53]

Both men, finally, were ardent proponents of religious toleration, but here also we may observe different motivations: Franck sees all external religion as false and irrelevant per se, so persecution can serve no conceivable purpose. The core of Schwenckfeld's advocacy of toleration is the freedom of the Spirit.[54]

In a 1574 tract, Coornhert praises Franck and Schwenckfeld, but he adds two caveats:

> I find in Franck, in Swenckfelt, indeed in all of you something good that pleases me. Does that mean that I agree with all of you on everything? Frankly, no. For in all of you, also in Franck and in Swenckfelt, I find fallacies that displease me. But that you [he addresses his Calvinist and Lutheran counterparts in this dialogue]... in your bitter slandering of those men act in open violation of the kindly nature of love, is quite obvious to anyone who

[48]R. Emmet McLaughlin, "Sebastian Franck and Caspar Schwenckfeld: Two Spiritualist *Viae*," in Müller, ed., *Sebastian Franck*, 73.

[49]See K. van Berkel, "Aggaeus de Albada en de crisis in de Opstand (1579–1587)," *Bijdragen en mededelingen betreffende de geschiedenis der Nederlanden* 96, no. 1 (1981): 11; the Dutch *stilstand* as a term indicating postponement of positive action also was used by David Joris: see Williams, *Radical Reformation*, 542.

[50]McLaughlin, "Sebastian Franck," 73.

[51]Ibid., 76.

[52]Franck, *Paradoxes*, 144; see e.g. paradox 85: "Therefore Christ was born only now, suffered now, heaven was opened only now and with it came the Holy Spirit and God's grace...."

[53]McLaughlin, "Sebastian Franck," 78–79.

[54]Ibid., 77.

understands her (love's) goodly nature. Furthermore, it [this slan-
der] also seems to contradict the truth as regards Franck, with
whose books I am more familiar than with those of Swenckfelt.[55]

Schwenckfeld's ideas, however, also reached Coornhert through another
channel, namely his Schwenckfeldian friend, the Groninger jurist Aggaeus van
Albada (c. 1525–87).[56] Much like Coornhert, Albada drifted away from the
Catholic Church without ever making a formal break.[57] In the 1560s he
became a Schwenckfeldian.[58] He was friends with the irenic humanist Cassander and corresponded with Marnix of St. Aldegonde. He became an imperial official at the Reichskammergericht in Spiers and councilor of the bishop
of Würzburg, Germany.[59] This position provides a good illustration of the
conformism of which Schwenckfeldians were capable, for the external church
was not of great importance to them.[60] Coornhert struck up a friendship with
Albada during his exile in Cologne (1567). Albada was part of the States General delegation to the failed peace negotiations in Cologne between Spain and
the rebellious Netherlands in 1579. Due to his fluency in Latin and German, he
acted as the spokesperson for the States General, offering an eloquent defense
of the Revolt. At the behest of the States General, Albada made a protocol of
the documents that had been exchanged at the negotiations to demonstrate to
the Holy Roman Emperor, Rudolph II, that the failure of the negotiations
could not be blamed on the nascent Dutch Republic. The States approved the
protocol's publication. Albada augmented the final version with copious annotations, drawn from various sources containing much monarchomach, irenic,
and pro-toleration material.[61] For the *Synod*, which he published the next
year, Coornhert drew heavily on this wellspring of highly relevant material,
containing quotations from Castellio's *De haereticis an sint persequendi*, and
from a missive by Schwenckfeld.

---

[55]Coornhert, *Wercken*, vol. 3, fol. cccxlviD.
[56]On Albada, see Wiebe Bergsma, *Aggaeus van Albada (c. 1525–1587), schwenckfeldiaan, staatsman en strijder voor verdraagzaamheid* (Meppel: Kripps Repro, 1983).
[57]Van Berkel, "Aggaeus de Albada," 3.
[58]Ibid., 4, 12–13.
[59]Bonger, *Leven en werk*, 62.
[60]Bergsma, *Aggaeus van Albada*, 18.
[61]It was published in Latin in 1580 as *Acta Pacificationis*; in 1581 in Dutch, entitled *Acten vanden Vredehandel gheschiet te Colen…*. See Van Berkel, "Aggaeus de Albada," 4, and see ibid., 4–9, for the sources that Albada used.

Albada and Coornhert agreed on some significant and, at the time highly controversial, issues. The two drew a sharp dividing line between the inner and the outer man; they asserted that governments ought to have no power over the inner man (his spirit) and must only safeguard citizens from the attacks of others; they felt strongly that faith is a *donum Dei* (a gift from God), falling outside of the competence or reach of the government; they firmly believed that more than one religion could and should be allowed to coexist in a state. These were all arguments for toleration that the two men shared.[62] But they also disagreed, especially on the meaning of Christ's incarnation and on original sin. In a 1583 letter, Coornhert urges his friend to come to Haarlem and stay for a few weeks so they can discuss these matters. He was particularly keen on discussing original sin, which, he writes, Albada may consider trivial, but which Coornhert saw as being of the utmost importance "since the misunderstanding of this issue is the fertile mother of many pernicious errors."[63] Coornhert was bent on refuting the notion of original sin because it went against his perfectibilism, that is, his cherished concept of humanity's ability completely to obey God's commandments.

Great affinity existed between Albada and Coornhert with regard to their advocacy of toleration, but in their life stories they drew opposite conclusions from analogous assessments of the intolerant direction into which the new Dutch Republic was going. Coornhert immersed himself in debates and polemics, aimed at reversing a trend that he regarded as pernicious. Albada opted for a clear conscience, declining invitations to take up important positions in the Dutch Republic and remaining in Cologne as an outsider.[64]

The incipient sixteenth-century debate on freedom of religion accelerated suddenly in the wake of the well-known incident of the burning at the stake of Michael Servetus, the "total heretic," in Geneva (1553). This execution provided the occasion for the publication of Castellio's famous compendium of arguments for toleration, *De haereticis an sint persequendi*. The case of the anti-Trinitarian Servetus[65] challenged the emergent Reform to show its true

---

[62]Van Berkel,"Aggaeus," 7–8; Bergsma, *Aggaeus de Albada*, 95–105.

[63]*Wercken*, vol. 3, fol. 110B; quoted in Bonger, *Leven en werk*, 239. Rejection of the concept of original sin is also the reason for Coornhert's refusal to translate the Schwenckfeldian Johann Sigismund Werner's *Postille*. For other differences between Albada and Coornhert, see Bergsma, *Aggaeus van Albada*, 13, 87–89.

[64]Van Berkel, "Aggaeus," 20.

[65]On Servetus, see Roland H. Bainton, *Hunted Heretic: The Life and Death of Michael Servetus 1511–1553* (Boston: Beacon Press, 1953).

colors at a time when Geneva and other centers of the movement were under pressure to show that they were the nuclei of a well-ordered new polity, and not the harbingers of unbridled religious anarchy and sedition. When the extent of Calvin's flexibility was put to the test, the outcome was the stake.[66] Bouwsma, however, in his biography of Calvin, suggests that the Reformer's tolerant, fideist, humanist side was bothered by the perceived necessity to act with rigor against Servetus.[67] In 1536 John Calvin published his *Institutes* with the express purpose, as he would later write in the introduction to his Commentary on the Psalms, of refuting those who accused all victims of persecution of being Anabaptists and fomenters of sedition. Calvin set out, instead, to vindicate those "godly persons" who had laid down their lives for the true faith. In Geneva between 1536 and 1538, and then from 1541 until his death in 1564, he tried to build the structure of God's Church on the foundations laid down in the *Institutes* and the *Ecclesiastical Ordinances.*

Confronted with the Spanish heresiarch, the Reformed notion of the freedom of conscience showed its limitations: this freedom was circumscribed by the demands of God's honor. Calvin defines conscience as a medium between God and the individual. This conscience, Calvin and Beza thought, ought to be free from any human determination. This did not imply the freedom to worship God according to one's whims because, as Beza stated, freedom of conscience is the freedom to obey God, and the pure worship of God was seen as having been reestablished in the Reform. Calvin's "freedom of conscience" is an inviolable sanctuary, but not an inalienable right.[68] Beza characterized the religious liberty, such as that demanded by a Castellio, as the freedom for everyone "to go to hell in his own way." The main Reformers did not recognize the right of an "erring conscience": conscience only has validity when it is based on knowledge, as taught in the Scripture-based church. "Heretics," Bainton summarizes, "have only a fictitious conscience."[69]

On church discipline, Calvin writes, in the *Institutes,* that minor infractions should not be treated too severely, but in all cases obstinacy is condemnable

---

[66]Andrew Pettegree, "Michael Servetus and the Limits of Tolerance," *History Today,* 40 (Feb. 1990): 40–45.

[67]Bouwsma, *John Calvin,* 27, 244 n. 115.

[68]See Alain Dufour, "La notion de liberté de conscience chez les Réformateurs," in *La liberté de conscience (XVIe–XVIIe siècles): Actes du Colloque de Mulhouse et Bâle (1989),* ed. Hans R. Guggisberg et al. (Geneva: Librairie Droz, 1991), 18, 28.

[69]Roland H. Bainton, "The Struggle for Religious Liberty," *Church History* 10 (1941): 97, 108.

because people must not be allowed merely to follow their own whims. Such license would, he feared, lead to a breakdown of all order.[70] In the ideal polity the sword of the Church is strengthened by the operation of the civil sword. It is the duty of the civil authorities, Calvin writes, to safeguard society against blasphemy and "other public offenses against religion." This, he emphasizes, does not contravene earlier statements on Christian liberty, for civil authorities may not craft laws on religious matters. However, he goes on, "I approve of a civil administration that aims to prevent the true religion which is contained in God's law from being openly...violated and defiled with impunity...."[71] Calvin, and indeed most religious leaders of his day, regarded Servetus as a flagrant violator of the law of God, and saw permissiveness toward heresy as cruelty.[72]

In his *Defensio Orthodoxae Fidei*, written in 1554 in defense of the execution of Servetus, Calvin states that as long as there is hope that a sinner will mend his ways, we should not punish.[73] Only those guilty of crass impiety must be purged from the community in order to prevent the spread of their pollution.[74] Ananias and Sapphira were justly smitten (Acts 5:5–10), for they had sinned against the Holy Spirit, and therefore God's honor was at stake. If, the argument goes, judges are appointed to protect the rights of human beings, then should they leave God's honor open to attack?[75] The heretic, Calvin claims, is not forced to believe, as some of his critics charged. It is the heretic's outrage against God's honor that is justly punished.[76] When the same critics point out Christ's meekness, Calvin in turn argues that Jesus cleansed the temple by force. Jesus' meekness, Calvin writes, never was intended for the malicious and the obstinate.[77] Castellio would point out quickly the difference between Calvin's attitude toward apostates and his milder stance vis-à-vis the Turks and other "open enemies" of Christianity: the latter's "deviance" was condoned, whereas "religion's friends" were destroyed.[78] Calvin defends this difference in response: heretics are, in his view, more pernicious than Turks or

---

[70]Calvin, *Institutes*, 2:1229–30; cf. Ozment, *Mysticism and Dissent*, 182–83.

[71]Calvin, *Institutes*, 2:1488.

[72]See Robert White, "Castellio against Calvin: The Turk in the Toleration Controversy of the Sixteenth Century," *Bibliothèque d'Humanisme et Renaissance* 46, no. 3 (1984): 574.

[73]Calvin, *Defensio Orthodoxae Fidei*, CR 8:462.

[74]E. Doumergue, *Jean Calvin: Les Hommes et les Choses de son Temps*, 6 (Neuilly-sur-Seine: Editions de "la Cause," 1926), 417.

[75]Calvin, quoted in E. Doumergue, *Jean Calvin*, 6:412.

[76]Ibid., 6:413.

[77]Ibid., 6:414.

[78]White, "Castellio against Calvin," 585.

Jews, because they "bore from within."[79] This relative mildness may confirm the observation by Kühn that intolerance increases in proportion to the level of danger which the "other" is thought to pose to people's "vital essence."[80] The Turks were perhaps too remote from Calvin's world to be perceived as a real threat, whereas the threat from Anabaptists and other radical groups was all too real.

The career of the Savoyard humanist, Sebastian Chateillon, better known as Castellio (1515–63), somewhat resembles that of Franck and Schwenckfeld. He, too, first became a follower of the Reform, only to become disillusioned later.[81] As a young humanist, he converted to the Reform, moved by the persecutions in France. While in Strasbourg in 1540, he fell in with the circle around Calvin, who was there in temporary exile from Geneva.[82] Two years later, was appointed rector of the collège in Geneva, but due to theological differences Castellio's request to be ordained as a minister was refused. Around the same time, during the winter of 1542–43, when Geneva was visited by the plague, Castellio volunteered to minister to its victims. The duly ordained ministers were reluctant to expose themselves to the danger—one minister had already died. But Castellio's offer was turned down because he had not been ordained. He later resigned as rector and departed for Basel.

The execution of Servetus prompted Castellio's response, Calvin's heated defense, and subsequent written exchanges, including one by Coornhert (the second part of his *Trial of the Killing of Heretics*).[83] Castellio stressed that the issue was not Servetus's heresies, but the fact of his execution.[84]

What weighs heavily for Castellio is the ethical imperative. He regards deeds as the test of creeds,[85] and it is the immorality of persecution and the dignity of man that concern him. In his refutation of Calvin's *Defensio,* writes Ozment, "authority is ceded to those who are experts in the art of living well, not in the arts and sciences." With his own treatment at the hands of the Genevan Reform probably never far from his mind, Castellio charges that Calvin

---

[79]Ibid., 583–84; cf. Calvin, *Defensio,* 476.

[80]Kühn, "Geschichtsproblem," 5.

[81]Ferdinand Buisson, *Sébastien Castellio, sa vie et son oeuvre (1515–1563): Étude sur les origines du protestantisme libéral français,* 2 vols. (Paris, 1892) is still a useful biography.

[82]Ozment, *Mysticism and Dissent,* 168.

[83]Coornhert, *Proces vant Ketterdoden ende dwang der Conscientien,* vol. 2, *Ecclesiastical* in *Wercken,* vol. 2, fols. 114–70.

[84]Ozment, *Mysticism and Dissent,* 173.

[85]Roland H. Bainton, *The Travail of Religious Liberty* (New York: Harper & Bros., 1958), 118.

tolerates vices but severely punishes heresy, as, for example, when he considers rebaptism a more deadly vice than adultery. As physicians are judged by their healing skills, so should theologians and religious leaders be judged by their fruits, tangibly expressed in ethical deeds.[86]

This moral imperative and Castellio's pessimism regarding the current state of affairs in Europe in general, but in France particularly, bring to mind the concerns that had impelled Sebastian Franck to give up his position as a Lutheran preacher. Franck did exert considerable influence on Castellio, who refers to him often in *De haereticis*. Franck's argument that people who have often been persecuted and executed as heretics were actually true Christians, and that therefore all persecution should stop immediately, is very similar to Castellio's views on the matter.[87] Both men refer to the biblical allegory of the wheat and the tares, pose the relativity of the concept of heresy, and the right of individuals to follow the promptings of their consciences, even if it is erroneous.[88] The difference between them is mostly one of degree: for Castellio there were certain absolute boundaries, and he did believe that heresy existed and was odious.[89] In Castellio's views, doctrinal bones of contention such as those surrounding baptism, the Eucharist, justification are no reason to reject or persecute fellow Christians. If they were indeed of such fundamental importance, God would have forestalled doctrinal bickering by making their meaning crystal clear. These differences ought to be tolerated, and Christians must concentrate on a practical "imitation of Christ," holding on to the fundamentals contained in Scripture and providing loving counsel and admonishment to the erring.[90] Those who violate these fundamentals by denying the existence of God, his creation of the world, the immortality of the soul, and the Ascension, must first be admonished, and—if that does not produce the desired effect—excommunicated. Ultimately, the secular government may fine and, in the worst cases, banish the offender, but never execute him. In taking such measures, the magistrate does not judge heresy, but

---

[86]Ozment, *Mysticism and Dissent*, 180, 183–84. A similar theme can be found in Coornhert's *Aertzenij der Zielen* in *Wercken*, vol. 1, fols. 472–85.

[87]Guggisberg,"Sebastian Franck und Sebastian Castellio: Ein Diskussionsbeitrag," in Müller, ed., *Sebastian Franck (1499–1542)*, 293–302.

[88]Cf. Müller, *Sebastian Franck*, 298; Bainton, *Travail*, 119.

[89]"Odi ego haereticos," he writes in *De haereticis*, quoted in Guggisberg,"Ich hasse die Ketzer: Der Ketzerbegriff Sebastian Castellios und seine Situation im Basler Exil," in Silvana Seidel Menchi, ed., *Ketzerverfolgung im 16. und 17. Jahrhundert* (Wiesbaden: Harrassowitz, 1992), 253.

[90]Guggisberg, "Ich hasse die Ketzer," 254. See also D. Erich Seeberg, *Gottfried Arnold: Die Wissenschaft und die Mystik seiner Zeit*. Studien zur Historiographie und zur Mystik (Meerane i/Sa: E.R. Herzog, 1923), 291.

he may punish the atheist for sinning against the laws of nature, which present to human reason the unmistakable signs of God's omnipotence that only the recalcitrant and obstinate can fail to see. In other words, the nonbeliever is not punished for his faith, but for his lack thereof.[91]

Theologically, the focal point of Castellio's critique of Calvin is the latter's supralapsarian doctrine of predestination. Again, a chief component of this critique hailed from Castellio's ethical imperative. Castellio contends that upon Christ's return, he will repudiate people's doctrines and examine their moral behavior.[92] Another main component of Castellio's thought is rationalism: in his parables, Christ appealed to common sense. Therefore, Castellio writes in his last work (*De arte dubitandi*), if, in reading of Scripture, you grapple with an obscure passage, you should let your reason help you interpret it in accordance with what you know about God, namely that he is just, good, and merciful. Calvin's doctrine of predestination contradicts this knowledge, for if we entertain the notion that God creates great numbers of people only to punish them, we turn him into a brute. More than God's omnipotence, Castellio thought it important to safeguard his goodness and fairness. This position, combined with his perfectibilist belief in humanity's ability to attain full obedience to God's commandments (in a gradual progression), made Castellio susceptible to the charge of Pelagianism.[93]

Castellio's rationalism, displayed especially in his last work on the "art of doubting," is another aspect of his thought that connects Castellio with the early Enlightenment.[94] It is, he writes, by means of reason that Christ's basic teachings have been inscribed into the hearts of all people by the finger of God. To be faithful to reason is what makes us human, he claims. Calvin used his reason to come up with his conclusions regarding divine truth, so why should he deny us the use of our judgment? In this connection, Jesus himself, the "Word" or Λόγος, is directly associated with reason.[95]

In 1562, a year before his death, Castellio wrote a late, impassioned plea for toleration addressed to a France wracked by internecine religious warfare.

---

[91]Guggisberg,"Ich hasse die Ketzer," 257–58.

[92]Ozment, *Mysticism and Dissent*, 184.

[93]Ibid., 185–289. Castellio's stages in the growth to perfection in this life harked back to the three "ages" of Joachim of Fiore: Ozment, *Mysticism and Dissent*, 201. Coornhert translated Castellio's perfectibilist tract, *An possit homo per Spiritum Sanctum perfecte obedire legi Dei*, into Dutch: *Vande gehoorsaemheyt* (1583), not in *Wercken*.

[94]Guggisberg, "Ich hasse die Ketzer," 261.

[95]Ozment, *Mysticism and Dissent*, 196.

In this *Conseil à la France Désolée*, he implored the monarch to tolerate the Protestants alongside the Catholics, so people could choose freely.[96] The dignity of humanity figures prominently in this moving tract, in which Castellio adopts a protopolitique position with regard to the role of the state. He writes the government should have absolute control and stand above the religious disputes, allowing its subjects freedom of conscience.[97] Around the same time, the chancellor of France, Michel de l'Hospital (who had begun as an irenic, Erasmian striver for reconciliation between contending creeds), abandoned this hope and adopted a politique position because of the failure of the Colloquy of Poissy.[98]

Castellio's writings on toleration constitute an important milestone in the history of ideas, for they represent the beginning of a systematic conceptualization on issues of toleration and religious pluralism.[99]

Coornhert enhanced his own pro-toleration arguments tremendously by mining the treasures compiled and newly created by Castellio. He translated some of Castellio's works,[100] and in his toleration writings had frequent recourse to arguments or examples used by the "remonstrator" (as Bainton calls Castellio). Coornhert was the main conduit for the transmission of Castellio's thoughts to the circle around Arminius.[101] In one of his polemical writings against the Reformed minister Donteclock, Coornhert makes the well-known statement: "I gladly admit that, in one short page in Castellio's writings, I find more truth, more piety, and more that is elevating, than in all the books of Calvin and Beza."[102] But again, as was the case with Franck and Schwenckfeld, Coornhert rejects being labeled or deemed a follower. When, in his protracted exchanges with the Reformed ministers of Delft over the Heidelberg Catechism, they think to embarrass Coornhert by showing that Castellio's ideas on original sin and predestination differed from his, Coornhert retorts: "You confront me with Castellio's thoughts on this matter. His writings are not

---

[96]Sebastian Castellio, *Conseil à la France Désolée* (1562). I used the translation: idem, *Advice to a Desolate France*, trans. Wouter Valkhoff, ed. Marius F. Valkhoff (Shepherdstown, W. Va.: Patmos Press, 1975).

[97]Kamen, *Rise of Toleration*, 139.

[98]See Lecler, *Toleration and the Reformation*, 2:68–69; Guggisberg, "The Defence," 40.

[99]Guggisberg, "Ich hasse die Ketzer," 249.

[100]See Guggisberg, *Sebastian Castellio im Urteil seiner Nachwelt vom Späthumanismus bis zur Aufklärung*. Basler Beiträge zur Geschichtwissenschaft, vol. 57. (Basel: Helbing & Lichtenhahn, 1956), 63–64.

[101]Guggisberg, *Sebastian Castellio*, 63.

[102]Coornhert, *Vande Toelatinge*, in *Wercken*, vol. 2, fol. 538B.

a Bible. The Bible, and not what people say, has authority for me in matters of such great gravity."[103]

The Italian Jacobus Acontius (c. 1520–67)was another important contributor to the defense of toleration, who was indebted to some extent to Castellio, and from whom Coornhert borrowed in some of his writings. Sympathetic to Protestantism, Acontius was forced to flee Milan, and eventually entered the service of Queen Elizabeth in London, where he lived with a circle of Italian expatriates. In 1565 his great plea for toleration appeared, entitled *Satanae Stratagemata*.[104] Like Castellio, Acontius was dismayed by the unfolding tragedy of the religious wars in France.

Acontius's approach is along rational and methodical lines.[105] For documented support of his argument, he only has recourse to scriptural proof, seeing *Sola Scriptura* as a way to overcome the doctrinal bickering.[106] He also provides abundant current and historical evidence, intending to show that force does not work and is even counterproductive.[107] Although a church may condemn false doctrine, Acontius pleads for a wide tolerance based on certain fundamental articles. Nonbelief in secondary points should be tolerated. Violation of essentials (such as rejection of the Trinity or the Bible, and justification by faith alone),[108] can only be punished with excommunication and avoidance, and the magistrate—who, in Acontius's scheme, exercises control over religion—is in no position to use the sword in the defense of "orthodoxy." A trademark Acontian argument is that if clergymen should be allowed to lean on the civil authorities for the defense of doctrine, this would make them lazy, and it would make the people wonder if the Word of God is not strong enough in and of itself.[109]

---

[103]Coornhert, *Van de Erfzonde, Schulde, ende Straffe Duplyck,* in *Wercken*, vol. 2, fol. ccccxB. This passage also quoted in Bonger, *Leven en werk*, 250–51.

[104]This work was translated as: Jacopo Acontio, *Satan's Stratagems*, 2 vols., trans. Walter T. Curtis, introd. Charles D. O'Malley. Occasional Papers, English Series no. 5, parts 1 and 2 (San Francisco: California State Library, 1940).

[105]Charles D. O'Malley, "Introduction" to Acontio, *Satan's Stratagems*, iv.

[106]See Seeberg, *Gottfried Arnold*, 303.

[107]One often finds appeals to self-interest, as when Acontius warns that persecution makes men ill-disposed toward the church, and thus all the more inclined to incite others against it; e.g. Acontio, *Satan's Stratagems*, 1:62.

[108]Acontius made sure to exclude contentious issues such as the Eucharist and predestination from his "fundamentals"; see Seeberg, *Gottfried Arnold*, 304. But his inclusion of justification by faith alone opened the door for measures against Catholics; see Bainton, "Struggle," 104.

[109]Lecler, *Toleration and the Reformation*, 1:373.

Acontius adopts the optimistic premise that free inquiry will destroy Satan's kingdom because the many claims to a monopoly on truth that will ensue will cause the people to wonder and compare. The image conjured up by Acontius is that of a marketplace where various creeds contend peaceably. He reveals a humanist's confidence in man's ability to think and judge for himself.[110]

Briefly comparing Castellio with Acontius, we see that Castellio is more open to dogmatic formulas (however reductionist these are), and firmly believes that there is an absolute religious truth that is knowable and that will prevail in the end. Freedom, to Acontius, is not a necessary concession to the uncertainties inhabiting the realm of religion. It is, rather, a strategic victory over Satan, whose errors and ruses will stand no chance once the light of truth is allowed to shine unimpeded.[111]

In Coornhert's ideas on toleration, to which we will turn in the following chapters, we can hear echoes of the voices that spoke in this chapter, integrated into a new synthesis. This synthesis was inspired by his theologico-philosophical premises and his practical experience in a nation engulfed in a life-or-death struggle and seeking to define itself. In making his heartfelt case for the freedom of conscience, Coornhert eagerly mined the riches stored in an Erasmian humanist and mystical-Spiritualist tradition of tolerationist views.

[110]Acontio, *Satan's Stratagems*, 2:132; cf. Bainton, "Struggle," 111.
[111]Lecler, *Toleration and the Reformation*, 1:376.

4

"BE YE PERFECT"

THE THEOLOGICAL FOUNDATION

Theological concerns and religious issues predominate throughout Coornhert's works. In the last year of his life (1589–90) he wrote the most voluminous work of his oeuvre, *On Predestination* (*Vande Predestinatie*), a 774-page tome. He wrote this book in five weeks by working twelve hours a day.[1] Of the many writings contained in the three folio volumes of his works, a great number address topics such as original sin, predestination, and prayer. For him, the Revolt was fought first and foremost *religionis causa*, against the murderous constraints placed on men's freedom to worship as they saw fit. When he girded his loins to battle the forces of religious compulsion and made this struggle his chief goal in life, it was a fight that was well anchored in his religious convictions. His theology and his struggle against the constraint of conscience, however, were intertwined from the start. In 1584 he writes that the issue of killing heretics "was the prime, indeed (the Lord be my witness) the only cause which first impelled me to take up the pen against Calvin and Beza, and after that against you [he addresses the ministers in Delft with whom he was engaged in a long-running dispute], when I saw clear signs that you were planning to force conscience and to use physical punishment…."[2] It is therefore important to understand Coornhert's main

[1] See Bonger, *Leven en werk*, 139–40; Coornhert, *Vande Predestinatie* is printed in *Wercken*, vol. 3, fols. clxxi–cclxxxvii.

[2] Coornhert, *Van de Vreemde Sonde/ Schulde/ Straffe nasporinghe*, in *Wercken*, vol. 2, fol. cccclxxxii v.

theological concerns and ideas before analyzing his ideas on religious toleration.

The term "theology" needs, however, to be used with caution in Coornhert's case, since he emphasizes repeatedly that he is not interested in theological speculation for its own sake. Rather, his theology is bound inextricably to his view of ethics and of the individual's place and responsibility in this world. In the prologue to his *Zedekunst* (*Ethics*), he states that there are too many religious teachers who lose themselves in abstruse, speculative, "subtilizing" theology. "Isn't it about time," he writes, "that people should stop scaling the heights of doctrine, before having first progressed steadily, step by step, along the lowest levels?"[3] Coornhert employs a rational approach throughout his writings, which makes him reject abstract philosophizing or chiliastic speculation. In one dialogue, the host proudly reads to the guests gathered in his house a tract on the Trinity that he intends to publish. One of those present—the reader suspects Coornhert—asks the general question if someone who is unable to lift one hundred pounds, can lift one thousand. When this is denied, he asks if his host could please define for him what the soul is. When he cannot answer this question, the guest reminds his host that God is infinitely greater than the individual soul. So how can he claim to define God and the Trinity?[4] In another dialogue, a "Münsterite" (a millennialist Anabaptist) visits Coornhert and asks what he thinks about the establishment of Christ's kingdom here on earth. Coornhert answers that he does not worry about such things, and he offers biblical grounds for his refusal to pry and to speculate. When the Münsterite demands to know why Coornhert is not interested in finding out more about this heavenly Jerusalem, Coornhert replies: "Because I have a greater desire to learn how to live well, than to learn how to know much."[5] Thus, throughout his works there is an Erasmian emphasis on the moral imperative, that a good tree is known by its fruits.[6] To

---

[3]Coornhert, *Zedekunst, dat is Wellevenskunste: Vermids waarheyds kennisse vanden mensche, vande zonden ende vande dueghden, nu alder eerst beschreven int Neerlandsch*, ed. Bruno Becker (Leiden: Brill, 1942), 2.

[4]Coornhert, *Kruyt-Hofken*, dialogue no. 5: *Van te diep ondersoecken*, in *Wercken*, vol. 3, fol. lxxixAB.

[5]Coornhert, *Verscheyden t' samen-spraken*, no. 10, *Vande Hope opten oprechtinghe vanden rijcke Christi hier op aerden uytterlijck*, in *Wercken*, vol. 1, fol. 445C.

[6]Cf. Bonger, *Leven en werk*, 125.

know more does not make one better. What matters is that we act as we know Christ wants us to, according to our abilities.[7]

The essentials of Coornhert's perfectibilism appear now to be accepted generally as the core of his theology.[8] His ideas on perfectibility took shape at an early stage in his life. These ideas were so evident in a series of etchings that Coornhert made for Maarten van Heemskerck in 1550 that Ilja Veldman called the etchings *Jacob's Ladder* (after Coornhert's description of the graduated journey of the believer towards perfection, described below).[9] The idea of perfectibility clearly is present in Coornhert's *Apology for Roman Idolatry*, the early tract which had been denounced so vehemently by Calvin.

This idea is based on the conviction that people are able, in this earthly life, to attain perfect obedience to God's commandments through his grace in Christ. God is our ultimate and highest goal,[10] and virtues are our pathway for attaining this goal. "We have been put on this earth," Coornhert writes, "to become living images of God through virtues, to be united with God through this reflection of his image, and to be saved through this union with God …."[11] And in a letter to his friend, Cornelis Boomgaert, Coornhert states that the believer "is able, through God's grace in Christ Jesus, through his spirit of truth … to attain such a true and sincere obedience to God in this world, that he from then on truly fulfills God's commandment, in that he loves God above all, with all his heart and might, and loves his neighbor like himself, and that in this wise, unified with God through love in Christ, he is safe, calm, and as

---

[7]Coornhert, *Ooghwater,* in *Wercken,* vol. 2, fols. cccclxxiD–cccclxxiiAB. Here he counters the argument, used by his Reformed opponents, that some have a better understanding of Scripture than others.

[8]The term "perfectibilism," I believe, is to be preferred over "perfectism," used in Bonger, *Leven en werk,* and elsewhere. Here I agree with Willem Nijenhuis, *Adrianus Saravia (1532–1613): Dutch Calvinist, First Reformed Defender of the English Episcopal Church Order on the Basis of the ius divinum* (Leiden: E.J. Brill, 1980), 180–81, who describes the process of growth toward perfection. For this summary I rely chiefly on Bruno Becker, "Coornhert de 16de eeuwsche apostel der volmaakbaarheid," *Nederlandsch Archief voor Kerkgeschiedenis* 19 (1926): 59–84; Bonger, *Leven en werk,* part 2, chap. 1, "Denkbeelden over de volmaakbaarheid," and chap. 3, "Bestrijding van de dogma's der erfzonde en predestinatie"; and Coornhert, *Op zoek naar het hoogste goed,* ed. and introd. Bonger. Geschiedenis van de wijsbegeerte in Nederland (Baarn: Uitgeverij Ambo B.V., 1987). Coornhert saw as the foundation of his "structure" a number of Bible texts, collected by him, and listed in *Wercken,* vol. 1, fols. 211–13.

[9]See Veldman, *Maarten van Heemskerck.*

[10]This is the end station of the *Search for the Highest Good* (*Op zoek naar het hoogste goed*), Coornhert's five dialogues on this issue.

[11]Coornhert, *Wercken,* vol. 3, fol. 399D (quoted in Bonger, *Leven en werk,* 183).

completely without temptation as the very apple of God's eye."[12] In the *Zede-kunst* (*Ethics*), Coornhert explains the possibility of perfect obedience by pointing to the fact that God commands us to be completely obedient to him. Those, Coornhert continues, who claim that you can only do so in a very limited and incomplete way in this life, actually say yes and no. For if you obey your master's order incompletely, you actually disobey.[13]

The Bible text most often used in support of this belief in humanity's perfectibility is Matt. 5:48: "Be ye therefore perfect, even as your Father which is in heaven is perfect." Coornhert distinguishes clearly between human and divine perfection and does not equate the two. God is eternally perfect, humanity becomes so in time; God is perfect in himself, humanity receives perfection from God, and whereas God is self-sufficient and not in need of anything, humanity can keep growing in its perfections.

This idea of perfectibilism explains Coornhert's criticism of existing churches and sects. He believed those church leaders either shortchanged humankind's capabilities or deified themselves and insinuated themselves as prophets on a divine mission, without proof or justification. This is why Coornhert stopped taking part in mass, and said he could not understand how Protestants can pray the Lord's Prayer, which asks that "Thy will be done, on earth as it is in heaven," since Protestant leaders assured the flock that this goal was unattainable in this lifetime. These heartfelt objections induced him to embark on a struggle with the Reformed ministers that lasted for thirty years.

It is the believers' duty to honor God and to love their neighbors, and this leads automatically to the other great commandment, which is the "law of nature," or the Golden Rule.[14] This law of reciprocity is found in Matt. 7:12, "Therefore all things whatsoever ye would that men should do to you, do ye even so to them: for this is the law and the prophets." This idea is crucial to Coornhert's ideas on perfectibility. Perfectibility is the key to his ethical system, and provides a powerful argument for his plea for toleration.[15] This law is the *ratio superior* or supreme reason that God has infused into nature; because of this law pagans are able to attain salvation if they act in accordance with the spirit of Christ, which is eternal.[16] In the fifth dialogue of his *Search*

[12]Coornhert, *Wercken*, vol. 3, fol. 98CD (from Becker, "Coornhert de 16de eeuwsche apostel," 59).

[13]Coornhert, *Zedekunst*, ed. Becker, bk. 4, chap. 5, pp. 232–33.

[14]Becker, "Coornhert de 16de eeuwsche apostel," 62, 63, 78-79.

[15]See Bonger's introduction to Coornhert, *Op zoek*, p. 34.

[16]Bonger, *Leven en werk*, 187–88.

for the Highest Good (*Op zoek naar het hoogste goed*), Coornhert explains that true believers will love their neighbors, naturally disseminating the love that is constantly pouring down on them from God.[17] Obeying his reason, humankind will follow the Golden Rule and thus do what is right, bringing harmony to human society.[18]

Coornhert's belief in humanity's perfectibility is intertwined closely with his view of humanity's station on earth. People were created so that they may receive salvation and become one with God, a goal in which God wants all his children to share. In this connection, Coornhert often refers to 1 Tim. 2:3–4, "For this is good and acceptable in the sight of God our Saviour; Who will have all men to be saved and to come unto the knowledge of the truth." Coornhert believed people were placed on this earth to become the living images of God through virtue. Although he always states that we need God's grace through Christ, it is clear that Coornhert harbors an optimistic view of humankind which, he believes, is good by nature, and naturally inclined toward good, not evil.[19]

The road towards God consists of virtues and way stations, in its gradual climb to perfection. The idea of climbing up towards unification with God in stages was a familiar theme in mysticism, but Coornhert's practical system of six stages, described in *Jacob's Ladder* (1584) and elsewhere,[20] was unique in that his ascent did not entail mortification, spiritualization, or losing one's self but was fundamentally ethical and gradual.[21] Since it is important to know what stage of the journey one has reached, Coornhert greatly emphasizes the necessity of self-knowledge.

On the lowest rung of this "ladder" we find the "stubborn unbelievers, who continue to sin unrepentantly, who sin deliberately, and who rejoice in committing evil deeds."[22] The second station is that of servants who obey because they fear a beating: these are the weak beginners on this road, who have to be

[17]Coornhert, *Op zoek*, 110; see also 112.
[18]See Coornhert, *Zedekunst*, bk. 4, chap. 2, par. 16, p. 222.
[19]Coornhert, *Wercken*, vol. 2, fol. 471C (quoted in Becker, "Coornhert de 16de eeuwsche apostel," 64).
[20]Coornhert, *Ladder Iacobs, of Trappe der Deughden,* in *Wercken*, vol. 1, fols. 165–76; also in *Vre-Reden,* in *Wercken*, vol. 1, fol. ccccxxiC ff. See e.g. Castellio's three (st)ages, in chap. 3 above, p. 61,.
[21]Bonger, *Leven en werk*, 191; for the full description of the stages see Coornhert, *Ladder Iacobs,* 190–93.
[22]Coornhert, *Ladder Iacobs,* fol. 171C.

pummeled into obedience by copious threats.[23] Third is the "mercenary" who obeys God in hopes of a reward. In a letter to some *Doopsgezinden* (Anabaptists, followers of Menno Simons), Coornhert places Menno in this category. Menno had written in *Fondamentboek* that his only goal was that he should be saved, and many others with him. This, writes Coornhert, relegates him to the rank of a mercenary, because he loves his salvation (that is, his pay) more than he loves God. Thus, Coornhert concludes, this soul is egocentric and wants to use God as a means to an end. Coornhert even goes so far as to call such love "the love of a whore" (*hoerenliefde*), since a whore only "loves" a man for the money he gives afterwards.[24] What is lacking in this and the previous stations is true love, "without which...all is in vain,"[25] and both the servant and the mercenary ultimately only live and manifest love for themselves, not for their neighbor. "Neither the servant in fear of a beating, nor the mercenary craving a reward, but the loving child of God will inherit from the Father."[26]

The fourth stage follows regeneration, which he describes as a genuine killing of humankind's evil being and a calling forth (*levendmakinghe*) of God's good life in the sincerely contrite person.[27] The "inside" must be cleaned, a cleansing which can start once you profess your ignorance, abandon your will, and only desire to grow in obedience to God and to become free of self.[28] The traveler is thus reborn in Christ and has shed the "old Adam" of sin. This rebirth is a spiritual, nearly ineffable, event in which God and the individual are united. Such a reborn person is "perfect" and will inherit the kingdom of God, but—and here Coornhert's concept differs from mystical views of the *unio mystica*—rebirth does not bring about the instant death of sin. Old customs die hard, and the person still needs to traverse various stages. As of this rebirth, however, there is no going or falling back: the reborn person is changeable since he or she always can move from less to greater good, but cannot get worse nor sin. Such children in Christ may err, but not sin, because in Coornhert's conception one can only sin with deliberation. From this point in the journey onward, the travelers are saints; saints, because of their love for Christ and their enlightenment through truth, cannot sin deliberately.[29] Coornhert

---

[23]Ibid., fol. 171D.

[24]Becker, *Bronnen*, Letter 45, n.d., pp. 284–90.

[25]Coornhert, *Ladder Iacobs,* fol. 172A.

[26]Becker, *Bronnen*, Letter 45 (to Anabaptists), p. 287.

[27]Coornhert, *Vande Wedergheboorte, hoe die gheschiet...* , in *Wercken*, vol. 1, fol. 178v.

[28]Coornhert, *Brieven-boeck* (*Book of Letters*), Letter 43, in *Wercken*, vol. 3, fol. cviiD.

[29]Coornhert, *Ladder Iacobs,* fols. 172C–173D.

makes the subtle distinction between sinning and bearing sin (*sondighen* and *sonde hebben*), with an analogy to a wound and the act of wounding: the saint still carries wounds inflicted earlier on, "and such carrying of a sin is not imputed to such who have desisted from sinning."[30] As a good being, the regenerated can grow infinitely toward God's infinite goodness.[31]

The first station for the saint is that of the "weak child," who is freed from sin through the light of truth, but who may still err due to ingrained habits or ignorance. Since it took a long time for evil habits to grow through practice, likewise it will take time before they can be replaced by good habits. This stage is naturally followed by that of the "strong adult," whom God has given the intention and the power to conquer evil.[32] Finally, a few will reach the highest station, that of the "wise elders," who obey God completely and have reached true peace. The life of these "elders" resembles that of Christ, and thus can serve as an example to others, for "they do no harm to anyone, but good to everyone, including their enemies, out of love, as true subjects of the Kingdom of Christ."[33]

These saints remain humble because they realize that nothing is gained through personal merit, and they only do what they are supposed to do. Coornhert's synergism is patently clear from this scheme. God can reach us in many ways, but we must cooperate; this is an action, Coornhert explains, in which there is as little merit as there is merit in the action of a beggar who has to stretch out his hands to receive his alm.[34] Humankind can accept or reject God's gifts (faith being one of them). In this regard, Coornhert accepted the Roman Catholic position.[35]

As stated earlier, throughout Coornhert's writings, the rational element plays a central role. He wrote that ignorance (*onverstand*: the negation of intelligence or perception) is a roadblock on the way to perfection, and to remain ignorant is humankind's chief sin and the prime source of error.[36] Reason, he

[30]In Coornhert, *Hert-spiegel godlijcker Schrifturen,* in *Wercken,* vol. 1, fol. 24A. A very similar passage is also quoted in Bonger, *Leven en werk,* 189–90, but this passage is from a letter to Spieghel d.d. 1588.

[31]Coornhert, *Op zoek,* 57–58.

[32]Coornhert, *Ladder Iacobs,* fol. 174C.

[33]Ibid., fol. 175B.

[34]This simile is in Coornhert, *Wercken,* vol. 1, fol. 180B. Elsewhere, Coornhert uses the analogy with light: the light comes from God, but man must open his eyes to see: Becker, "Coornhert de 16de eeuwsche apostel," 67.

[35]See Bonger, *Leven en werk,* 253.

[36]Becker, "Coornhert de 16de eeuwsche apostel," 64.

said, is a spark of the divine light, and we all harbor some of this "divine seed" within ourselves. It is what distinguishes humanity from the animal, for humans "have been ennobled, above all other earthly creatures, with the light of reason, so that we obey it, practice virtue, acquire a divine nature, and enjoy divine prosperity."[37] Reason is a guide that points man toward the good. This quality of reason as a guide to moral behavior shows that reason is to be distinguished from mere intelligence which can only tell truth from lies.[38] Supreme reason (*ratio superior)* is the law of nature or Golden Rule, mentioned earlier.[39] The *ratio inferior* applies to humankind and is neutral or intermediate (*middelbaer*), meaning that it can focus on material things and other externals which tend to make humans more evil, or on goals that lift them up and make them better.[40] Wise people reflect every time before they act.[41] Reason and understanding, without which there can be no obedience to God, let people discover God's will as revealed in his written Word.[42]

This reliance on reason also shows Coornhert's great confidence in truth, whose power will make a person choose "what he knows to be best."[43] This dedication to truth also extends to the citing of his sources and the assurance to his readers that he does not distort or misquote them. In his *True Abandonment of Sins* (*Waarachtighe aflaat van zonden*), Coornhert relates how a Reformed visitor tells him he has heard that Coornhert misquotes Calvin and other Reformers. Coornhert then shows the visitor the edition of the *Institutes* that he used and lets the visitor borrow it to compare and make certain the quotations are correct.[44] Coornhert believed force could never change a person's false judgment, but a proof based on truth could, and only a judgment based on truth could be deemed good judgment.[45] The will, he believed, always followed knowledge or insight, and virtue could not be acquired unless

[37]Coornhert, *Wercken*, vol. 3, fols. 399D–400A, quoted in Bonger, *Leven en werk*, 183.

[38]See Coornhert, *Zedekunst*, bk. 1, chap. 2, p. 15, par 10.

[39]See Coornhert, *Zedekunst*, bk. 2, chap. 2: "Reason," par. 17: reason commands us to obey our Creator and to do unto each other as we wish them to do unto us.

[40]Bonger, "Introduction" to Coornhert, *Op zoek*, 27.

[41]"Action before reflection is wrong" (*Daad voort beraad is quaad*): Coornhert, *Zedekunst*, bk. 2, chap. 3, par. 9. Also, ibid., bk. 6, chap. 5, p. 513, par. 41: "He, who only chooses what he knows that he knows, cannot be deceived."

[42]Coornhert, *Wercken*, vol. 1, fol. 15B (2d pagination), quoted in Bonger, *Leven en werk*, 188.

[43]Coornhert, *Op zoek*, 94.

[44]Coornhert, *Wercken*, vol. 1, fol. 250A; the Dutch word *aflaat* means both an "indulgence" and, literally, "abandoning sin."

[45]Bonger, *Leven en werk*, 188–89; Coornhert, *Zedekunst*, bk. 2, ch. 4, p. 463, pars. 3–4..

one knew it.[46] Reason should not, however, try to probe the depths of the divine mysteries: in this limitation lies true wisdom, encapsulated in Coornhert's adage, *Weet of rust* (know or let go).[47] He believed you should do what you know to be right, and refrain from doing what you know to be wrong, but in those areas where you know that you do not know—in other words, where you realize, in the Socratic way, your ignorance—you should calmly resign yourself and let go, and refrain from acting on a basis of uncertainty.[48] This course will keep the believer from sinning: when asked whether someone could reach such a state of sinless perfection, where one does not even sin unwittingly, Coornhert answers that one must, first of all, know what it is that one knows, and also know what things one does not know. Then one should do only those things one knows are good, and not act in uncertainty, for "in doing what he knows for a certainty to be good, he cannot sin."[49]

No matter how self-assured and hard to convince Coornhert was in daily life, in theory at least he subscribed to the principle of healthy doubt and of thinking for yourself at a time when numerous religious groups were vying for people's souls. In an introductory poem to his *On What God Permits and What He Decrees* (*Van de toelatinge ende decrete Godts*) (1572), Coornhert exhorts his readers:

> Test the pretenders, don't believe them all,
> don't believe me either, be nobody's thrall,
> believe in God, and you will know.
> I don't believe everything people profess—
> this makes me such a bothersome pest:
> they wish to hear yes, but I say no.[50]

Coornhert's goal is not to make people doubt everything and be left without any certitudes. In a written dialogue between Coornhert and his conscience, his conscience asks him: "What is the purpose of your writing? Do you

[46]On the vital connection, for Coornhert, between knowledge and virtue, see C. J. *Wijnaendts Francken, Vier Moralisten: Confucius-Plutarchus-Montaigne-Coornhert* (Amsterdam: Wereldbibliotheek N.V., 1946), 173.

[47]A collection of texts by Coornhert, translated into modern Dutch, was given this adage as a title; see *Weet of rust: Proza van Coornhert*, ed. H. Bonger and A. J. Gelderblom (Amsterdam: Querido, 1985).

[48]Bonger, "Introduction" to Coornhert, *Op zoek*, 28, mentions the Socratic element.

[49]Coornhert *Brieven-boeck*, Letter 33, fol. ciiB.

[50]Coornhert, *Wercken*, vol. 2, fol. 525v, also quoted in Bonger, *Leven en werk*, 72 (translated with some poetic license.)

want to make everyone full of doubt?" Coornhert answers: "No, but I want to help diminish everyone's false certitudes (as much as I can)."[51]

It is impossible, said Coornhert, that anyone should want something without knowing it. This statement brings us to another cornerstone of his structure, that is, the freedom of the will. The will is the "queen of the soul," and reason will determine whether she is good or evil.[52] The will is essential, and to speak of a "free will" is in fact tautologous, for it cannot exist in the presence of necessity, and where the will is absent there can be no virtue or sin either. Only when the will is free can there be moral responsibility. Sinning is a voluntary matter, or else it cannot be considered sinning. Thus, newborn infants cannot sin, and to do evil means to desire, want, or do something knowingly against God's will. Similarly, injustice is not simply the absence of justice, but always implies volition (of the wrong kind).[53]

In one of his dialogues, Coornhert appears as a dissatisfied Anabaptist. His church does not have an acceptable solution for the problem of sin, and neither does his interlocutor, who voices the Reformed doctrine of imputed justice. According to this doctrine, our debts are forgiven in Christ, although our sinfulness is not removed. But, objects the "Anabaptist," the feeling of remorse is valuable, and if God takes that feeling away from us, but leaves the sin, then he removes what is good and leaves what is evil. To make his point, he uses an allegory: a renowned physician has a son who just cannot stop gorging himself, even though his father forbids him to do this. The son keeps getting sick, but afterwards his father always smiles and forgives him, and withholds the punishment he had promised. In this way, how will the son ever mend his ways? Would it not be much better for the father, who possesses the requisite skills, to cure the son's brains of his fallacy, that is, of the "evil desire" *(kwade lust)* that causes him to sin? Then the punishment would no longer be needed, because, the cause being removed, the sin (bringing along its own inevitable punishment) would be prevented. In no church, the "Anabaptist" concluded regretfully, did he find this answer. Therefore, he must go straight to his Lord.[54]

An important consideration, in connection with Coornhert's concept of the free will, is that, for him, faith is a *donum Dei* (gift from God) and there-

---

[51]Coornhert, *Wercken*, vol. 1, fol. 121B.
[52]Coornhert, *Zedekunst*, bk. 2, chap. 1.
[53]Ibid., p. 220.
[54]Coornhert, *Verscheyden t'samen-spraken*, fol. 439BCD.

fore cannot be forced. Yet, human volition plays an essential part in the receiving of this gift. In Bonger's analysis of the difference between Castellio and Coornhert, he concludes that it is because of Castellio's concept of faith as primarily a matter of volition that he was unwilling to show forth tolerance toward the atheist.[55] This view needs to be elaborated, however, because as we have seen, volition is indispensable for Coornhert as well. But for Castellio, reason plays a more important role: reason, with the aid of natural law, will present the observer with incontrovertible evidence of God's existence. Therefore not wanting to recognize this evidence makes one obstinate, and such obstinacy must not go unpunished. For Coornhert, the stress is on humankind's being receptive and willing to receive, and on God's giving his gift. Thus, in Coornhert's view it is an act of cruelty to punish those who are still deprived of this gift, and if one is not open to receive the gift, his will cannot be forced.

Harmonizing the postulate of human free will with God's "prescience" (a misnomer according to Coornhert) has been a perennial challenge to theologians, and Coornhert's theology is not free of "cracks" either.[56] His basic argument against the assertion that all that happens, happens necessarily, because God knows everything beforehand, is that for God there is no "before" or "after," an argument that goes back to Boëthius and Aquinas.[57] Knowledge of an event, Coornhert reasons, does not cause it to happen, but the event produces the knowledge of it. Humankind's virtues, Coornhert asserts, are from God, but its sins are its own.[58] When in one dialogue the Reformed interlocutor states that it was necessary or inevitable that Adam in paradise sinned voluntarily, Coornhert states that this can be interpreted in two ways: an acceptable one, which holds that Adam could only sin in freedom, and one which holds that Adam had to sin due to God's will: a proposition that Coornhert sees as a logical corollary of the Reformed doctrine, but one which he rejects, because it makes God the author of evil.[59] Free will, so fundamental to

[55]Bonger, *Leven en werk*, 226.

[56]See E. Dekker, "Wilsvrijheid volgens Coornhert in het traditiehistorisch licht van de scholastiek: Een kleine dieptepeiling," *Nederlands Theologisch Tijdschrift* 45 (1991): 112, where Dekker points out that on the one hand Coornhert claims that God is *by his nature* good, yet at the same time he states that God wanted to be good, which implies at least the possibility of evil.

[57]Ibid., 113. This explains why Coornhert rejects the term "Providence," or "prescience."

[58]Coornhert, *Wercken*, vol. 2, fol. 531C (quoted in Bonger, *Leven en werk*, 249–50, with some inaccuracy); see also Coornhert, *Zedekunst*, bk. 2, chap. 1.

[59]Dekker, "Wilsvrijheid," 114.

Coornhert's ethical system, thus exists because God has chosen to rest in certain areas and to allow room for free will to operate.[60]

In response to the age-old question of the origin of evil (*unde malum*), Coornhert cannot allow the possibility of a connection of evil with God, and neither does he externalize it as some concrete devil pushing his schemes. Analogous to Franck, or Tauler, he regards evil as an absence, as a *privatio boni* (absence of the good). Presented with the problem of the obvious effects and activity of this evil which he claims to be nothing—and with the seemingly contradictory exhortation, in the Bible, to kill sin (a nonentity), Coornhert states that sin is not an object, but an act, and he again compares it with a wound.[61]

Coornhert distinguishes sharply between natural inclinations and "artificial" desires. The flesh and its drives—such as hunger, thirst, and sex—are not evil but God-given. The evil begins when one starts to fantasize, creating "appetite without hunger, and the desire to drink without thirst, and to copulate without a natural urge. Following and repeating these desires often creates drunkards, who get thirsty from drinking, gluttons who stuff their body with food, and lechers who waste their physical force."[62] These primary drives thus belong to the "intermediate" or neutral things, good if put to their intended use, evil if abused (similar to the condition of the *ratio inferior*). Sinning is a matter of the soul, not of the flesh.[63] Mortality also, Coornhert asserts, is not a punishment for sins, but a natural condition, and Adam and Eve were mortal creatures from the beginning.[64] Here again, it is the will that must ride in the saddle and follow the light of reason.

We can see how fundamental the safeguarding of man's free will is to Coornhert as he states repeatedly that its absence would mean the breakdown of the moral fiber of society. In the second dialogue of his *Search for the Highest Good*, Coornhert explains that if we say that we are merely a tool through which God does his good work, or the devil his evil, then there is no room for human volition, and that would mean "that there would be...no virtue and

---

[60]Ibid., 114–15. Dekker indicates Coornhert's probable sources: Duns Scotus and Thomas Aquinas.

[61]Coornhert, Letter 46, *Wercken*, vol. 3, fol. 111ABC (quoted in Bonger, *Leven en werk*, 189–90).

[62]Coornhert, *Op zoek*, 77.

[63]See Coornhert, *Van des Menschen Natuerlijcke vleesch Wondersproock*, in *Wercken*, vol. 1, fols. 139–147, esp. fols. 140B–141A.

[64]Becker, "Coornhert de 16de eeuwsche apostel," 65; Bonger, *Leven en werk*, 185.

sin, punishment and reward, and consequently that there would be a confusion of good and bad, honor and shame, and that the distinction between things would be blurred."[65]

Becker adamantly rejects the contention that Coornhert, in his *Zedekunst* and elsewhere, presents a moral system that does not much need a Redeemer or God. He points out how absolutely "crucial" Christ is for the perfectibilist. To Coornhert, Christ is not just an example, but indispensable for our salvation, which he gives us the power to attain. Indeed, one recurring reproach leveled by Coornhert at the Reformed is that they, by saying that man can never reach perfect obedience in this life, manifest a lack of faith in Christ's power to redeem.[66]

Much of Coornhert's work is cast in the combative, negative mode. He is almost constantly battling foes, mostly consisting of Calvinist ministers, but at times also encompassing a famous Leiden professor (Lipsius), the Anabaptist brethren, or the founder of the Family of Love (Hendrick Niclaes). Even when there is no practical need, he chooses the dialogue form for many of his works.

Whereas in the above pages, I have presented the positive, essential elements of Coornhert's theology, much of his energy was vested in disputes and controversy. Bonger even suspects that, in 1589, while living in Gouda, Coornhert deliberately provoked the Reformed synod assembled in that town with a *Remonstrance* in which he first told the ministers gathered there that they had no right to call themselves teachers of God's true church because they lacked a special divine calling, and then requested to be allowed to resume his debate with Saravia, cut off six years earlier. Their negative response—a foregone conclusion—provided Coornhert with a convenient excuse for writing yet another anti-Calvinist book, *On Predestination*.[67] Coornhert wrote against the Heidelberg Catechism, which the 1578 Synod of Dordrecht of the Reformed church had decided would be presented to the congregation from the pulpit as the official creed.[68] He rejected article 115 of the Catechism, which stated that humankind can never hope to attain to perfect obedience of God's commandments in this life, a view diametrically opposed to his perfectibilism. "The Scriptures," he wrote, "are for here, for this time, and for this world, and they will not be there afterwards in heaven. Thus they must be implemented now,

---

[65]Coornhert, *Op zoek*, 73; the same thought for example in Coornhert, *Zedekunst*, 102, 107.

[66]See Becker, "Coornhert de 16de eeuwsche apostel," 66, 74, 77.

[67]Bonger, *Leven en werk*, 139. The *Remonstrantie* and the Synod's peremptory response are printed in *Wercken*, vol. 3, fols. 461–64.

[68]See Van Deursen, *Bavianen en Slijkgeuzen*, 48.

in time, or never, and here, in this world, or nowhere."[69] Coornhert took special aim at the doctrines of original sin and predestination. It is sufficient just to outline Coornhert's arguments against these doctrines since they follow directly from his perfectibilist outlook.[70]

Coornhert sees original sin as a human invention, which cannot be found anywhere in the Scriptures.[71] His arguments against this "invented doctrine" can be summarized as follows: (1) Adam was created in God's image, not as God's image. If he had been created as God's image, he could not have sinned, but he was created in his image, that is, with the capability of living up to that image. (2) Death is not God's punishment for the Fall in paradise: As discussed earlier, Coornhert argues that mortality and suffering were part of humankind's nature from the very beginning. (3) The Bible does not state that God damned man after the Fall. (4) The body and its appetites are not sinful in themselves, but they are intermediate; sin occurs in the soul, and believers in original sin must prove that we physically inherited our soul from Adam. (5) If we must sin of necessity, we cannot feel genuinely remorseful. Coornhert proposes that adherents of the doctrine of original sin alter the text of the Lord's Prayer to: "Forgive us Adam's debt" (or sin).[72] At the most, a sinner imitates Adam: that, to Coornhert, is the only true original sin. (6) Coornhert rejects the moral consequences of the doctrine, which dooms innocent children and turns God into a tyrant and an unjust judge. (7) Belief in original sin undermines the significance of Christ's expiatory death and attributes more power to humans (to lead astray) than to Christ (to heal). (8) Calvin admits that original sin implies a severe judgment by God but adds that we may not question God's *arcanum consilium* (hidden, or secret decree), incomprehensible and cruel-seeming to man. Coornhert claims that the overt, revealed "decrees" or pronouncements of God, found in the Bible, rule out this "hidden" judgment imagined by Calvin. The following long passage makes this point. It also serves to illustrate Coornhert's pugnacious style:

> If God's hidden judgment is incomprehensible to all people, then
> so it is for you [meaning the Protestant ministers].... How can

[69]Coornhert, *Wercken*, vol. 3, fol. 289A (quoted in Bonger, *Leven en werk*, 192).

[70]See Bonger, *Leven en werk*, pp. 233–46 on original sin, and 246–53 on predestination.

[71]Awareness of the diversity of opinion on original sin was, according to Coornhert, what first prompted him to study Latin so he could read the patristic sources, since he could not find any mention of it in the Bible: Coornhert, *Wercken*, vol. 2, fols. dliv–dliir.

[72]Bonger, *Leven en werk*, 241.

you deem just what you do not understand? Because (you say) it is the judgment of God, whose acts are all just, even though we may not understand them. But how do you know that it is indeed the judgment of God? ... First of all, we must make sure that it is God's judgment, and not your own. Furthermore it is a fact that the judgment of God which has been revealed to us in the Holy Writ is also God's judgment, therefore is also just. Now your imagined judgment of God, which you term "hidden," is in clear conflict with this revealed judgment of God: thus, one or the other must be unjust. Which one? The one revealed in the Holy Scripture? In that case we must reject the Bible as untrue, and follow your dreams as the truth, and thus we must hold for a duplicitous and false God, who through his Holy Spirit testifies in the Scripture to a justice and judgment that differ from the truth ... which is hidden. ... If such sophistries with regard to the Sacred Scripture be allowed, then what certitude will be left to us? This takes us quite some distance from the words of your Calvin, [who states] that we ought to ask, think, and speak of God "in the Word, with the Word, and through the Word." Because in this way, we leave the Word and artfully speculate about God outside of the Word, without the Word, and even blatantly against the Word.[73]

This passage demonstrates Coornhert's favorite line of attack, using the tools of his opponents (in this case, Calvin's *Institutes*) against themselves.

Coornhert's passionate rejection of the doctrine of predestination is a logical corollary of his belief in free will, discussed earlier. He mostly attacks the moral consequences of this doctrine, which takes away man's responsibility for his actions. If God did not only foresee but also wanted Adam's fall, this would make God a hateful tyrant. God does not ask of us anything that cannot be attained: how can we deny the possibility of full obedience and of free choice without denying God's omnipotence?[74]

---

[73]Coornhert, *Wercken*, vol.2, fol. 505D (quoted in Bonger, *Leven en werk*, 243). Similarly, in *Van de Toelatinge ende Decrete Godts*, Coornhert first quotes Augustine and Tapper, who both state that this issue (original sin) is beyond any creature's comprehension: then states that, since both Augustine and Tapper themselves are creatures, people should not follow their lead in this matter, since they themselves acknowledge that they are blind; see *Wercken*, vol. 2, fol. 552v.

[74]See Coornhert, *Zedekunst*, bk. 1, chap. 1, p. 10, par. 18; bk. 4, chap. 5, p. 234, par. 23.

For Coornhert, the relationship between the individual and God supersedes all interhuman relations. This paramountcy is clear, for example, in his play, *Abrahams uytgangh* (c. 1570), wherein Abraham comes to the conclusion that an individual can only judge his own relation to God, but never the relationship between God and others. In this belief, we have the basis of and precondition for the requirement that we tolerate our fellow human beings and that we do not judge them.[75]

.   .   .

Although at times practical arguments appear in Coornhert's argumentation, and he often resorts to dialectical and commonsensical reasoning, the deepest motivation for his restless crusade against the repressive forces that he encounters wells up from the bedrock of theological convictions sketched in this chapter. His scheme of successive steps that will lead humankind to perfection here on earth, coupled with his trust in reason and the individual's self-reliance in this quest, show us his confidence in humankind's God-given faculties, and conversely, mistrust of all those who claim spiritual authority over others. This same faith in humankind's adequacy and Christ's power underlies his defense of the freedom of conscience. Coornhert never compartmentalized his activities nor did he circumscribe his intellectual pursuits.

[75]See Anneke Fleurkens, *Stichtelijke lust: De toneelspelen van D. V. Coornhert (1522–1590) als middel tot het geven van morele instructie* (Hilversum: Verloren, 1994), 248.

5
Coornhert's
Toleration Writings

THE THEME OF RELIGIOUS TOLERATION is so important to Coornhert[1] that it occurs throughout the *Wercken*. The first impassioned plea for peace and concord, and the laying aside of petty differences, appeared in his *Peace Tract* (*Vre-Reden*).[2] Coornhert extols the spirit of charity, forbearance, and patience that should pervade Christ's church, and he supports this plea with numerous biblical passages. Evincing the true spirit of Christian brotherhood is more important, he writes, than being right on some subtle or obscure points of theology and doctrine. He cautions his readers that the spectacle of Christians persecuting Christians sets a bad example to the non-Christian world of Turks, Jews, and pagans, and will serve to repel rather than attract. The tract was published anonymously, and its style is rather un-"Coornhertian," but Bonger concludes, in *Leven en werk,* that Boomgaerdt was correct in attributing this document to Coornhert.[3]

In the *Tribunal* (*Vierschare*), appearing c. 1574, the theme of impartiality—who has the right to judge—is discussed.[4] The "judges" consist of "all impartial minds," the plaintiff is "Charitable, Good Hope" (*Lieven, goede hoop*), represented by his lawyer, "Ernst-Who-Sticks-To-The-Word" (*Ernst Woordthouder*). The defendant is "Fanatical Premature Judgment, Mynaertsz"

---

[1] Bonger, *De motivering*, 1–29, gives a detailed survey of most of the relevant writings.

[2] Coornhert, *Vre-Reden of Onderwijs tot Eendracht, Vrede ende Liefde, in desen tijden hooghnoodigh* (*Peace Tract or Teachings for Solidarity, Peace, and Love Supremely Necessary in These Times*), in *Wercken*, vol. 3, fols. 415–21, followed by the second part (written later), fols. 421–28.

[3] Bonger, *Leven en werk*, 159–60 n. 31; Bonger, *Motivering*, 129–33, had argued that Coornhert was not the author. Bonger does not explain what made him change his mind.

[4] Coornhert, *Wercken*, vol. 1, fols. 420v–433.

(*Yver, stout oordeel, Meynaertsz*), represented by "Coenraedt Bible Interpreter" (*Coenraedt Schrift-gloser*). The only two witnesses called to the bench are the Old and New Testament.[5] The basic theme would resound throughout Coornhert's toleration writings: that only the "true church" has the right to judge heresy, but that there is no impartial authority to pass judgment on the various claimants to that status.

While in Germany, Coornhert expressed his ideas on ceremonies and "external" religious practices in *Schijndeught der Secten* (*Falsity of the Sects*).[6] The book consists of eight dialogues taking place during a trip on the Rhine. Participants in these dialogues are a Calvinist, a Lutheran, an Anabaptist, and an "impartial Catholic" in whom the reader recognizes Coornhert. The central argument is, that ceremonies are meant to unify Christians, and that when they become a source of dissension and abuse, abstention from outward ceremonies is to be preferred. Coornhert's distinction between the "sign" (that is, external ceremony) and the "signified," and his defense of Sebastian Franck and Caspar Schwenckfeld clearly reflect his Spiritualism.[7] Coornhert does not deny the wrongs in the Catholic Church, but he states that even if he wanted to leave, he would not know where to go, since they who present themselves as alternatives are sects, not churches, and lack a clear calling.[8] All these self-proclaimed churches show intolerance, and Coornhert suggests that even the Anabaptists, were they to find themselves in a position of power, would be intolerant, due to their claim to a monopoly on truth.[9] The impartial "Catholic" charges that Luther, Zwingli, Calvin, and others, in following their own prompting and insights regarding the ceremonies, have hatched the eggs of the many-headed serpent Hydra. He asks, would it not have been better if they had "refrained from action" (*stille stonden*) in such a weighty matter?[10]

---

[5]Ibid., fol. 420v.

[6]*Schijndeught der Secten met hare verwerde twistigheden om de Ceremonien* (*Falsity of the Sects with Their Confused Quarrels about Ceremonies*) (1574), in *Wercken*, vol. 3, fol. cccxlii-ccclv (*Bibliotheca Belgica*, 736–37, C 102). The title page contains two Bible passages (Jer. 7:21 and Matt. 24:13), both warning against false Messiahs. Coornhert pretends the dialogue was translated from German and the author is deceased. See also: Bonger, *Motivering*, 8.

[7]The Calvinist refers to a booklet by Anastasius Veluanus, attacking Franck, entitled *De corte Weghwijzer* (*Quick Guidance*) (1564).

[8]Coornhert returned to this theme of the absence of a divine calling of religious teachers in a 1581 booklet, *Toetzsteen der ware Leeraren* (*Touchstone of True Teachers*), in *Wercken*, vol. 1, fols. 45–70.

[9]Coornhert, *Schijndeught*, in *Wercken*, vol. 3, fols. cccxliiiiD–cccxlvA.

[10]Ibid., fol. cccxlviiiD.

It is understandable that some who were confronted with Coornhert's stated views on ceremonies and his rejection of self-proclaimed leaders of sects asked him for his ideas on what sort of church organization he envisioned. Coornhert outlined his answer in two brief sketches, one in a letter and the other in the form of a short dialogue between a father and his son.[11] Coornhert sees an analogy between the current situation in Europe, where sects have proliferated, and that of the Jews as they were wandering through the desert, when no permanent abode for God could be constructed. He deplores this situation, but feels he cannot start his own church, for he lacks the wisdom and, more importantly, he has not received a divine summons. But he would not mind contributing to the establishment of "a church that remains totally free and impartial." So he reluctantly presents his rough draft of such a church, but qualifies this effort by stating that such an endeavor, although inspired by love, would need some form of authorization, for why should people voluntarily subject themselves to someone else's insights?[12] Perhaps his fundamental doubt as to the viability of this project explains why it never got beyond the theoretical drawing board.

The above sketch distinguishes between the invisible church of all those who are united in true love for Christ, and the visible church, which welcomes true believers as well as hypocrites. The visible church will need some form of doctrine. The only sources permitted in this regard in Coornhert's "ideal church" are the canonical books of the Bible, and the apostolic creed. The members of this church will not be allowed to speculate about verities of the faith such as the virgin birth, or how there will be enough housing in God's kingdom for all believers.[13] They also will avoid those who consciously and deliberately teach things that go against God's honor; the examples given here are all doctrines held high by the Calvinist church (original sin, predestination). For the weak ones—those who need such externals—this church would maintain, on a strictly voluntary basis, the two ceremonies of baptism and the

[11] *Insicht, over't op-rechten van een Alghemeyne uyterlijcke Christen-Kercke* (*Idea regarding the creation of a General external Christian Church*), a letter dated 19 September 1578, which contains the "Bewerp eender onpartijdigher Kercken Christi…soo men die in den woestijne deser secten menighvuldigheyt eenighsins soude moghen hebben" ("Sketch of an impartial Church of Christ … such as would be possible to have in the desert of this multitude of sects"), in *Wercken*, vol. 1, fol. 554. The dialogue, *Ruygh Bewerp eender onpartijdiger Kercken onder verbeteringhe* (*Rough Draft of an impartial Church*), in *Wercken*, vol. 3, fols. 1–3, is a bit more elaborate. See also Bonger, *Motivering*, 8–9.

[12] Coornhert, *Wercken*, vol. 1, fol. 554B

[13] Coornhert, *Ruygh Bewerp*, fol. 1B.

Lord's Supper. The church would not have any preachers, but Coornhert explains that in this there would not be any real difference with the current situation since the ministers of the new "churches" were self-appointed and without authority.[14]

This idea of a "temporary" lay church found concrete expression early in the seventeenth century in the Rijnsburger Collegianten. When a congregation in Warmond (in the province of Holland) found itself without a minister, one of the elders and his brother decided "to come together without any minister and hold a meeting of a free congregational type."[15] The movement started by these brothers, who were influenced by the ideas of Castellio, Acontius, and Coornhert, lasted until ca. 1800. In the meetings of the Collegianten, whose ranks swelled with Mennonites as well as Remonstrants, everyone could speak, the Eucharist was celebrated, and baptisms by immersion were performed. Freedom of thought and the absence of dogmatism were hallmarks of this movement.[16]

In 1579 Coornhert became involved in an indirect way in the conflict between the town government and the Reformed church of Leiden about the power to appoint ministers, elders, and deacons.[17] This conflict, known as the Coolhaes affair, is an episode in the establishment of the new political order in the emergent Dutch Republic, and forms part of the tug of war between Reformed consistories and the town regents: the latter often tended to treat the Calvinists as one of several denominations under their care, although a particularly favored one.[18] In the 1570s, church law was still in its infancy, and the politico-religious situation was in flux. Competency conflicts with the town magistrate erupted around the issues of church appointments, education, the press, and marriage law.[19]

The appointment of the more liberal Coolhaes as Calvinist minister in Leiden led to a conflict between the town government and the Reformed consistory. The dispute included issues such as the town input in the appointment

[14]Ibid., fol. 1D.
[15]Rufus M. Jones, *Spiritual Reformers in the 16th & 17th Centuries* (London: Macmillan, 1928), 115.
[16]See e.g. Israel, *Dutch Republic*, 395.
[17]On this conflict, see Bonger, *Leven en werk*, 95–102; Lecler, *Toleration and the Reformation*, 2:263–69. On Coolhaes, see H. C. Rogge, *Caspar Janszoon Coolhaes, de voorlooper van Arminius en der Remonstranten*, 2 vols. (Amsterdam, 1856–58).
[18]Christine Kooi, "Popish Impudence: The Perseverance of the Roman Catholic Faithful in Calvinist Holland, 1572–1620," *Sixteenth-Century Journal* 26 (1995): 76.
[19]See Van Gelderen, *Political Thought*, 230, for background.

of ministers, elders, and deacons, and the requirement by the town government that two delegates (confessing members of the Reformed church) attend consistorial meetings on its behalf.

During an impasse in the conflict, Jan van Hout, town secretary of Leiden, asked Coornhert to write a defense of the town magistrate's position. The result was the *Justification of the Magistrate of Leiden in Holland* (*Justificatie des Magistraets tot Leyden in Holland*).[20] The document was sent to all the town governments in Holland. For his efforts—which, however, failed to bring the two sides in the conflict any closer—Coornhert was rewarded with a written expression of gratitude and a gold medal with Leiden's coat of arms.[21] In the document, Coornhert presents the town's version of the conflict, but also pursues his own agenda. The tone of the *Justification* is far from conciliatory, and Pieter Cornelisz, the town's great Reformed antagonist in the clash, is described unflatteringly as a venomous snake, a rancorous hate monger, and a man of questionable morals.[22] The nature of Coornhert's position evinced in this document was essentially Erastian.[23] Lecler saw an eventual change in Coornhert's stance from an Erastian one in the *Justificatie*, to one emphasizing the individual conscience.[24] Güldner denied that there is a contradiction between Coornhert's position in the *Justificatie* and his later writings, but he notes a shift in Coornhert's priorities: after 1579, the magistrate no longer plays a role of importance in his thinking.[25] Of course, time and again, Coornhert makes it clear that the state has no right to impose a religion on its subjects, and that it does not want to dominate or determine the teachings of the church. The magistrate needs power over appointments, he explains, because

[20]Coornhert, *Wercken*, vol. 2, fols. 189–209 (*Bibliotheca Belgica*, 715–16, C 65). It appeared anonymously and was sent to the governments of all Holland towns (1579). The fact that the *Justificatie* appeared anonymously is only one reason why Bonger's statement (in *Leven en werk*, 99) that Coornhert was selected by Leiden because of his impartiality, is not very plausible. Coornhert acknowledged his authorship of the *Justificatie* in 1590; see Coornhert, *Verantwoordinghe van 't Proces*, in *Wercken*, vol. 3, fol. cccclxxxiiiB.

[21]Bonger, *Motivering*, 10–11.

[22]Coornhert, *Justificatie*, fol. clxxxiiir (misnumbered; should be clxxxiiiir).

[23]Thomas Lüber, alias Erastus, rejected the idea of what he regarded as the subjection of the state to Calvinist or Catholic notions of a church-based polity. Instead, he believed that the magistrate's authority in and of itself was divinely ordained; see Tracy, "Magistracy," 490B.

[24]Lecler, *Toleration and the Reformation*, 2:264 n. 1.

[25]Güldner, *Toleranz-Problem*, 75. Bonger, *Motivering*, 54–56, also presents Coornhert's views on church-state relations as having been consistent and unchanging.

it must weed out the seditious and keep the peace.[26] But Leiden's whole position in the *Justification* is predicated on the fact that the Reformed Church has been adopted as the "favored" religion. A clear line is drawn between the time before the revolt, when there was tyrannical rule, and the current situation, under a Christian magistrate. So "Christian" is here synonymous with Reformed.[27] A committee of the States of Holland already had argued in 1576 that, since the state paid the ministers' salaries, they should be appointed by the authorities.[28] More important to Coornhert is the argument that, if the magistrate has no power over appointments, he becomes the blind executioner who must totally subject himself to the church's judgments. Coornhert compares the situation to the Jews who wanted Jesus put to death and told Pilate that he should not bother to investigate their reasons because he would not understand anyway. In the church, Coornhert argues, wolves may enter under the guise of shepherds. If the magistrate wishes to use his power correctly and to avoid protecting the wolves and killing the sheep, then he must be able to examine critically those whom the church wants to entrust with leadership over the flock. Coornhert here accepts the identification of town and nation with one of the contending creeds, despite his emphasis on freedom of religion and on the obligation of the church to preach and persuade, and not to rely for the dissemination of their truth on the strong arm of the government. Sometimes this identification appears in subtle form, as when Coornhert discusses the decision by the 1574 Reformed Synod that the appointment of ministers must be handled by the consistory rather than by the whole congregation, to avoid confusion. Yet, Coornhert remarks, when the magistrate plays his rightful role in these appointments of ministers, such confusion will easily be avoided since the entire community is represented in the magistrate. Thus, again, an analogy is drawn that seems to imply that Reformed Church and community are identical.[29] He summarizes his view in a letter to Coolhaes, in an analogy between the role of the authorities *in religiosis*, and that of a father: it is not the father's task to force his children into his religion, but to attract them into it by his example and his admonitions. Furthermore, a father accepts his children equally, as long as they abide by the rules of the house.[30]

---

[26]Coornhert, *Justificatie*, fol. clxxxxB; the magistrate wanted to ensure "that seditious spirits would be kept out of the consistory."

[27]Coornhert, *Justificatie*, fol. clxxxxiC.

[28]Van Gelderen, *Political Thought*, 230.

[29]Coornhert, *Justificatie*, fols. clxxxxiiC–clxxxxiiD.

[30]Coornhert, *Brieven-boeck*, fol. 146D (Letter 46).

Of course, the fact that Coornhert's name was not attached to the document and that he was in essence a hired gun should not be forgotten in assessing this tract. After all, where else in Coornhert's writings does one encounter words of praise for Calvin?[31] But Coornhert appears to recognize the inherent danger of his Erastian-politique position. Indeed, he makes what seems to be an oblique reference to the treatment to which he himself was being subjected, when he denounces the tendency on the part of the Reformed to use the civil power as a crutch in the defense and imposition of dogma. Two Reformed documents are appended to the *Justificatie* to demonstrate that although the Reformed expect the freedom to criticize Mennonites, Catholics, and others, none of these last groups must, in the Reformed view, be allowed to reciprocate. This position violates the law of nature, as well as people's conscience, which tells them to combat error that they discern in the church. Now, writes Coornhert, those whose conscience compels them to raise their voice against error "risk loss of property, incarceration, and physical punishment...."[32]

The Coolhaes affair ended in a compromise,[33] but in 1582 Coornhert took up the pen once more to write a *Remonstrance*, addressed to the States of Holland, which indirectly attacks the Reformed church and its pretenses. The document was signed by Jan van Hout, Leiden's secretary.[34] The theme is similar to the *Justification,* but much broader: it is a protest against the decisions made by the National Synod of the Reformed Church held at Middelburg in 1581. Indeed, the Remonstrance rejects the Reformed claim that this had been a National Synod, for it had not been convened officially by the States General.[35] Thus Coornhert once more takes up the theme of the Reformed wanting to turn the authorities into their vassals. But the tone in this document moves away from the more clearly Erastian tenor of the *Justification:* Coornhert's Spiritualist convictions shine through more visibly, and the religious constraint that is seen as the inevitable result of the Reformed insistence on

[31]Ibid., fol. clxxxxiiiiB; of course, elsewhere Coornhert does employ pro-toleration arguments proffered by Calvin, Luther, etc., but in those cases his ironic intentions are always clear!

[32]Ibid., fol. clxxxxiiA.

[33]Jones, "Reformed Church," 123. Later, the situation resolved itself, more or less, as more and more of the magistrates themselves became elders in the Reformed church.

[34]Coornhert, *Remonstrance of Vertoogh by die van Leyden,* in *Wercken,* vol. 2, fols. 184–88; the *Remonstrance* was dedicated to the delegates at the States of Holland (*Bibliotheca Belgica,* 735, C 98).

[35]See Olivier Fatio, *Nihil Pulchrius Ordine: Contribution à l'étude de l'établissement de la discipline ecclésiastique aux Pays-Bas, ou Lambert Daneau aux Pays-Bas (1581–83)* (Leiden: Brill, 1971), 37.

unity of faith is rejected. He repeatedly labels such insistence as the imposition of a new papacy, this time Genevan, and rejects the sole domination by any church. Thus, as a ventriloquist, Coornhert has the town government of Leiden disseminate his convictions, which are at this point latitudinarian rather than Erastian.[36]

On behalf of the Reformed ministers, Arent Cornelisz responds with a tract, also addressed to the States of Holland, in which he emphasizes the church's independence, and reiterates the position taken in this regard at the Middelburg synod and in several pamphlets that had circulated before. Cornelisz and the ministers assert that the church does not want to impose its decisions on the magistrate and, in fact, had sent the synod's resolutions to the states so that the latter could promulgate them after having examined and approved them. They reaffirm the national character of the Middelburg synod by referring to the official authorization of the Reformed church by the government. They also defend again the right of the church to elect its ministers although they will permit the magistrate to approve of their choice, provided the magistrate in question is a member of the Reformed church. The church, they state, cannot sit idly by when the magistrate allows ministers to stay on and preach who have been deposed by the church.[37] Furthermore, they firmly reject the notion, expressed in the *Remonstrance,* that the essence of liberty is the freedom of conscience and opinion, for this policy would only engender licentiousness and atheism.[38]

In the same year that the *Justificatie* was published, the States of Holland tried to silence Coornhert by forbidding him to publish any theological tracts without their approval. This prohibition was closely linked with the disputes with Reformed ministers in which Coornhert had engaged since his return from Germany. The wording of the States' decision to end a debate in Delft in February 1578 between Coornhert and some Reformed ministers states that it is motivated by the desire to prevent "scandal and rebellion."[39] The dispute in Leiden with Cornelisz in April about the characteristics of the true church did have official sanction, but it was unilaterally broken off by Coornhert, who was frustrated because he was not allowed to quote Calvin and Beza. Responding

[36]Ibid., 70. Fatio infers that the positions of the Leiden magistrate and Coornhert's were entirely congruous, but I doubt that they entirely accepted Coornhert's viewpoint.

[37]Ibid., 178–79 n. 39.

[38]Van Gelderen, *Political Thought,* 237–38.

[39]Becker, *Bronnen,* no. 106 (25 February 1578), p. 70: "in view of the fact that such disputations tend to cause scandal and rebelliousness in the community."

in November to a request by Coornhert to be protected against Reformed slander hurled at him, even from the pulpit, the States of Holland had replied that no harm would come to him as long as he did not publish anything on the topic of religion.[40] This resolution is repeated by the States on 23 August 1579, with the express admonition that he is not to attack the Reformed church and its ministers, and that if he does, he will be regarded as a "disturber of the public peace" ("*perturbateur vande gemeene rust*").[41] Coornhert's statement about a "harmful peace," quoted earlier, seems to be a direct reference to this admonition, and he voices his dilemma in a letter to his friend, Nicolaes van der Laen (mayor of Haarlem), who is also the interlocutor in Coornhert's first important tract on toleration, published later that year, *On the Beginning of the Constraint of Conscience in Holland* (*Van de aangheheven dwangh in der conscientiën binnen Hollandt*).[42] In the aforementioned letter he complains to Van der Laen that the men who have to "preapprove" his writings on religion are the same ones whose false dogmas he targets. Yet, he writes, he cannot keep quiet, since he is moved by love for his neighbor, which impels him to speak out. Thus, once again, it is the law of nature or reciprocity that motivates him: he must write against these false human opinions (such as predestination).[43] He explains to Van der Laen his dilemma: we must obey God more than man (Acts 5:29), yet the authorities will treat him as a disturber of the peace if he follows his conscience in this matter and speaks out. He emphasizes that "no man on earth has the power, jurisdiction, or dominion over another's conscience. The latter is eager to be attracted, but not to be forced...."[44] In another letter to a friend, he explains that the only reason why he ever took up the pen against Calvin and Beza was that he did not want people to accept "this

[40]Bonger, *Leven en werk*, 90; Becker, *Bronnen*, 84 n. 4.

[41]Becker, *Bronnen*, 295 n. 2, Resolution of the States of Holland dated 23 August 1579.

[42]The letter: Coornhert, *Brieven-boek*, Letter 44, fol. 145; *Van de aangheheven dwangh*, in *Wercken*, vol. 1, fols. 469–72. Part of the dialogue was translated and incorporated in Kossman and Mellink, eds., *Texts concerning the Revolt of the Netherlands*, no. 43, pp. 191–96, "About the constraints upon conscience practised in Holland: A conversation between D. V. C. and N. V. L., 7 November 1579."

[43]Coornhert, *Brieven-boek*, Letter 44, *Wercken*, vol. 3, fol. 145B; again in Becker, *Bronnen*, Letter 51, 297, where he writes that he does not act out of vindictiveness, but "only out of love for a general freedom of conscience."

[44]Coornhert, *Brieven-boek*, Letter 44, fol. 145C. In describing his dilemma to Van der Laen, he uses the same simile used by Castellio in his *Advice to a Desolate France*, of a piece of bread stuck on a knife held to the fire; it can go neither backward nor forward.

lethal doctrine of theirs on the killing of heretics...."[45] He sounds the martyr when he describes the personal hardships he must undergo due to this irrepressible urge to follow the dictates of his conscience.[46] He is not out to destroy or to weaken the Reformed faith, he claims, but he vigorously defends his speaking out, claiming that it is the blatant teaching of error that is truly disturbing the peace. And he claims that giving him the label "disturber of the peace," is only a subterfuge, used by the authorities to avoid being accused of constraint of conscience. In another letter he writes bitterly that the term "disturber of the public peace" is now being employed in the same way that they used to invoke the crime of lèse-majesté.[47] In his letter, and in the tract, he repeatedly manifests anger over the fact that he is being treated as guilty of something so serious without receiving a fair hearing or due process. However, it seems as though Coornhert fell into a hole that he had dug for himself in the *Justificatie*, by supporting the notion of a state with an officially sanctioned church, in which freedom of expression could be curbed under the cloak of the maintenance of "law and order."

With regard to the issue of church-state relations, this pivotal tract (*Van de aangheheven dwangh*) shows the transition from the Erastian position taken up in the *Justificatie* to the exclusive focus on the freedom of the individual conscience that we find in Coornhert's best-known works on religious toleration, the *Synod on the Freedom of Conscience* and the *Trial of the Killing of Heretics*. The transition can be seen in two conflicting passages in the 1579 tract: at the start, Coornhert voices the Spiritualist objection that Van der Laen (as mayor), and the authorities in general, are mixing the two realms (secular/spiritual) by interfering in spiritual matters. "Concern yourself," he admonishes, "with what has been given to you as your charge, that is, with political matters: What business do you have with controlling, commanding, or protecting the church of God?"[48] To be sure, Coornhert consistently maintains that the state may never force anyone to believe. But later in this tract, he

---

[45]Becker, *Bronnen*, Letter 51, 297; Bonger, *Leven en werk*, 208–9, quotes extensively from this important letter.

[46]Becker, *Bronnen*. The tone here is quite similar to the one adopted during the later clash with Lipsius, when his friends urged him to let the matter rest, and he replied that he was unable to do so.

[47]Becker, *Bronnen*, 295.

[48]Coornhert, *Van de aangheheven dwangh*, fol. 470A; Güldner, *Toleranz-Problem*, 75 ff., quotes this passage, but does not pay attention to the contradictory statement on fol. 471B. Similarly, Bonger, *Leven en werk*, 91, only invokes the opening paragraphs of the tract where the state is described as the neutral and impartial referee.

describes a state which, instead of being neutral in religiosis, makes a positive choice: "Let the Government choose a religion that it likes the best, and protect the Ministers of this faith, when they preach and practise this religion, with its political power and its Sword of Justice: but let the Ministers themselves, being physically protected in this manner, protect their doctrine with the spiritual sword of truth."[49] Such a state is evidently not neutral: it has chosen one religion and protects it, although this favored religion's truth is in the hands of the preachers. Coornhert's own experience demonstrated what could happen when the authorities did not or would not walk the fine line of endorsement without enforcement.

Coornhert responded to the perilous situation in which the rebellious provinces found themselves in 1580[50] with a political statement entitled *Consideration of the Netherlands' Crisis and Its Solution* (*Bedencke vander Nederlanden Noodt ende Hulpe*).[51] In it, he discusses several possible solutions for the crisis, and expresses his preference for one-man rule under an indigenous leader who can unite the land (or prevent it from falling further apart). Although he does not mention his name, it seems clear that William of Orange is intended here.[52] With regard to religion—an essential topic to Coornhert, who regards religious constraint as the primal root of the Dutch Revolt—he prefers the Polish solution; but, as a second option, he still clings to the Erasmian ideal of a free religious colloquy: a gathering that would only admit the Bible as evidence, and where the congregants would rid themselves of all man-made accretions but keep the gold.[53] He issues grave warnings against the new forms of constraint that are being imposed on the new state. Reformed fanaticism, he argues, alienates Catholics and adherents of other faiths, who have faithfully supported the struggle against Spain, but who now realize that it is the Reformed who are taking from them their highest good, namely their freedom of worship; this fanaticism plays into the hands of the enemy. Those who do not belong to the Reformed church, he asserts, lose their respect for authority, because they see that the Reformed can perpetrate crimes without being

[49]Coornhert, *Van de aangheheven dwangh,* fol. 471B.

[50]The previous year included the failed peace negotiations with Spain in Cologne, Parma continued to be successful in his *reconquista,* and in March 1580, the "treason" of Rennenberg, governor of Groningen and Friesland, took place; see Israel, *Dutch Republic,* 206–7.

[51]Coornhert, *Wercken,* vol. 1, fols. 518–520.

[52]See the description of the "ideal man for the job," in ibid., fol. 518A.

[53]Coornhert, *Wercken,* vol. 1, fol. 519D. At this colloquy, the ideas expressed in Coornhert's *Rough Draft of an Impartial Church,* discussed earlier, would of course be highly relevant.

(seriously) prosecuted. The Reformed themselves, on the other hand, also disrespect the authorities, for the same reason and with similar potentially seditious consequences. Finally, all this acrimony may well lead to a hopeless civil war, much to the benefit of the enemy.[54]

In 1581 Coornhert drew up a request for toleration on behalf of the Catholics of Haarlem, who felt increasingly threatened. Their freedom of worship and the mutual toleration between Catholics and Protestants had been guaranteed by the treaty *(Satisfactie)* with Orange of 1577, whereby the Catholic town government of Haarlem had joined the States of Holland. The prince actively pursued a policy of reconciliation in predominantly Catholic Haarlem, also as a means of demonstrating the viability of his *religievrede* (religious peace) to other towns. But gradually, Catholics disappeared from the Haarlem town government (*vroedschap*). The *religievrede* was more in the nature of a truce, and whereas the Calvinist services in their newly acquired church were not disturbed, Catholic worshippers in the St. Bavo church were increasingly harassed. A violent, anti-Catholic eruption occurred in May 1578—the so-called *Haarlemse Noon* (an event to which Coornhert also alluded in his *Bedencken*, as an example of the Reformed getting away with crime)[55]—during which the Catholic churchgoers were robbed and molested by Beggar soldiers, and one priest was stabbed to death. Some of the perpetrators eventually were prosecuted and punished, but the church remained closed, only to be handed over to the Reformed in the fall of 1578.[56] Although the Catholics' right to free worship was reiterated once more (3 June 1578), the situation had polarized and the position of the Catholics in Haarlem kept deteriorating. Increasingly, the Reformed church acquired the characteristics of a public church, which put the situation in Haarlem more in line with other Holland towns.[57] In the spring of 1581, the treaty describing the *religievrede* was annulled by Orange and the States of Holland, and a new treaty negotiated by

---

[54]Coornhert, *Wercken*, vol. 1, fol. 518D.

[55]Coornhert, *Bedencke*, in *Wercken*, vol. 1, fol. 519A; see also Coornhert, *Minute aen Niclaes Verlaen*, in *Wercken*, vol. 1, fol. 550A, where he writes that in Haarlem fifty-one people got away with pillaging; and *Advertissement*, in *Wercken*, fol. 548A, where Coornhert claims that many Haarlemmers regarded the handing over of the St. Bavo to the Reformed as an approbation of the *Noon*.

[56]Spaans, *Haarlem na de Reformatie*, 50–59. The States of Holland handed over the church to the Reformed, with the approval of the town government. The reopening of the church occurred on 31 October, Reformation Day.

[57]Ibid., 63. Still, Spaans regards the fact that the Haarlem *religievrede* continued 1577–81 as a sign of success; ibid., 68.

which the de facto position of the Reformed church became law, and the other denominations were relegated to the status of tolerated churches. Thus, the *religievrede* in Haarlem came to an end and public Catholic worship formally was forbidden in April.[58] The written request by a group of twenty prominent Catholics, headed by Gerrit Ravensberghe, former mayor and former alderman (*schepen*), was a last-ditch effort to maintain the status quo of the *religievrede*. Coornhert was asked by Ravensberghe to write the request because of his experience as a notary in the crafting of petitions and his reputation as a staunch defender of toleration.[59] Coornhert and the request's signatories were summoned to city hall, rebuked, and made to realize the futility of the request in the light of the official annulment of the *satisfactie*, which had not been known to them at the time when the request was written. In response, Coornhert tore up a copy of the request there and then.[60]

The tone of the request is respectful and deferential, yet to the point and specific. It starts and ends with the reminder to the States that the Catholics with their viewpoint on this matter represent a majority of the population of Haarlem. Relations between the Reformed and Catholic citizens of Haarlem during the past four years, it stresses, have been friendly and demonstrate "that two religions can indeed coexist peacefully in one town."[61] For the sake of peace, the Catholics are willing to acquiesce in the loss of the St. Bavo as long as they can retain the freedom to worship.

This request naturally made Coornhert all the more despised by the Reformed. In his defense, he emphasizes that this was the Catholics' Request, that he was only a conduit, and that whoever knows him can attest to the fact that he rejects Catholic doctrine and regards that church as a "murderers' den" (*moort-kuyle*).[62] Still, he stands behind the principle defended in the request.

This aborted attempt to achieve reconciliation and the imposition of a new state church in Haarlem form the context for Coornhert's most comprehensive and polished treatment of the topic of religious toleration, a

---

[58]Ibid., 71–73. See also Jones, "Reformed Church," 116.

[59]Coornhert, *Requeste der Catholijcken tot Haarlem…Aen mijn heere den prince van Orangien stadthouder van Holland* (*Request by the Catholics of Haarlem…to my lord the Prince of Orange stadholder of Holland*), in *Wercken*, vol. 1, fol. "537" (should be 545)–546v. See Bonger, *Leven en werk*, 105–6.

[60]Bonger, *Leven en werk*, 106.

[61]Coornhert, *Requeste*, fol. 545-b.

[62]Coornhert, *Wercken*, vol. 1, fol. 547C, 548C; see also Coornhert's defense in *Levende Kalck" contra Daneus*), in *Wercken*, vol. 3, fol. 361B.

work that stands out in the sixteenth century as one of only a few such thorough and multifaceted exposés: the *Synod on the Freedom of Conscience* (*Synodus vander Conscientien Vryheydt*), which appeared in 1582.[63] H. Bonger places the *Synod* alongside Castellio's *De haereticis an sint persequendi* (1554), Acontius's *Satanis Stratagemata* (1565), and Jean Bodin's *Heptaplomeres* (1590). Gerhard Güldner, in *Das Toleranz-Problem,* calls it one of the most impressive works written in defense of religious toleration.[64]

Two years prior to the publication of the *Synod,* Coornhert already had stated that he believed the problem of religious fragmentation could be solved by a religious colloquium, to be convened by the government. At this colloquy, anyone would be allowed to take part in a free debate based only on the Bible. This proposal followed on a warning of the political consequences of losing the support for the government by non-Protestant Dutch, once they realized that it was taking away their freedom of worship.[65] The dream of the restoration of church unity was apparently not quite dead yet.[66]

As stated earlier, in 1582, before the *Synod* and at the behest of Van Hout, the Leiden magistrate, Coornhert had written his *Remonstrance* against the decisions of the national Reformed synod of Middelburg to reject the term "national synod" since the gathering had not been convened by the States General, and therefore was not national. Indignation at the arrogance with which the Reformed, according to Coornhert, claimed to represent the nation, may have played a role in the form he chose for the *Synod,* namely that of a panoramic survey of the differences to be overcome before something like national harmony could be attained. It is in this connection perhaps significant that the *Synod* is dedicated "to all devout and impartial people (*onpartijdigen*) and to all sensible ministers of the Protestant religion in the Low Countries."[67]

---

[63]Coornhert, *Synodus vander Conscientien Vryheydt,* in *Wercken,* vol. 2, fols. 1–42 (*Bibliotheca Belgica,* 738–39, C 104). An excellent and virtually complete French translation exists: Thierry Coornhert, *A l'Aurore des Libertés Modernes: Synode sur la Liberté de Conscience (1582),* ed., trans., and introd. Joseph Lecler and Marius-François Valkhoff (Paris: Editions du Cerf, 1979).

[64]Bonger, *De motivering,* 18; Güldner, *Toleranz-Problem,* 79–80. Reading this book through, he states, one cannot escape the conclusion, "eines der eindruckvollsten Werke zur Verteidigung der religiösen Toleranz gelesen zu haben."

[65]Coornhert, *Bedencken van der Nederlanden Noodt ende Hulpe,* in *Wercken,* vol. 1, fol. 518B; cited in Bonger, *Leven en werk,* 107.

[66]See Lecler, *Toleration and the Reformation,* 1:217 ff. on the humanist inspired policy of colloquies in the Holy Roman Empire.

[67]Coornhert, *Synod,* fol. A2 (before the pagination of the *Synod* starts), as translated by Lecler, *Toleration and the Reformation,* 1:278. Here, Lecler reminds us that "*onpartijdig*" (impartial) was a favorite term of Sebastian Franck.

In the *Synod*, the participants debate in nineteen sessions on many aspects of the issue of religious constraint.[68] The presentation of the *Synod* shows the dialectic development of Coornhert's thought, starting with the most extreme support for religious constraint proposed by the Catholic side, countered with Protestant objections, followed by evidence that the Protestants committed the same errors wherever they were in a position of power, and culminating in Gamaliel's thoughts on how the Scylla and Charybdis of Catholic and Protestant intolerance may be avoided, and why this should be done.[69] The vice president, Iezonias, chairs the meeting in the absence of the chairman, Master Daniel, who represents Christ, and is expected to return after the synod and pronounce his verdict on who had been right. At the end of each session, Iezonias summarizes the outcome of the discussions in a *procès verbal*, to be presented to Daniel upon his return. The original 1582 edition contained a rebus on the title page, which stands for: "Synod or Balance between the Old and the Reformed Church on the Freedom of Conscience."[70] That edition also ended with a "balance" which juxtaposed sixteen Catholic errors in one column with sixteen Protestant statements in the other column manifesting the same error.[71] The format clearly reflects Coornhert's often expressed concern that we should not judge prematurely (based on 1 Cor. 4:4, "he that judgeth me is the Lord"). Since everyone takes up a position and is partial, no one is able to determine which is the true church.[72]

The synod takes place in the imaginary town of *Vrijburgh* (Freetown). According to the title page, the first part concentrates on how, in the past as well as in the present, people have sought to exercise dominion over other people's conscience. Part 2 focuses more on the role of the government in religious matters.

Participants in the synod are Iezonias, the vice president; a Doctor Consistorium Catholicum; a Magister Consistorium Reformatorum; Theodore Beza, John Calvin's successor in Geneva (1519–1605); Melchior Canus (otherwise known as M. Cano, a Dominican, d. 1560); Stanislaus Hosius, Polish cardinal and delegate at the Council of Trent (d. 1579); John Calvin; Wolfgang Musculus, reformer in Germany and Switzerland (d. 1563); Johannes Brenz, a Lutheran from Württemberg (d. 1570); Bullinger, successor

---

[68]Cf. Lecler, *Toleration and the Reformation*, 2:278.

[69]See, on the dialectic progression, Güldner, *Toleranz-Problem*, 79.

[70]See Bonger, *Leven en werk*, 171 n. 258; also the introduction to *A l'aurore*, 55 ff.

[71]Lecler, *Toleration and the Reformation*, 2:278.

[72]Bonger, *Leven en werk*, 109.

of Zwingli in Zürich (d. 1575); Du Plessis-Mornay (d. 1623, moderate French Reformed leader and statesman, who was in close contact with William of Orange), and Ruardus Tapper, chancellor of the University of Louvain and inquisitor general for the Low Countries (d. 1559). Coornhert appears under the guise of Gamaliel, the Pharisee who counseled nonaction against the Christians.[73] This choice of alias underscores two basic arguments against persecution that can be deduced from Gamaliel's counsel (in Acts 5: 34–40) and that figure prominently in the *Synod*: first, that God's truth will triumph without human aid, and second, that man is not in a position to judge heresy.[74] These debaters quote from their books, which Coornhert lists at the beginning of the synod. Gamaliel, in his contributions, frequently quotes from Albada's *Acta* of the failed Cologne peace negotiations of 1579 between the Spanish and the States General. The annotations of the Schwenckfeldian jurist Albada, published with these *Acta* formed an eloquent defense of toleration, but Coornhert probably also had other motives for using this source: it carried special weight, because it had been formally accepted by the States General. Using the *Acta* was also an indirect way of introducing arguments formulated by Castellio (hated by the Reformed ministers to whom the *Synod* was dedicated).[75]

Around the time of the *Synod*, Coornhert engaged in an extended and heated exchange with the Reformed ministers Cornelisz and Donteclock of Delft regarding his critique of the Heidelberg Catechism. His point by point criticism of the Catechism was titled *Proeve vande Heydelberghsche Catechismo* (*Examination of the Heidelberg Catechism*),[76] printed in November 1582, but not published until the spring of 1583.[77] In the dedication of the *Proeve*, Coornhert addresses the delegates to the States of Holland and wishes for them the wisdom of Solomon in determining who is the real "mother" (church). He pleads for free criticism of perceived wrongs in the institution that claims to be the national church. He also explains the grave reasons that impel him to

---

[73]Cf. Lecler, *A l'aurore*, 31.

[74]See Bonger, *Leven en werk*, 212.

[75]See Lecler, *A l'aurore*, 25–26; for Albada, see Bergsma, *Aggaeus van Albeda*; on the aforementioned motive for Coornhert's use of the *Acta*, see Bergsma, *Aggaeus van Albeda*, 139.

[76]The full title is *Proeve vande Heydelberghsche Catechismo omme te verstaen, of die voortgekomen is uyt de Godtlijcke Schrift, dan uyt het menschelijcke vernuft* (*Examination of the Heidelberg Catechism, in order to find out whether it is based on Divine Scripture or on human invention*), printed twice in *Wercken*: vol. 2, fols. 224–36, and vol. 3, fols. 465–78 (*Bibliotheca Belgica*, 734, C 97).

[77]See Becker, *Bronnen*, 210 n. 7.

launch his attack on the Catechism's fallacies with which young minds will be poisoned, since this Catechism was to be introduced into all the schools. Coornhert says that he considers the Reformed plan to constrain conscience and to teach the Catechism to youth as "more harmful than an enemy invasion or a disastrous fire in a good town."[78] Coornhert considered his book as the cry of the watchman against such an imminent danger.

At the end of the *Proeve*, Coornhert's first, brief defense (*Cort betoogh*) is printed against the *Remonstrance* which Cornelisz and Donteclock had sent to the delegates to the States of Holland.[79] *Theriakel*, also appearing in 1583, is Coornhert's extensive refutation of the same *Remonstrance*, which is printed at the beginning of *Theriakel*.[80]

In their *Remonstrance*, the ministers almost consistently refer to Coornhert as the *Wederspreker* (Gainsayer). They give the states their version of their encounters with Coornhert and of what had happened at the 1578 Leiden dispute between Cornelisz and Coornhert. They especially complain about Coornhert's incredible productivity, stating that refuting all his writings would be a fulltime job and also a waste of time. They complain about the Gainsayer's method of arguing, such as his trick of using the Reformers' own writings against themselves. And they refer to Scripture, which advises believers to avoid a heretic after the first and second admonition. They suggest that the States suppress Coornhert's writings,[81] and they argue that Coornhert is unpatriotic and dangerous since enemies of the Reformed church are also enemies of the common cause. Books that calumniate against the church, they warn, only play into the hands of the enemy.[82] Although they acknowledge that they cannot force people to believe, they emphasize that they and the authorities can and must prevent public calumny, which will foster discord and quarreling. Coornhert's "alternative," they write, is nothing less than unbridled license.

---

[78]Coornhert, *Wercken*, vol. 3, fol. cccclxvi r.

[79]Coornhert, in *Wercken*, *Cort betoogh*, fol. cccclxxviii: ; the same text is printed again in *Dolinghen des Catechismi*, in *Wercken*, vol. 2, fols. cclxxv–cclxxiv.

[80]*Theriakel Teghen het Venijnighe Wroeghschrift, by Arent Cornelisz ende Reynier Donteclock Delfsche predicanten (die dat noemen Remonstrantie)* [*Theriac Against the Venomous Libel" by the Delft ministers Arent Cornelisz ende Reynier Donteclock (who call it Remonstrantie)*], in *Wercken*, vol. 2, fols. ccxxxviiD–cclvii (*Bibliotheca Belgica*, 740–41, C 107). Coornhert's dedication of the *Proeve* to the delegates to the States is here reprinted: fols. ccxxxix r–ccxl r. The *Remonstrance* is printed on fols. ccxl-ccxliii.

[81]Ibid., fol. ccxli V.

[82]Ibid., fols. ccxli v–ccxlii r.

In his first, brief reaction, printed at the conclusion of the *Proeve,* Coornhert focuses on the charge by the ministers that he "Pelagianizes": he seeks to prove (with appropriate quotations from the church fathers mentioned) that he does not "Pelagianize," "but that he at all times Augustinizes, Jeromizes, Cyprianizes, Basilianizes, and so forth, and that therefore it is the ministers who, in this matter, are calumniating and certainly not Christianizing."[83] He summarizes his criticism of the Heidelberg Catechism by referring to question 5 of the Catechism, which asks if we are able perfectly to obey God's law of love: the Catechism answers "no," Coornhert says "yes."[84] Coornhert's criticism of the Catechism led to the great disputation with the noted theologian Saravia in The Hague in 1583.

In 1585 Coornhert wrote what would become his most famous book, the *Zedekunst, dat is Wellevenskunste* (*Ethics, or the Art of Living Well*), during exile in Emden after the assassination of William of Orange (his protector from Calvinist fury).[85] The book—the first work of ethics published in a European vernacular—appeared in 1586 under a pseudonym that was rather easy to decipher. It contains no biblical passages. His friend Spieghel, who had encouraged Coornhert to write the book, had asked him to refrain from using the "weapon of respectability" (*geweer van grootachtbaerheyt*) and to use instead the "natural weapons of reason" (*natuerlijcke wapenen van rede*),[86] but another reason for not directly referring to Scripture may have been a desire to avoid controversy and renewed troubles with the Reformed ministers and the States. This was the time of Leicester's presence in the Netherlands, and the fervent Calvinists were in the ascendant.[87] As a practical guide for morality and an explanation of its foundations, the *Zedekunst* does not address the issue of religious toleration directly, but it sets certain parameters for it.[88]

---

[83]Coornhert, *Wercken,* vol. 3, fol. cccclxxixC.

[84]Ibid., fol. cccclxixD. Coornhert also refers to the controversy around the *Proeve* in a letter to D. J. van Montfoort, written in the spring or summer of 1583; see Becker, *Bronnen,* Letter 7, pp. 210–12. In it, he writes that he is not surprised that the ministers will take action against the *Proeve*; after all, they are paid well to do so, and the *Proeve* strikes at the root of their theology. (The rest of the letter is linked with the Coolhaes affair.)

[85]Coornhert, *Zedekunst,* in *Wercken,* vol. 1, fols. 268–335; the edition by B. Becker appeared in 1942.

[86]Quoted in Bonger, *Leven en werk,* 125.

[87]See Becker's introduction to the *Zedekunst* (1942), p. xiii.

[88]Coornhert, *Zedekunst,* part 2, chap. 2: "On Reason" ("Vande Reden"), and chap. 4: "On Judgment" ("Van het Oordeel"); part 4, chap. 3: "On True Religion" ("Vande ware Godsdienst of Religie"), 4: "On False Religion" ("Vande valsche Godsdienste"), and 7: "On Truth" ("Vande Waarheyd").

Also at Spieghel's request, Coornhert does not use biblical references in the dialogue with "Splinter" (that is, Spieghel) that he wrote c. 1587.[89] The theme of their debate is whether a State ought to disallow freedom of the press through censorship. Coornhert advocates full freedom through a wide range of arguments. Towards the end, however, he gives a familiar Spiritualist twist to the debate by stating that the entire argument—about whether a State ought to suppress free expression or not—is futile, because through repression the government is trying to cut the soul with a sword, or to cane the air.[90] This policy, he writes, is doomed to fail and even will produce results opposite to what is intended, as has been proven time and again in the past.

In the last year of his life (1590), before he embroiled himself in a bitter clash with Justus Lipsius, Coornhert presented his view with regard to the root cause of the Dutch Revolt—namely, the constraint of conscience—in a dialogue entitled *Wortel der Nederlandsche Oorloghen* (*Root of the Dutch Wars*).[91] Three former friends take part in the dialogue: *Ghereformeerde* (Reformed), *Catholijc* (Catholic), and *Pacifijc* (Pacific, in whom we recognize Coornhert). The fact that these friends have drifted apart due to the religious quarrels demonstrates that the intent of the dialogue goes beyond merely stating what Coornhert regarded to have been at the root of the struggle against Spain. The same injustice that had led the Dutch to rise up and fight has now created discord among the Dutch themselves. Pacifijc, who is saddened by their mutual estrangement, plays one party against the other to show that "they (Catholic and Reformed) agree on the issue of the killing of heretics, but deny each other the right to do so."[92] He also tries to serve as a bridge between the former friends, and the dialogue ends with a plea for humility and peace.

The confrontation between Coornhert and the famous humanist scholar, Justus Lipsius, over the passage in the latter's *Politica* that advocated allowing only one religion in a state, resulted in a last, massive exposition by Coornhert, now living in Gouda, of his ideas on toleration. This book, *Proces vant Ket-*

---

[89]In the *Wercken*, this dialogue appears under the title *Oordeelen van een ghemeen Landt Leere*, preceded by a brief text in which he addresses the issue about whether truth is relative; see *Wercken*, vol. 1, fols. 461–66. According to Bonger, *Motivering*, 11–12, only that brief text (fol. 461ABC) dates from 1579, and the dialogue from 1587 or later. He bases this on internal evidence: on fol. "643A" (read 463A) there is a reference to the start of Luther's protest as having taken place "more than seventy years ago." However, in *Wercken*, vol. 1, fol. 461B, *in margine*, there is a reference to the dialogue. One might ask if the entire document dates from 1587 or later.

[90]Ibid., fol. 465D.

[91]Coornhert, *Wercken*, vol. 2, fols. 173–83.

[92]Bonger, *Motivering*, 22.

terdoden ende dwang der Conscientien (*Trial of the Killing of Heretics and the Constraint of Conscience*), vol. 1 (*Political*),[93] may not present any new arguments for toleration when compared with the *Synod*, but it is still an impressive achievement. The clash between Coornhert and Lipsius, and the writings pertaining to it, will be discussed in a later chapter.

When the printing of the *Proces* was almost completed, Coornhert learned about a booklet in Latin by Pamelius,[94] containing ideas that were similar to the ones Coornhert had criticized in the *Politica,* and evincing, in Coornhert's words, "more error than scholarship."[95] The critique, appended to *Proces,* volume 1, is a point by point refutation, citing *Pamelius* translated into Dutch. The tenor is aggressive and very anti-Catholic.[96] Much of this refutation is a tirade against Roman Catholic persecution and injustice, with Coornhert calling the Catholic Church the servant of the Antichrist and enemy of truth, due to its status as champion-persecutor.[97]

The second volume of the *Trial* (*Ecclesiastical*),[98] which was combined with the first in one book, is unrelated to the above-mentioned confrontation. The format is, once again, that of a dialogue (or dispute) between Coornhert and "Wolfaert Bisschop" (Wolfaert Bishop; it should be noted that "Wolfaert," although a normal first name, literally means "having the nature of a wolf"). Wolfaert is Theodore Beza's advocate, and in this book Coornhert targets the Reformer's *Anti-Bellius*, Beza's 1554 denunciation of Castellio's reaction against the burning of Servetus (1553), *De haereticis an sint persequendi.* Coornhert did not know of Castellio's refutation of the *Anti-Bellius*, which then existed only in manuscript and was not recognized as having been written by Castellio until 1938.[99] "Thus," writes Bonger, "we have two refutations of Beza's book, written independently of one another, and composed by the two great protagonists of toleration in the sixteenth century."[100]

In the second part of the *Proces*, Coornhert describes Calvin as a Prometheus who has stolen the fire for the burning of heretics from the

[93]Coornhert, *Proces*, 2, *Wercken*, vol. 2, fols. 43–114 (*Biblotheca Belgica*, 733, C 95).

[94]Pamelius, *De religionibus diversis non admittendis* (Antwerp: Plantin, 1589).

[95]"meer verkeerheyt dan geleertheyt": *Wercken*, vol. 2, fol. cR; the critique: fols. c–cviii; cf. above, chap. 3, on this anti-intellectual motif.

[96]See, for example, Coornhert, *Wercken*, vol. 2, fol. ciB.

[97]Ibid., fol. ciiC.

[98]Coornhert, *Wercken*, vol. 2, fols. 114–70.

[99]See Bonger, *Leven en werk*, 151–52; in pt. 2 of his biography, pp. 215–27, Bonger compares the two refutations.

[100]Bonger, *Leven en werk*, 152.

Catholic "heaven" and brought it to Geneva, but only "after he had reached a position there of safe power enabling him to do to others what he had first complained about when it happened to him."[101] As in most of his polemical work, Coornhert makes ample use of the device of using his opponents' writings against themselves. Thus, the Reformed admit that their church may err; the Catholic Church claims infallibility, but Beza and the other Reformers do not accept this. Therefore, Coornhert concludes, either of you may err, one of you must certainly err, so in wanting to protect or eradicate one of the two religions by physical force, one may be promoting or destroying the true faith.[102] Here, Coornhert actually advocates the embracing of the uncertainty principle: in persecuting, you may be wrong, and in not persecuting you do not run the risk of committing a fatal error.

Towards the end of the book, Wolfaert Bisschop is swayed increasingly by Coornhert's arguments: at one point he agrees, for example, that killing is not Christ's way, and acknowledges that he himself has "always trusted more in the Word, than in murder, being more intent on the healing of souls, than on death and destruction."[103] And from this point on, Bisschop himself also is bringing up evidence in support of toleration.

The book ends with a set of characteristics marking the truly Reformed, juxtaposed with a set of features marking the "Deformed" (that is, Reformed who favor persecution).[104] Coornhert's own story is interwoven subtly with the argument for the "truly Reformed." The "truly Reformed," in the left column, request a colloquium where they can defend their beliefs only with the sword of truth. The "Deformed" ministers of Holland, in the right column, prematurely interrupt a colloquium in progress (referring to the disputation with Saravia in The Hague, 1583, about the Heidelberg Catechism), and ignore Coornhert when he admonishes them to continue.[105]

---

[101]Coornhert, *Wercken,* vol. 2, fol. cxliA.

[102]Ibid., fol. cxlviC.

[103]In Dutch, these sentences rhyme: "altyt meer toeverlaets gehadt opt woort dan opte moort. Meer siende opt ghenesen der zielen, dan op doodens vernielen"; ibid., fol. clxiiiC.

[104]Ibid., fol. clxx ff.

[105]Ibid., fol. clxxiC.

6

THE SWORD OF THE SPIRIT

THEOLOGICO-PHILOSOPHICAL ARGUMENTS FOR THE FREEDOM OF CONSCIENCE

NO DRAMATIC SHIFTS CAN BE DETECTED during Coornhert's life in his stance against constraints on conscience. His beliefs are a constant theme, which only intensify and become more prominent after 1572. His most productive years with regard to his toleration writings were during the 1580s. The following chapters present an in-depth analysis of Coornhert's ideas on toleration here, now that the background of Coornhert's life up to this point has been described, and other major currents of pro-toleration thought as well as Coornhert's optimistic, perfectibilist theology outlined in the previous chapters.

The panoramic view of Coornhert's ideas falls into two broad categories. First, in this chapter, the emphasis will be on the theologico-philosophical arguments for toleration.[1] This section will examine the relative importance to Coornhert of scriptural as compared with patristic and other sources. It will pay specific attention to the Gamaliel-motif and the parable of the wheat and the tares in Coornhert's writings, as well as the Golden Rule or the law of nature, which is omnipresent in his statements on toleration. We will look at

---

[1]Guggisberg, "The Defence," 37, distinguishes between three categories of pro-toleration arguments: theologico-philosophical, politico-pragmatic, and economic arguments. This chapter discusses the first, the next chapter the second category. The third category (economic) was not significant in Coornhert's thinking on the topic.

three Spiritualist convictions: (1) belief in the all-subduing power of truth; (2) the notion of a complete dichotomy between the world of the flesh and that of the Spirit, and (3) the idea of the impossibility of objective judgment of heresy. We will trace Coornhert's struggle against virtually all contemporary sects and the most prominent arguments used therein. The problem of certain judgment at a time when an impartial criterion is lacking because of a plurality of faiths is another essential theme that I will follow. And finally, since the concept of heresy takes such an important place in his writings, I will analyze Coornhert's specific ideas on heretics and on why they should not be persecuted. Naturally, any format one uses to represent another's ideas is a device, and the one given below plausibly will show more system than Coornhert's mercurial and sometimes rambling writings really do.

Freedom of Conscience

Explaining his actions in connection with the aborted 1581 Catholic Request in Haarlem, Coornhert asserts that he could never regard the constraint of conscience "as just or scriptural in any way, but still … consider it to be contrary to reason, to the law of nature, and to the Divine Scriptures."[2] He adds that their promotion of persecution was the prime reason why he took up the pen against Calvin and Beza.[3]

Coornhert describes conscience as the tree of the knowledge of good and evil that God has planted in humankind's heart and the built-in judge of all one's actions.[4] At times he appears to be using the terms "conscience" and "religious conviction" interchangeably.[5] He distinguishes between a good conscience based on certain knowledge—rooted in love of God and in the knowledge of the death of the old sinful self in Christ—and a conscience based on uncertain knowledge, derived from what other people tell it, or from what it imagines. Such an uncertain conscience can still be good and true if anchored in Christ, but it can also be false if it lacks this foundation. In the latter case, it is fickle, restless, and shifting.[6] But conscience may not be manipulated or "cured" from outside. An impure heart can only be purified from within, for "purification must come from the same place from which the infection

---

[2]*Advertissement,* fol. 548B.

[3]Ibid.; also in the dedication of the *Synod,* fol. A2 v.

[4]Coornhert, *Ware beschrijvinghe der Conscientien,* in *Wercken,* vol. 2, fol. ccxr.

[5]Bonger, *Motivering,* 45.

[6]Coornhert, *Ware beschrijvinghe,* fol. "ccxiCD" (should be ccxiiCD).

came."[7] This is a notion that we find in Spiritualism (for example, Sebastian Franck). It is alien to a Beza, who distinguishes between a conscience that is good and a conscience that is objectively bad.[8] Luther, Calvin, Menno, he writes in the same tract, all show that they feel that you can cleanse souls externally, favoring "a deplorable murdering of the unwise [but] well-intentioned souls...."[9] Here he mentions almost in one breath the "killing of heretics" and the emphasis on ceremonies, referring to Matt. 23:25.[10] Trying to clean the exterior will only cause the disease to break out again in another spot.

It is clear from his definition that for Coornhert the notion of conscience contains a strong rational element ("knowledge"). Its light is rational, and this emphasis leads Christiane Berkvens-Stevelinck to call him a "rationalistic spiritualist."[11] Conscience belongs to God's domain, and when his friend Spieghel objects to Coornhert's proposed freedom that it is not right that people should despise the government, Coornhert counters that it is not right either that the government should despise God. And it despises God if it usurps his place by wanting to have dominion over people's conscience.[12] He states the principle very clearly in his *Constraint of Conscience* (1579): "Only God has the right to be master over man's soul and conscience; it is man's right to have freedom of conscience."[13] When Van der Laen argues that in the Dutch Republic there is indeed freedom of conscience, albeit no public worship for each and every sect or church, Coornhert counters that such "freedom"—without the right to worship or organize publicly—is worthless and means that nothing has been gained from the struggle against Spain. After all, during the failed peace negotiations in Cologne (1579), the Catholics had likewise offered not to persecute or pursue those who held heretical beliefs in private. And Coornhert rejects the argument that persecution in the Republic is less severe than previously, because there are no burnings, for example. It is, he asserts, the principle of toleration that matters, and without it treatment of heretics may still get worse.[14]

---

[7]Ibid., fol. ccxxiB.

[8]See Bonger, *Motivering*, 42–45.

[9]Coornhert, *Ware beschrijvinghe*, fol. ccxxiB.

[10]Matt. 23:25: "Woe unto you, scribes and Pharisees, hypocrites! for ye make clean the outside of the cup and of the platter, but within they are full of extortion and excess."

[11]Christiane Berkvens-Stevelinck, "Coornhert, een eigenzinnig theoloog," in Bonger et al., eds., *Dirck Volckertszoon Coornhert*, 18.

[12]Coornhert, *Oordeelen van een ghemeen Landts Leere*, in *Wercken*, vol. 1, fol. "643C" (should be 463C).

[13]Coornhert, *Vande aangheheven dwangh*, fol. 471B.

[14]Ibid., the same argument is in *Wercken*, vol. 2, fols. ccliiiiBC, ccccclxxxiiC, and cclD.

SOLA SCRIPTURA

Coornhert was a firm adherent of *Sola Scriptura*, believing that Scripture is the only and ultimate criterion of doctrine.[15] The Reformers, of course, believed this also. Coornhert would apply this same principle in order to reject some of the main tenets held high by his Reformed opponents.

Just leafing through the thousands of folio pages making up Coornhert's writings, one is struck by the prominent role played therein by Scripture. Naturally, it also figures prominently in his defense of the freedom of conscience. In his *Tribunal* (*Vierschare*), the only two witnesses permitted are the Old and the New Testament. In *Toetzsteen* he explains his view of the importance of Scripture, by asking "if it is not a secure gold balance to distinguish with certitude, by its lightness, the counterfeit of lies from truth's gold, then in what other way can Holy Scripture serve us?[16]

As stated earlier, he cherished as his life's work—never to be finished—his massive *loci communes*. The specific goal of this endeavor was to make the Bible more accessible without human intervention in the form of commentary.[17] With regard to knowledge of Scripture it was difficult to find Coornhert's match. On two occasions, at Spieghel's request, Coornhert refrained from quoting any Scripture.[18] Typically, in the first of these two, a debate with Spieghel, he then refers to pagan authors as, for example, "your Plato."[19] In the *Synod,* one by one, the other possible proofs for doctrine are discarded (in Sessions 2 through 7): proofs based on Antiquity, custom, tradition, nonscriptural institutions and ceremonies, patristic sources, councils and consensus, examples from Church histories, and finally pagan authors. The Reformed debaters all claim the *Sola Scriptura* principle, but when it comes to defending such doctrines as infant baptism (and, of course, the killing of heretics), they have recourse also to nonscriptural sources.[20] Coornhert believes that whatever is essential to our salvation is revealed in Scripture: in this matter, he feels,

[15]Euan Cameron, *The European Reformation* (Oxford: Clarendon Press, 1991), 137.

[16]Coornhert, "Toetzsteen," *Wercken*, vol. 1, fol. 66D.

[17]See Fleurkens, *Stichtelijke lust*, 109–15.

[18]This is the case in the tract *Oordeelen van een ghemeen Landts Leere,* in *Wercken*, vol. 1, fols. 461–66, and in the *Zedekunst.*

[19]Coornhert, *Oordeelen,* fol. 462A.

[20]See *Synod,* session 2, fol. iiiiD; in *Theriakel*, fols. ccliD–ccliiA, Coornhert first quotes at length a tract by Du Plessis, where he ridicules the Catholic Church for needing commentaries in order to mask that there is no scriptural ground for purgatory, the veneration of saints, the papacy, etc. You applaud, he writes about his Reformed opponents, because Du Plessis here scores for you. But when I make the same point about your need for commentaries, you are blind: and he proceeds to repeat the quotation, but for the Catholic dogmas he substitutes Reformed beliefs that he

we may not rely on people, for we risk imperiling that salvation.[21] An important text for Coornhert in this regard is Matt. 15:9: "But in vain they do worship me, teaching for doctrine the commandments of men." When his opponents accuse him of being a Pelagian (because of his belief in the perfectibility of man), Coornhert rejects this label and asserts that he bases his understanding of perfectibilism on the Bible alone, not on Pelagius. Do you, he defiantly asks his Reformed enemies, Cornelisz and Donteclock, derive your concept of the Eucharist from Berengarius, or your opposition to the veneration of saints from Vigilantius?[22]

The central importance of the Bible to Coornhert is evident from a proposal made in 1582 in his *Middel tot minderinghe der secten* (*Means toward a Reduction of the Number of Sects*),[23] for which his Reformed antagonists attacked him. The *Middel* is a dialogue between "Romanista," a Roman Catholic, "Secte," representing the sects that had cut themselves off from the Catholic Church, and "Catholijck," in whom we recognize Coornhert who, in reply to Romanista's complaint that he is usurping his name, explains that "Catholic" merely means "general," a term that suits him well, he says, since he feels that true Christians can be found in all churches.[24] After the three have unanimously complained about the rampant errors, the proliferation of sects, and the strife and warfare that these have caused, "Catholic" proceeds to unfold his plan. While asserting that the ideal is that people attract each other to faith by gentle persuasion, and that they overcome the lie by truth, he proposes a temporary solution to reduce sect-forming and mutual execration among sects by means of an "Interim" that would apply until a general and impartial council would have agreed unanimously on doctrine. The only thing that all sects and the Catholic Church can agree on, says "Catholic," is on the validity of the canonical Bible. All see it as the product of the Holy Spirit. The Bible is the only source of true knowledge, a pure spring, but human glosses are "like

---

regards as unscriptural: original sin, predestination, the damnation of innocent children, the unfree will, our supposed tendency to hate our neighbor, and of course the killing of heretics and the constraint of conscience. ...

[21]Coornhert, *Synod*, session 2, fol. viiC.

[22]Coornhert, *Theriakel*, fol. cclviiA. Berengarius of Tours (c. 1000–88) was a French theologian who denied transubstantiation; Vigilantius (who lived c. 400 in Gaul) opposed the cult of saints and relics.

[23]Coornhert, *Wercken*, vol. 3, fol. 396v ("397AB"; should be 399AB).

[24]Ibid., fol. cccxcviiA.

cisterns, not exempt from impure slime and dirt seeping from the corrupt understanding of man."[25] In the proposed Interim, all preachers will be forbidden to preach anything but the clear text of Scripture, without any additions or deletions. Thus, in one stroke, one would be rid of all false teachers, factionalism, and sects, "and all would no longer be known as Zwinglians, Lutherans, Papists, Anabaptists, but as Christians...."[26] All citizens must be forced to turn in to the authorities any treatises or books they possess that contain anything but pure Scripture, or be fined. Such a measure would not hurt anyone, for it can be compared to the closing of all muddy cisterns and compelling people only to use water from the pure fountain itself.[27] The Delft ministers fiercely attacked this proposal[28] by ridiculing it and claiming that Coornhert wants to reintroduce the Inquisition. In his *Ooghwater opten etter des voor-oordeels* (*Eyewash for the Pus of Prejudice*), Coornhert defends his proposal.[29] He holds his Reformed critics firmly to the *Sola Scriptura* principle they themselves claim, quoting the ministers themselves, who had written that what is human must be doubted, but not that which is divine.[30] Scripture, he asserts, stands in no need of human commentaries; it can stand on its own, and all he (Coornhert) did in his *Middel,* he writes, is to point the way to this solution.[31] The ministers charge that in his proposal of a general council or synod—this is the year that his great defense of toleration entitled *Synod on the Freedom of Conscience* is published—Coornhert conveniently forgets what he says elsewhere, namely that in their decisions synods generally go along with the (impious) majority. To this, Coornhert somewhat lamely retorts that he never said that such concord could not be attained with the help of the Holy Spirit, and that a Gamaliel might rise up and sway the other attendees.[32] The

---

[25]Ibid., fol. "cccxcviC" (should be cccxcviiiC).

[26]Ibid., fol. "cccxcviiA" (should be fol. cccxcixA).

[27]Ibid.

[28]*Ondersoeck des onghehoorden middels, onlancx versiert ende wtghegheven door D. V. Coornhert* [*Examination of the unprecedented measure, recently invented and published by D. V. Coornhert*]. Cf. Bonger, *Leven en werk,* 209.

[29]Coornhert, *Ooghwater opten Etter des vooroordeels in den Ooghen van de ondersoecker der Delfscher Predicanten,* in *Wercken,* vol. 2, fols. 556–76.

[30]Ibid., fols. dlxvD–dlxviA.

[31]Ibid., fol. dlxviiBC contains a beautiful simile, in which Coornhert compares himself with a pilot who warns a traveler to avoid all the lakes, ponds, whirlpools, reefs, and to head for a narrow, tranquil, and safe little river that leads to his destination.

[32]Ibid., fol. dlxviiCD. The ministers have a valid point here, and it underscores the utopian character of Coornhert's proposal, which in the *Middel* itself (apparently unfinished), Coornhert seems also partially to acknowledge: see *Middel,* in *Wercken,* vol. 3, fol. "cccxcviiB" (should be fol.

ministers also object that such a general council would once again result in a human document, which would again, according to Coornhert's ideas, be the beginning of error.[33] In his response, Coornhert emphasizes that at such a council, doctrine would be established in mutual concord, and he outlines the kind of document that would result from it: it would state that Scripture alone and by itself is sufficient for salvation, and that all human preaching or writing must be doubted as long as there is no legitimate proof that they come from God.[34] And he wonders how we can go wrong with such an Interim even if the desired synod and concord would never occur.[35] He firmly rejects the ministers' accusation that he wants to introduce the same kind of coercion by the government that he has always rejected, and he reminds his attackers that his proposal was only meant as a second best. The best thing was for religion and conscience to remain free, but seeing the real state of things, with the power of the Reformed church in the ascendant, Coornhert claimed to have simply proposed equality among all citizens in matters of religion.[36] The ministers' accusation is hypocritical, Coornhert asserts, for it is their preeminence and their coercion that made Coornhert come up with his proposal in the first place.[37] When the ministers object that one can forbid manifestations of sects, but that the sectarian spirit and understanding will remain, Coornhert asks

---

cccxcixB), where his Roman Catholic and sectarian interlocutors object that his proposal is unrealistic, due to the fact that all governments have already taken sides with one or the other of the contending religions, and "Catholic" concedes that it is indeed unlikely that his proposal will be accepted—"but each of these churches is free to do this and would benefit from it."

[33]It seems that in this *Ondersoeck*, the ministers take a page from Coornhert's book, i.e. that they are applying the line of criticism he loved to use, attacking his opponents by using their own writings against them.

[34]Coornhert, *Ooghwater*, in *Wercken*, vol. 2, fol. dlxviiiB.

[35]Ibid., fol. dlxviiiC.

[36]Ibid., fol. cccclxixACD. He compares the two alternatives—absolute religious freedom, and the solution of the Interim—with a town government that, faced with an abundance of quacks, either allows these quacks free rein (so people can make up their own minds), or compels the citizens only to consult the one qualified town physician.

[37]Bonger, *Leven en werk*, 209, states that Coornhert retracted his proposal with regard to the rounding up of forbidden books, but I feel his "retraction" is at best conditional. For while apparently "retracting," Coornhert explains that, actually, it was the Reformed who were responsible for such a questionable solution. Coornhert will seldom acknowledge an error on his part, and then it is mostly on minor matters. In "Ooghwater," *Wercken*, vol. 2, fol. cccclxxiiiB, he does admit to having been guilty of a slip of the pen, when he wrote in the "Middel" that, thanks to the Interim, all sects would *immediately* disappear; and he points to the full title of "Middel," which indicates that this disappearance would take place gradually.

sarcastically why, if they believe this, the Reformed strove so hard to have public Catholic worship prohibited.[38] The logical corollary from his Reformed opponents' refusal to allow freedom of religion on the basis that allowing everyone freely to read and interpret the Bible as they see fit would lead to a proliferation of individual interpretations, writes Coornhert, is that, instead, the ministers want to impose their own interpretation exclusively. Such coercion will not, Coornhert stresses, reduce the number of sects, but rather increase it, as can be proved from the results of the tyrannical Roman Catholic repression.[39] The ministers in their tract defend the necessity of exegesis and commentary through an analogy with Philip (in Acts 8:26–40) who explains the Old Testament to the Ethiopian. Coornhert counters that: (1) Philip was clearly a preacher sent by God, whereas the ministers still have to prove their mission [a theme to which we shall return], and (2) Philip explained the Old Testament (namely Isaiah) to the Ethiopian eunuch. Since we now have the New Testament—it did not yet exist at the time of Philip—to explain the Old Testament to us, he asks, do you claim to be able to better the New Testament in this regard?[40] Thus Coornhert claims that in his proposal he only points out the one path that is secure. For Coornhert, *Sola Scriptura* was an important tool to overcome sectarian strife and find unity among Christians. Of course, it is also crucial to his struggle for toleration, because Coornhert is convinced that the Bible provides no grounds whatsoever for religious persecution. In this regard, he is much closer to a Schwenckfeld, and especially to Acontius who, in *Satan's Stratagems,* also deliberately refrains from quoting anything but Scripture, than to Franck, for whom the Bible is much less central.

The crux of Coornhert's biblical proof that toleration and forbearance are the right attitude toward heretics is the fact that the term heretic does not occur in the Old Testament, and that the only punishment for heresy prescribed in the New Testament is banishment (Titus 3:10–11).[41] Beza, Coornhert argues, takes for example a statement by David, in the Old Testament, on "evildoers," and makes it apply to heretics (since they also do evil).[42] Coornhert shows where this argument will logically lead: all offenses against "God's"

---

[38]Coornhert, *Ooghwater,* fol. ccccclxxiiiB.

[39]Ibid., , fol. ccccclxxiiiC.

[40]Ibid., fol. ccccclxxiiiiA.

[41]Coornhert, *Proces* 2, in *Wercken,* vol. 2, chap. 7, fols. cxxviiC–cxxxiiiB; the same argument e.g. in his *Wortel der Nederlantsche oorloghen,* in *Wercken,* vol. 2, fol. clxxvA.

[42]Coornhert, *Proces* 2, fol. cxxviiBC; the passage is Ps. 101:8.

law would become punishable by death, since the tiniest offense against God's majesty is worse than the greatest offense against humans.[43] This shows, he adds, that Beza's God is cruel and harsh, and not the merciful God of Israel.[44] He lists other purported scriptural support often given for persecution: Exod. 22:20 and 31:14; Deut. 13 and 17; Lev. 24:15, and Num. 15:30, and breaks down the cases for which capital punishment is meted out to six types of offenders[45]: the list does not include heretics. When Coornhert's interlocutor in the *Trial of the Killing of Heretics,* "Wolfaert Bisschop," defends Beza by stating that the latter equates idol-worshipping (one of the punishable offenses listed above) with heresy, Coornhert scoffs at such a liberal interpretation, which will, little by little, "turn a man into a cow."[46] He elaborates by conceding that if we state that both man and cow belong to the animal kingdom, then we are right in a generic sense: but that still does not mean the two are identical. The same applies to an idol-worshipper or a blasphemer as distinct from a heretic.[47] Further on, Coornhert states that in equating idol-worship with heresy, Beza makes of himself a new idol of cruelty, against the Bible and Christ, and that whoever follows Beza in this regard becomes an idol-worshipper for following Beza instead of God's Word.[48] Since Beza allegorizes idolatry and makes it applicable to crimes of a spiritual nature, he should also, Coornhert argues, apply Christ's spiritual, instead of a physical, sword in combatting such a transgression.[49] Furthermore, if God had intended capital punishment for the heretic, it would have been stated unequivocally in the Old Testament and been confirmed in the New.[50] In his dialogue on the root causes of the Dutch Revolt, Coornhert's (former) friends try to defend that they still want to follow the purported Old Testament examples of the persecution of heretics, since in Christianity we still adhere to the ethical (as opposed to the ceremonial) laws of the Pentateuch. But Coornhert shows that there are other clear laws of the Old Testament that have been rescinded (e.g. polygamy). So what right do they

[43]Ibid., fol. cxxviiiC. Cf. Bainton, "Struggle," 98.
[44]Coornhert, *Process* 2, fol. cxxviiiD; cf. ibid., fol. cxxxA.
[45]Ibid., fol. cxlviiiC.
[46]Ibid., fol. cxlixB.
[47]Ibid., fol. cliB; the same argument can be found in the *Synod,* session 17, fol. xxxviAB.
[48]Coornhert, *Proces* 2, fol. clviAB; when in fol. clviC—Beza's argument, that heresy is the "mother of all idolatry"— is mentioned, Coornhert predictably counters that the mother is not the same as the daughter: why mete out the same punishment for both? And since ignorance is really the mother of heresy, does this mean we have to put to death all who manifest ignorance?
[49]Ibid., fol. clviB.
[50]Ibid., fol. cliiA; the same argument in Coornhert, *Aangheheven dwangh,* fol. 470C.

have to still observe a "law" for which the Old Testament never clearly provided?[51] Christ never had to abrogate this "law" of the killing of heretics, because such a law did not exist.[52] After refuting evidence given by his opponents of Old Testament examples of the killing of heretics, Coornhert often gives counterexamples of kindliness, forgiveness, and mercy shown there.[53]

Besides arguing that heretics do not occur and are not implied in the text of the Old Testament, Coornhert furthermore rejects the notion that we are still subjected to Old Testament laws in such matters because the dispensation of Christ has superseded it. The Israelites lived in a visible kingdom, but Christ's kingdom is not of this world, and we are concerned with spiritual matters.[54] So even if the Old Testament text had been correctly interpreted to refer to heretics, Coornhert would still not have accepted the conclusion that heretics ought to be killed. Beza, Pamelius, Lipsius, and others, he writes, consider Christ's yoke to be too light, and therefore they want "once more to subject the kings' necks to the heavy and unbearable yoke of Moses."[55] Coornhert labels such reverting to Old Testament laws "Ebionizing," after the Ebionites, a group of early Christians who wanted to keep Christians subjected to the Judaic laws.[56] In the treatment of scriptural passages, as in the use made of writings by the Reformers themselves, Coornhert often deftly applies what his opponents invoke as evidence against them. A good example is Beza's reference to 2 Samuel 6 on the Ark of the Covenant. Beza cites this text to show that King David—as a biblical model—did indeed involve himself with external religion in ordering the Ark to be moved. But Coornhert asks if Beza does not realize how this example hurts rather than helps his cause, for the Bible makes clear that David, in this matter, acted on his own initiative, and not with divine approval. And in fact, God shows his disapproval as he strikes dead Uzzah, when he reaches out to the Ark to keep it from falling. Thus, for Coornhert, the lesson of this story is, that "someone [here] wanted, on his own initiative, to protect the Ark from falling—the same way that Beza now advises his

[51]Coornhert, *Wortel der Nederlantsche Oorloghen,* in *Wercken,* vol. 2, fol. clxxviA.
[52]Ibid., fol. clxxvC.
[53]Coornhert, *Proces* 2, , fol. clvA.
[54]Ibid., fol. cxxviiB, with a reference to John 18:36.
[55]Coornhert, *Proces* 1, supplement (*Bijvoeghsel*), ibid., fol. cviCD.
[56]Coornhert, *Aangheheven dwangh,* , fol. 470B.

princes to protect his own falling Church—and, due to his audacity, fell himself, through God's punishment."[57]

In a further effort at undermining his opponents' arguments derived from the Old Testament, Coornhert states that in following these precepts, they cannot arbitrarily choose which provisions they want to follow. If you follow, he asserts, the juridical laws of the Old Testament, then you must also accept the practice of polygamy or reject land ownership. And, following the letter of the law of Deuteronomy 13 (a key text for those supporting religious constraint, as the parable of the wheat and the tares was for its opponents), the ruler should wipe out entire cities where people are found to be engaged in "idol-worship."[58]

There is, Coornhert believes, no justification in a matter of such gravity as the killing (or persecuting) of heretics for such a "liberal" interpretation of the text of the Old Testament and such disdain for the express course of action prescribed in the New. In Titus 3:10–11, Paul mentions the heretic, and tells the community to avoid him after two admonitions. "This is," he concludes with indignation, "a law on the punishment for heresy, undeniably given to us by God's Spirit through this apostle. Moses never recorded any law on this matter: and yet you do not hesitate to depart from this clear evangelical law on heretics, and to look for, yea invent, one that does not exist with Moses."[59] Thus, persecutors are followers of human invention rather than God's Word, and Christ's words apply to them, when he says that "whosoever killeth you will think that he doeth God service."[60] Elsewhere he cites 2 Thess. 3:6, where the believers are told to shun "every brother that walketh disorderly," adding that we are told to avoid, not to hate them.[61] Generally, members of the early church were not cut off easily, and the believers were exhorted to manifest great patience, love, and compassion toward the erring, and cases of avoidance mostly regarded cases of gross immorality rather than doctrinal error.[62]

---

[57]Ibid., fol. cxxixB. When his opponent tries again, this time with the example of Solomon who discharged Abiathar (1 Kings 2:27), his high priest—thus showing involvement with external religion—Coornhert, with a reference to the Coolhaes affair, immediately and cynically counters by asking whether the Reformed then want to be treated in the same way.

[58]Coornhert, *Aangheheven dwangh*, fol. 470B; the same argument—about selectivity—in letter 95 to Coolhaes, in *Brieven-boeck*, in *Wercken*, vol. 3, fol. 145D.

[59]Coornhert, *Aangheheven dwangh*, fol. 470D.

[60]Ibid., the Bible verse is John 16:2.

[61]Coornhert, *Vre-Reden*, fol. ccccxviiiA.

[62]Ibid., fol. ccccxxAB (with a reference to 1 Corinthians 5).

When the Reformed proponent of the utilization of the secular arm for the extirpation of heresy by the Church argues that the New Testament cannot provide any clear supporting evidence for this policy because at the time it was written there were as yet no Christian magistrates, Coornhert counters that in a matter of such importance, there would have been a clear indication of such a future situation since Christ knew the future. Did not Moses give rules for the king to abide by long before the Israelites had a king?[63] When Pamelius writes that at the time of Christ a secular prince's help could not be solicited because there were no Christian princes, Coornhert's rebuttal is somewhat different: could not, he asks rhetorically, God have smitten his enemies, and rained fire upon them, if he so desired?[64] The reason that he did not is that under this dispensation only the weapons of the Spirit may be used.[65] However, in the *Justification*, where on behalf of the Leiden town government Coornhert makes the argument that the magistrate should have the final say in the appointment of Reformed ministers, he appears to be using the same line of argument that he elsewhere condemns in his opponents. Pieter Cornelisz and his supporters argued for church autonomy in the appointment of ministers or deacons, because in the elections of the apostles of the first church (recorded in Acts), we cannot see any involvement of the magistrate in the process either. Coornhert concedes this, but then states that at that time, the church did not bother the authorities either by demanding that they defend the church or approve of the synods. The other side will then argue, he writes, that times have changed, for at the time there was no Christian magistrate. For the same reason, Coornhert concludes, we do not see any involvement of the secular authorities in the appointment of church officials.[66] But not satisfied with this reason alone, Coornhert continues with the familiar argument, that if his opponents insist upon following the New Testament example, they cannot pick and choose: they must then follow all precepts, including, for example, the community of goods (as described in Acts).[67] Of course in this case,

---

[63]Coornhert, *Synod*, session 17, fol. xxxvD; he refers to Deut. 17:14 (provisions made for kings), and Isa. 11:4 (interpreted as regarding the coming Messiah, whose "weapon" shall be truth).

[64]Coornhert, *Proces* 1, supplement, *Wercken*, vol. 2, fol. cviB; the references are to Luke 9:54; John 18:6; Matt. 26:53; Acts 5:22 and 13:11.

[65]Coornhert, *Aangheheven dwangh*, fol. 470D, refers to Matt. 10:28 and 16:19 to prove that the apostles were only granted authority in spiritual matters.

[66]Coornhert, *Justificatie*, in *Wercken*, vol. 2, fol. clxxxxiA.

[67]Ibid.

his opponents could have stated, that if in the future magistrates were supposed to play a role in the appointment of ministers, then surely the New Testament would have given a provision for that situation.

His opponents naturally also found New Testament texts in support of their position. Beza cites two examples from the apostles: the stories of Ananias and Sapphira (in Acts 5:5–10), and Elymas the sorcerer (Acts 13:11), in which the first two are struck dead for their disobedience by the word of Peter, and the sorcerer is blinded through the word of Paul. Coornhert, in his rejoinder, objects that they were not killed for heresy and that the apostles only used the power of the Word. Beza argues that Elymas, in trying to seduce the proconsul and turning him away from the faith, was also a heretic. He adds, however, that this story presents an extraordinary situation since normally it would be the secular, not the ecclesiastical authorities, that would mete out the punishment.[68] In his rebuttal, Coornhert calls Beza a "magician" for turning a sorcerer into a heretic. But, he continues, even if I grant you that this is so, and also that instead of the apostle, it is the secular government, as "God's instrument," that must punish the sorcerer/heretic, then we must also conclude that the government may only punish such a transgressor with temporary blindness.[69] And when Beza gives no further New Testament proof, and states that there must have been more examples but that they were not written down, Coornhert denies this, saying that this dearth of examples is explained by the spirit of kindliness and forgiveness that is so prevalent in Christ's dispensation and is epitomized in Christ himself, "who never gave any cruel example to anyone, and who did not break the little bruised reed, but looked for the lost sheep, put it on his shoulder, and brought it to the fold."[70]

Under Christ's dispensation, Coornhert believes, teachers of the faith are only permitted to use the armor of the spirit and of Scripture for the promotion or the defense of truth. When an opponent quotes Proverbs 23:13 to prove that the Bible condones force to discipline a child or servant, Coornhert retorts that such discipline in one's house is good and well, but that Christ never enjoins us to force wife and child to believe, for faith is God's gift which may not be enforced.[71] Coornhert uses Christ as his example: when many left his side, he never tried to force his followers to stay with him but asked his

---

[68]Ibid., fol. clixC.
[69]Ibid., fol. clxB.
[70]Ibid., fol. clxiC.
[71]Coornhert, *Proces* 1, fol. cvAB.

disciples if they also wanted to leave him (John 6:66–68). Furthermore, the disciples, and Paul, often engaged in debate.[72] Such debating is more needed now, at a time of proliferating sects, than ever before, and "Gamaliel" (i.e. Coornhert) scolds Catholics and Protestants, who are reluctant to engage in such debate, for their laziness. He compares them to shepherds who take a nap while their sheep are under attack by vicious wolves.[73] Tranquillity will only come about when the teachers teach the truth, thus doing away with fallacy. Coornhert denounces the false, artificial "peace and quiet" surrounding the established church that does not want to be criticized with a reference to Matt. 10:34: "Think not that I am come to send peace on earth: I came not to send peace, but a sword."[74]

To allow criticism means to acknowledge that one may err. To err is human, states Coornhert (referring to James 3:2), and if all error were punishable by death, then who would be saved?[75] The Catholics, in the first session of the Synod, deny that the Church can err, and although Coornhert disagrees, at least he appreciates their intellectual honesty, for the Reformed scold the Catholics for their opinion in this matter, demanding the right to criticize Catholic error, but do not allow free criticism of their own doctrine.[76] To make the point that the Catholic Church can indeed err, Coornhert uses the analogy with the Jewish faith: surely, until the coming of Christ, this was the true church, but it erred most grievously, and then committed the worst error of all in crucifying Jesus. So we do not have to allow that the Catholic Church is not God's church when we admit that it may err.[77] Coornhert emphasizes that to err does not mean that one separates oneself from God, for, as we have seen earlier, those who have been reborn in Christ will not apostatize. But he concludes that if one individual can err, we must infer that the collective body of the believers (the Church) may also err.[78] The fact that Paul himself at first persecuted Christ in His members ought to be a warning, for if such a blessed tool for the promotion of the Christian faith could make such an error, then

---

[72]Coornhert, *Synod,* session 14, fol. xxxB; the Catholic delegates, in this same session, denied that one should debate doctrine, for that in itself would already be an admission of the *possibility* of error: fol. xxixA.

[73]Ibid., fol. xxixD.

[74]Coornhert, *Aangheheven dwangh,* fol. 471B.

[75]Coornhert, *Synod,* session 19, fol. xliiB.

[76]Ibid., session 1, fols. iA–iiiC.

[77]Coornhert, *Proces* 1, fol. ciiiA. The text Coornhert refers to elsewhere (*Vierschare,* in *Wercken,* vol. 1, fol. 421D) when making the point that we all err, is James 3:2.

[78]Coornhert, *Synod,* session 1, fol. iiiAB.

why should any of us be exempt?[79] The chief apostles erred when, after having received the Holy Spirit, they initially refused to believe Christ had risen from the dead. This was, Coornhert asserts, most definitely a grievous error according to the Bible, and yet Christ forgave them for this.[80] Why then should the current church leaders, of whom it is not at all certain that they also received the Holy Spirit, be infallible?[81] And if they themselves are prone to error, these leaders are in no position to pass judgment over others (Matt. 7:1–2). In doing so, they usurp God's function since they have as yet to prove (before an impartial tribunal) their station as true teachers.[82] Indeed, their mutual condemnations, discord, and internecine fighting—which Coornhert compares to a civil war, where brother fights against brother (referring to Isa. 19:2)—prove that Zwingli, Luther, and Anabaptist leaders are people "of the flesh" instead of people "of the spirit," and "[i]t is impossible that those of the flesh should judge correctly on spiritual matters."[83]

The apostles' faith was simple, writes Coornhert, and he decries the fact that so many articles have since been added to complicate that faith.[84] The Gospel is replete with examples of the humility, meekness, and nonviolence of Christ and his followers. Referring to many passages manifesting that spirit, "Gamaliel" at the end of the *Synod* deplores the fallacy that thinks cruelty can be overcome by cruelty. Were this so, he argues perhaps somewhat facetiously, the world would have been free of cruelty long ago. In Castellian fashion he concludes that "there is no other remedy against killing than to stop the killing."[85] Christ did not persecute, but was persecuted, and he did not crucify, but was crucified: by using violence and force, one chooses the side of the Antichrist and shows that one is a child of the flesh, not of the spirit.[86] This theme is prevalent in Coornhert's writings. In the *Toetzsteen*, a

---

[79]Ibid., session 19, fol. xliiB; he refers to 1 Cor. 15:9. He also refers to Augustine of Hippo, who erred in his youth.

[80]Coornhert, *Vierschare,* in *Wercken,* vol. 1, fol. 421CD, and "417C" (it must be 430C).

[81]Ibid., fol. 421CD.

[82]Ibid., fols. 421D and 424CD.

[83]Ibid., fol. 432D.

[84]Coornhert, *Vre-Reden* 1, fols. ccccxviiiA–D; he quotes, *i.e.,* Matt. 16[:16] and 1 John 5.

[85]Coornhert, *Synod,* session 19, fol. xliiB. The biblical references include 1 Pet. 5:5; Luke 14:8; Matt. 20:26, and 11:29; Gal. 6:1. In *Vre-Reden* 1, fols. ccccxviCD, other New Testament quotes may be found to support the notion that Paul wants us to be kind and tolerant: 2 Tim. 4[:5]; Gal. 4; Phil. 2 and 4:7; 2 Cor. 13:11, and 1 Cor. 13:1–13.

[86]Coornhert, *Synod,* session 19, fol. xliC: here the Reformed delegate speaks, his words being taken from the *Acta* of the peace negotiations in Cologne written by Aggaeus van Albada. Biblical references include Matt. 16:24; John 16:33; 2 Tim. 3:12.

dialogue about the qualities of a true religious instructor, Coornhert states that he realizes the cause and not the persecution makes the martyr, and that often false teachers are probably persecuting other false teachers. But, he adds significantly,

> I also know from the full testimony of H. Scripture, that true fol-
> lowers of the Lamb do not persecute anyone, but that they are per-
> secuted, and that no authorities, be they spiritual or secular, can
> produce proof that they were commanded by God to persecute or
> physically kill anyone for their misbelief (I am not speaking of
> misdeed), be he an instructor or a student. Thus those who are
> persecuted are always, according to the Scripture, more likely to be
> true Instructors than those who persecute others.[87]

Christ is a shepherd, Coornhert writes elsewhere: he does not lead a pack of wolves.[88] Thus, the persecutors stand in danger of losing their soul, for "we do indeed read 'Blessed are those who suffer persecution,' but nowhere that those are blessed who persecute others in my Name."[89] In their treatment of the Catholics, the Reformed often repaid the persecution they had suffered in kind, and that, Coornhert asserts, is not the Christian way. The Reformed should not put on the "worn-down shoes of the Catholics": there are two sides in this matter, with Christians on the one hand and tyrants and murderers on the other.[90]

Some invoke texts that show there is only one church, but Coornhert explains that this refers to the invisible church of Christ's children. The visible, outward church, where the ceremonies are administered, comprises the good and the bad, the true believer and the hypocrite. The invisible Church of sincere Christians (be they outwardly known as Catholic, Reformed, Lutheran, Anabaptist, etc.) is known only to God.[91]

---

[87]Coornhert, *Toetzsteen,* in *Wercken,* vol. 1, fol. 64D. In my translation I use "misdeed" instead of crime to mimic the Dutch juxtaposition of "mishgeloof" (misbelief) and "misdaad."

[88]Coornhert, *Van de aangheheven dwangh,* in *Wercken,* vol. 1, fol. 471B, with references to 2 Tim. 3:12 (again), John 15:18, and Matt. 10:16 (about the disciples being sheep among the wolves), and 17: "But beware of men: for they will deliver you up to the councils, and they will scourge you in their synagogues...."

[89]Ibid., fol. 471AB. The quotation is from Matt. 5:11: the first of the beatitudes.

[90]Ibid., fol. 471B.

[91]Coornhert, *Vre-Reden* 1, fol. ccccxxAB.

Gamaliel's Counsel

Of particular significance in Coornhert's scriptural defense are the counsel given by Gamaliel, the parable of the wheat and the tares, and the Golden Rule.

The importance of Gamaliel's counsel is made sufficiently clear by Coornhert's using his name as an alias in the *Synod*. Gamaliel, leader of the Sanhedrin and teacher of Paul (Acts 22:3), had counseled against persecuting the Christians, reminding the other Pharisees of other sects that had come and gone, and warning that in fighting the Christians they might inadvertently find that they had been fighting God (Acts 5:34–39).

Wheat and Tares

In the parable of the wheat and the tares (Matt. 13:24–30, and 36–43)—a crucial text for the defenders of toleration, as Roland H. Bainton has amply demonstrated[92]—Christ warns against wanting to separate the "children of the wicked one" from the "children of the kingdom" before the time of the end when he will send his angels to do this and to cast the tares into "a furnace of fire." To Coornhert, this is an express command given by Christ himself against the killing of (supposed) heretics, and he gladly admits that he wants to postpone the weeding out until God sends his angel, considering such tarrying to be "the safest route."[93] This is the text with which he counters Pamelius's reference to Prov. 20:26, where it is said that "a wise king scattereth the wicked, and bringeth the wheel over them," asking if God commanded the king to separate the wheat from the tares.[94] He exhorts the Reformed ministers in the fledgling Dutch Republic, if they cannot clear their doctrine from all blemishes in a public debate, to suffer other religions to coexist with them, "until the time that the Lord himself will ensure a certain extermination of the weeds through his angels. ..."[95] He also denounces the effort made to interpret the parable in an intolerant way: Luther and Melanchthon claimed that the Christian magistrate protects the wheat by severely punishing the heretic.[96] Here, these Reformers equate the authorities with the angels of the parable, and the

---

[92]See Bainton, "Parable of the Tares."

[93]Coornhert, *Theriakel*, , fol. ccliiD.

[94]Coornhert, *Proces* 1, fol. cviA.

[95]Coornhert, *Proeve, Wercken*, fol. ccxiiiiV.

[96]Coornhert, *Proces* 2, fol. cxxxvB. Another argument used by those who gave an intolerant interpretation of the parable was, that the "overly zealous" servants mentioned therein referred to the ministers, and thus left the (Christian) magistrate free to weed out the tares: Bainton, "Parable of the Tares," 67, 79, 82.

The Sword of the Spirit

tares with heretics, but Christ clearly defers this purging until the time of the end. The reason why Christ commanded us to wait, Coornhert explains further, is that we have no certain way of telling wheat from tares. And thus Calvin, in having Servetus burned, acted against Christ's express command, and so did all who were instrumental in the death of people for their faith.[97] Furthermore, he concludes, imagine what would happen if all sides acted on the belief that the tares may be eradicated now: this would lead to general carnage, with each church killing off all the others wherever it finds itself in a position of power.[98]

Coornhert elaborates that, with the tares, Christ cannot have meant the evildoers (such as murderers or thieves), because it *is* possible to weed them out, and this must indeed be done if society is to maintain law and order. The tares, he claims, are the hypocrites, heretics, and seducers, who cannot be outwardly distinguished from true Christians and often outshine them in apparent virtue and piety. Among these, he considers the sincere heretics (who err "honestly") to be the least offensive.[99] He explains that the essential distinction between the doer of evil and the erring is that doing evil implies volition, but that one who errs does so involuntarily, thinking that he is indeed on the right track. If someone killed or robbed another person involuntarily or in ignorance, then the act should in fact be labeled as "erring."[100] One might argue that in this view, one exculpates the terrorist who errs by sincerely believing that he honors God by killing what he regards as evildoers. But such an act of violence, Coornhert would argue, violates the law of nature, as we will now see, and can therefore never be condoned.

THE GOLDEN RULE

In Matt. 7:12, Christ tells his audience: "Therefore all things whatsoever ye would that men should do to you, do ye even so to them: for this is the law and the prophets." This ethical law of reciprocity, known as the Golden Rule and equated by Coornhert with the law of nature, plays a key role throughout his writings.[101] "Let everyone follow," he writes, "the law of nature: if you do not like being forced in your conscience, then do not force others either in word or

---

[97]Coornhert, *Proces* 2, fol. cxxxviA.
[98]Ibid.,
[99]Ibid., fol. cxxxviC.
[100]Ibid., fol. cxxxviD.
[101]Bonger, *Motivering*, 57, calls it Coornhert's most often used argument for religious freedom.

in deed."[102] Indeed, this law determines the format of some of his major works which revolve around the observation that the Reformed, who were formerly persecuted (and did not like it), return the favor to the Catholics and others wherever they find themselves in a position of power. Several times, Coornhert chooses to make his point in a form that is similar to court proceedings. This stylistic device in itself brings out the fact that there is basic injustice in intolerance because it violates the principle of reciprocity, and at the same time because there is no impartial judge. He applies this "judicial format" in his greatest work on toleration, the *Synod,* but also in his other massive defense, the *Trial of the Killing of Heretics,* and in smaller works.[103] In one of his theological writings, Coornhert explains that the love toward their neighbor that Christians are commanded to manifest comes naturally. It is, he states, our natural inclination to be with each other. In the human body each member cooperates for the good of the whole. When two Haarlemmers, he continues, run into each other outside Haarlem, they feel a natural, mutual sympathy; when two Hollanders (inhabitants of the province of Holland) meet in Flanders, when two Netherlanders meet in Italy, when two Christians meet in Turkey, or when two human beings encounter each other in the desert, they rejoice. So in giving us the commandment to love our neighbor, God asks us to do what is natural: after all, he writes, pagans also have this moral rule and call it the law of nature, which implies that it is natural. And if it is natural, it must also be easy.[104]

In a dialogue *On the Salvation of Pagans,* a Reformed person debates this theme with a Zwinglian by scolding the latter for praising Socrates. He believes that all heathens are doomed because they did not believe in Christ, either because they lived before his time, had never heard of him, or refused to accept him (and he refers to Romans 10:13: "For whosoever shall call upon the name of the Lord shall be saved"). The Zwinglian bases his defense of the notion that some of these pagans were saved on (1) the general goodness of God, who at any time and anywhere provides man with the ability and opportunity to strive to become his image. If this were not so, he argues, God would be a tyrant who

---

[102]Coornhert, *Vre-Reden* 2, fol. ccccxviiA. Of course, this conditional phrasing is meant to be rhetorical, for in *Toetzsteen, Wercken,* vol. 1, fol. 56C, he writes: "[I]n religious matters people do want to be attracted, but in no way do they want to be forced."

[103]See for example his relatively early tract, *Vierschare* [*Tribunal*], *Wercken,* vol. 1, fols. 421–33, discussed above, p. 105.

[104]Coornhert, *Dat Godts Gheboden licht zijn ende leerlijck* [*That God's Commandments are light and learnable*], in *Wercken,* vol. 1, fol. 227C.

automatically damns people by not giving them the means for their salvation; (2) the testimony given by creation of God's glory (Psalms 19:1; the text erroneously refers to verse 5), and (3) the law of nature which is universal: all pagans endowed with reason have had access to this law, which comprises the love for God and neighbor. Since Christ says that this law embraces "the law and the prophets," the pagans thus also had everything that was needed for salvation at their disposal. When his Reformed opponent objects that these pagans did not know Jesus, the Zwinglian counters that Jesus is also comprised in the Golden Rule, since Christ is of all ages, and just as someone may know everything about the "historical" Christ without having Him in his heart, one may also have Christ in his heart without knowing the historical Christ.[105]

In the *Synod,* the pattern repeated throughout is that first the Catholic delegate pronounces himself on the theme at hand and advocates the intolerant stance; then the Protestant delegate denounces him, whereupon in his rejoinder the Catholic proves, by quoting Protestant writings, that the Protestants in reality practice the same intolerance. The *Synod's* sessions then end with Gamaliel's plea for toleration, and Iezonias's summary of the debate. Therefore, a constant theme in the background of these pleas is the Golden Rule, since both sides denounce intolerance when it is inflicted on them. The *Synod* is dedicated to "all God-fearing, impartial and wise ministers of the Reformed religion."[106] Although this tactic might be seen as a provocation (since Coornhert was not very popular among the Reformed), I believe he is sincere in his subsequently expressed wish that these ministers will at least hear him out because they themselves would certainly like to be heard before being condemned.[107] Similarly, in *Wortel der Nederlantsche Oorloghen,* Pacifijc (i.e. Coornhert) passionately invokes the Golden Rule, which both the Reformed and the Catholics choose to forget. He reminds his former friends that Christ tells us that we should love our enemies (Matt. 5:44). If your love is not so great that you can accomplish this love, are you not at least able to tolerate heresy "in your father, your mother, your friend, sister, brother, or children?"[108] If you can do this for a part, you should also be able to do this for the whole—or

[105]Coornhert, "Verscheyden t'samen-spraken" ["Various Dialogues"], no. 21, *Vander Heydenen salicheyt,* in *Wercken,* vol. 1, fol. 458C–460B.

[106]Coornhert, *Synod,* fol. A2 r.

[107]Ibid., fols. A3 RV; he makes this statement after relating some of the slander by Reformed enemies that he had been subjected to, e.g. that he had been involved in a fistfight, and that he slept with his own daughter (although the Coornherts were childless).

[108]Coornhert, *Wortel,* in *Wercken,* vol. 2, fol. clxxxiC.

is, he asks rhetorically, "the body less than its members?"[109] By persecuting a part, he warns further, you will bring the whole down.

Coornhert felt that the Golden Rule also applied in a very specific way to his own life and activities. It is this law of nature that prompts someone who knows—or imagines that he knows—that the church is erring to speak out in order to avoid the eternal damnation of his soul. Therefore, Coornhert must speak out. Should someone who sees that the enemy is approaching his town not go and warn the magistrate? Similarly, Coornhert feels it to be his duty to criticize error and to warn the authorities against the intentions and actions of a church that wants to dominate the state and make it the blind executioner of that church's bloodthirstiness.[110] Toward the end of his life, in a reflective dialogue employing the third person to discuss Coornhert and his motives, he gives two reasons for his writing and criticizing: the Golden Rule, and the divine commandment to speak truth to our fellowman (Zech. 8:16).[111] In a tract written against the pretenses of Henry Niclaes, Coornhert wonders why none of the Reformed ministers had taken the trouble to warn people against the grievous errors of Niclaes and his sect: he deplores such laziness, for these Reformed ministers live on a salary, but they leave it up to him, who does it pro bono, to refute the errors of such sects.[112]

Coornhert believes that he renders a valuable service by pointing out the error of Reformed doctrine, especially with regard to the issue of constraint in matters of conscience, for he hopes to be instrumental in preventing the imprisonment of conscience in the newly established Dutch Republic.[113] Some accused Coornhert of a predilection for quarreling and of pride in his mental acuity. Coornhert counters that such statements, without proof, are mere slander and must be disregarded. But he also states that even if there should be an element of pride and vainglory in his actions, that does not alter the fact that the issue that he addresses (intolerance) is all too real. He uses the allegory of a woman who has fallen into the water. She cannot swim and is

---

[109]Ibid.,

[110]Coornhert, *Synod,* session 8, fols. xxviiiAB, xxviiiCD, xxxiiiC, and passim; the analogy with someone who sounds the alarm when he detects a that a fire has started in one part of town is given (among other places) in *Proeve,* fol. ccxxiiiir, and in a letter to the mayors of Haarlem, *Wercken,* vol. 2, fol. ccccclxxxiiD; also in *Toetzsteen,* fol. 48A; *Theriakel,* fol. "cclviiC" (should be ccxlviiC); *Ooghwater,* fol. dlxviiA.

[111]Coornhert, *Wagen-Spraeck (Conversation in a Coach),* in *Wercken,* vol. 2, fols. ccccclxxviA–ccccclxxxD; cf. Bonger, *Leven en werk,* 136–38.

[112]Coornhert, *Spiegelken van de ongerechtigheyt,* in *Wercken,* vol. 3, fol. lviiiV

[113]Coornhert, *Synod,* fol. A3R; see also Coornhert, *Ooghwater,* vol. 2, fol. dlviiiC.

about to drown. Coornhert can swim and knows he can save her, but meanwhile a crowd has gathered, and he fears that he will only jump in the water because of the praise and acclaim that will follow his act. Should he, under such circumstances, just let the woman, whom he feels he can save, perish?[114]

In the course of his long-running dispute with the Delft ministers, Coornhert defends his criticism of the ministers' doctrines, and adds that if his criticism is justified, then they ought to thank him for pointing out their error, and if it is not, they should have no problem refuting him with the truth.[115] He therefore decries the suppression of free speech in the name of keeping the peace of the church and calls such suppression "an insufferable tyranny" and a "godless constraint of conscience."[116] He sees freedom of religion as the chief attainment of the Revolt. This freedom "consists…in letting people speak the truth modestly and freely in matters of faith, without fear of punishment, and for the benefit of one's neighbor."[117] Coornhert emphasizes that such teachers who admonish based on the Golden Rule—among whom he counts himself—do not have any authority to command or to forbid: they can only counsel and admonish in a gentle way.[118] In forbidding him to perform this duty—that is, to criticize and warn—the authorities place Coornhert in a terrible dilemma, for in obeying the government he would be disobeying God, to whom he owes supreme allegiance (Acts 4:19).[119] Faced with this dilemma, when the States of Holland forbid him (in 1578) to publish anything on religion without their express approval, while at the same time Daneus and other Reformed enemies are able to issue libellous statements against him with impunity, Coornhert requests (in 1583) permission from the States of Holland to go into voluntary exile to a country that is not an enemy of the Republic, so he will not have to disobey the

---

[114]Coornhert, *Kleyn-Munster,* in *Wercken,* vol. 3, Prologue, fol. xxviiB.

[115]Coornhert, *Aengheheven dwangh,* fol. 469B; see also Coornhert's Letter 95, in *Brievenboeck,* fols. 145D and 146B, where Coornhert defends his (gentle) criticism of Coolhaes by saying he would, himself, also appreciate it if others pointed out his errors; and Becker, *Bronnen,* Letter 51, p. 297.

[116]Coornhert, *Proeve, Wercken,* fols 223–36; in Coornhert, *Synod,* session 15, Gamaliel advocates freedom of the press.

[117]Coornhert, *Proeve,* fol. ccxxiiiiV

[118]Coornhert, *Toetzsteen,* fol. 48AB.

[119]Coornhert, *Synod,* , session 8, vol. 2, fol. xxviiiCD; the same argumentis in *Theriakel,* fol. ccliiiiA, stating that such a policy of coercion creates martyrs on the one hand, and hypocrites on the other hand; also in his request to the States of Holland after the suspension of the debate in The Hague (1583), *Wercken,* vol. 1, fol. 4A.

government by following his conscience.[120] Exile, to him, was only a final, desperate solution. He wants the States to hear him personally, since they have already heard so much from the other side. The issue of correct doctrine is, after all, no trifling matter, he asserts, since it concerns "neither cows nor pigs, but rather people and the salvation of souls, and God."[121] Did not, he often asks, the Reformed themselves attack Catholic doctrine when they found it to be full of error? Thus, they should allow him, or any other sincere Christian, to do the same. "Or are you the only ones to have received permission to do unto others what you will not accept from anyone?"[122]

In one instance, Coornhert rejects someone's appeal to the Golden Rule. In a dialogue on backbiting, which occurs during a voyage by canal-boat, a Catholic passenger begins to cast aspersions on a certain (absent) Reformed person. Challenged by a Reformed passenger, the Catholic has to admit that he does not personally know the man he is calumniating. But he defends his backbiting by invoking the Golden Rule, for would not everyone, for example, appreciate it if they were warned against a certain corrupt merchant? So, counters his Reformed challenger, you do this out of religious zeal, the same way that the Pharisees calumniated Jesus. He finally gets the Catholic to admit that love does not commit evil in order to obtain the good, and that in attacking someone's character without firsthand knowledge we are transgressing since we may be repeating someone else's fabrications.[123]

The Power of Truth

In Coornhert's writings, his Spiritualist beliefs are very much in evidence although they are combined with ceaseless polemical activity, different from the *weltfremd* aloofness with which Spiritualism is often associated. Bonger, in his introduction to Coornhert's *Op zoek naar het hoogste goed*,[124] states that Coornhert is not a mystic, despite for example his concept of Jacob's Ladder.

---

[120]Becker, *Bronnen*, no. 132, Coornhert's letter to the States of Holland, 1583, p. 86; this letter is very similar to his letter written to the mayors of Haarlem, in Coornhert, *Wercken*, vol. 3, fols. 400 ff. Cf. Bonger, *Leven en werk*, 111–12. Shortly after this, the States decided that Coornhert would be allowed to debate with Saravia on the Catechism.

[121]Becker, *Bronnen*, no. 132, Coornhert's letter to the States of Holland, 1583, p. 86.

[122]Coornhert, *Theriakel*, fol. ccxlixD; earlier he had already asked them to produce the privilege that gave them this right: ibid., fol. ccxlixC; see also *Ooghwater*, fol. dlxiiiiC.

[123]Coornhert, *Kruyt-Hofken*, no. 14, "Van achterclap" ["On Backbiting"], *Wercken*, vol. 3, fol. 81. Thus, here, we see a rare example of Coornhert's taking the side of the Reformed participant in a dialogue.

[124]Bonger, introduction to Coornhert, *Op zoek*, 24.

For Coornhert, there is no ultimate loss of self-consciousness or "dissolution" of the individual in the *unio mystica*. During the successive stages of a person's spiritual development the individual's consciousness, rationality, and self-knowledge remain and are even sharpened with every new step, and there is no separation of the individual from society.[125]

One area where we see his Spiritualist proclivity revealed is in his frequent affirmation of the power of truth, emanating from God's Spirit which does not need the crutch of secular support. That truth will prevail is, of course, also the message of the counsel given by Gamaliel (in Acts 5:36–39). In the *Zedekunst* Coornhert rhymes: "The fog of lies will flee, wherever truth's glow makes its entry."[126] Speaking the truth, however hard it might be for the persons addressed, is what Coornhert sees as his supreme obligation. He realizes full well that his life would have been much easier, had he relented, as some of his friends urged him to do, but he cannot shirk this duty.[127] He reserves his most bitter reproofs for those who cloak and veil the truth, who accuse him without having given him a chance to defend himself and use slander and invective against him. In one letter he urges someone who has slandered him behind his back to tell him these things to his face, so he can counter them with truth.[128] His defense of freedom of the press is also strongly colored by his conviction that the truth must be unimpeded. In the dialogue *Oordeelen*,[129] Coornhert opposes censorship, of which his friend "Splinter" (Spieghel) is a supporter. He first has Splinter admit that not all writings are detrimental to the commonweal. If we could know for sure which writings are evil, then we should certainly weed them out: but now we risk weeding out the good and promoting the evil (here we hear an echo of the wheat and tares motif). This risk is too great: "Should one thus discard the gold, of which there is little, because of the foam that exists in much greater quantities?"[130] Since to err is human,

---

[125]Bonger, introduction to Coornhert, *Op Zoek*, 24.

[126]Coornhert, *Zedekunst*, quoted in Bonger, *Motivering*, 119: "Des loghens nevel verdwijnt, zo waar des waarheyds glants verschynt"; also Coornhert, *Zedekunst*, bk. 4, chap. 7, p. 483. In *Kleyn-Munster*, an attack on David Joris, Coornhert states that he is not afraid of posthumous attacks on his writings, for the truth is its own best defense, and his writings are not the Gospel: *Wercken*, vol. 3, fol. xxviiiB.

[127]Coornhert, *Waghen-Spraeck*, fol. ccccclxxviiA; see also Bonger, *Leven en werk*, 137.

[128]Becker, *Bronnen*, Letter 20 (no date), 229–30; he warns that if N. continues his slander, Coornhert will expose his lies in a book showing N's true character and actions, "so that your children's children will be ashamed of your name."

[129]Coornhert, *Wercken*, vol. 1, fols. 461–66.

[130]Ibid., fol. 462A..

who, Coornhert asks, could be entrusted with the power to separate the good from the bad? The authorities—which Splinter would endow with such powers—are not necessarily more knowledgeable on spiritual matters than their subjects, for their task is secular, and they have dominion "over body and material things, but not over the heart."[131] Sedition and strife are brought about by oppression and not by freedom of expression.[132] It was the Roman Catholic reliance on the sword rather than the Word which made the people mistrust the ecclesiastical authorities, feeling that they lacked confidence in the veracity of their own teachings.[133] Truth, Coornhert contends (quoting Plato), is always good and cannot be the cause of evil, and to forbid free publication means that you forbid people to do good.[134] When you realize that the spirit is far more important than matter, you will teach the truth no matter what, and you will also realize that what the government attempts to do when it imposes censorship is ultimately futile, for you cannot stop the truth from expressing itself and from vanquishing in the end. In discussing censorship, we are, he concludes, actually discussing an impossibility, for "aiming to force the understanding and to obstruct teaching is the same as wanting to kill the soul with a sword, or to flog the air with a rod."[135]

The truth is generally reviled, ignored, or persecuted.[136] In a concrete way, Coornhert applies this notion to his concept of perfectibility and the possibility of attaining complete obedience to Christ's commandment to be perfect. In a dialogue dedicated to his Reformed brother Frans,[137] the Reformed participant states that experience teaches that nobody on earth is perfect. Coornhert counters that, in the first place, nobody can claim to know the thoughts and deeds of everyone on earth: so there is no empirical evidence that no earthling is without sin. The Reformed antagonist then challenges Coornhert to give one example of someone who is without sin, but Coornhert states that, because the Reformed do not believe that sinlessness is possible, his interlocutor would

[131]Ibid., fol. 462B.
[132]Ibid., fol. "643A" (should be fol. 463A).
[133]Ibid., fol. 463A.
[134]Ibid., fol. "643BC" (should be fol. 463BC).
[135]Ibid., fol. 465D.
[136]See, for example, Coornhert's *Toetzsteen* in *Wercken,* vol. 1, fol. 58B, where one of the marks of a "true teacher" is, that he does not hate anybody, nor does he persecute, but that he is hated and suffers persecution, "for the sake of Christ's truth."
[137]Coornhert, *Vande waarachtighe Aflaat* [*On the true Indulgence*], *Wercken,* vol. 1, fols. 249–67. The Dutch word for "indulgence" has the literal meaning of "letting go or abandoning," that is, of sin.

simply refuse to accept any claim to such sinlessness. Christ was recognized by those of his contemporaries who looked upon him with the eyes of faith as the Son of God, but the Pharisees saw him merely as a sinner and a seducer. Thus, he says, it is "your unbelief that keeps you from seeing this true abandonment of sin in the holy members of Christ."[138] He asks his counterpart if he believes that we can visibly locate Jesus somewhere on this earth. No, replies the Reformed, that is why we object to the Roman Catholic concept of the Eucharist. Then Coornhert uses this as an analogy to make the point that the truth is also usually despised and persecuted:

> Just as we are unable to indicate the Head of the Christians with our finger, and show him to physical eyes, we are equally unable to do the same with regard to his members, who are at present already walking in heaven, while in the flesh they are still living here on earth: And just as the Jews could not recognize Christ as holy and innocent, the unbeliever and the world cannot recognize Christ's members as holy and innocent.[139]

When his Reformed opponent accuses Coornhert of calling him an unbeliever, Coornhert replies that this adherent of the Reformed faith himself acknowledges that he is one, by saying that he cannot believe that anyone is truly without sin.[140] The connection between truth and suffering is fully explained in Coornhert's tract on the characteristics of a "true teacher" (that is, a preacher).[141] True teachers suffer because they teach the unadorned truth, which the people and the government generally do not want to hear. Therefore, the "new Pharisees," who hold great credit with the powers that be, hurl their false accusations and calumnies at them by accusing the real children of Christ of sedition, blasphemy, and the like.[142] True teachers are subjected to hunger and thirst, to incarceration, flogging, and a shameful and bitter death, "the reward that the world with its hypocrites is wont to give to God's true saints...."[143] If such was the state of the world at the time of Christ, he adds,

---

[138]Ibid., fol. 252C.

[139]Ibid., fol. 252C.

[140]Ibid.; it is clear that Coornhert did not ingratiate himself with the Reformed by such an argument.

[141]Coornhert, *Toetzsteen der ware Leeraren* [*Touchstone of True Teachers*], chap. 18, "Van der ware Leeraren Cruys, Lijden ende Vervolginghe," *Wercken*, vol. 1, fol. 64BCD.

[142]Ibid., fol. 64C.

[143]Ibid.

we cannot expect to be treated any better by this world.[144] But true teachers are intrepid warriors in a spiritual battle and serve no other master but God. They make no use of prisons or swords of steel, for "[w]ho can wound or kill the air?"[145]

Theologians and scholars make things unnecessarily complicated, for the truth and the message of the Gospel are simple: Coornhert regularly emphasizes this simplicity by reminding his readers that Christ's first followers were simple fishermen, and invoking the popular motto *Hoe geleerder hoe verkeerder* (freely translatable as "Intellectuals are usually not much good").[146] In this context, Coornhert often and, it seems, proudly, refers to his own lack of schooling, calling himself an "unlearned idiot." In *Aertzenij der zielen* (*Healing of souls*), a sick man gets advice from his untitled brother "Eumenes" but discards it, saying: "Am I not mad to follow you, an unlearned idiot, and turn my back on the learned doctors…?"[147] Eumenes—who clearly represents Coornhert, with his evangel of perfectibilism—counters by asking why his brother should leave the house for help when he can find the remedy inside. His brother, however, sends for the "true doctors" anyway: "Doctor Pope," "Doctor Luther," and so on, with predictable results.[148]

Two Worlds Apart

A Spiritualist theme found throughout Coornhert's writings, and also crucial for his view of the polity (which will be explored later) is that of the absolute dichotomy between the world of the flesh and the world of the spirit. It leads him to advocate the killing of heresy and not the heretic, and to see evil as the absence of the good (*privatio boni*, a concept already propounded by Augustine). The true admonisher and preacher of God's Word does not need the executioner's sword, nor does he need to lean on the secular power, since he robs the strong of their "furniture of false opinions through the strength of sincere truth," since he is "in direct possession of the power to avenge all disobedience

---

[144]Ibid., fol. 64D.

[145]Ibid., fol. 65A. This is followed by the statement that "only God can kill the soul," which is the title of a chapter on Coornhert's toleration, by Bergsma, in Bonger et al., eds., *Dirck Volckertszoon Coornhert*, 32–43.

[146]See, e.g., Coornhert, *Hemel-werck*, in *Wercken*, vol. 2, fol. cccxlv.

[147]Coornhert, *Aertzenij der zielen*, in *Wercken*, vol. 1, fol. 472B. See also, for example, *Schijndeught der secten*, im *Wercken*, vol. 3, fol. ccccxliiiD, speaking in third person about Coornhert, that "unlearned idiot and…loutish Hollander."

[148]Coornhert, *Aertzenij der zielen*, fol. 472B. The rest of this dialogue is discussed below.

with the two-edged sword of the all-powerful truth."[149] Conversely, in relying on the civil sword for the advancement of spiritual ends, one manifests a lack of faith in the power of God's Word and blindness to the fact that only God has dominion over soul and conscience.[150]

Due to this focus on the spiritual essence of Christ's message Coornhert manifests indifference to, even disdain for, chiliast speculation or expectation. When a friend asks for his opinion on God's one-thousand-year kingdom on earth, Coornhert responds that people who are so intent on these things are like mercenaries, craving God's gifts (thus fitting them into the scheme of Jacob's Ladder). They love God for the reward He gives instead of for His own sake.[151] He admits that he has never been able to understand John's Apocalypse and that he has better things to do with his time than to speculate about the predictions contained therein. He lists the following reasons for leaving such speculation alone: (a) the matter is obscure; (b) when the time comes, it will be clear enough; and (c) prior knowledge of the coming of God's kingdom here on earth is useless if, by wasting my time on researching these issues, I keep myself from becoming "a sincere member of Christ's Kingdom, and thus, lacking my wedding clothes, I shall have to remain outside, or be expelled from it."[152] This position is also linked with his ethical imperative, for he concludes his words on this topic by stating that "not to know much, but to be virtuous is what makes us well-prepared for Christ's Kingdom."[153] Elsewhere, Coornhert refers to the tragic results of the Anabaptist hopes for the establishment of God's kingdom on earth, in Münster.[154]

[149]Coornhert, *Toetzsteen,* fol. 58B.

[150]Coornhert,*Synod,* session 17, fol. xxxvA; it is the Reformed delegate who speaks these tolerant words, taken from the *Acta pacificationis,* the account of the peace negotiations in Cologne written by Albada (1579).

[151]Coornhert, *Brieven-boeck,* Letter 91, "Van't duysent-jarighe Rijcke Godes op Aerden...," fol. 143B.

[152]Ibid., fol. 143C.

[153]Ibid., fol. 143C..

[154]Ibid., Letter 92 (against Hendrik Niclaes), fol. 144A; in the next letter (93), fols. 144B–145A, probably to his friend Montfoort, Coornhert ranks the topic of the origin of evil, about which the addressee had asked him, with speculative matters that we do not need to pursue.

The Many-Headed Hydra: Coornhert against the Sects

Not a level playing field

Far from being indifferent to the manifold divisions into which Christianity was being transmuted, Coornhert waged a constant battle against what he regarded as sects. He never joined or started one, and remained a nominal Catholic. Instead of presenting here a detailed account of Coornhert's interactions with the various sects,[155] I want to trace some of his general reasons for attacking and rejecting the sects (of which he, of course, saw the Reformed Church as the most dangerous).

Although he always professes that there should be absolute freedom for any religious conviction and vaunts his impartiality, it is clear that he does not regard all error as equal. Boomgaert, in the short biography preceding the *Wercken*, states that Coornhert nearly joined the *Doopsgezinden* (the pacific Anabaptists in the Netherlands, such as the Waterlanders), because of their "impartiality."[156] He clearly felt more sympathy for this last sect (also due to their sufferings) than for the Reformed even though he also wrote with his customary sharpness against certain Anabaptist beliefs and practices. Using his own perfectibilist theological convictions as a Procrustean device, he rejected the sects. Rather than impartiality, Coornhert manifested a firm conception of "the truth" which he could not find perfectly reflected anywhere. He remained an individualist who never collected a sizable following (and did not attempt to either), and in the debates against the Reformed ministers he stood alone.

Another sign that Coornhert did not adopt a truly level playing field between religious groups is that he still placed the Catholic Church, however much corrupted, above (or, rather, before) the sects. Among the visible "churches" (he actually denies the appellation "church" for what he regards as the Reformed and other sects), the Catholic Church may have become weighed down with encrustations and accretions, but it still goes back to the true apostolic church, "for the dirt does not remove the substance, but sticks to it."[157] Another comparison he uses is that in the Catholic Church great amounts of foam have covered up the original gold—but the gold is still there, whereas the Reformed, for example, are merely "foam without gold."[158]

---

[155]For this, see Bonger, *Leven en werk*, pt. 2, chap. 4, pp. 257–91, "Coornherts plaats in het godsdienstig leven van zijn tijd. De kritiek op de 'vergodete' profeten."

[156]Boomgaert's prologue to *Wercken*, vol. 1, fol. 9r.

[157]Coornhert, *Bedacht schynende met te brenghen dat die Roomsche kercke beter zy dan der Ghereformeerden*, in *Wercken*, vol. 1, fol. 484C.

As stated earlier, Coornhert never formally left the Roman Catholic Church although as of the early 1570s, he most likely never attended services anymore.[159] In one of his dialogues, he describes "a certain man living in exile in Germany," who was wont to attend the sermon but would then leave church before the mass. Then, noticing that in doing so he offended certain people, he stayed away from church altogether. When one of the newly appointed bishops in the Netherlands heard about this, he wrote him a letter of reproof. The bishop assumed, writes Coornhert, that the addressee was *papistelijck,* whereas in fact he was only *Catholijck.* The bishop warned him that he could not consider himself a Christian, nor be saved, if he did not attend Church and take communion regularly. The exile, in his response, referred to St. Paul the Hermit (died c. 347 A.D.), the recluse who lived in a desert cave for well-nigh one hundred years, never attended church services during all that time, and yet had the rank of sainthood conferred upon him by the Catholic Church. He asked the bishop to write back and prove that the Catholic Church had erred. There was no response, so this man "continued to live quietly in the little town, did not attend church and never regretted his staying away from the services, for he realized full well that the essence of church ceremonies would not be lost if you let go of their external form. What matters is to hold on to the inner significance. If you do that, you can safely go without the outside."[160]

"Ceremonialistians instead of Christians"

The last quotation brings us to one of Coornhert's favorite themes in his attacks on all the "visible churches" around him, viz. their abuse of ceremonies. In *Schijndeught der Secten,* "Catholic" (Coornhert) cleverly plays his interlocutors against each other, with the Anabaptist and the Reformed both rejecting transubstantiation, and the Lutheran more or less siding with the Roman Catholic position on this topic, and the Reformed and Lutheran agreeing on infant baptism, which the Anabaptist rejects on biblical grounds.[161]

---

[158]Ibid., This tract is followed by a similar one: *Ander ende corter bewys,* ibid., fol. 485v–"485 v" (must be 486 v).

[159]See e.g. Coornhert, *Schijndeught der secten,* in *Wercken,* vol. 3, fol. cccliiA.

[160]See the "dialogue" (in letters), "Wter Kercken dienst blijven" ["Not going to Church services"], in *Verscheyden t' samen-spraken,* in *Wercken,* vol. 1, fol. 444BC; a translation into modern Dutch of this dialogue is given in Coornhert, *Weet of rust,* ed. Bonger and Gelderblom, 12–14, and 127–128 (annotations). The quotation is translated from this modern rendering, p. 14.

[161]Coornhert, *Schijndeught,* fol. cccxliiiB.

Thus, different interpretations of ceremonies have become a major source of strife. In the *Zedekunst,* Coornhert distinguishes between external and internal religion, stating that external religion consists in a saintly way of life and in making use of ceremonies: of these two, it is the ceremonies that are the cause of strife and division, which is a sad thing, for "not in appearances, but in the essence do we find true religion."[162] The comparison Coornhert regularly uses is that between the shadow and the object casting it, or between the sign pointing to the wine cellar and the wine itself. He who is fixated on ceremonies is like a person who is constantly staring at the sign, and thus never gets to taste of the wine.[163] Anyone, even the devil himself, he writes elsewhere, can perform and fake ceremonies, but true, heartfelt love toward God and one's neighbors cannot be faked.[164] However, a varnish of divine zeal is often used to disguise fanaticism.[165] To the objection that both body and soul must be clean, Coornhert replies that according to the Bible, the soul comes first: when the soul is pure, the body will automatically become pure as well, but the body can appear to be clean on the outside and yet hide an impure soul.[166] Calvin, Coornhert charges, is inconsistent, for on the one hand he writes that our heart always remains a fiery oven filled with desires, but on the other hand he states that God does not look at the outside, but only at one's purity of heart. How dare Calvin offer this heart, which he first states to be forever filthy, to God? How can God ever accept our ceremonies, he asks, when Calvin claims that God only accepts them if they come from a pure heart?[167]

Due to different interpretations and abuse, it is hard to partake in ceremonies without the risk of offending God. Coornhert explains this plight in a story of an immoral priest, who consecrates the host without having confessed and done penance. A lady who witnesses this—she followed the priest after he had spent a night of debauchery and noticed that he went from there straight to the celebration of mass—challenges him. The priest tries to save himself by saying that in such cases, priests did not really consecrate the host. The woman

[162]Coornhert, *Zedekunst,* ed. Becker, 226. This argument was also at the root of Coornhert's "Verschooninghe" against Calvin, that elicited a vehement response from the Reformer: see chapter 1, above..

[163]Coornhert, *Schijndeught,* fol. cccxlviiiAB; also *Vre-Reden* 2, fol. ccccxxiiiiD; and same reasoning in Letter 24, Becker, *Bronnen,* 241–43.

[164]Coornhert, *Toetzsteen,* fol. 55B.

[165]Coornhert, *Schijndeught, Wercken,* fol. ccliiiiD.

[166]Ibid., fol. cclD.

[167]Ibid., fol. cccliB.

says that in that case she is determined never to attend mass again, to avoid the risk of worshipping a mere piece of bread and thus engaging in idolatry. From now on, she will just skip intermediaries and pray directly to God in heaven.[168] We see here the reflection of Coornhert's adage, *Weet of rust* (Know or let go). Everyone knows, Coornhert writes in a letter to Dirck van Egmont, that the Roman Catholic Church has been corrupted, but since none of the new would-be churches has received a clear mandate to rectify and purify these ceremonies, we have no way of knowing if they are better. Thus, it is better to abstain from something when you have no way of knowing whether it is right: in desisting, you cannot go wrong.[169] After all, Christ gave ceremonies to foster unity among the believers. When ceremonies cause disunity instead, it is better to refrain from them altogether, and just focus on the real thing.[170] It is better, Coornhert scoffs, that those who are so bent on abusing the ceremonies and on using them as a yardstick and an instrument of division, no longer call themselves Christians, but instead adopt the name Ceremonialistants.[171] In an impassioned plea for toleration concluding session 3 of the *Synod*, "Gamaliel" (Coornhert) acknowledges that most people are in need of external acts and ceremonies. One would wish, he continues, that we only use ceremonies according to God's decree, but since this is not so, "one must either tolerate or vanquish the other," an observation immediately followed by the plea: "Oh, if only we could tolerate one another...."[172]

Lack of proof

A recurring argument against the sects is their purported lack of validation or mission. Similarly to the way in which in France the Huguenot church was known officially as "l'Eglise prétendue Réformée," to Coornhert the Anabaptists, Lutherans, Reformed have not produced proof to substantiate their claim to church status. He often refers to the Reformed ministers and other leaders of these sects as teachers who "walk on their own intiative," e.g. in "Schijndeught der secten," where "Catholic" (Coornhert) approvingly refers to Sebastian Franck and Caspar Schwenckfeld, who "saw...that the teachers of all three

---

[168]Coornhert, "Van de ongheconsacreerde Hostie in der Missen," in *Het Kruythofken,* in *Wercken,* vol. 3, fol. lxxxiB; this story is also in Coornhert, *Weet of rust,* 14–15 (notes on p. 128).

[169]Coornhert, Letter 53, in Becker, *Bronnen,* 302–304.

[170]Coornhert, *Schijndeught,* fol. cccxlixB.

[171]"Ceremonialisten" instead of "Christen": Coornhert, *Schijndeught,* fol. cccxlixA.

[172]Coornhert, *Synod,* session 3, fol. viA. The implication from the context is that vanquishing by force is intended.

of your congregations walked in the Lord's vineyard unsent, on their own initiative."[173] These new, so-called leaders needed to produce proof of their mission: either clear textual proof, or miracles, but they could produce neither. To the Reformed assertion that the words spoken by Christ to the apostles also apply to the current teachers in Christ's cause, "Catholic" answers that in that case, these new teachers should be like the apostles in all respects: perform miracles, have all their worldly goods in common, and so on.[174] The Reformed, Coornhert writes elsewhere, imagine that their faith is the only true one and all others false. You must, he challenges them, first "give legitimate proof that your religion is the true one."[175]

Besides the teachers claiming a direct mission from God there are teachers who have been sent by the true church.[176] The problem with these latter teachers is, of course, that one must be absolutely certain that the church that sends them is the true one: the entire *Synod* revolves around the idea that this church cannot be identified with certainty at the present time, and the Catholic Church is such a corrupted relic of the apostolic church that its teachers are naturally suspect as well.[177] Acclaim and success for Luther and others are in themselves no proof of the veracity of someone's mission: the Arians, or Mohammed, writes Coornhert, also attracted a massive following.[178] What we now witness is the blind leading the blind. Such blindness can be seen, according to Coornhert, in the many revisions of the *Institutes* by Calvin, and in the claims made by such leaders as David Joris, by Menno Simons in his *Fondamentboeck,* or by Hendrik Niclaes in his *Spiegel der gherechticheyt.* Simons,

---

[173]Coornhert, *Schijndeught,* fol. cccxlviiB. See also *Toetzsteen der ware Leeraren,*" fols. 45–70; on fol. 47 C, e.g., the same warning against false teachers who "walk on their own initiative." Cf. Sebastian Franck, in an oft-cited letter to John Campanus, where he writes, against so-called church leaders, that "they all run uncalled and enter into the sheep[fold] unsent": Franck, "A Letter to John Campanus," in Williams, ed., *Spiritual and Anabaptist Writers,* 154.

[174]Coornhert, *Schijndeught,* fol. cccxlviiCD.

[175]Coornhert, *Theriakel,* fol. cclC.

[176]Coornhert, *Toetzsteen,* fols. 47CD and 56C. A third category are the "Golden Rule teachers" who can claim no authority: see above, p. 102. See also Coornhert, *Vande Sendinghe* (two dialogues), *Wercken,* vol. 1, fols. 377–83.

[177]Therefore, in reading Coornhert's *Toetzsteen,* which lists all the qualities of "true teachers" backed up by numerous scriptural quotations, one gets a sense that this is an exercise in futility, for if someone is not a teacher direct from God, whose miracles attest to his divine message, then he must be indirect, sent by the "true church," which we already know Coornhert feels cannot be identified. If not an exercise in futility, perhaps it can be seen as a utopian sketch of the kind of teachers that could rise up once the "truly Catholic," i.e. impartial, church has emerged?

[178]Coornhert, *Toetzsteen,* fol. 56CD.

Coornhert charges, paints himself and his followers as much more saintly than is warranted, and he calls his book a "foundation." Does this not imply, writes Coornhert, that the Gospel is obscure, and that Simons' writings are a necessary supplement to the sacred text?[179] Similarly, Coornhert attacks Niclaes's pretense that he completes Christ's revelation, for this suggests that something had been missing in that revelation. He ends his prologue to the tract "Spiegelken vande ongherechtigheyt..."[180] with a warning to "hold on to the truth, which is Jesus Christ, and not to H. N. (Hendrik Niclaes), Henric Jansz. (i.e. "Hiël," Hendrik Jansen Barrefelt, leader of a sect that broke away from Niclaes), nor any other human being, which definitely includes me, being human as well...."[181]

As stated earlier, of all the sects, Coornhert felt closest to the *Doopsgezinden*, in particular the Mennonite sect known as the Waterlanders.[182] In a dialogue titled "Conversation with the Waterland Community,"[183] Coornhert states that he had long considered the church of the *Doopsgezinden* to be one of the most impartial of the new churches.[184] However, he strongly objects to their practice of the "ban," the isolation of church members deemed sinful or unorthodox, which even prescribed the shunning of a "banned" wife by her husband or vice versa (a form of the ban known as *echtmijdinghe*).[185] Coornhert emphasizes that only if it can be proven that one reborn person may know the reborn status of a fellow believer, a visible church of saints can be erected. Until that time, the church will inevitably contain true believers as well as hypocrites. When his

---

[179]See Coornhert, Letter 45 to some *Doopsgezinden*, in Becker, *Bronnen*, 284–90.

[180]Coornhert, *Little Mirror of Injustice* (the title alludes to Niclaes's "Mirror of Justice") *Wercken*, vol. 3, fol. lviii–lxxii.

[181]Ibid., fol. lviiiV. In Letter 42, *Brieven-boeck*, fol. 144A, Coornhert rejects the fact that Niclaes acts like a "God on earth," and that he "rules over the hearts of the blind, who have blindly placed themselves under his blind leadership." See also *Toetzsteen*, fol. 58A.

[182]Coornhert, *Openinghe Van den grondt der Waterlandtsche Kercken*, in *Wercken*, vol. 1, fol. 433B.

[183]Coornhert, *Gesprake met de Waterlantsche Ghemeente*, in *Wercken*, vol. 1, fols. 365–70.

[184]Ibid., fol. 365A.

[185]Coornhert, *Van 't Overheydts Ampt*, in *Wercken*, vol. 1, fol. 387AB. For Anabaptist church discipline, see Krahn, *Dutch Anabaptism*, 233–34; differences over the severity of discipline had caused the less severe *Waterlanders* to break away from the strict disciplinarian Mennonites led by Leenaert Bouwens and Dirk Philips. Coornhert still thought them too strict, or rather, he considers the principle of such discipline false, because it presupposes the existence of a true church. Coornhert mediated when schism threatened the Waterland community due to a conflict over the status of "admonishers" (ministers): see Bonger, *Leven en werk*, 130–33; Coornhert's account of his mediation efforts in *Openinghe Van den grondt*, fols. 433–38.

Anabaptist interlocutor asks him if it would, then, have been better if Luther had stayed within the Roman Church, Coornhert confirms this. When the Bible proclaims that we should avoid the unbeliever (2 Corinthians 6: 17), he says, what is meant is to avoid him with your heart, not with your feet (by running away).[186] The erection of new churches everywhere, without a clear and incontrovertible divine summons, is the major cause of this bloodshed all over Europe.[187] The Anabaptist practice of the "ban" goes against the basic precept, given by Christ, that we should love even our enemy.[188] In a letter to some *Doopsgezinden*, Coornhert excoriates them for their use of the ban and their condemnation of others. "Will you finally stop," he implores them, "making all others out to be carnal and worldly people, and pulling the weeds out of other people's gardens? Tend to your own garden, and begin with judging yourselves; then you will not be judged."[189]

Perfection is of the essence

In his treatise on "true teachers" (that is, ministers, admonishers), Coornhert makes sure to include, as one of the criteria for what constitutes such a teacher, the stipulation that his aim must be the perfect obedience in Christ. Whoever teaches that such perfection is unattainable here on earth, he insists, cannot be a true teacher.[190] Thus, Coornhert's perfectibilist creed is a hallmark of the true church, and it is this conviction that of course also inspired his intense, persistent quarrel with the Reformed ministers (whom he likes to call "Deformed"[191]). The Reformed ministers, Coornhert complains, want people to accept their interpretations as though they were the same as Scripture, but they must be put to the test. One test, he continues, namely that of correct prophesying, they fail miserably, for they promise that their doctrine will make people healthy, but at the same time their catechism teaches that people will always be inclined to hate God and their neighbor. Wherefore, their promise can never come true, for a soul that still contains the germ of the disease cannot be deemed healthy.[192] Since their path does not lead to the desired destination, Coornhert likes to call such would-be healers of the soul

---

[186]Coornhert, *Wercken*, vol. 1, fol. 366ABC; see also Coornhert, *Vre-Reden* 1, fol. ccccxviiCD.
[187]Coornhert, *Gesprake*, fol. 367A.
[188]Ibid/. fol. 366D.
[189]Coornhert, Letter 45, Becker, *Bronnen*, 290.
[190]Coornhert, *Toetzsteen*, fols. 53A, 62D.
[191]See, e.g., Coornhert, *Ooghwater, Wercken*, fol. dlviiiD.
[192]Ibid., fols. dlxiiiD–dlxiiiiA.

"quacks" [*Lapsalvers*].[193] At times, Coornhert accuses his Reformed opponents of what some of them hold Coornhert for: a Libertine.[194] Such an accusation does not flow from his pen in the form of unreasoned invective, but as the logical conclusion of his argument: if we cannot completely fulfill God's commandments in this life, and should not even strive to do so, as the Reformed Catechism claims, and if full compliance will only take place in the hereafter, then we must conclude that people do not sin in not trying to live virtuous lives. The Libertines also claim that the commandments were only given in order that we get to know our own weakness, and that we are not expected to try to live up to that divine standard. Thus the Reformed position is "the same as saying," he writes, "that sin is not sin," and that is, also by the Reformed definition, Libertinism.[195]

The same association between Calvinism and Libertinism is made in an entertaining and witty dialogue that brings together many of the themes discussed in the previous pages. In the dialogue, *Aertzenij der zielen* (*Healing of souls*),[196] a "sick person," (Crancke) wants to send out "Desiderium Sanitatis" to go find him a qualified physician, no matter what the cost. His brother, Eumenes ("Good will," i.e. Coornhert), advises against this strategy because of the unreliability of the doctors' opinions. He will be wasting his time and money, Eumenes warns, for these doctors all disagree among themselves. But "Crancke" is stubborn and sends for the doctors anyway: he tells his servant to go get "the great doctor Pope," and the renowned doctors Luther and Calvin at the official apothecary. But next, his servant must also proceed to an obscure apothecary, where he will find some quacks: Menno, Libertine, Henry Niclaes, and others.[197] When these doctors arrive, they immediately begin to quarrel. Soon the fighting intensifies and even becomes physical.[198] The fight starts on the theme of credentials: "Magister noster," who represents the pope, infuriates

---

[193]Ibid., fol. dlxiiiiA.

[194]The term Libertine was used somewhat similarly to the way an epithet such as "fascist" is today. I, therefore, have avoided putting this label on Coornhert, because "Libertine" is a "shoe that fits many feet." Benjamin Kaplan, *Calvinists and Libertines: Confession and Community in Utrecht 1578–1620* (Oxford: Clarendon Press, 1995), chooses to use the appellation, and I think his definition, p. 14, of Libertines as "people who rejected ecclesiastic discipline" is apt, but still, with regard to our topic, this only covers a part of Coornhert's multifaceted position.

[195]Coornhert, *Hemel-werck, ofte Quay-Toe-Verlaet,* in *Wercken,* vol. 2, fols. ccclxvD–ccclxviA.

[196]Coornhert, *Aertzenij der zielen, Wercken,* vol. 1, fols. 472–75.

[197]Ibid., fol. 472B.

[198]Ibid., fol. 473A.

the others by calling them all quacks. They try to assert their authority: Luther by referring to his status as a former Augustinian monk, Menno because he used to be a Roman Catholic priest, Calvin because … he represents Zwingli, who used to be a priest as well. Don't you claim, the Roman Catholic then asks, that our school is utterly false and cannot heal? This they unanimously confirm. In that case, concludes the pope's delegate, you have no real mandate, and thus you are all quacks. This silences the others for just a spell.[199] The spell is broken by Crancke, begging them to please tell him what it is that ails him, and how he can be cured. All except the Roman Catholic say that he has syphilis (*pocken*), and that he was born with this incurable affliction. The cause of the disease is the philandering of his father. Here the Roman Catholic disagrees, saying that he is able to cure the disease entirely through penitence after confession, but that the cure will only be temporary. The others offer to cure him, but only outwardly, so that he will only appear to be healthy. But when they discuss the salve to be used for this external healing (that is, the ceremonies), the bickering starts anew and turns ugly: each doctor produces his own medicine chest, and Roman Catholic punches Doctor Luther in the face.[200] This causes the patient to wonder, "surprised that, wanting to cure his wounds with their salves, they wounded one another, making themselves needy of salve."[201] In the course of this struggle, Luther and the Roman Catholic side with each other on the Eucharist, at least on the bread and wine being the true flesh and blood of Christ. Naturally, Calvin and Menno rave against this misconception. When Menno notices that he has curried the learned Calvin's favor by teaming up with him against the fallacy of transubstantiation, he becomes rather cocky and starts to praise his own remedy as the purest, especially with regard to adult baptism. This causes all hell to break loose over Menno, with Luther and Calvin getting particularly angry. The latter even "became so livid with rage that he unsheathed his knife and stabbed Doctor Menno a few times in parts of his body."[202] While this bloody scene is taking place, Roman Catholic is trying to win Crancke over by pointing out that all his rivals can do is fight among themselves, so why not follow his advice? After all, he adds, you are endowed with free will! Luther and Calvin, upon hearing this, forget their quarreling and explain that free will does not exist, because it

[199]Ibid., fol. 472C.
[200]Ibid., fol. 472D.
[201]Ibid., fol. 473A.
[202]Ibid.

detracts from God's omnipotence. This is the moment that Libertine has been waiting for. Since God is responsible for everything that happens, he explains, no one on earth can actually ever do wrong. Calvin fumes: What about sin? he asks, and "how dare you, O murderous and venomous quack, hum along with learned people?"[203] But Libertine persists and manages to catch Calvin in his own net. Don't you hold, he asks Calvin, that God is good? Of course, Calvin replies. Can the good Lord do evil? he continues. Calvin denies this. And do you not claim that nothing happens without or against God's will? Indeed, agrees Calvin, but he adds that often what appears to be evil to us, is not evil in reality. The Libertine then concludes that there are three possibilities: (1) God himself commits evil and sin; (2) God is not responsible for everything that happens; or (3) Nothing that happens is evil. Calvin, having rejected the first two possibilities, must therefore embrace the third and find himself in the Libertine's camp.[204] No matter how persuasive Libertine's argument sounds to the reader, he has to make a quick, premature departure as all the others turn against him.

At this point, the unlearned Eumenes cannot stand it any longer and intervenes, prompted by heartfelt concern for his sick brother. Addressing all of the doctors, he gets them to give a collective response. You all want to heal my brother? he asks them. We do, they reply. And you believe that he is in mortal danger should he follow the wrong counsel, and therefore has to make absolutely sure that he makes the right choice? They also affirm this. Well then, says Eumenes, is an unlearned person able rightfully to judge your learned disputations? No, they collectively reply. This means, concludes Eumenes, that it is impossible for my brother, who understands neither Greek, nor Latin, nor Hebrew, to make a reasoned choice between your purported remedies, as long as you yourselves, being scholars, disagree. The wisest course of action is thus for him not to use any of your remedies, and to wait "until sweet peace will have blotted out all your hateful quarrels."[205] Realistically speaking, he adds, this means that my brother will most probably die first. That being the case, Eumenes then proposes a cheap alternative, and proceeds to explain Coornhert's concept of the gradual attainment of perfection in Christ. This remedy, he asserts, cannot be harmful, for although he, Eumenes, is indeed an unlearned idiot, he has received this remedy from the only authentic

---

[203]Ibid., fol. 473B.
[204]Ibid., fol. 473BC.
[205]Ibid., fol. 473D.

Hippocrates, who said: Leave yourselves behind and follow me. He explains that evil and sinfulness form the true roots of the disease. They consist in the sick person being determined to follow his own bad judgment, his own desires, his own will. These are the things he must be willing to leave behind. The cure consists of goodness, for the true Hippocrates, the Word incarnate, is goodness itself. His brother, asserts Eumenes, is already on the right track (or rung, if we think of Jacob's Ladder) because he realizes that he is sick, that his own sinfulness is the cause of the disease, that Jesus is the true medicine, and that where there is light no darkness can remain. He advises his brother to endeavor "to desist from what you now know or believe to be evil, and to do what you know or believe to be good."[206] This can only mean, Eumenes continues in Platonic vein, that he will leave behind the idle speculation and bickering over dogma, "and depart from this dark cave of ignorance and of the blind desires of error, and will go towards the light of life ... and that all who thus act in accordance with the truth will attain to the light."[207] When Eumenes asks if the doctors have any objection to his proposal, they remain silent. He asks them if anyone can possess true knowledge as long as he is in darkness. They all deny this. Lacking such knowledge, he continues, can one make a reasoned decision about what to do and what not to do? When they also deny this, Eumenes insists that from now on they leave his brother alone. Let him leave behind your quarrels over ceremonies and abstruse speculation, and let him do what he knows is good, and let him desist from what he knows to be evil: then he cannot go wrong. These, he concludes, are the ABCs that everyone must first master, in order to be able to read.[208]

Sometimes, a sect came close to what Coornhert believed about perfectibilism, or—in one case—they went too far. Arent Barentsz from Harderwijk, leader of a sect that started in 1574, taught that the old Adam was full of sin, but that when he is reborn in Christ, in one moment—immediately—he is freed from all sin, and thus perfect.[209] The regenerated are thus absolutely sinless, but whoever continues to fight evil inclinations is equated with the Antichrist. Coornhert, claiming that freeing oneself from sin is a gradual process, wrote two sharp tracts against this sect, whose followers were sometimes called

---

[206] Ibid., fol. "479C" (should be 474C).

[207] This same cave-allegory is in Coornhert, *Schijndeught der secten,* in *Wercken,* vol. 3, fol. cccliiiiB.

[208] Coornhert, *Aertzenij,* fol. "479CD," should be 474CD.

[209] See Bonger, *Leven en werk,* 288.

perfectisten.[210] Bonger links the sharp tone of these treatises to Coornhert's close affinity with this line of thought, for he battled his own inclinations.[211] This interpretation is necessarily hypothetical yet plausible. What may, however, have played an even greater role was Coornhert's need to dissociate himself from such sects that were generally discredited in the public eye because of their lack of humility and their tendency to condemn everyone else.

"Turn towards that sweet peace…"

An argument sometimes stressed against sectarian strife is that it cannot be squared with the Christian spirit of charity and concord, a spirit that the "true teachers" will try to instill in the congregants.[212] It is better to tolerate or suffer certain "opinions" than to fight against your Christian brothers.[213] We should consider how inter-Christian animosity and disharmony will repel the Jews or the Turks, for "we give the unbelievers little opportunity to be attracted to the true faith…."[214] Coornhert is less concerned about winning over Jews, Turks, and pagans than about shaming the "partial" by making them aware of how all this religious strife must look to "the outside world." In their rejection of one another, and in mutual execration and recrimination, the sects prove that they are all wrong. In the *Vre-Reden,* a relatively early tract, Coornhert appeals to all Christian sects to manifest kindliness and love, and to "turn towards that sweet peace, and towards that gentle love, from which you have strayed so far" and he continues his plea to "make amends with your brother, who forms one body with you and has been ransomed with so dear a price, to wit: with the precious blood of the immaculate Lamb Jesus Christ."[215]

"Judge Not Before the Time…"

Underlying this appeal to tolerance, there is always Coornhert's awareness that he and his contemporaries are living in a time of uncertainty. In the matter of

[210]Coornhert, *Dat yemandt te strijden magh hebben teghen zynen zondelijcken lusten ende des niet te min een warachtigh Christen mach zijn,* in *Wercken,* vol. 1, fols. 472C–473D, and *Klockegheslagh Tegen den smoockenden brandt eender (nieuwer) gemackelijcker Secte…,* in *Wercken,* vol. 3, fols. xlv-xlix.

[211]Bonger, *Leven en werk,* 291.

[212]See Coornhert, *Vre-Reden* 1, fol. ccccxviC; *Toetzsteen,* fol. 63D.

[213]Coornhert, *Vre-Reden* 1, fol. ccccxixA.

[214]Ibid., fol. ccccxviiiB. Again on fol. ccccxviiiC this concern, that the Turks will not feel moved to accept the true faith if the Christians themselves do not live in concord and harmony with each other.

[215]Ibid., fol. ccccxviiD.

ceremonies, or other issues that cause people to split up into sects, we should postpone our judgment and "tolerate each other mutually, that each...follow his conscience, until he has received a wiser judgment...."[216] This advice is of course also based on biblical precept, for we are told to "judge nothing before the time, until the Lord come...." (1 Cor.: 4:5).[217] In the *Synod*, Gamaliel gives biblical examples of forgiveness, and of God's circumspection; that is, in his treatment of Sodom and Gomorrha.[218] Of course, it is a strange dilemma if you want to condemn someone for his condemnation of others: in the *Vierschare*, the plaintiff, "Charitable-Good Hope," speaks just once in order to clarify that he only wants Meynaerts (that is, "Fanatical, Premature Judgment") to acknowledge that he does not have the right to judge and condemn others for the sake of peace and concord. Thus his conscience prompts him. But that same conscience forbids him to judge and condemn Meynaerts.

The theme of the postponement of, or abstention from judgment runs like a *fil rouge* through Coornhert's work. As stated earlier, this theme even determines the form of some of Coornhert's best-known, and some of his lesser works: the *Vierschare* (*Tribunal*, 1574), the *Synod on the Freedom of Conscience* (1582), and the *Proces vant Ketterdoden* (*Trial of the Killing of Heretics*, 1590). His magnum opus on the topic, the *Synod*, is centered around this very theme, every session ending with a summary of the proceedings that will be presented to "Master Daniel" (Christ) upon his return. Toward the end of session 14 of the *Synod*, Gamaliel advocates postponing judgment by describing the current religious situation as an "eclipse of the sun of truth," pending which "we should delay for a while these bold and erroneous judgments, until President M. Daniel is available to give his final judgment in all these matters."[219] Thus, Coornhert incorporates an eschatological element into his toleration scheme: not one with speculative overtones, leading to chiliastic fantasies, but one that will, if accepted, have the beneficial practical effect of increasing people's humility and forbearance.

According to Coornhert, since everyone accepts the canonical Scriptures, the mutual condemnations and attacks all revolve around differing (human) interpretations of God's Word and are based on an unverified, exclusive claim to the truth.[220] In a short dialogue between a Licentiate and a layman, the

---

[216]Coornhert, *Vre-Reden* 1, fol. ccccxxviD.

[217]Ibid., fol. ccccxixB.

[218]Coornhert, *Synod*, session 8, fol. xivA.

[219]Ibid., session 14, *Wercken*, vol. 2, fol. xxxivC.

[220]Ibid., session 5, fol. ixA, and Coornhert, *Vierschare*, 1, fol. 423B.

doctor tries to convince the layman that he errs, that he is blind in divine matters, and should therefore let himself be guided by others who are learned. The layman replies: Let us assume that I am indeed blind, and that at your side would be Luther, Zwingli, Calvin, Menno, Schwenckfeld, Joris, Niclaes, Barentsz; would they not all claim to be endowed with sight? But how would I, being blind, be able to trust one above all others, since each one will claim that all the other would-be guides are blind too?[221]

The aforementioned dialogue concerns the uncertainty of the individual citizen, but in a wider sense the same argument applies to mutual attacks, persecution, rejection, and judgment in general. Under the current circumstances, a fair trial is impossible. For such a trial to take place, we must be assured of three separate parties independent of each other: the defense, the prosecution, an impartial judge.[222] In the religious persecution occurring today, Coornhert argues, there can be no true impartiality. The Roman Catholic Church was not condemned by an impartial judge, and neither was there an objective verdict over who was right in the conflict between the Reformed and the Lutherans over the Eucharist. The Servetus case regularly serves as an illustration of the absence of "due process," for most people realize "the kind of judge and the kind of prosecutor that served Servetus in Geneva."[223] Coornhert, in his personal encounters with the Reformed ministers, often levels the same accusation at them, viz. that they want to be prosecutor and judge at the same time.[224]

This subjectivity and lack of certainty, precluding any justification for the condemnation of fellow Christians, will last, Coornhert asserts, until a free council, before impartial judges, will have produced a verdict.[225] He usually brings up such a council in a negative form, asking his Reformed opponents, for example, the rhetorical question, what general and free council has authorized and validated their claims to orthodoxy.[226] To Coornhert, such a council

[221]Coornhert, *Verscheyden t'samen-spraken*, no. 1, *Wercken*, vol. 1, fol. 439AB; this dialogue also in Coornhert, *Weet of rust*, 18–20.

[222]Coornhert, *Synod*, session 16, fol. xxxivA; see also Coornhert, *Vierschare*, fol. 423D; Coornhert, *Proces* 1, fol. cliD, and passim.

[223]Coornhert, *Synod*, fol. xxxiiiC.

[224]Coornhert, *Theriakel*, fol. ccliiiiC. See also the prologue to Coornhert's *Vande Zendinghe der Lutheranen, Swinglianen, ende Mennonisten…*, in *Wercken*, vol. 3, fol. ccclxxxix, where he states that he is willing to defend himself at any time, but not before partial commissioners, "much less before Judges who are themselves parties and prosecutors…."

[225]Coornhert, *Synod*, session 5, fol. ixA.

[226]Coornhert, *Theriakel*, fol. cclC.

no longer represents the kind of real possibility and hope that it did to a Michel de l'Hospital (at least before the colloquy of Poissy). Thus he writes that to solve the interreligious strife a national council could be called, but immediately adds that nothing good would come of this, due to the prevailing spirit of partisanship.[227] In the *Synod,* the Roman Catholic delegate is able effectively to turn the tables on his Reformed opponent with regard to the Protestant persecution of heretics through the government. Your persecution, he asserts, justifies our actions when we did the same to you. And you—the Protestants—cannot argue, the Roman Catholic contends, that you alone possess the true faith, because this has never yet been proven before and accepted by an objective and impartial tribunal.[228]

Underlying Coornhert's urge not to judge is also his spiritualist conviction that there are true Christians in all churches, who together form the invisible Church of Christ, the living members of his body.[229] Even outside European Christendom pure souls can be found, since the Spirit is unrestricted geographically or timewise. Such a realization may serve to humble us, to make us less insistent upon our different understanding of points of doctrine, and to make us more aware of the perils of strife and the bounties of concord. Good souls may assuredly be found, Coornhert asserts, "among those that live today among the Greeks, the Muscovites, the Armenians, the Abyssinians, Prester John, or in India. The Lord knows his own, he who alone is…a knower of the hearts."[230] All sects harbor sincere people, but they understand God's Word the way it is refracted to them through their teachers, meanwhile leading sincere and tranquil lives.[231]

Finally, as has been stated earlier, with regard to making religious choices under the current circumstances, Coornhert believes that these choices are up to every individual, and not just to a learned elite. The people must judge: this idea would infuriate a Lipsius, who, as we will see (in chapter 8), vehemently objected to Coornhert's decision to write in the vernacular and to open their dispute on church and state to the rabble. In *Aengheheven dwangh,* Coornhert's interlocutor, Van der Laen, objects to the former's belief that the

[227]Coornhert, "Vre-Reden" 2, *Wercken,* vol. 3, fol. ccccxxviBC.

[228]Coornhert, *Synod,* session 8, fol. xiiiC.

[229]Coornhert, *Schijndeught der secten,* fol. cccxlvD, where he rejects the equation of church with dogma and ceremony; see also *Gesprake met de Waterlantsche Ghemeente,* ion *Wercken,* vol. 1, fol. 365A.

[230]Coornhert, *Vre-Reden* 1, fol. ccccxviiB [my emphasis].

[231]Ibid.

people must judge on religious error. "They are an unwise judge'" he says, whereupon Coornhert retorts: "But a necessary one. This concerns all people; it concerns the salvation of everyone's soul. Therefore, all people should also have a say-so in this matter."[232] Coornhert manifests an optimistic confidence in everyone's rational capabilities and earnest striving. He claims that there are only two options: either the people must be forced to believe everything that might please the ministers, or they must be kindly invited and attracted through persuasive teaching. Naturally, for Coornhert only the second option is a real one since faith should always be based on free choice.[233] The people's yardstick and gauge is Scripture, "a sure touchstone to distinguish between the true and false spirits."[234] No false teacher will deceive openly, so one cannot just trust their claim. Coornhert reminds his readers of the fact that it was the Jewish teachers, standing in the "true" succession of what was at the time the true church, who condemned Jesus to death. Therefore, these self-proclaimed teachers are not to be trusted on their word, and a claim to "apostolic succession" is by no means a guarantee that they are indeed right.[235] If the judgment were not up to us, Coornhert argues, God would not have admonished us to beware of false prophets. Having received this admonition, we must also consider ourselves capable of telling true from false, for how could we otherwise ever be found guilty for following false teachers?[236] Vigilance, examination, judgment are the duty and concern of everyone. Since government exists to serve the people, it can and should not take away from them this right to judge. In this matter people should not even "follow the opinion of the prince, who exists because of the people...."[237] At the end of his *Toetzsteen* (about the criteria for true teachers), Coornhert states emphatically that it is the right of every individual to judge in matters of faith and to decide "either to stay with or leave his God (who does not force anyone to believe)."[238] Of course in exercising this choice, people must know what they may know, what is uncertain, and what is beyond their knowledge and yet to be believed (because it is

---

[232]Coornhert, *Aengheheven dwangh*, fol. 469C.

[233]Ibid.

[234]Coornhert, *Toetzsteen*, fol. 66D.

[235]Ibid., fols. 66C–67A.

[236]Ibid., fol. 67AB.

[237]Ibid., fol. 67C. Coornhert's view of the role of the government will be probed more specifically in the next chapter.

[238]Ibid., fol. 68B. In the *Synod*, Gamaliel presents the same argument: since there is no (independent) judge among the Christians, there is no alternative to allowing the people to judge for themselves, though never for someone else: *Synod*, session 9, fol. xvCD.

related in the Bible). As long as you are unsure about something, you should not judge or act in that area, in order to avoid the risk of unknowingly committing an error. Thus, he here again advocates his adage, *Weet of rust* (Know or let go).[239]

Such freedom, Coornhert acknowledges, would not free us from the multitude of sects that are a test to the believers, but it would end religious strife and prevent the eternal damnation of unwise souls.[240]

HERETICS[241]

All the theologico-Spiritualist arguments discussed above play a role in Coornhert's treatment of the victims of persecution, the "heretics." That heretics must be persecuted is something upon which virtually all churches were in agreement; they only differed about how heretics ought to be defined.[242] Coornhert, in his writings, tries to demonstrate that such definition touches the core of the problem. He also presents several reasons why the use of (physical) force against "heretics" is inappropriate, ineffective, nefarious, and generally counterproductive, and to a lesser degree he indicates the right attitude towards heretics.

In the second part of the *Trial of the Killing of Heretics*, Coornhert's antagonist, Wolfaert Bisschop, tries five definitions of the term "heretic," and one by one his opponent rejects them, primarily because of the subjective nature of the definition. The first definition, taken from Peter Martyr Vermigli, states that heresy means to choose and stubbornly defend teachings that conflict with Scripture, due to ignorance or contempt. Coornhert asserts that in this case, it must first be proven that heretical doctrine goes against the Bible. To do this, the purported heretic must receive a fair hearing, and for the verdict to have any validity the heretic must have an impartial and knowledgeable judge. We have already seen that according to Coornhert the "judges" will always be partial. Once more, the Servetus case is mentioned, and although Coornhert concedes he does not feel competent to judge the issues on which Servetus was

---

[239]Coornhert, *Synod,* fols. xvD–xviA. This adage is written above Goltzius's famous portrait of Coornhert (used on the cover of this book).

[240]Coornhert, *Toetzsteen,* fol. 68B.

[241]The term "heretic," in sixteenth-century parlance, denotes someone who propagates dogmatic error; an "apostate" is one who has relapsed from the "true" faith into unbelief; "infidels" are followers of Islam or Judaism, and "pagans" are people outside the pale of monotheistic religions, who worship spirits or idols: cf. Guggisberg, "Defence," 36–37.

[242]Coornhert, *Schijndeught,*" fol. cccxliiiiD–cccxlvA.

condemned, he feels that what matters is that Servetus remained constant and never admitted to being a heretic. Servetus's accusers called such constancy stubbornness. Bisschop then tries a second definition, given in Bullinger's *Hausbuch*. A heretic, he contends, is he who accepts, defends, and spreads heterodox teachings of his own invention against Scripture, the articles of faith, and the healthy doctrine of the community. This brings Coornhert back to the problem of the impartial judge, and he objects to the description that Bullinger gives of the heretic's inner motives; Coornhert asserts that only God is the knower of hearts. A third definition, by Beza, meets the same objections. The fourth definition is taken from Calvin, who posits that heretics are opponents of the unity of the church and refers to Titus 3:10 in support of this view. Coornhert objects to the use made of this passage since Paul speaks of a schismatic rather than a heretic. But even in the case of a schismatic, Coornhert is not convinced, for schism may be healthy if the old church is erring. And he makes sure to quote Musculus, who states that the Reformed do not deny that they are schismatics who opposed the unity of the Roman Church. The fifth and final definition attempted is one given by Beza in his *Traité de l'Autorité du Magistrat*, defining heretics—as distinct from schismatics, unbelievers, or hypocrites—as persons who appear to be full of zeal, but who do not follow the healthy admonitions of the church and insist on disturbing the peace and unity of the church by producing false teachings. This definition quickly leads to a discussion of the role of the civil authorities, for Coornhert objects that if the latter have no authority to judge heresy for themselves, they will be the blind executioners of one church's subjective viewpoint (a topic to which we will return in the next chapter). The pattern of the argument in *Proces* 2 is repeated ad nauseam: "Bisschop" states that those who stubbornly persevere in attacking dogma and in calling it devilish are heretics and punishable by death; Coornhert counters that in that case, the Roman Catholics have the right to condemn and execute the Reformed as such stubborn attackers; "Bisschop" answers, "Certainly not, for we represent the truth and are thus justified in our criticism"; Coornhert again counters, "So you admit that one is indeed able to denounce doctrine without automatically becoming a blasphemer?"[243]

Coornhert is so deeply engaged in attacks on others' views, that it is at times hard to pinpoint what his own view is on certain issues. In the case of heresy, he feels that a heretic is someone who may err, but is convinced in his conscience that he has the truth, and since it is our religious duty to follow our

---

[243]See Coornhert, *Proces* 2, fol. cxviA–cxviiiC, passim, for this paragraph.

conscience, no force may be used against the heretic.[244] When the Reformed ministers object to Coornhert's proposed freedom and aver that a person cannot be allowed to believe whatever he wants, Coornhert retorts that "then he must believe what pleases someone else…."[245] However, the difficulty of arriving at a satisfactory definition of heresy is for Coornhert in itself an important argument against persecution, for "without true and indubitable knowledge of this [i.e. of what constitutes heresy or the true church] it is impossible for the government to kill someone as a heretic, except at great risk of error."[246] The fact that there is no objective criterion for labeling someone a heretic is in itself a powerful argument for refraining from persecution. But there are more reasons, Coornhert believes, why such persecution is wrong. As stated earlier, the opinion that the government must combat heresy based on the dictates of the Church, Coornhert argues, validates in retrospect the persecutions by Charles V and Philip 2.[247] More importantly, Coornhert is convinced, as we have seen, that there are no clear biblical grounds for the killing of heretics, and in a grave matter such as this, one may not act except through the express command of God.[248] In not persecuting, one does not run the risk of fatal error, for it is better not to punish than to punish unjustly.[249]

Persecution of heretics, Coornhert believes, evinces an un-Christian spirit. The end does not justify the means, and we may only defend God's honor in ways that conform with God's demands. It is Christian to hate evil, "but not to hate the evildoer."[250] In another dialogue an Anabaptist decries the "wolf mentality" that predominates in the other churches and states that it has always been true that wolves will bite the sheep, and not vice versa. He invites Coornhert to his sheep pen (i.e. the Anabaptist faith), for, he predicts, he will only be suffered to stay on in one of the wolves' caves for just a little while longer. Although one senses his relative sympathy for the Anabaptists, Coornhert declines because of their exclusivism. Using the horrific example of Münster, he throws doubt on the Anabaptists' sincerity when it comes to toler-

---

[244]See Bonger, *Motivering*, 46–47; also Coornhert, *Proces* 2, fol. cxlviiC: heretics, writes Coornhert, do not consciously or maliciously lead people astray.

[245]Coornhert, *Theriakel,* fol. ccliiiC.

[246]Coornhert, *Proces* 2, *Wercken*, fol. cxixB.

[247]Ibid., fol. cxlviB.

[248]Ibid., fol. clvD.

[249]Ibid., fol. cxxB.

[250]Coornhert, *Wortel der Nederlantsche Oorloghen*, in *Wercken*, vol. 2, fol. clxxviB; the quotation is from ibid., fol. clxxiiiiC. The same view is expressed in *Proces* 1, fol. lxvB; and in *Proces* 2, fol. cxliiB, where Coornhert charges that Beza has more "puffed up anger" than "humble love."

ation. He acknowledges that there is no proof based upon which the current Anabaptists can be associated with the outrage that occurred in Münster, but he fears that, once you have attained to a position of power, you will not tolerate anyone beside you who is unwilling to say yes to all your opinions. This is my reason: The mean tongues of your people, as well as the pen of Menno and D. P. (Dirck Philips) spew forth such deadly venom in slandering, convicting, and damning all those who are outside of your community,

> that I have no doubt that if you should find the external sword in
> your hands, you would not save the bodies of these [outsiders],
> similarly to the way that now you do not save their names with
> your two-edged and defaming tongues.[251]

Yet another reason why heretics should not be put to the sword, Coornhert claims, is that in cutting off the heretic's earthly life, one deprives him of the time in which he could have become the recipient of God's gift, that is, of faith. *Kruyt-Hofken,* a collection of short moralistic stories and dialogues, contains the story of an old Anabaptist, Lucas Lambertsz, executed for heresy in Amsterdam in 1544.[252] One of the court officials present at the execution tries to persuade the Anabaptist to recant by assuring him that he errs and that he will go to hell. The Anabaptist gets the official to admit that faith is God's gift which cannot be forced, and which some receive early, others late. If, by killing me, you prevent me from receiving this gift, the heretic asserts, "who else then but you are the murderers of my soul?"[253] A favorite scriptural passage in this regard is the parable of the laborers in the vineyard (Matt. 20: 1–16): persecuting someone for lack of faith is the same as if the laborers who had been called to the vineyard first came back and slew those still waiting to be hired.[254] Another allegory Coornhert likes to use is that where the heretic is compared with a blind person: he should be guided and helped, and not punished for his blindness (he refers to Deut. 27: 18: "Cursed be he that maketh the blind to

---

[251]Coornhert, *Schijndeught,* fol. cccxlvA.

[252]Coornhert, *Van't dooden eens Ketters* (*On the killing of a Heretic*), in *Kruyt-Hofken,* in *Wercken,* vol. 3, fol. lxxxiBC; the story is included in Coornhert, *Weet of rust,* 64–66; the historical background of the story is in ibid., 136. Lambertsz was burned, but in the story he is beheaded.

[253]Coornhert, *Kruyt-Hofken,* fol. lxxxiC. The same argument in Coornhert, *Vande Leydtsche Disputatie,* in *Wercken,* vol. 3, fol. clviA; *Proces 1, Wercken,* vol. 2, fol. lxxxviiC; and *Wortel der Nederlantsche oorloghen,*" in *Wercken,* vol. 2, fol. clxxviiiB; in these passages, Coornhert calls it true tyranny to deprive someone of this period in which God's grace might yet be vouchsafed to him.

[254]Coornhert, *Wortel,* fol. clxxviiiB.

wander out of the way…"). But the authorities burn and kill the blind and the seeing alike.[255] Here we see the reason for Coornhert's belief that even the atheist should be tolerated.

Another compelling reason not to persecute heretics, Coornhert argues, is that coercion simply does not work and is even counterproductive. Persecution fans the flames of heresy, Coornhert claims, always pointing at the great proliferation of sects due to violent suppression.[256] Because of the harsh, unChristian attitude of the Roman ecclesiastical authorities, many started to regard themselves as true teachers, Coornhert explains, and all others as godless seducers (*verleyders*). The people seemed willing to believe anything, Coornhert states (with some hyperbole, it seems), as long as it went against the Roman Catholic Church.[257] He touches on human psychology when he states that to forbid people to do something is virtually tantamount to commanding them to do that same thing.[258] In the *Zedekunst*, Coornhert writes that compulsion cannot change someone's judgment, but rational proof can.[259] God wants to be praised voluntarily. People become godless due to persecution, for they forsake God to save themselves. Persecution, besides killing heretics, also breeds hypocrites, people who only feign that they have abandoned their former opinions.[260] Persecution embitters people, some of whom will be tempted to resort to violence when they see their "highest good" [their freedom of conscience] taken away from them and notice that the ministers' arguments take the form of magistrates' placards.[261] Those in authority must consider, Coornhert warns, that a heresy that is driven underground becomes much more dangerous than public and visible heresy, the same way, he adds, that dangerous mutinies thrive in the dead of night.[262]

The real remedy for the problem has already been touched on earlier. Christ's dispensation is a strictly spiritual one, so his battles must be fought with spiritual weapons. The idol worship by the disobedient Israelites in the Old Testament was physical and elicited physical punishment. Under Christ,

---

[255]Ibid.
[256]Coornhert, *Process* 2, fol. cxliiiiA.
[257]Coornhert, *Wortel*, fol. clxxviiD.
[258]Ibid., fol. clxxxiA.
[259]Coornhert, *Zedekunst*, chap. 4, bk. 2, p. 463.
[260]Coornhert, *Aengheheven dwangh*, fol. 471A.
[261]Coornhert, *Synod*, session 14, fol. xxxA.
[262]Coornhert, *Wortel*, fol. clxxxA.

idolatry has become spiritualized, with Paul, for example, who labels avarice as idol worship. Therefore the "punishment" should also be spiritual.[263] Instruction and gentle and loving persuasion are the ways to approach the heretic and to try to cure him from his blindness. Should the blind person reject the guiding hand, "then one can let him wander about, fall, and suffer the punishment for his obstinacy."[264] This is how we should go about killing the heresy, not the heretic.

Sometimes, Coornhert pleads with the adherents of the major faiths to manifest more simple Christian love and to pay more heed to the many things they have in common as Christians, such as their belief : (1) in Scripture; (2) in the Trinity; (3) in the twelve articles of faith (the apostolic credo); (4) that Jesus died for us. Why should you treat each other worse for relative trifles such as ceremonies than you do the Turks or Jews who totally disagree with you? Forgiveness, Coornhert asserts, is better than severity.[265] These appeals to Christians to overlook their mutual differences sound somewhat disingenuous, coming from someone who found fault with everyone around him and harped on the smallest cause for disagreement rather than areas of agreement. Still, I believe that the wish for an irenic attitude was genuine on the part of Coornhert. Most of the time his own confrontational nature, however, made it impossible for him to practice what he preached in this regard.

---

[263]Coornhert, *Proces* 2, fol. cliiC. Although not stated here, with the "spiritual punishment" he probably means the avoidance of a heretic mentioned in the New Testament.

[264]Coornhert, *Wortel,* fol. clxxviiiB.

[265]Ibid., fol. clxxxiD.

7

FREEDOM OF CONSCIENCE IN THE
POLITICAL SPHERE

C OORNHERT'S LIFE WAS ONE OF ACTION and full immersion in the
tumultuous reality of a new polity then being born. He rarely developed his thoughts about toleration—with all the spiritualist and theological elements—in isolation. The new political order taking shape in the
emerging Dutch Republic greatly concerned Coornhert. He followed the
unfolding events closely, and he played an active part in these events
through his debates, petitions, and other writings.

After his return from exile in 1577, Coornhert did not resume his active
role as a public official. He carried on his notarial activities, and devoted the
rest of his time and tremendous energies to his writing and other pursuits. The
relative freedom that the *wederspreker* (gainsayer) had from the responsibilities
of public office, his stature as a self-made man, and his proud independent
spirit allowed Coornhert to assume the ideal position for the proper functioning of the new nation—especially the safeguarding of the absolute freedom of
conscience within it. Coornhert was not subjected to great external pressures
urging him to compromise, and he did not have to be overly concerned as to
what would work under current circumstances, unlike a Calvin or Beza (or for
that matter a Donteclock[1]) who were charged with the constitution of a viable
church organization, and unlike even Lipsius, who held a highly visible and
politically sensitive position at a prestigious public institution. Thus, Coornhert's ideas on the relationship between church and state are generally lucid
and consistent. They manifest the working out in practice of his Spiritualist
and humanist beliefs in the absolute chasm separating the *civitas Dei* from the

[1]Reformed minister in Delft; discussed in chapter 8, below..

secular world, and in the paramount importance of man's freedom of will and choice. These ideas stand out as unprecedentedly radical in their rejection of any compulsion in matters of conscience (even where it concerns the internal discipline within a church organization, for example, among the Anabaptists), and in the all-encompassing nature of the toleration they advocate. This toleration embraced even the atheist, a position where Coornhert finds himself virtually alone among his contemporaries. Coornhert's constant vigilance, his relentless attacks on what he perceived as constraint and spiritual tyranny, and his refusal to compromise spurred a greater awareness of and sensitivity to these issues in his day, which carried over to the next century and beyond. At the same time it appears that Coornhert's influence or effectiveness was limited by his position on the fringe, outside the pale of mainstream organizations, and by the perception in some circles that Coornhert was only out to destroy and was disinclined to proffer anything constructive (a perception that also persisted after his death). We can see this attitude at work when the Reformed synod, held in Gouda in 1589, brushed Coornhert off when he "bothered" them again with a request to continue the debate suspended some six years previously. They only graced his request with a peremptory note, not even addressed directly to him, and stating that he should go to the States to complain, for the synod had better things to do.[2]

The current chapter will set forth Coornhert's ideas regarding the proper relation between church and state, placed in the context of contemporary developments in the emerging Dutch Republic. The analysis will outline what, according to Coornhert, pertains to the state's domain and what falls outside its pale; it will show the political limitations that he places on toleration, and highlight Coornhert's reaction to the proliferation of sects in the Netherlands. The realities of war and political strife are never far from Coornhert's consciousness, so I will separately profile his views of historical and contemporary situations and events: the historical exempla often serve his rhetorical analogy, and in his assessment of contemporary facts he manifests his concerns and unfolds his agenda as to the politico-religious situation that he envisages. The

[2]Coornhert, *Wercken*, vol. 2, fol. cccxxxviA; see also Bonger, *Leven en werk*, 139.

next chapter will then analyze Coornhert's main activities during the last fourteen years of his life.

$$\bullet \qquad \bullet \qquad \bullet$$

The position of the Reformed church in the emerging Dutch Republic
after 1572 was increasingly that of a privileged, public church, but not that of a
church "by law established."[3] As towns in Holland and Zeeland were liberated
in 1572, the Beggars negotiated agreements with the town magistrates, typically resulting in compromises. The mostly Erastian magistrates of these towns
were reluctant to give much power to the Reformed church, and many felt
that, once Holland was liberated, there was no longer any need for Reformed
consistories since the town government represented the now recognized
church. While under the cross, the Reformed had developed an independent
and strong ecclesiastical government, but the authorities in the towns were
wary of such independence.[4] The States of Holland initially strove for a general
church of the people, where everyone who had lived for two years in a town
would automatically be admitted to the Lord's Supper, but the Reformed
church rejected this concept from the onset.[5] It mistrusted the magistrates,
many of whom did not (yet) belong to the Reform, and they maintained their
consistorial discipline, reserving admission to the Lord's Supper for the carefully screened (the *lidmaten*) who, as full members, stood apart from the *liefhebbers* (sympathizers) who only attended the sermons.[6] The application of
church discipline—to which the *liefhebbers* for example were not subjected—
is just one of the reasons for the slow growth of the Reformed faith in the liberated provinces, with the Reformed accounting for less than 10 percent of the
population in Holland around the time of Coornhert's death.[7] Article 36 of the
Reformed Confession of Faith presented the state as the servant of God with
the task of protecting the true church and having the Gospel preached

[3] Duke and Jones, "Towards a Reformed Polity," 213. See also W. Nijenhuis, "De publieke
kerk veelkleurig en verdeeld, bevoorrecht en onvrij," in *Algemene Geschiedenis der Nederlanden*,
6:27.

[4] Jones, "Reformed Church and Civil Authorities," 113.

[5] See Van Deursen, *Bavianen en slijkgeuzen*, 23–24.

[6] Duke, "Ambivalent Face," 130. Thus, the Reformed opted to maintain their "sect-type" of
organization: see Bainton, *Travail*, 25.

[7] Duke, "Ambivalent Face," 109, 112–13, presents an explanation of the reasons for this slow
growth; from the beginning there was diversity of faiths, and the Dutch Republic was never a
"truly Calvinist" nation: see G. J. Schutte, "Nederland: Een calvinistische natie?" *Bijdragen en
mededelingen betreffende de geschiedenis der Nederlanden* 107, no. 4 (1992): 690–702.

everywhere,[8] but the Reformed church, in its attitude and self-image, was oscillating between the role of public church and that of the "gathered few."[9] Politically this led to the basic paradox in the Reformed position, which expected the magistrate's support for the official church, yet insisted on that church's freedom from government interference. The synod held at Dordrecht in 1578, for instance, posited the church's autonomy in all "internal matters."[10] To the Reformed of course this was not a contradiction but rather a matter of safeguarding the purity of the church at a time when the orthodoxy of many of the town regents was still questionable. Thus, although this was mostly a natural evolution from the circumstances in which they found themselves, the Reformed saw the "Zurich model" of church-state relations as inapplicable, and to a certain extent followed the Genevan model, as "a church that defined its own boundaries" in an effort to effectuate "the seamless unity of a Christian community within a divided body politic."[11]

The peculiarity of the situation in the Dutch Republic, with its compromises between a magistrate jealous of its power and a church unwilling to yield the independence it had shed blood for under the cross,[12] explains the frustration of a Lambert Daneau, who had been a student of Calvin in Geneva (1559–1561). When he was called to serve the new University of Leiden, he saw this as an opportunity to help build up a church order along the lines of Geneva. To Daneau and other Reformed ministers, the church order was ordained by God, and therefore the power of the magistrate, too, was circumscribed and limited by this divinely appointed order. The election of ministers, elders, and deacons, the maintenance of church discipline, these belonged to the church's domain. In an ideal polity—that is, one with a "Christian" (Reformed) magistrate— the relation between church and state would be like the coordination between one's eyes and hands.[13] Daneau's consistent pursuit of what he regarded as the order intended by God—as when he set up a consistory for the French congregation in Leiden without notifying the authorities, or protested

---

[8]Van Deursen, *Bavianen en slijkgeuzen*, 13.

[9]Duke and Jones, "Towards a Reformed Polity," 213.

[10]D. Nauta, "Religieuze situatie bij het begin van de strijd, 1568–1579," in *Algemene Geschiedenis der Nederlanden*, 6:210–11. See also Van Gelderen, *Political Thought*, 229.

[11]Tracy, "Magistracy," 492B.

[12]See Jones, "Reformed Church and Civil Authorities," 112–14. Cf. Tracy, "Magistracy," 489A.

[13]Fatio, *Nihil Pulchrius Ordine*, 3–4, 68; the analogy with eyes and hands in a commentary by Daneau quoted in ibid., 163 n. 27.

vehemently against the Leiden magistrate's inaction against what he (and the Middelburg synod of 1581) considered to be a heterodox minister—quickly brought him into acrimonious conflict with the magistrate and led to his resignation. To a Jan van Hout, Leiden's town secretary, the Reformed "pretenses" smacked of a "new Inquisition," this time sent from Geneva.[14] To the Reformed, it was the magistrate of Leiden that tried to usurp the rights of the church.[15]

In the years after 1577, Orange's *religievrede* further eroded, leading in many instances to Calvinist dominance, as in Antwerp where in May 1578, the Jesuits and the Friars Minor were expelled.[16] In the north during the years after the Pacification of Ghent, the "Dutch Revolt Holland style," that is, with the exclusion of the public practice of Catholicism, was triumphant. The Union of Holland and Zeeland that took place in June of 1575 foreshadowed the wider-ranging Union of Utrecht. It signalled the establishment of an exclusively Protestant state, albeit a state recognizing individual freedom of conscience (that is, without the freedom to express this in public acts of worship).[17] When the States of Holland in 1575 conferred on Orange the status of "sovereign"(*hoge overheid*), they specifically instructed him to maintain "the practice of the Reformed Evangelical Religion, suspending and putting an end to the practice of all other religions that are contrary to the Gospel...."[18] The Union of Utrecht explicitly stipulated that the provinces of Holland and Zeeland were not bound to the conditions of the *religievrede*.[19]

It is in this context of a growing de facto Protestant religious monopoly, combined with tensions between Reformed ministers and an Erastian magistracy, that Coornhert sets forth his ideas on church and state. In these ideas

---

[14]Fatio, *Nihil Pulchrius Ordine*, 4, 84. Often, such accusations will mention reintroduction of the Spanish Inquisition, whereas the Spanish Inquisition had actually never been introduced to the Netherlands. On the functioning of this topos, see F. E. Beemon, "The Myth of the Spanish Inquisition and the Preconditions for the Dutch Revolt," *Archiv für Reformationsgeschichte* 85, (1994): 246–64.

[15]Fatio, *Nihil Pulchrius Ordine*, 9; Jones, "Reformed Church," 114.

[16]A. J. Tjaden, "De reconquista mislukt De opstandige gewesten 1579–88," in *Algemene Geschiedenis der Nederlanden*, vol. 6, 245. See, for the *religievrede* in Antwerp, Fl. Prims, ed., *Register der Commissie tot onderhoud van de Religionsvrede te Antwerpen (1579–81)* (Brussels: Paleis der Academiën, 1954).

[17]See Israel, *Dutch Republic*, 188–98; Duke and Jones, "Towards a Reformed Polity," 225.

[18]Quoted in D. Nauta, "Religieuze situatie," 208.

[19]Duke and Jones, "Towards a Reformed Polity," 225; see Kossman and Mellinnk, eds., *Texts concerning the Revolt*, document 37, "Treaty of the Union, eternal alliance and confederation," article 13, 169–70.

there appears to be great constancy, except for a shift away from the concerns of the state, noticeable at the time of the "Justification," to a more exclusive concern with the paramountcy of the individual conscience.

.   .   .

In a letter to Spieghel, Coornhert reproduces an exchange between him and his friend on the topic of freedom of conscience.[20] The letter probably reflects a discussion that had actually taken place. As in the *Zedekunst*, here also Spieghel had requested that in their argumentation they refrain from using Scripture. If you strip away Spieghel's arguments and formulate Coornhert's defense of the freedom of conscience positively, you get an uncharacteristically pithy survey of the latter's chief ideas on the matter. They are as follows (in rearranged order):

1. By nature everyone is free to speak and teach what he wants.

2. To attest to the truth is one's right, and to suppress this right is an injustice. By forbidding people to speak "lies," truth-speakers will also be throttled, since the government is no infallible judge.

3. Whoever is well versed in Scripture is in the best position to understand issues relating to conscience; but Coornhert denies emphatically that by this he means theologians, because

4. Those who are formally trained in Scripture (i.e. theologians) are also the most partial in matters of faith.

5. When doctrine is faulty, every pious man has the moral obligation to counter it with truth.

6. Freedom of teaching and attesting to the truth cannot harm anyone, but it may benefit many.

7. The government has authority over body and worldly goods *(Lijf ende Goedt)*, not over the hearts of its subjects.[21]

8. God reveals the truth through prophets, not through the government.

---

[20]Coornhert, *Brieven-boek*, Letter 99 to Spieghel, in *Wercken*, vol. 3, fols. 148B–150D.
[21]Ibid., fol. 148D.

9. Matters of faith are not the domain of the political government: those who know the truth should counter lies with arguments.

10. The authorities[22] make themselves hated by the use of force in matters of conviction; excessive force equals tyranny and is therefore always wrong.

11. The government generally knows little on matters of faith; within governments as in society at large, the wise and pious form a minority.

12. The people are more important than their ruler. Equality among subjects creates stability, inequality breeds strife, and therefore to cater to the wishes of some but not of others (concerning the freedom to worship) means to create enmity between groups in society.

13. Persecution fosters irreligion and increases the number of heretics.

14. The proscription of free speech and free teaching results in persecution, under which the pious also suffer as the government has no way of distinguishing truth from falsehood.

15. It is better to allow some false teaching to occur than to run the risk of killing a teacher of truth.

16. Leaders of false doctrine fear criticism, for they stand to lose benefits and honor. Coornhert disagrees with Spiegel's assertion that sedition and riots are worse than the suppression of freedom needed to prevent them; Coornhert says: "I know of no worse evil than the lie and the banishment of truth."[23]

17. Sedition and riots are not the result of freedom of teaching, but of tyranny and oppression. The Peasant War in Germany, Coornhert explains, was the peasants' response to tyranny and

[22]In Dutch there is a clear distinction between the nonpartisan apparatus of the state (*overheid*) and the government wielding power at a given moment (*regering*). In almost all instances here translated with "government" or "authorities," Coornhert uses the term *overheid*.
[23]Coornhert, *Wercken*, vol. 3, fol. 150A.

oppression by the nobility. Those, however, who teach against the fundamentals of political society are punishable.

18. Many countries allow more than one faith and are at peace; therefore, such peace does not necessarily lead to strife.

In the points listed above, one sees once again the evident importance of "truth" (and for Coornhert this always means religious truth) that underlies the whole argument. In points 7 and following, however, he delineates and delimits the role of the state. These themes resound throughout the *Trial of the Killing of Heretics*, the *Synod on the Freedom of Conscience*, and many other writings.

Coornhert believes that the government derives its authority from God, and does not carry the sword in vain (based on Rom. 13:1–7). He views the tasks and functions of government in highly moral terms: it has to protect the poor, prevent crime, and so on. Obedience to the government does not depend on its religious coloring: Christians must also obey a non-Christian government since Christian as well as non-Christian authorities are ordained by God.[24] And since to serve the government means to serve your neighbor, a Christian ought not to refuse if called upon to serve the state. He therefore strongly rejects the Anabaptist position forbidding adherents to take any government positions and teaching that any use of the sword is illicit. Neither Christ nor his apostles were called upon to serve in government, and although the apostles were forbidden to use the sword (since such weaponry does not become true teachers), Peter did not, for example, demand that the Roman centurion Cornelius lay down his sword after he had converted (Acts 10). It is in the law of nature, Coornhert feels, that we should not want others to do for us what we do not wish to do for them, and since everybody needs protection against crime, the authorities need the means to prevent it. To serve the government in that respect also is a moral duty.[25]

Thus, the government must be obeyed as the guarantor of law and order in society. At the same time the government does not have the right, Coornhert asserts, to impose on everyone its interpretation or choice of religion, since there is no impartial criterion for determining the true faith. Even in the

[24]Coornhert, *Van 't Overheydts Ampt. Oft een Christen mach bedienen, ende oft de ghene die 't bedienen Christenen moghen wesen*, in *Wercken*, vol. 1, fol. 383; also *Justificatie*, in *Wercken*, vol. 2, fol. 146A; cf. Bonger, *De motivering*, 48.

[25]Coornhert, *Van 't Overheydts Ampt* fol. 384B, 385C; this tract is addressed to the *Doopsgezinde* Hans de Ries.

Justification, Coornhert's endorsement of the choice made by the government for the Reformed faith is premised on the provision that the government will not impose this preference, and that it will allow the people the freedom to follow the promptings of their own conscience.[26] Coornhert writes that the government ought to follow the precepts of the *Acta* (1579), a document endorsed by the States General, and render unto God what is rightfully his, that is, "dominion over the soul and conscience, and to render unto itself also what [rightfully] belongs to it, to wit: dominion over the bodies and goods of their subjects, in accordance with their privileges."[27] The political government should act as an impartial referee to ensure that the various religious groups do not try to tyrannize the others and that a new church does not put on the well-worn shoes of the popes of old.[28] We see here, again, Coornhert's firm belief in the existence of two realms that ought not to be mixed or confused. The secular government has not received a divine mission as religious teacher.[29] The authorities also err grievously in their efforts to silence him, Coornhert writes, "because you are usurping the dominion of the spiritual realm of God, in which the Lord Christ alone and no secular government may exercise dominion."[30] Prophets and apostles received the care over souls and power in spiritual matters, but not the secular government, which "cannot kill, wound, catch, or banish the soul."[31] The Reformed religious leaders who advocate a role for the state in the suppression of religious deviants want to build the church on the quicksand of human power instead of on the rock of Christ's truth.[32] The analogy by which Reformed and Roman Catholic advocates of persecution alike claim that, if common murderers are executed, then the same should certainly happen to the "murderers of souls," is faulty, Coornhert contends, for a murderer consciously transgresses, whereas the heretic errs in good faith. Therefore, the murderer must be punished, but the heretic must be instructed. Besides, he adds, real crimes (murder, rape) are visible and

[26]Coornhert *Justificatie,* in *Wercken,* vol. 2, fol. 146A.

[27]Coornhert, *Advertissement"*(written in defense of his drawing up of the 1581 pro-Catholic request), *Wercken,* vol. 1, fol. 548C. Another locus where he states this very clearly ion *Proces* 2, *Wercken,* vol. 2, fol. cxxviiB: subjects must fully obey the government's laws and stipulations, but with regard to the church the magistrate may not force anything against the conscience of his subjects.

[28]Coornhert, *Aengheheven dwangh,* in *Wercken,* vol. 1, fol. 470A.

[29]Coornhert, *Proces* 2, fol. cxxiC.

[30]Coornhert, *Aengheheven dwangh,* fol. 470A.

[31]Ibid., fol. 470D.

[32]Coornhert, *Justificatie,* fol. 146D.

recognizable, but "what certain knowledge may the worldly judges have of heresy? of who is a heretic? and of whether one should kill a heretic? or are most sovereigns and judges also theologians?"[33] Furthermore, if we allow the lawful government to impose what it regards as the true religion on the people, then it follows that the Dutch, and especially the Reformed, were rebels for refusing to abide by this imposed religion. They had been unwilling to follow the religion that was offered, and "would not abandon the one that was prohibited by the king of Spain, who, as the count of Holland, is or was our lawful sovereign...."[34] In the Coolhaes affair, Coornhert also found fault with Coolhaes' *Apologia*, since the latter acknowledges the state's right to impose church order, and calls the magistrate the "Nurturer of the Church"(*Voedtster-heeren der Kercken*). Coornhert objected that he thought that this role belonged to the genuine shepherds who feed their flock with divine words.[35]

Coornhert sees the role of the government with regard to the church more in negative than in positive terms: its chief concern is to keep the Reformed in check and to insure that they will not impose a new tyranny of conscience. When the ministers accuse Coornhert of inconsistency, because he, who is against government interference in matters of religion, has threatened to take his complaints about them to the States if they do not respond, he asserts in his rejoinder that the government should certainly involve itself in religious matters, in the sense that it should keep the Reformed zealots under control and prevent that they should follow in the footsteps of the popes of old.[36] In the many exchanges caused by the debates between Coornhert and the ministers, Coornhert often brings up this skewed situation, where the state sides with the Reformed church and is becoming its "accomplice." In the Coolhaes affair, as represented in Coornhert's *Justification*, the chief issue between the magistrate and the Reformed revolves around competency. "Leiden" contends that the Reformed want the magistrate to defer to them and accept their viewpoint.[37] But the magistrate, Coornhert writes, does not wish to subject itself to a new

[33]Coornhert, *Wortel der Nederlantsche Oorloghen,* in *Wercken,* vol. 2, fol. clxxiiiiD.
[34]Coornhert, *Justificatie,* fol. 146A. The same point is made in *Ooghwater,* in *Wercken,* vol. 2, fols. dlixD–dlxA.
[35]Coornhert, *Brieven-boek,* Letter 96 to Coolhaes, in *Wercken,* vol. 3, fol. 146BCD.
[36]Coornhert, "Sendtbrief" (regarding the Leiden disputation of April, 1578), *Wercken,* vol. 2, fol. cclxviB.
[37]Coornhert, *Justificatie,* fol. clxxxxiiB. Later, he argues that the courts to which one appeals are always superior to the ones from which one appeals: the consistory places its jurisdiction above the magistrate's, "Leiden" contends; see ibid., fol. clxxxxiiiC.

tyranny of conscience.[38] The Reformed regarded Leiden's position as a frontal
attack on their presbyterian church organization.[39] Coornhert, however, regularly reminds the Reformed that their church has the government to thank for
its preeminent position, and not vice versa. And yet, he argues, now the
Reformed synod (he refers, in this instance, to the one held in Middelburg,
1581) "tries to become the head of the government."[40] Always quick to point
out inconsistencies in his opponents' argumentation, Coornhert stresses the
fact that in Geneva, which the Reformed claim as their example, the magistrate's approval for the appointment of ministers is needed and accepted.[41]
Later, the emphasis in Coornhert's writings is more on what he sees as the
incipient manipulation of the government by the Reformed, who through
trickery try to abuse the power of the government in having all other faiths
outlawed.[42] A government that may not exercise its own discernment in the
eradication of religious dissidence becomes the blind executioner of others'
cruelty, similarly to what had been the function of Catholic princes, whom
Calvin had called "executioners of the Catholic cruelty."[43] The Reformed
attempt to steal the sword from the state, leaving it only the scabbard or only
its shadow.[44] In so doing, Coornhert asserts, the church remains responsible
for the harm done to heretics, even if it works through the government.

The ministers thus function as what Coornhert calls, somewhat cryptically,
the magistrate's "conscience makers"(*conscientiemaeckers*): this may refer to the
forcing of conscience, or to the fact that since they are the true architects of this
policy, the guilt rests on their conscience.[45] People should not let themselves be
fooled by the beautiful front which hides these persecutors' murderous activities.
The latter will mask the ugly reality with splendid words such as their "holy zeal"
to protect God's honor.[46] The distinction they make between the political and
ecclesiastical governments is, according to Coornhert, mere subterfuge, an effort
to hide their true intentions. When his Reformed opponents label Coornhert a
"threat to the nation"(*Lant-verderver),* the latter scoffs that this is the kind of

---

[38]Ibid., fol. "clxxxxiiiiD" (read fol. clxxxxviD); also in Coornhert, 2, fol. cxxiiB.

[39]Fatio, *Nihil Pulchrius Ordine,* 48, 54; Van Gelderen, *Political Thought,* 233.

[40]Coornhert, *Remonstrantie of Vertooch,* in *Wercken,* vol. 2, fol. clxxxviiC; also fol. clxxxvii.

[41]Coornhert, *Justificatie,* fol. "clxxxxiB"—should be fol. clxxxxiiiiB.

[42]See Becker, *Bronnen,* Letters 18, 226, to a Reformed minister in Zierikzee.

[43]Coornhert, *Synodus van der Conscientie Vrijheid,* session 10, *Wercken,* vol. 2, fol. xixC.

[44]Coornhert, *Sendtbrief,* in *Wercken,* vol. 2, fol. cclxiB.

[45]Coornhert, *"Proces* 2, , fol. cxxiiiA.

[46]Coornhert, *Toetzsteen,* in *Wercken,* vol. 1, fol. 52C.

epithet they will hurl at anyone who exposes their erroneous ways and who disturbs the "external peace" of their church, "in accordance with the nice distinction that you...make between the political and ecclesiastical government."[47] To prevent a Reformed religious monopoly, Coornhert writes, is the main task he has set himself, and he repeatedly asserts that all is not yet lost, for the States have not yet entirely bought into the intolerant views of some Reformed leaders, and might "employ [their] power justly in order to prevent this killing of heretics that you have in mind...[48] The government must realize that the realm of conscience and religious conviction is not an area where it should actively or forcefully intervene, as Coornhert writes in the *Synod,* calling advocates of such constraint "blood councilors" and "wolves in sheep's clothing."[49] Gamaliel, through whom Coornhert speaks these words in the *Synod,* goes on to remind the teachers on both sides, Catholic and Protestant, that they have the means clearly to expose heresy through God's Word, and that in so doing, they will be able effectively to free the lost from error, "and render the unrepentant heretical serpents entirely harmless by ripping out their lethal fangs and by chilling the pernicious venom of the soul that is mixed in with their teachings."[50] In this way, you can only win: the government does not run the risk of bloodying its hands with the persecution of true Christians, the repentant wandering souls will be protected through good teachers who will open their eyes, and the stubborn archheretics will be left alone, and even they may still convert at a future date, as did a St. Paul or a St. Augustine.[51]

To illustrate the arbitrariness of a state's choice of an official religion in the absence of an independent judge, Coornhert sketches an imaginary scenario. In a certain land, he writes, a Christian emperor with absolute powers is pained by the religious strife that wracks his country and summons the representatives of the four main churches in his realm, who appear before him with full mandate. He tells them that they should unite in peace if they want to keep the name of "Christians": "We, oh friends, are all called Christians. Christ is a prince of peace, not of strife. You are engaged in constant mutual strife. Therefore, let all of you now unite in peace, or acknowledge that you are not Christians."[52] In

---

[47]Coornhert, *Theriakel,* in *Wercken,* vol. 2, fol. "cclvCD" (read: fol. ccxlvCD).

[48]Ibid., fol. "cclviA" (read fol. ccxlviA).

[49]Coornhert, *Synod,* session 10, , fol. xixCD.

[50]Ibid., fol. xxB.

[51]Ibid., fol. xxB.

[52]Coornhert, *Proces* 2, fol. cxviiiB. This brings to mind the theme of Lessing's *Nathan der Weise* (1779).

response, each of the four steps forward and says that this would be a great idea, were it not for the fact that the others are at fault. Whereupon the emperor tells them that they cannot be their own judges, and he suggests that they accept God as a judge. Asked how they are to know God's verdict, the emperor responds: by drawing lots on the matter (and he quotes Proverbs 16:33). It goes without saying that none of the four is willing to accept this strategy.[53]

To judge and to choose in matters of faith, Coornhert believes, is the right of every individual—and it stands to reason that he therefore, according to the law of nature, also grants the magistrate this right, a right that in no way should impede the individual's right to choose differently. The only "proper means" for the promotion of spiritual truths are gentle and loving admonition and sincere teaching.[54] Since judgment is based on knowledge, and everyone who judges based on conjecture sins, people must examine doctrine for themselves. Coornhert is not a relativist, and certainly not a Pyrrhonist:[55] he does not believe that there are various "truths" or more than one way to salvation, "[f]or the truth and the way are unique, but the lie and the roads that lead astray are manifold."[56] In this crucial matter of religious choice—sometimes indicated by Coornhert as the "highest good"—people should not just follow religious leaders but their own understanding.[57] Their salvation depends on this choice—and in this connection Coornhert often sounds a monarchomach theme, emphasizing that the people were there before the government, that a government without people is nothing (but the people without the government are still the people).[58]

[53]Coornhert, *Proces 2, Wercken,* vol. 2, fol. cxviiiBC.

[54]Ibid., fol. clxviB; *Ooghwater,* fol. dlixB; and *Aengheheven dwangh,* fol. 470D, where he also implies that the state is certainly free to argue against what it perceives as doctrinal error.

[55]See, on Pyrrhonism and scepticism: Richard Popkin, *The History of Scepticism: From Erasmus to Descartes,* rev. ed. (New York: Harper & Row, 1968). Coornhert does not speak favorably of Montaigne: e.g., in a letter to Spieghel he speaks of Montaigne's "baneful paradoxes"("verderflycke paradocxen"); see Becker, *Bronnen,* Letter 27, p. 248.

[56]Coornhert, *Oordeelen van een ghemeen Landts Leere,* in *Wercken,* vol. 1, fol. 461B.

[57]This is, I believe, the basic message of this tract, *Oordeelen van een ghemeen Landts Leere* (*To Judge a Country's Established Doctrine*). Bonger, in *De motivering,* 11, writes that this document is incomplete and breaks off before answering the question (namely, whether the individual should just follow religious leaders, or if he should examine carefully if, or in how far, the established religion is true or false), but the context makes clear that the question is rhetorical and that Coornhert's answer is a resounding "yes" to independent investigation; otherwise the individual falls into the ditch together with the blind teachers.

[58]Coornhert, *Synod,* fol. xxxivB. See also *Oordeelen van een ghemeen Landts Leere,* fols. 462C, and "643D" (read 463D), where he invokes the example of Tarquinius Superbus, ousted by the

In contrast with most of his contemporaries, Coornhert believes that it is the constraint of conscience that creates discord, weakens the nation, and undermines the government. Taking away their privileges and their "highest good" embitters former supporters of the fledgling state against such injustice, Coornhert claims, "weakens these lands and strengthens the enemies...."[59] Obviating this trend towards constraint thus means, necessarily, fostering concord and strength.[60] It is a simple matter of equality among the citizens: giving some privileges in matters of faith over all the others fosters strife and is "a pestilence upon the...commonweal."[61] If this repression, this partisanship, this constraint continue, Coornhert warns repeatedly, the only outcome can be a general bloody war, an internecine holocaust that he describes in Apocalyptic terms and often compares with the massacre wrought among the Midianites (Numbers 31),[62] for the magistrate "will tyrannize, the people will rebel against that, and one arm will eat, devour, and consume the other."[63] Things will only be aggravated by the fact that the Reformed as a religious group are by far "the smallest minority" (*het kleynste hoopken*), and will thus, due to their fear of Catholic retaliation, want to hire soldiers to protect themselves against this perceived threat, a move that the Catholics in turn will resist....[64] It is to counteract this slide toward the abyss, he writes in another dialogue on the root causes of the Dutch Revolt, in a barely veiled reference to himself, that under the current circumstances those "of irenic disposition"[65] have to act as disturbers of the public peace.[66] There is such a thing, Coornhert contends, as a "false peace" that he sees it as his duty to disturb, a façade established

---

Romans, who then became stronger than ever before, and reminds the reader that in Athens the tyrannicides were lauded. For an interesting reflection of Coornhert's thoughts on the desired qualities in those who serve the country, see *Gesprake van Liefhebbers des ghemeynen nuts*, in *Wercken*, vol. 3, fols. ccclxxxixC–ccccxcvD.

[59]Coornhert, *Theriakel*, fols. ccxlixD–cclA. See also Coornhert, *Wortel der Nederlantsche Oorloghen*, in *Wercken*, vol. 2, fol. clxxviiiC, where he states that "by nature" people hate tyrants.

[60]Ibid., fol. cclA. The same point made in *Remonstrantie of Vertooch*, in *Wercken*, vol. 2, fol. clxxxviA.

[61]Coornhert, *Ooghwater*, in *Wercken*, vol. 2, fol. ccccclxixB.

[62]Coornhert, *Theriakel*, fol. ccliiiAB.

[63]Coornhert, *Wortel*, fol. clxxxiiC.

[64]Coornhert, *Bedencke van der Nederlanden Noodt ende Hulpe*, in *Wercken*, vol. 1, fol. 518C.

[65]"de Pacifijcken," as a reference to "Pacifijc," one of the three participants in this dialogue, *Wortel der Nederlantsche Oorloghen*.

[66]Coornhert, *Wortel* fol. clxxxiiC.

through coercion.[67] Uncertainty is to be preferred over a false security, because at least it will make the people wary of all the misguided teachers, and induce them actively to search for truth.[68] In *Theriakel* (written against the Delft ministers), Coornhert sums up as the chief objectives of his disputations and publications: (1) To lessen the renewed constraint of conscience on the part of the Reformed; (2) To warn the authorities against their "new popery"; (3) To foster concord in the land through "equality of privileges"; (4) To keep out the fearful eternal slavery of the Spaniards; and (5) To keep people's minds from being corrupted and poisoned by Reformed doctrine.[69] He undertakes these actions for the common good at his own expense, whereas the ministers, he charges, work to the detriment of the common good. Therefore Coornhert in his turn calls them and their actions "pernicious to the nation"(*Lant-verderf-lijck*),[70] returning tit for tat, but he adds that they act at the taxpayers' expense, since they were paid from the public coffers.[71]

Applying constraint in matters of conscience will also result in the creation of a nation of hypocrites (and hypocrites, Coornhert feels, are worse than unbelievers).[72] The lax enforcement, in many towns, of a placard against heretical books ca. 1582, is welcome news, writes Coornhert, but it would be much better if such toleration were the official policy, because non-enforcement of ordinances engenders a loss of authority on the part of the government.[73] On the other hand, Coornhert also manifests concern for the salvation of rulers, who in applying religious constraints put their soul in mortal peril. If the ruler does not use force in religion, he argues, he can never go wrong, since he will then not run the risk of committing evil. After all, you will not, Coornhert states, be condemned on Judgment Day for not having killed![74]

The limitations that Coornhert places on toleration that is to be meted out by the government revolve around the subjects' obedience to the political laws of the land. The magistrate's purpose is to ensure that all churches coexist in concord and peace, enjoy freedom of their faith and worship, as long as they

---

[67]In *Sendtbrief,* fol. cclxiiiB, Coornhert calls "their so-called external peace of the church" a "painted mask" that hides lust for power, sloth, and cupidity.

[68]Coornhert, *Oordeelen over een ghemeen Landts Leere,* fol. 464A.

[69]Coornhert, *Theriakel,* fol. cclC.

[70]Ibid., fol. cclvB; the ministers had first accused him of the same: fol. "cclvC" should be ccxlvC.

[71]Ibid., fol. cclvD.

[72]Coornhert, *Remonstrantie,* , fol. clxxxviB.

[73]Ibid., fol. clxxxviC; also in "Ooghwater," *Wercken,* vol. 2, fol. dlxBC.

[74]Coornhert, *Proces* 1, fol. lxxxvA (this statement in a quotation from Albada); also: fol. lxiC.

do not go against the political laws.[75] However, after 1579, having himself been subjected to efforts to silence him, efforts inspired by Reformed sentiment but cloaked as measures to preserve the "political peace," Coornhert often warned against what he saw as attempts by the Reformed to cloud the issue and to mask their coercion of conscience by labeling any form of criticism of their doctrine a "disturbance of the public peace."[76] Conversely, we can see Coornhert apply a similar strategy in the Coolhaes affair, when in the *Justification*, written on behalf of the Leiden magistrate, he describes Pieter Cornelisz as a "Catiline," a "venomous snake" who openly incited the people to disobey the magistrate and thus forced the latter to dismiss him.[77] Coornhert, as Leiden's mouthpiece, here brings in a class argument as well, charging that Cornelisz and his supporters with their agitation stirred up the lower classes and turned them into rebels. According to the Leiden magistrate, from the pulpit Cornelisz had cast doubt on the legality of the town government's actions. This had brought about the real danger of "contempt of the magistrate by the credulous, and pernicious sedition by the rebellious."[78] Cornelisz's action is here portrayed as an infringement on the authority of the political government, but of course in the view of Cornelisz's faction, what was at stake was a fundamentally spiritual matter (namely, the independence of the church).

From Coornhert's belief that faith is a gift of God which depends on man's receptiveness, it follows that Coornhert also wants the person who is devoid of faith to be tolerated. Since nobody can believe for you, and since no one can open or close heaven or hell for you, "likewise nobody can force you to believe or not to believe."[79] Therefore it behooves the government "to tolerate everybody: that they may believe what they want or are able to believe."[80] When his opponents accuse Coornhert of wanting to promote "atheistic chaos"(*een Atheische verwilderinghe*) by urging people not to go to church if they are not sure that it is the right one, Coornhert quickly puts this charge back on his opponents' doorstep by asserting that it is their policy of not allowing other faiths to worship freely that forces Catholics and others into atheism (or

---

[75]Coornhert, *Aengheheven dwangh*, fol. 470A.

[76]See for example Coornhert, *Ooghwater*, fol. dlxBC.

[77]Coornhert, *Justificatie*, , fol. "clxxxxiiiiD" (read fol. clxxxxviD).

[78]Ibid.

[79]Coornhert, *Proces* 1 fol. lxiA.

[80]Ibid.

hypocrisy, or skepticism—the term "atheism" is rarely used).[81] In his tract on the roots of the Dutch Revolt, Coornhert asks, through Pacifijc:

> Whoever leads a blind person from the right path incurs the people's deserved wrath. So what punishment is due him who will kill a blind person, [just] because he has strayed and fallen? Has the seer endowed himself with vision? or can the blind man provide himself with sight? would it not be of greater help to the blind person if we kindly offer him our hand and lead him (if he be willing) on the right path? And if he does not want us to help, then we can let him wander, fall, and undergo the punishment of his obstinacy.[82]

In the *Synod* Gamaliel invokes the example of Abraham who pleaded with God to save the notoriously godless inhabitants of Sodom, and his plea did not displease God, who is not a "respecter of persons."[83]

A significant, and to many of his contemporaries rather provocative element in Coornhert's views of the relationship between church and state is that for Coornhert, diversity of faiths in a country is not just a negative situation that needs to be "tolerated" to prevent strife. On the contrary, he often presents such pluralism in positive terms. This view of toleration as a positive thing reflects Coornhert's Spiritualism.[84] As stated earlier, this does not mean that he feels truth is relative, or that diversity of faiths in itself is good (in our modern sense). It is obvious that he deplores the disunity among Christians, and he emphasizes that a Christian may not love the heretic as heretic: he must love him as a sheep that has gotten lost.[85] But plurality of faiths is both an opportunity and a challenge. Citing a passage from Acontius's *Stratagemata Satanae* in his *Trial of the Killing of Heretics*, Coornhert stresses that force in religious matters tends to make people lazy. What incentive is there to study the Bible, to testify, to make an effort, if the

---

[81]Coornhert, *Sendtbrief*, fol. cclxviiA.

[82]Coornhert, *Wortel*, fol. clxxviiiB.

[83]Coornhert, *Synod*, session 8, fol. xiiiD: "aenziender der persoonen." This is based on Acts 10:34. That God is no respecter of persons and would also save pagans and infidels is also a theme in Sebastian Franck's work: see e.g. Franck's remark to John Campanus (1531), in Williams, ed., *Spiritual and Anabaptist Writers*, 150, that "God is no respecter of persons...but instead is to the Greeks as to the Barbarian and the Turk, to the lord as to the servant...."

[84]See Zijlstra, "Tgeloove is vrij," 41–67.

[85]Coornhert, *Wortel*, fol. clxxxB, where he adds that similarly, a Christian may love the virtue in pagan, Moslem, or Jew. Cf. Castellio on heretics, in Guggisberg, "Ich hasse die Ketzer."

authorities are at your beck and call to defend your orthodoxy? On the contrary, Coornhert stresses that God's church can surely survive without the crutch of government support.[86] The presence of sects in a realm puts the pious to the test.[87] Experience teaches us, he states, that repression only leads to the proliferation of sects, for "the number of sects in the Netherlands multiplied the most rapidly, when they [i.e. the authorities] tried their hardest to reduce and suppress them with bloody placards."[88] Or do you think, he cynically asks his Reformed opponents, that Philip II of Spain, or Charles V, were not dedicated enough in their efforts at stifling and stamping out heresy?[89] Repression will at the most succeed in driving dissident thought underground, which makes it more dangerous, for then one no longer knows what doctrine (possibly subversive) is being taught.[90] However, if we follow Christ's precepts, and use only teaching and admonition in the fight against error, this will lead to a reduction of the number of the erring and the evildoers.[91] Again, Coornhert stresses that such forbearance will also motivate citizens to support the struggle against Spain, for they will notice that their interest, i.e. the preservation and protection of their freedom of conscience, is served.[92] Needless to say, he seizes every opportunity to point out the violation of the Golden Rule committed by the Reformed, who themselves acknowledged the feasibility of allowing more than one faith in a country while they were still living under the cross, but who reverse themselves now that they have what they want.[93] This perceived injustice, this Reformed "change of mind," not only inspires Coornhert with anger: it also regularly incites him to rhetorical flourishes which employ near-homophones that are each other's opposites, in order to contrast the position

[86]Coornhert, *Proces* 1, fol. lviiiA. Also fol. lxxxivC; and *Proces,* supplement ("Bijvoeghsel"), fol. ciD.

[87]"Sects are also necessary as a test for the pious," says Vryemondt: Coornhert, *Proces* 1, fol. lxxxiiC.

[88]Ibid., fol. lxxxixC; ibid., fol. lviiiC, where he gives the example of the Anabaptists; also Coornhert, *Ooghwater,* fol. dlxiAB; Coornhert, *Tweede Verantwoordinghe Eens eenigen Sendbriefs,* in *Wercken,* vol. 3, fol. cccxxiiiV; *Aengheheven dwangh,* fol. 471A; *Wortel* fol. clxxxiA.

[89]In one instance, Coornhert puts the number of those who were executed for their beliefs, prior to 1566, at "more than 36,000," claiming he had heard this from a well-informed high official: Coornhert, *Wortel,* fol. clxxviiiB. The actual number of people executed for heresy in the Low Countries (1523–65) is estimated at 1,300: see Israel, *Dutch Republic,* 100.

[90]Coornhert, *Synod,* session 13, fol. xxviiiD.

[91]Coornhert, *Proces* 1, fol. lxxxiiCD.

[92]Ibid., fol. lxxxiiiC.

[93]Coornhert, *Ooghwater,* fol. dlxD.

taken by the Reformed while they were still "under the cross" with the one claimed after they had attained a position of power: their *kerck* (church) has now changed into a *kercker* (prison), and their *bidden* (praying) into *ghebieden* (commanding)![94]

Coornhert, therefore, sees no danger to the state in allowing a multiplicity of faiths to coexist. He also sees the fact of such a plurality of faiths as a challenge for teachers to do their best, and as a reason for the individual seeker of truth to exercise great caution before entering one of the available "external churches." Clearly, he employs this need for caution as an argument to validate his own position outside any formal church, with only a nominal membership in the Roman church. You must wait until you know with certainty which is the right path, he warns, and not allow yourself to be put under pressure by ministers who threaten that there is no salvation outside a certain church. It is much better to "stand still" and not to act until such certainty is obtained.[95] But, he adds, when you act, act with deliberation, realizing that you can still go back if the road chosen is not spiritually satisfying.[96]

· · ·

As will also be apparent later in his encounter with Lipsius, Coornhert did not accept historical precedent as a sufficient justification for actions in the present. Nonetheless, he regularly refers to events in the distant, but especially in the more recent, past. Historical precedent provides him with models of mistakes to be avoided and enlightening examples to be emulated. Thus, Coornhert always has recourse to the past for an affirmation or illustration of a truth he has already established. The message is simple. History teaches us, Coornhert claims in the *Trial of the Killing of Heretics,* part 1, "that religious coercion is always detrimental to a nation, and that on the contrary freedom of conscience which allows the exercise of other religions has [always] been the cause of peace."[97]

In his attack on Pieter Cornelisz and his supporters during the Coolhaes affair in Leiden, Coornhert draws an analogy between the growing inclination

---

[94]Coornhert, *Theriakel,* fol. cclD: first "doen ghy in 't *bidden* waart," then "nu ghy in 't *ghebieden* komt"; and on ibid., fol. cclviA, he speaks of people who move from one "kercke" to another "kercker."

[95]Coornhert, *Ooghwater,* fol. dlxiiB; this notion of "*stilstand*" was an important concept used by the Spiritualist Caspar Schwenckfeld: see above, chapter 3..

[96]Coornhert, *Ooghwater,* fol. dlxiiB.

[97]Coornhert, *Proces* 1, fol. lxxxviiD.

on the part of the Reformed to try to "place their own chair in city hall" and the way the popes had initially been satisfied that magistrates confirm them in their position, and then later arrogate to themselves the right to confirm the magistrates in theirs. Just as these Reformed ministers, Coornhert continues, now want the magistrate to step in and defend "true dogma" for them through censorship and other restraints, similarly the popes and bishops, once they had grown rich and decadent and had started to stray from the truth, began to appeal to the magistrate to help them against "heresy," using the secular power as their executioner.[98] These corrupt bishops and other clergy, whom Coornhert describes as "Epicurean pigs wallowing in their filth," labelled those who protested against their behavior and actions as "agitators"(*perturbateurs*) and wanted them persecuted since they disturbed their false peace.[99]

In his representation of medieval church-state relations, Coornhert is not interested in (or aware of) a gradual historical evolution, a process culminating at the time of Pope Gregory VII when the church reached the height of its power. Nuances do not serve the rhetorical use he intends to make of these examples, and so we see a pope who, right from the start, turns the emperors and later rulers into lackeys of his cruelty. Constantine the Great meant well, he writes, when he put the pope in the saddle in Italy, but this papal position of power quickly resulted, he continues, in a situation where the flock was entrusted to the wolves, and the riches of the church devoured its mother.[100] Even the Council of Nicaea (325 A.D.), which is so widely praised, he asserts, only contributed to the strengthening of the Arians and of their resolve, and this shows that coercion always produces an effect contrary to the one intended. From the onset popes put kings in place at will. It was a pope who made Pippin the Short, bastard son of Charles Martel, king of France, Coornhert explains, bypassing the rightful heir, King Childerik III. A pope crowned Pippin's son, Charlemagne, emperor of Rome. This contributed to the schism between Latin christendom and the Byzantine Empire. Thus some claim that the Western emperors had become vassals of the pope.[101] This extended analogy with the early Middle Ages, written in 1582, aims to demonstrate that the holding of a self-styled "National Synod" in Middelburg by the Reformed in 1581, where the latter, according to Coornhert and the Leiden magistrate,

---

[98]Coornhert, *Justificatie,* fol. clxxxxiD.
[99]Ibid..
[100]Coornhert, *Remonstrance,"* fol. clxxxviiA.
[101]Ibid..

arrogated to themselves powers rightfully belonging to the secular government, is the beginning of a fatal road.[102] Besides these more specific historical
analogies, we often find the almost stereotypical epithet "new popery" given to
the Reformed church and its purported efforts to dominate the state.[103]

That force in matters of conscience does not work, and is indeed counterproductive, also finds support in exempla from the distant and recent past.
Augustine, battling the Donatists, resorted to force, invoking the *compelle
intrare* (Luke 14:23), and indeed, many heretics did become nominal Christians from fear. But as a result, Coornhert contends, sometime later, when
Islam engulfed the area, Christianity vanished from North Africa, leaving
hardly any trace.[104]

The contemporary Ottoman Empire serves Coornhert as proof of his
point that to allow more than one faith in a state is not a sign of weakness and
does not undermine it, "[f]or the great Turk, who is indeed quite able to exercise dominion over us, also suffers [*lijdt*] Christians and Jews."[105] Giving an
example of forbearance in the non-Christian world could of course also have
been intended to embarrass his opponents. But closer to home, he uses the situation in the Holy Roman Empire to make his point that repression leads to
war, and that toleration promotes peace and tranquillity. Charles V's efforts to
stop the spread of heresy initially brought war over Germany.[106] But the subsequent permission of the peaceful coexistence of faiths has led to some forty
years of peace so far, he writes in 1590.[107] Here, also, it is striking how little
nuance there is. Coornhert does not mention the limited nature of the toleration extended under the territorial solution provided for in the Peace of Augsburg (1555). After all, the *cuius regio, eius religio* principle meant freedom for

---

[102]Ibid., fol. clxxxviiB. On the synod see Nijenhuis, "De publieke kerk," 337; Fatio, *Nihil Pulchrius Ordine*, 36–44.

[103]E.g., Coornhert, *Justificatie*, fol. clxxxxB: let us avoid, writes Coornhert, "a new papacy."
For the prevalence of this argument among those who refused to subject themselves to the discipline of the new church or of the old, see Benjamin Kaplan, "'Remnants of the Papal Yoke': Apathy
and Opposition in the Dutch Reformation," in *Sixteenth Century Journal* 25 (1994): 653–69.

[104]Coornhert, *Proces* 1 supplement, fol. cviiiB.

[105]Ibid., fol. ciD.

[106]E.g. Becker, *Bronnen*, Coornhert's Letter no. 55 to Utrecht's mayors (June, 1590): here,
Coornhert protests against a 25 guilder fine that had been imposed in that town on whoever practiced a religion other than the Reformed faith. Why should you succeed with such compulsion,
Coornhert asks, when Charles V, Philip II, and the kings of France with all their might were unable
to do this?

[107]Coornhert, *Proces* 1, supplement, fol. cviiiC; also Coornhert, *Synod*, session 13, fol. xxvi-
iiA; session 17, fol. xxxviiD; Coornhert, *Advertissement*, fol. 548B.

the territorial princes only. This peace only honored the conscience of the princes; their subjects had no choice except emigration should they find themselves unable to accept the religion of their prince. Besides, the choice was limited also in the sense that it had to be between the Catholic and the Evangelical faiths only.[108]

Finally, France also presents examples of the solution on the one hand—he makes favorable mention of the Peace of Beaulieu (1576), which had meant a victory for the politiques with its authorization of Protestant worship (Paris and environs excepted)[109]—and of the bloody "alternative" on the other hand, for the French king had felt compelled by circumstances to grant this freedom. Coornhert thus employs the French civil war as a warning. In the case of Coolhaes, he writes in another reference to the conflict in Leiden, the only thing that Leiden citizens were petitioning for was that Coolhaes be allowed to preach again. "But," he adds, "how much greater the disturbances, caused by a refusal, would be, can be easily seen in the aforementioned case of France, where they have been forced to accommodate everybody, or else steadily continue in a mutual slaughter."[110]

Among the protagonists of the Dutch Revolt, there was no consensus as to the primary motive of the struggle. In an analysis of the role of political theories in the Dutch Revolt, M. E. H. N. Mout notes that in the pamphlets, as the war wore on, the emphasis was increasingly placed on the preservation of privileges and liberties as the rationale (the *haec libertatis ergo*), and not on religion (the *haec religionis ergo*).[111] The reason could have been the fact that help from Protestant princes was not forthcoming, or that the leaders of the Revolt did not want to alienate Catholics, who would most likely see the aforementioned "religion" as a synonym of the Reformed church. However, for Coornhert there was no doubt as to the essential cause and rationale for the Revolt, for it was nothing else but "the constraint of conscience...."[112] Thus, for Coornhert we can say that the Revolt was *conscientiae ergo*. When he contemplates solutions for the problems confronting the newly liberated provinces, and looks for inspiration elsewhere, his first concern is with the safeguarding of the

[108]See Lecler, *Toleration and the Reformation*, 1:93.
[109]Coornhert, *Wercken*, vol. 1, fol. 552A; Becker, *Bronnen*, letter to D. J. van Montfoort (written in 1583), p. 212; see also (for the Peace of Beaulieu) J. H. M. Salmon, *Society in Crisis: France in the Sixteenth Century* (New York: St. Martin's Press, 1975), 198–99.
[110]Becker, *Bronnen*, letter to van Montfoort, 212.
[111]Mout, "Van arm vaderland," 355.
[112]Coornhert, *Justificatie*, , fol. clxxxxiiA.

freedom of each individual's conscience. In a tract that he intended for Orange in March 1580,[113] Coornhert lists three options for resolving the crisis in which the country finds itself: (1) to accept the peace offered by Philip II, and to subject the nation in slavery to Spain's bloody tyranny; (2) to seek a foreign potentate to protect the Dutch; (3) and finally, the only option seen as viable, to find a native *(inheymsch)* leader who can unite the land or prevent it from falling further apart.[114]

For this creation of unity in the land, Coornhert presents two scenarios: the first is the Polish solution, applied under King Stephen Báthory, extending freedom of religion to everyone, as long as people respect the laws and each other's rights—and Coornhert here emphatically includes adult baptism as an allowed practice.[115] When the Reformed, Coornhert recounts, saw that they held a majority in the Polish king's council, they asked the latter to proscribe the Catholic faith, deemed idolatrous, but were rebuffed by the king, who spoke the famous words that he was a ruler over people, not over consciences.[116] Batory was indeed tolerant, and the 1573 Pact of Confederation of Warsaw did guarantee freedom of religion.[117] However, in this instance too, the nuance is missing in Coornhert's presentation, for Polish freedom, also, was chiefly freedom for the nobles, and their peasants were often forced to accept the religion of their landlords.[118] Still this Polish scenario, presented in ideal terms, is Coornhert's favorite solution. The second option consists of the convocation of a religious colloquy where all those belonging to an "external church" could safely appear and participate. This is the Erasmian solution that had been tried and had failed repeatedly in Germany and France. Coornhert still sees such a gathering as a way of reaching Christian harmony. At this colloquy, the "foam" and the accretions found in the four gathered religions would be removed from the churches' doctrines and ceremonies, leaving only

---

[113]Becker, in his introduction to *Bronnen*, xvi; Coornhert, *Advertissement*, fol. 548D: here Coornhert writes that, having found the prince unwilling to consider the proposals contained in his tract, he had decided not to submit it to him.

[114]Coornhert, *Bedencke vander Nederlanden Noodt ende Hulpe*, in *Wercken*, vol. 1, fol. 518A. I agree with Bonger that with this "native leader" Coornhert must have had Orange in mind: Bonger, *Motivering*, 13.

[115]Coornhert, *Bedencke*, fol. 519C.

[116]Coornhert, *Ooghwater*, fol. dlxviiD.

[117]Kamen, *Rise of Toleration*, 120.

[118]Lecler, *Toleration and the Reformation*, 1:121–22; and Janusz Tazbir, "Poland," in Bob Scribner et al., eds., *The Reformation in National Context* (Cambridge: Cambridge University Press, 1994), 173, who adds that Catholicism remained the official religion.

a "nugget of pure gold" which would constitute a new, truly catholic church acceptable to all.[119] If we add that Coornhert specifies that Schwenckfeldians, Franckists, indeed even Libertines, would all be tolerated in his putative general church of Christendom, it is not too surprising that Orange was not amenable to Coornhert's proposal. However, it is significant that in both scenarios sketched by Coornhert, it is the freedom to believe according to conscience that would establish the national unity, under one dictatorial but just leader. This freedom would enable the Dutch successfully to resist the Spanish.[120]

In the later 1570s and the 1580s (after the prohibition of the Catholic faith), Coornhert often contrasts the current unequal state of affairs, contained in the loss of the essential privilege of freedom of conscience for Catholics and other non-Reformed groups, with the early days of the Revolt, when Roman Catholic and Protestant "patriots" fought shoulder to shoulder against the Spanish foe, united in their common goal, "to keep peace in the land, and to help, shield, and protect each other, irrespective of religion, against all violence and assault by the enemies."[121] He refers, for example, to the Three Million Guilders Request, to show that back in 1566 the Protestants still professed to believe that a tranquil coexistence of Reformed and Catholic was possible.[122] In a tract on the current state of affairs in the Dutch Republic written shortly after the assassination of Orange (1584),[123] Coornhert analyzes the options that present themselves in this desperate situation now that the prince is dead and the Spanish under Parma are quickly gaining ground in the South. Because of Spanish successes, he feels, peace with the king of Spain is out of the question, for Philip II feels too strong after subduing Flanders and Brabant and will never allow "the second religion." We can try to go it alone and protect ourselves, without soliciting foreign assistance against the king's power, but this strategy is not likely to meet with success—and here Coornhert contrasts "then" with "now": when the provinces were still together and rich, we were not able adequately to protect ourselves, let alone now that we have lost Hainault and Artois, and nearly all of Flanders and Brabant. Moreover, we no longer have one leader with authority to maintain concord within and among the provinces, and enthusiasm for the war is on the wane, for "currently in the

---

[119]Coornhert, *Bedencke* „ fol. 519D.

[120]Bonger, *Motivering*, 13.

[121]Coornhert, *Remonstrantie of Vertooch*, in *Wercken*, vol. 2, fol. clxxxvi.

[122]Coornhert, *Wortel*, fol. clxxxiB.

[123]Coornhert, *Overweghinghe van de teghenwoordighe gelegentheyt der Nederlantsche saken*, in *Wercken*, vol. 1, fol. 550–554.

towns, discord over matters of religion is great, and the will of the citizens to shoulder the financial burden [i.e. of paying for the war] is minimal, since they do not see...that the taxes are spent appropriately."[124] Thus, Coornhert seriously believes that the measures against Catholics and others have considerably weakened the nation. He forestalls what he expects to be an analogy that those who disagree will employ, namely with the situation in 1573, when Holland and Zeeland managed to hold out by themselves against seemingly overwhelming odds. Yes, he concedes, God did help us miraculously back then, but at that time, he adds significantly, we were unified (*eendrachtigh*)....[125] Then, he writes, Catholics and Reformed together were enemies of the Spaniards; now "you"—he addresses the Reformed—have become enemies of the Catholics, and therefore the latter are withdrawing their support and are turning into a fifth column. The reason for the growing Catholic resentment, he explains, is that the Reformed have gone back on their promise (under oath) of freedom of worship, and that Catholics can no longer serve their country in important official functions. At least, he adds ominously, when the Spanish win, the Catholics will be allowed to worship again, and then some will certainly want to avenge themselves. It is interesting to see how in his analysis, he sees the Reformed measures against Catholic worship as the cause of what the Reformed (and Orange) felt they were (at least partially) the result of: the political danger posed by the Catholics, whose allegiance was in doubt.[126] It is telling that in all of Coornhert's writings, to my knowledge, there is not one reference to Rennenberg's "treason" (March 1580), an event that seemed to many of his contemporaries to illustrate the political untrustworthiness of Catholics, and in its practical effect actually strengthened the Revolt and the Protestant cause.[127]

In the aforementioned tract (*Overweghinghe*), Coornhert ends by advising that the States seek a powerful sovereign, and he recommends that they ask the king of France. In his defense of this recommendation, Coornhert lauds

---

[124]Ibid., fol. 551A.

[125]Ibid., fol. 551C. See for the importance of the notion of concord in the political thought at this time Van Gelderen, *Political Thought*, 228.

[126]See Otto de Jong, "Les idées du Taciturne sur la religion et la tolérance," in *Réflexions sur Guillaume le Taciturne*. Une série de conférences à l'Institut Néerlandais de Paris, mars 1984 (The Hague: Ministerie van Onderwijs en Wetenschappen, 1984), 99–101, who claims that this political aspect explains why Orange was more successful in protecting the freedom of Anabaptists than that of the Catholics.

[127]See Israel, *Dutch Republic*, 206–8.

Henry III's tolerance vis-à-vis the Huguenots and asserts that, not yet being king of France at the time, Henry III had not been involved in any way in the Bartholomew Day's massacre, nor was he to blame for Anjou's betrayal.[128] Again, this is not a very careful or honest analysis of a monarch who had been an accessory to the massacre[129] and had also fought many battles against the Huguenots. Coornhert does concede that offering sovereignty to Henry is a matter of a choice between bad and worse, and he suggests that the offer should be made conditional on a number of stipulations (that is, that the Netherlands will be able to choose their own governor, of royal blood, and one belonging to the Reformed faith—he names Henry of Navarre and the prince of Condé).[130] But his efforts to make the French king appear acceptable appear to be somewhat disingenuous even though the course charted by Coornhert was very similar to the policy pursued by the late prince, and to a proposal made by the States of Brabant on 3 September 1584.[131]

Coornhert's historical references and his use of contemporary examples were generally meant to illustrate the tenets of his *Weltanschauung*. They were selective and one-sided, and in this kind of usage of history as a sounding board he was by no means unique. What was new or different was his concept of the freedom of conscience, which he saw reflected in the annals of history that could be marshaled for his cause.

·   ·   ·

In the last years of his life that we are about to examine in the light of Coornhert's defense of toleration, he acquired renown as a feared debater and a "bothersome pest." His motivation, as we have sought to demonstrate, came from a deep font of Spiritualist faith and scriptural convictions. His wide reading, fierce independence and sense of fairness, and his practical grounding in the politics of the early phase of the Revolt, gave him a wide and varied arsenal of pro-toleration arguments.

[128]Coornhert, *Overweghinghe*, in *Wercken*, vol. 1, fol. 552C.

[129]Tazbir, "Poland," 173.

[130]It is indeed remarkable that no mention is made here of Maurice, the slain Orange's son, as a possible governor; see Bonger, *Leven en werk*, 121.

[131]See Tjaden, "De reconquista mislukt," 248; also Israel, *Dutch Republic*, 218, who writes that the States of Brabant also stressed that "Henri III, unlike the Spanish king, tolerated Protestant as well as Catholic worship."

8

THE CONTROVERSIALIST
AT WORK

1577–1590

THE TIME AFTER COORNHERT'S RETURN FROM EXILE in Germany until his death in Gouda can be subdivided into a period dominated by debates and disputes with Reformed theologians, and the last few years marked by the grand finale of his clash with Justus Lipsius. His first contact with Lipsius coincided with the Coolhaes affair (1579), and the exchanges and publications elicited by the disputations kept reverberating through Coornhert's many writings until his death. Close to the end, he sent the Reformed synod gathered in 1589 in Gouda, where he then resided, an exhortation that they resume the debate on the Heidelberg Catechism, which had started in The Hague in 1583, been suspended, but never been formally ended.[1]

DEBATE IN DELFT (1578)

The first of the three major debates was brought about by Coornhert's contention that the Catholic Church was to be preferred over the Reformed church.[2]

---

[1] Coornhert, *Remonstrantie D. V. Coornhert aan de Synodale vergaderinghe binnen der Goude Anno 1589*, in *Wercken*, vol. 2, fol. cccxxxviA–cccxxxviiD.

[2] Coornhert gives his account of the Leiden disputation in *Van de Leydtsche Disputatie Warachtigh Verhaal* (written in 1583), *Wercken*, vol. 3, fols. 155–70; in *Wercken*, vol. 2, fols. 483–

In 1577, he contacted Thomas Tilius, a Reformed minister stationed in Delft, but temporarily in Haarlem to organize the Reformed community there, to indicate his willingness to prove his point on scriptural grounds. Tilius claimed to be too busy, but sent the first of the two tracts he received from Coornhert on the issue[3] to Arent Cornelisz, his Delft colleague, and asked him to refute Coornhert's "blasphemy" with the assistance of Reinier Donteclock.[4] After Tilius had moved back to Delft, he invited Coornhert to come and debate the issue. When Coornhert presented himself (24 February 1578) for the debate at Tilius' residence, he found himself faced not only with Tilius, but also with the other two ministers, Cornelisz and Donteclock. Whereas one senses some sympathy, on Coornhert's part, for the former abbot Tilius, who was closer to him in age and had more experience than Cornelisz and Donteclock, the latter two, who were about 25 years his junior, were his enemies from the start and would remain his inveterate opponents until his death.

Arend Cornelisz (1547–1605) was an influential figure in the nascent Reformed church of the Dutch Republic. He was a noted theologian, trained at the seminary of the University of Heidelberg and at the Genevan Academy. Cornelisz was the main force behind the organization and buildup of the Delft church, and he played a prominent role at several synods (for example, as president of the National Synod at Middelburg, 1581).[5] Reinier Donteclock (c. 1545–c. 1614) started serving the Delft church a few years after Cornelisz and was his close associate for many years. Together, Donteclock and Cornelisz campaigned for strict conformity with the Heidelberg Catechism and the Belgic confession of faith of Guido de Brès (which Cornelisz translated into Dutch in 1583),[6] but they also took up relatively moderate positions, as in Cornelisz' defense of an infralapsarian doctrine of predestination, versus the supralapsar-

---

523 (esp. the dedication, fol. 483); *Sendtbrief van D. V. Coornhert*, in *Wercken*, vol. 2, fols. cclviiD–267AB; and *Theriakel*, in *Wercken*, vol. 2, fols. 237–267. See also Bonger, *Leven en werk*, 83–88.

[3]Coornhert, *Bedacht, schynende met te brenghen dat die Roomsche kercke beter zy dan der Ghereformeerden,"* and *"Ander ende corter bewys van mijne ghesproken ende qualijck ghenomen woorden, dat de Roomsche kercke beter zy dan der Greformeerden,* in *Wercken*, vol. 1, fols. 484C–486D.

[4]Bonger, *Leven en werk*, 84.

[5]For his biography, see H. J. Jaanus, *Hervormd Delft ten tijde van Arent Cornelisz, 1573–1605* (Amsterdam, 1950), and *Oxford Encyclopedia of the Reformation*.

[6]See P. H. A. M. Abels and A. Ph. F. Wouters, *Nieuw en ongezien: Kerk en samenleving in de classis Delft en Delfland 1572–1621*, 2 vols. (Delft: Eburon, 1994), 1:607, 609; and *Oxford Encyclopedia of the Reformation* (on Donteclock).

ian doctrine supported by Calvin and Beza.[7] But Donteclock's temperament and stridency made him a controversial figure. He provoked the ire of the Delft magistrate, an action that led to his resignation in 1590.[8] Coornhert repeatedly complains about the youthfulness of the two, their inexperience and insolence.[9] One senses that, in Coornhert's estimation, they did not give him the respect he was due. He regularly complains that they treat him like a schoolboy. Other times, they treat him like a heresiarch,[10] and he writes to them that he found them, upon their first encounter, to be "unripe grapes…sour and unfriendly."[11]

The debate in Delft was cut short on the second day (25 February), when it had just gotten off the ground. It was halted on behalf of the States of Holland which felt that "such disputations tend to scandalize and inflame the community, and that such public disputations ought not to be tolerated without prior consent.…"[12] The inimical and combative atmosphere already present at this first encounter can be deduced from the fact that Coornhert immediately suspected the ministers of collusion with the States in this suspension of the debate. When he ran into the ministers the next day on Delft's market square, the three got into a heated argument.[13] However, the ministers themselves asked the States permission to continue the debate in order to dispel Coornhert's mistaken impression, whereupon a debate was organized for April that year in the Academy building in Leiden.[14]

Debate in Leiden (1578)

The debate was carefully prepared by the States, and Coornhert negotiated with the commissioners in charge of the disputation about the conditions. They would discuss the features of a true church, justification, and perfectibility. According to Coornhert, he was put under pressure to accept the condition

[7]See W. Nijenhuis, "Variations within Dutch Calvinism in the Sixteenth Century," in *Ecclesia Reformata*, 2:164.

[8]This "vehemence" of Donteclock's can also be seen, for example, in a complaint voiced at the time of the discussions between a number of ministers and the latitudinarian minister of Gouda, Herman Herbertsz: see C. C. Hibben, *Gouda in Revolt: Particularism and Pacifism in the Revolt of the Netherlands 1572–1588* (Utrecht: HES Publishers, 1983), 124.

[9]Coornhert, *Vande Leydtsche Disputatie*, in *Wercken*, vol. 3, fols. clvii; clxiiA.

[10]Coornhert, *Theriakel*, fol. ccxliiiiD.

[11]Coornhert, *Van de Leydtsche Disputatie*, fol. clviiD.

[12]Becker, *Bronnen*, 70–71, no. 106, (25 February 1578).

[13]Coornhert, *Van de Leydtsche Disputatie*, fol. clviiiB.

[14]Jaanus, *Hervormd Delft*, 181.

that during the debate neither side would be allowed to discuss the doctrine of Calvin or Beza. The States justified this restriction, according to Coornhert in his own account of the debate, by claiming that Coornhert was a schismatic.[15] He saw the stipulation that they would only be permitted to cite Scripture as a ploy, for everyone knew that he did not want to "invoke" Calvin and Beza as authorities, but on the contrary to attack them for being unscriptural. His dilemma was, he explains, that if he said no to their conditions, there would be no debate, and it was clear that this would be misrepresented as timorousness on his part. So he accepted, but he admits that he was lucky that things turned out as well as he feels they did.[16]

There were more reasons why Coornhert felt frustrated and irked by the upcoming debate, even before it started. He had been the one who had originally taken the initiative—he was the *Aenclagher* (literally "prosecutor")—but increasingly, the roles were reversed, and he typically calls the debate that his opponents envisage an "Inquisition" rather than a free disputation.[17] But a graver issue for Coornhert was the fact that the topic he had wanted to discuss most of all—the killing of heretics—was effectively swept under the rug.[18] His account of what preceded the debate in Leiden starts with the description of a meeting he had in Delft, in February of 1577, shortly after his return from German exile, with two friends who were experienced statesmen and had recently joined the Reformed church. He expressed to them his concern over the fact that some of the most esteemed Reformed scholars and role models—notably Calvin and Beza—had advocated the killing of heretics by the political government. This made him fear, he told them, renewed persecution as the Reformed ministers gained clout and attempted to persuade the magistrate to "do their duty" in this regard. He would do everything within his power, Coornhert promised, to help prevent this feared development.[19] His friends then sought to allay his fears and beseeched him to keep quiet on the topic, to which Coornhert assented, but only for as long as he saw no clear signs of incipient constraint of conscience on the part of the ministers. Not too much later, he did see such signs, and during the negotiations prior to the April debate,

---

[15]Coornhert, *Van de Leydtsche Disputatie*, fol. clxiiiA.

[16]Ibid., fol. clxiiiD; also *Sendtbrief,* fol. cclviiiABC; *Theriakel,* fol. ccxliiiiCD.

[17]Coornhert, *Van de Leydtsche Disputatie,*fol. clxiiiiA.

[18]Coornhert, *Van de Vreemde Sonde,* in *Wercken,* vol. 2, fol. cccclxxxiiR. In the dedication of *Van de Leydtsche Disputatie,* fol. clvV, he combines the topic of the "calling" of the Reformed church in one sentence with his admonitions against ministerial intolerance.

[19]Coornhert, *Van de Leydtsche Disputatie*, fol. clviC.

Coornhert wanted "punishment of heretics" to be placed high on the agenda. The ministers, however, were against inclusion of the issue and claimed that the punishment of heresy was a political, not a theological issue.[20] He managed to keep the issue on the agenda, but it was relegated to the bottom of a long list of topics on which the ministers wished to debate him, and he suggests this was done on purpose, for they knew that they would never get around to it.[21] Coornhert suggests two possible motives for the ministers' reluctance to discuss constraint of conscience as advocated by Calvin and Beza: either they are ashamed to admit that two such great Reformed teachers have erred in so fundamental a matter, or they themselves in reality embrace the same intolerant Genevan doctrine, but do not want to admit this openly, realizing that this doctrine does not sit well with the Dutch people who are still smarting from the wounds inflicted by the recent application, by the Spanish authorities, of the same doctrine. Thus, he suspects the ministers, in this latter scenario, of biding their time, knowing that now the magistrates and States General are not yet receptive to their view. To counter the ministers' assertion that they have more important topics to discuss, Coornhert quotes Beza's *Traité de l'autorité du Magistrat,* where the Reformer states that laxity in the persecution of heretics will put the church in mortal peril, underscoring that for him at least this was a fundamental issue.[22]

The debate in Leiden took place on 14 and 15 April 1578, before an audience of several hundred, including the Leiden magistrates. Coornhert was not allowed to apprise the audience of the backgrounds of the debate, and was to dispute with Cornelisz, who would be assisted by Donteclock. Coornhert had earlier complained that he, almost sixty years old and suffering from a faulty memory,[23] had to take on two young opponents, but when he was offered the opportunity also to use an assistant, he avowed that he could find none and added: "that shows what kind of a schismatic I am."[24] On the first day,

---

[20]Ibid., fol. clxA. Coornhert comments *in margine* that this argument does not hold, because the ministers reserve unto themselves the right to tell the magistrate who the heretics are.

[21]Ibid., fol. clxAB; also *Van de Vreemde Sonde,* in *Wercken,* vol. 2, fol. cccclxxxiiR, where he lists the following topics that they agreed to discuss: original sin, free will, predestination, justification, the church, the "calling" (*zendinghe*), humility, and finally "the power of the government," which, Coornhert explains, was the euphemism employed by the ministers for the suppression of "heresy."

[22]Coornhert, *Van de Leydtsche Disputatie,* fols. clxiCD, clxD.

[23]Of such a purported "faulty memory" his writings and debates give no evidence whatsoever.

[24]Coornhert, *Van de Leydtsche Disputatie,* fols. clxiiC and clxviD.

exchanges took place on the features of the true church, with Cornelisz expounding on the true apostolic creed and correct use of sacraments which can be found in the Reformed church, and Coornhert explaining the difference between the visible and invisible church. The two did not get one step closer to each other. Indeed, one does not get the impression that such was ever the intention. During the morning session of the second day, some commotion erupted when Coornhert mentioned Calvin and Beza.[25] Later that morning, the incident took place to which, in later accounts, Coornhert would return again and again with sardonic glee:[26] the silencing of his opponent, Cornelisz. Coornhert had just eloquently made his point that the Reformed church was not a real church. He got his opponent to admit that at the time of Christ, Judaism was the "true" but deformed church, replaced by Christ. The Catholic Church, with its apostolic creed, baptism, its belief in the Trinity, he continued, remained the true church. It would remain so until someone could clearly prove to be the recipient of a divine summons to rebuild it. It in turn had become deformed and overgrown with abuses and error. If you admit these things, he concluded, should we not infer from the foregoing

> that the Roman church is a true, but deformed, church, and that the ministers' church is a false church without substance, to wit: in appearance reformed, but in truth a nonexisting and chimerical church? And in that case, would not the R. Catholics have the substance of a true church, but without its form, and those who call themselves Reformed a form of the true church, but without substance?[27]

Whereupon Cornelisz did not know what to say in response, sat down, blushed, and presented an image of utter perplexity and discomfiture.[28] For the remainder of that morning session, Donteclock had to take over from Cornelisz (although this was against protocol).

During the break, Coornhert accosted the commissioners and demanded that from then on he be permitted to refer to the teachings of Calvin and Beza.

[25]Bonger, *Leven en werk*, 87.
[26]Coornhert, *Van de Leydtsche Disputatie*, fols. clxviiiA, clxixA; *Sendtbrief*, fols. cclviiiD, cclixBCD, cclxiiiiD–cclxvA; *Theriakel*, fols. ccxliiiiD; "cclvA" (should be ccxlvA).
[27]Coornhert, *Van de Leydtsche Disputatie*, fol. clxixA.
[28]Coornhert, *Van de Leydtsche Disputatie*; see also Geeraert Brandt, *The History of the Reformation and Other Ecclesiastical Transactions in and about the Low Countries* 1 (London: T. Wood, 1720): 336; Moorrees, *Dirck Volckertszoon Coornhert*, 73.

A bitter exchange ensued, in which the commissioners accused Coornhert of disrespect for the States, and Coornhert insinuated that they were playing favorites to the ministers. Coornhert told them, when they would not accede to his peremptory demand, that he regarded a continuation of the debate to be useless, and he left in a huff.[29] When Coornhert did not appear for the afternoon session—he writes that the commissioners knew full well that he had already taken the canal-boat back to Haarlem, but reconvened the meeting anyway for maximum effect—some claimed that he had shamefully deserted the battlefield. But Coornhert writes that this last assertion is preposterous since that morning everyone had seen how he had quite effectively knocked his opponent out of the saddle.[30] Still, it seems naive on Coornhert's part to have thought that the commissioners would be willing to give in to his demand that they change the rules of the debate in midstream, even though he could argue that his opponents had also violated the rules by letting Donteclock take over from Cornelisz.

Coornhert would have to wait five years before he was allowed to publish an account of this debate. He would then often, and bitterly, refer to it and dwell on the events leading up to the disputation. He repeated the charge that the authorities in this whole affair had been anything but impartial, and that the States followed the ministers' promptings. This contention is made in his correspondence with the ministers, whom he also accuses of arrogance, for assuming that the authorities were already on their side. This inner contradiction in his exchanges with his Reformed opponents indicates the tenuous status of relations between the Reformed church and the new Republic. "Do you already consider yourselves," Coornhert asks his opponents, "to be the Lords of the States, so that your actions must be deemed the States' actions? And that the Lords of the States are obliged to allow and execute anything you or your churches decree and decide? It is surely still too soon for that." All was not yet lost, Coornhert feels, and he refers to the Leiden magistrate, who had objected to "Reformed meddling."[31] But things were moving in a dangerous direction. Thus, he sharply attacks the ministers' distinction between political and ecclesiastical government by making the point that the "disturbers of the external peace of the church," whom they want to punish with fines and imprisonment, are merely all those who disagree with the Reformed interpretation of Scrip-

[29]Coornhert, *Van de Leydtsche Disputatie,*fols. clxixAB, clxixC.
[30]Ibid. He uses the imagery of a joust.
[31]Coornhert, *Sendtbrief,* fols. cclviiiCD, cclxiiB, cclxiiA.

ture.[32] When they complain about his productivity, Coornhert accuses them of laziness.[33] When the ministers argue that all this writing back and forth is rather useless, because the people, in general, are too lazy to read so many books, especially on religion, Coornhert asks why, in that case, the ministers are so keen on preventing the publication of his books.[34] He, Coornhert, did all this writing and debating pro bono, and to his own detriment, he reminds them, while they receive a salary yet fail to do their job.[35] They would rather use the political government as a shield than defend the truth themselves. And quick to remind the ministers once again of Cornelisz' dumbfoundedness during the Leiden debate, he suggests pusillanimity on the part of his opponents.[36]

Of course, Coornhert had a personal reason for his bitter contention that the government was on the ministers' side, for it was around this time that he himself was given the label of a potential "disturber" of the peace, and ordered not to publish any more tracts against the ministers. The tone of *Theriakel,* a response to the *Remonstrance* that Cornelisz and Donteclock had sent to the States of Holland,[37] is especially acrimonious, with Coornhert explaining that naturally the ministers would find the truth a bitter pill to swallow.[38]

The debate and his publications helped to make Coornhert widely known, and from their pulpits the Reformed ministers helped spread his notoriety as an "impious fellow" and a "freethinker."[39] In 1579, at the same time that he lent his pen to the magistrate of Leiden for a defense of the town's position against the Reformed church's demands of autonomy, the States of Holland tried to silence him. Coornhert reacted with his tract on the beginning of the constraint of conscience in the young state.

DEBATE IN HAARLEM (1579)

The second debate, on 6 February 1579, was a much smaller affair, and should actually be seen as a preparation for the great disputation with Saravia that

[32]Ibid., fols. cclxD–cclxiAB.

[33]Ibid., fol. cclxvC; he gives a none too subtle reference to Isa. 56:10 ("His watchmen are blind: they are all ignorant, they are all dumb dogs, they cannot bark; sleeping, lying down, loving to slumber").

[34]Coornhert, *Theriakel,* fol. ccxlviiiD. Or are you, he adds subtly and ironically, trying to stimulate the people's interest in my books by forbidding them?

[35]Ibid., fol. cclviD—must be ccxlviD.

[36]Coornhert, *Sendtbrief,* fols. cclxiB, cclxiiiiC.

[37]For *Theriakel* see above, chap. 5.

[38]Coornhert, *Theriakel,* fol. cclvB.

[39]Brandt, *History of the Reformation,* 337.

would take place four years later.[40] The document that unleashed this chain of events was the Heidelberg Catechism, commissioned by the elector of the Palatinate, Frederick III, in 1563. Coornhert read this summary of Reformed religious doctrine in 1578, the same year that the synod of Dordrecht accepted it and the decision was made that it would be taught at the schools. From the onset, Coornhert regarded the doctrine contained in the Catechism as poison for the young minds in Dutch schools. He voiced his criticism in conversations with his (Reformed) friend, the Haarlem mayor Nicolaes van der Laen, who then organized and moderated the debate that took place at his home in Haarlem, with only few participants. Coornhert's chief interlocutor was the Haarlem minister Damius, with whom he debated for five hours straight on original sin and perfectibilism.[41] Although this debate did not bring about any kind of rapprochement either, the atmosphere appears to have been less contentious than in Leiden the previous year, perhaps also because of the more informal setting.

Debate in The Hague (1583)

The years leading up to the debate in The Hague saw an explosion of activities on Coornhert's part. Much of this activity was directly connected with the ongoing exchange with the Delft ministers on points of doctrine. The ministers challenged Coornhert on his views on original sin, expressed in earlier writings, and he responded with an extensive refutation of the doctrine, finished in May 1581.[42] His views on a possible solution for the proliferation of sects, expressed in *Means toward the Reduction of Sects* (*Middel tot minderinghe der secten,* 1582), elicited another bout of sharp exchanges with the ministers, particularly Coornhert's *Eyewash* (*Ooghwater*), which again clearly exhibits Coornhert's anti-Reformed animus. In this document, he reasserts that he is against giving any government power to punish people politically for speaking their conscience in matters of religion, and contends that the logical outcome of the ministers' position is persecution and bloodshed against conscience.[43]

---

[40]The account of this second debate, written by Coornhert's friends Jan van Zuren and Gerrit Stuver who attended the debate, published in 1610, was not included in the *Wercken*. Only two copies of it are extant, one at the University library of Ghent, the other at the University of Amsterdam; see Bonger, *Leven en werk*, 168 n. 218; Spaans, *Haarlem na de Reformatie*, 86.

[41]See above, chap. 4, for Coornhert's views on these matters.

[42]Coornhert, *Van de Erf-zonde, Schulde, ende Straffe* [On Original Sin, Guilt, and Punishment], *Wercken*, vol. 2, fols. 407–50. This book was preceded by a shorter treatise on the subject, *Bootgen wt Het Schip van de tweede Antwoorde....* [*Dinghy from the Ship of the second Answer....*": this "dinghy" announced the impending arrival of the larger vessel], *Wercken*, vol. 2, fols. 393–406.

[43]Coornhert, *Ooghwater*, fol. dlxBC.

Referring to his forthcoming tract against the Catechism, Coornhert writes in *Ooghwater* that the ministers may claim to possess the pure foundations of Christianity, but that soon their errors will be clearly exposed.[44]

In 1582, another challenge of his view of the "external church" came from Lambert Daneau, doctor of theology and minister of the French congregation in Leiden (as of 1581) who had earlier examined the orthodoxy of the views of Caspar Coolhaes and had been co-instrumental in the latter's excommunication at the provincial synod of Haarlem (March 1582).[45] Indirectly, the two men had already found themselves in opposite camps on the question of the relation between church and state, since Coornhert had drafted the *Remonstrance* (1582) to the States of Holland on behalf of the magistrate of Leiden, reiterating the position that had earlier been expressed in the *Justification*. An ugly duel between the two men ensued that was more like a slanging match than an exchange of views. Even some of Daneau's colleagues cringed at the language employed by Daneau in his *Calx Viva* (*Quicklime*), for one of them, Hagius, wrote to Arent Cornelisz in Delft: "I must tell you, brother … that this quicklime is a bit too hot, and we risk burning ourselves with it …."[46] Initially, when the exchange was still somewhat civil, Daneau employed arguments against Coornhert's ideas on the invisible vs. the visible church that were similar to the ones Calvin had used in the exchange provoked by Coornhert's 1558 tract (*Apology for Roman Idolatry*). At the end of Coornhert's first rebuttal of Daneau's critique, it seems as though Coornhert deliberately added fuel to the fire, by printing an artful rhetorician's poem he had written with the refrain: "Why should he in bondage remain/ who may be free from fetter or chain."[47] To a man like Daneau, this of course was nothing but the provocative flaunting of unbridled license by a notorious Libertine.

---

[44]Ibid., fol. dlviiiD.

[45]Fatio, *Nihil Pulchrius Ordine*, 68.

[46]Ibid., 183 n. 40, letter dated 10 March 1582. See also Van Gelderen, *Political Thought*, 251; Bonger, *Leven en werk*, 102–4. The documents generated by this duel are *Zeepe opte vlecken by Lambert Daneus, Doctor in Theologie tot Leyden, ghestroyt op een Sentbrief…*"[*Soap for the stain that Lambert Daneus, Doctor of Theology in Leiden, left on a Missive…*], *Wercken*, vol. 3, fol. l– "xlixD" (must be lvii-D); and *Levende Kalck* [*Quicklime*, Coornhert's translation of Daneau's *Calx viva*, with his rejoinder], *Wercken*, vol. 3, fols. ccclvi–ccclxii; on fol. ccclviiD–ccclviiiD, Coornhert gives an anthology of epithets hurled at him by his opponent. In this exchange, Coornhert was supported by his friend Aggaeus van Albada, who sent a letter to Daneau to which the theologian did not deign to respond: see Van Berkel, "Aggaeus de Albada," 12.

[47]Coornhert, *Zeepe*, in *Wercken*, vol. 3, fol. lviiC–"xlixD" (must be lviiD): "Wat behoeft hy Bant die onghebonden leven can" (freely translated).

Coornhert's notoriety among the Reformed increased further when he drew up the "Request," the abortive defense of the freedom of worship of Haarlem Catholics. It was doubtless this experience, as well as the 1581 national synod of the Reformed in Middelburg (not recognized, by Coornhert or the magistrate of Leiden, as a national synod, since it had not been officially convened by the authorities), the efforts to stifle his criticism (apparently not too successful), the label of "disturber of the peace" put on him, and the reluctance of his Reformed opponents to address the issue of the constraint of conscience, that culminated in the creation, in 1582, of Coornhert's most eloquent defense of toleration, the *Synod on the Freedom of Conscience.*

Coornhert's thorough refutation of the Heidelberg Catechism—the *Examination* (1582)—addressed especially the fourth and fifth questions and answers, which denied the possibility of complete obedience to God's commandments in this world.[48] He sent this book to his friend Nicolaes van der Laen, who notified Coornhert in February of the next year that the majority of the States of Holland wanted him to send the *Proeve* to "a Leiden professor," so that the latter would be able to prepare himself, with the assistance of some ministers, for a disputation on the criticism contained therein. On 26 August 1583, perhaps in response to a request by Coornhert for such a debate,[49] the States of Holland resolved that Coornhert would be allowed to defend his book at a public disputation in October.[50] The States went to great lengths to prepare for this debate, which can almost be regarded as a national event.[51]

Coornhert, having learned from the Leiden disputation, accepted the proposed debate only tentatively and in September sent a memorandum with his conditions. He stipulated that the commissioners would not be allowed to pronounce judgment on the outcome of the debate since they were not special experts. Furthermore, since most of them belonged to the religion whose doctrines Coornhert attacked, they would be prosecutors and judges at the same time. Let the people who attend the debate judge for themselves, he writes.[52]

[48]Coornhert, "Proeve," *Wercken*, vol. 3, fol. cccclxxviiiC; on fol. cccclxxviiiB he calls the Catechism "lethal venom to the soul."

[49]Becker, *Bronnen*, no. 132, 1583, Request by Coornhert to the States of Holland, pp. 84–86.

[50]Ibid., 86 n. 3, resolution dated 26 August 1583. For the debate in The Hague, see: Bonger, *Leven en werk*, 110–17; W. Nijenhuis, "Coornhert and the Heidelberg Catechism," in *Ecclesia Reformata*, 1:188–206, with a concise explanation of Coornhert's theology; Brandt, *History of the Reformation*, 1:393–94; Van Gelderen, *Political Thought*, 243–49.

[51]Bonger, *Leven en werk*, 113; Van Deursen, *Bavianen en slijkgeuzen*, 54.

[52]Coornhert, *Disputatie over den Catechismus*, fol. ccccxxxivA; in a letter to his wife, dated 26 October, he writes that the commissioners will not be judges of the content of the debate, but

The result of the ensuing negotiations was that Coornhert would debate his opponent on two points: "first, that it is impossible to keep the commandment of love towards God and our neighbor perfectly; secondly, that we are all inclined by nature to hate God and our neighbor."[53] Both parties would have a recording secretary and sign the protocol after each session. Coornhert's opponent would have two assistants, the inevitable Cornelisz and Donteclock. Again Coornhert was also entitled to two assistants, but claimed that he could not find any, so he would debate unassisted.[54] His opponent would be Adrianus Saravia,[55] the noted peripatetic Reformed theologian, who was minister and professor in Leiden between 1578 and 1587. From the time that he started his professorate at Leiden University in 1582, there were tensions with the magistrate, who held the university under tight control; especially the town secretary of Leiden, Jan van Hout, who also served as secretary to the University's curators, and who had been the driving force behind the town's rejection of Cornelisz's attempts to safeguard the Reformed church's autonomy during the Coolhaes-affair, ensured such control. Saravia, who from 1584 to 1587 would be professor and rector magnificus, did not much heed a provision he had signed forbidding Leiden professors to engage in "disputes that would cause dissension." He mediated in several cases involving doctrinal controversies, such as the one regarding the minister Herman Herberts who refused to use the Heidelberg Catechism and believed in perfectibility.[56] Saravia's position would become untenable—indeed, he would become a "wanted man"—during the Leicester intermezzo, due to his active support for Lord Dudley, and he would return to England.[57]

The States asked for the input of the *vroedschappen* (town governments) of the towns of Holland, and most were in favor of the debate.[58] On 20 October, Orange gave his permission for the debate, which would begin on 27 October

---

judges of the procedure; see ibid., fol. ccccxxxvC. Of course the theme of the absence, under current circumstances, of an impartial judge, runs through the *Synod on the Freedom of Conscience* that Coornhert had published the previous year.

[53]Nijenhuis, "Coornhert and the Heidelberg Catechism," 194–95; also Brandt, *History of the Reformation*, 394.

[54]Coornhert, *Disputatie over den Catechismus*, fol. ccccxlixA.

[55]On Saravia see W. Nijenhuis, *Adrianus Saravia*.

[56]Ibid., 72.

[57]See ibid., 26, 47–50, 69.

[58]See Becker, *Bronnen*, nos. 133–43, pp. 86–90, for the "vroedschapsresolutiën" that are extant.

and last for a total of eleven days.[59] Orange's appreciation for Coornhert's past services may have prompted him to accommodate the controversialist when the latter requested to be given a fair hearing.[60] As recently as 1582, Coornhert had proved his patriotism by traveling posthaste to The Hague to warn the States of an impending pro-Spanish conspiracy in Enkhuizen.[61] But apart from Coornhert, the existing Erastian and Erasmian proclivities among the magistrates, which had given rise to conflicts and tensions that were far from resolved (as noted above), may also have contributed to the authorities' willingness to demonstrate to the world their fairness and their reliance on rational means instead of on force for the promotion of the true faith. They could also have meant to make a point to the ministers, giving them to understand that they should not take their position for granted, even though the wording of their decision to hold a debate the States clearly indicated that they supported the Catechism and utterly rejected Coornhert's position.[62]

Coornhert's hopes for the debate were high,[63] and the importance the authorities attached to the upcoming event can be seen in the calibre of those who attended it in an official capacity. That morning of 27 October in the council chamber of the *Hoge Raad*[64] in The Hague, those present included six members of the *Hoge Raad,* one member of the *Hof van Holland* (Court of

[59]Ibid., 87; Bonger, *Leven en werk*, 112.

[60]H. Bonger, "Prins Willem van Oranje en Coornhert," in Bonger et al., eds., *Dirck Volckertszoon Coornhert*, 55.

[61]Coornhert, *Theriakel*, fol."cclvC," must be ccxlvC, refers to this incident to counter the ministers' accusation that he was "pernicious to the nation" (a *Lant-verderver*, a word that in meaning comes close to "traitor"). See also Bonger, *Leven en werk*, 108.

[62]See e.g. Becker, *Bronnen*, 86 n. 3, resolution of the States of Holland, dated 26 August 1583, where they state that Coornhert "may be heard against the ministers, before the States or their commissioners and the [delegates of the] Court [meant is the *Hoge Raad*], on what is in some booklets that said Coornhert has published as a great insult to Christ's church and to God's S[acred] Word and Doctrine."

[63]See Coornhert, *Theriakel* (written at the time of preparations for the disputation), fol."cclviA" (must be ccxlviA), where he optimistically interprets the initiative for the debate taken by the States as a sign that the authorities were finally starting to take measures against the ministers' errors.

[64]The *Hoge Raad* [Supreme Court] was established in 1582, because as a result of the Revolt and the Abjuration the northern provinces were no longer able to appeal to the *Grote Raad* in Mechelen. The intention was for there to be one central court to which cases from provincial courts could be appealed, but only Holland, and (as of 1587) Zeeland acknowledged the authority of the *Hoge Raad* (and therefore "Supreme Court" would be a misleading translation). This situation would lead to recurring competency conflicts due to the parallel existence of the *Hof van Holland & Zeeland* (Court of Holland and Zeeland) and the *Hoge Raad*.

Holland), eight members of the States of Holland, and a representative of Orange.[65] The room was filled to capacity with spectators, who were keenly interested in this debate on theology.[66] The authorities had taken the preventive measure of confiscating Coornhert's books for the time being, lest curiosity stimulate sales.[67]

A further sign of the importance of the debate is the mere fact that in the middle of a war with a mighty adversary, who was reducing the area of the Revolt almost daily, the authorities felt they had to invest time and resources into such a disputation. The rebellious northern provinces had gone their own way under the Union of Utrecht (1579). In 1581, after the échec of the 1579 peace negotiations in Cologne with Spain, the States General, which by then, due to the continued successes of Parma in the south, had relocated to The Hague, had formally disavowed their allegiance to Philip II in the "Act of Abjuration."[68] Parma's reconquista, however, had continued unabated (and would continue until 1589), and had brought Spanish fortune back from the low point where it had been at the time when Don John had had to send back all Spanish troops (in 1577).[69] Starting with his victories at Gembloux (1578) and Maastricht (1579), by 1583 Parma had pushed the Revolt so far back that the area of the *Generaliteit* (under the States General) had become nearly the same as the area of the Union of Utrecht.[70] Constitutionally, the rebellious provinces seemed to be drifting towards anarchy; Anjou, brother of the French king Henry III, had accepted sovereignty (with many restrictions) over the new state in 1581, but Holland and Zeeland had refused to acknowledge him. He proved to be a military failure, and after his failed attempt to take several towns in order to strengthen his position, by 1583 he was "a spent force."[71] Orange's standing and popularity had also plummeted, for he had been the great advocate of the offer of sovereignty to Anjou. Thus, the year 1583 marked a low point. With both his religious peace and his pro-French strategy in ruins, Orange that year was compelled to move his headquarters first to The Hague,

[65]See Nijenhuis, "Coornhert and the Heidelberg Catechism," 195; Bonger, *Leven en werk*, 113.

[66]See Van Deursen, *Bavianen en slijkgeuzen*, 54, for the public interest in and enthusiasm for such disputations in general, and in particular for this debate in The Hague "between true champions such as Coornhert and Saravia...."

[67]Bonger, *Leven en werk*, 114.

[68]See Tjaden, "De reconquista mislukt," 251.

[69]Parker, *Dutch Revolt*, 187.

[70]Ibid., maps, 210–12.

[71]Ibid., 206; Israel, *Dutch Republic*, 213.

then to Delft.[72] Under such dire circumstances, one must wonder what Orange and the States hoped to gain from this debate, especially since it was rather evident that Coornhert, the challenger, would not be likely to change his mind or be converted.[73]

The 1583 disputation was held in a polite enough manner, without angry outbursts or vituperation, a fact that may have been caused, at least partially, by Saravia's reasonable and flexible personality. But despite such polish, the stakes were high, and in private correspondence during and after the debate, both sides describe the events in the council chamber in martial imagery: Saravia brags afterwards in a letter to Cornelisz and Donteclock about how, in The Hague, they had made this archcontroversialist bite the dust.[74] And Coornhert, in a letter to his brother Frans, writes, with regard to the interruption of the debate due to the illness of his wife, that he regretted having the debate suspended, "which went so well (*for they have already been slain*)."[75]

The debate revolved around the question of complete compliance with, or obedience to, God. Saravia defended the Reformed eschatological conception, i.e. the idea that such perfection can only be reached after man has left his mortal frame, and Coornhert made his point that such perfection is indeed attainable in reality, here on earth. Coornhert rejected the idea of "imputed righteousness" which claims that our sins are cloaked by the righteousness of Christ,[76] defended by Saravia, and replaced it with his belief in "actual righteousness." Saravia defended the Calvinist position that God gave man his laws in order to reveal to him his inability to live up to them, thus leading him to the shelter of Christ's grace. For Coornhert, on the other hand, the laws were given in order to be obeyed, thus gradually leading the reborn man to perfection.[77]

---

[72]Israel, *Dutch Republic*, 213; Tjaden, "De reconquista mislukt," 252–53.

[73]Nijenhuis, *Adrianus Saravia*, 88, states that such disputations were never real dialogues: "The other side's propositions were attacked from positions of unshakable prejudice." This view finds solid support in the accounts of Coornhert's debates.

[74]Ibid., 275, document no. 7, Saravia to Arent Cornelisz, Leiden, 23 April 1584 (from *Gemeentearchief Delft*, no. 112), in reference to Coornhert's contact with Lipsius regarding the latter's *De Constantia*: "Interea *dum ab hac disputatione Cornhertius feriatur* querit alium antagonistam" (my italics).

[75]Coornhert, *Wercken*, vol. 3, fol. 448v (my italics).

[76]For a clear description of the Reformed doctrine of imputed justice, see Cameron, *European Reformation*, 121–25.

[77]Nijenhuis, "Coornhert and the Heidelberg Catechism," 88; Van Gelderen, *Political Thought*, 249; see also above, chap. 4.

After seven days of debating, with only a break on Sunday, a messenger came with an urgent message for Coornhert, who had temporarily settled in The Hague so as not to lose too much time traveling back and forth. He was called to Haarlem where his wife, who had been ill for a while, expected her imminent death and wanted to see her husband one last time before her passing. Remaining with his ailing wife for several weeks, he wrote to a friend: "Now my wife is still in bed, dying. When the Lord has taken her, I intend to go back to The Hague."[78] But towards the end of November she had sufficiently recovered for Coornhert to return to The Hague, where the debate resumed on November 28. However, Coornhert would no longer speak. Quoting numerous biblical passages dealing with sin, Saravia now held the floor for four days straight. Due to this prolixity, which was certain to be reciprocated by Coornhert, the States then decided to suspend the debate.[79] They told Coornhert to send a written rejoinder, which the ministers would answer, whereupon both sides were to read their responses before the people. Coornhert delivered his response to the commissioners before the agreed deadline, but thereafter nothing happened (the ministers' reply would finally come in 1585), and the debate was not resumed.

In May of the following year (1584), to facilitate resumption of the debate Coornhert even moved to The Hague with his wife, still gravely ill.[80] On June 18, he writes to the *Hoge Raad* to give expression to his frustration and indicate his intention to move back to Haarlem at the behest of his wife, whom he does not want to refuse in her condition.[81] In letters to the States of Holland and Orange he denounces what he sees as the development of the Reformed faith into a state religion. He assures the prince that he can understand if the debate is not continued for the time being, due to the critical war situation.[82] But if he

---

[78]Coornhert, *Disputatie over den Catechismus,* letter to "a friend" dated 10 November 1583, fol. ccccxlixD. See also ibid., letter to his brother, Frans, dated 11 August 1583, fol. ccccxlviiiCD.

[79]Nijenhuis, "Coornhert and the Heidelberg Catechism," 197–98. Before the resumption, Coornhert had rejected a proposal to limit the debaters to just one argument, for then his opponents could pick what kind of argument and thus limit him: see Coornhert, *Disputatie over den Catechismus,* fol. ccccxlviiC (Bonger, in *Leven en werk,* 116, erroneously suggests that this happened after the indefinite suspension of the debate). Earlier (*Disputatie over den Catechismus,* fol. ccccxxxiiiB), before the debate began, he had already stated that he would not accept restrictions on what he could talk about—as he had in Leiden, 1578—"for such a Disputation would not be free but gagged, indeed it would be an Inquisition."

[80]Coornhert, *Disputatie over den Catechismus,* fol. ccccxlviiCD.

[81]Ibid., fol. ccccxlviiCD. The *Hoge Raad* tells him to write to the States and Orange.

[82]Ibid., fol. ccccclixD: "by a change in the national state of affairs"; for his letter to the States, see *Het leven van D. V. Coornhert,* in *Wercken,* vol. 1, fol. 4A, where this letter is printed.

is no longer allowed to utter public criticism of the errors that he sees in the Reformed teachings, and thus to "enjoy the freedom of conscience, bought at such a cost ...,"[83] he wants his passport so he can settle abroad although he does not look forward to such a move because of his wife's condition and his own advanced age.[84] Throughout the letter, he complains about the ministers' temporizing and suggests that they have no adequate way to counter his critique and do not want the people to realize their failure by a resumption of the debate. This last letter also was to no avail and remained unanswered—it was sent quite close to the date of Orange's assassination (10 July 1584), and it may well be that it never reached him. After three years, Cornelisz and Donteclock finally produced the *Wederlegginghe* (*Refutation*), their promised response to Coornhert's rejoinder, and more broadly to his *Proeve* which had occasioned the debate.[85] This booklet does not contain anything new: the ministers complain about Coornhert's enormous productivity—which will of course be countered with Coornhert's charge that the ministers are lazy—and about his habit of quoting Calvin and Beza in support of his own argument. They indignantly reject Coornhert's charge that they make themselves guilty of a new "popery" since, they assert, they are merely servants of God's Word. But, they add, it would be criminal consciously to expose the people to seductive spirits, and it is the responsibility of the government as "God's magistrates and vassals of the Lord Christ," they claim, to silence such seducers.[86] For the rest, they reiterate their arguments against the notion of perfect obedience to God's commandments, a notion defended by Coornhert in his response, which was not published until much later.[87] This response does not present new arguments either, but just as in other writings related to the debates, one sees a clear link between the debates and Coornhert's struggle against what he perceives as coercion of conscience, for he repeatedly makes the point that the main purpose of his unmasking of gross doctrinal error on the part of the Reformed is to open the eyes of the government so that it will not let this err-

---

[83]Coornhert, *Disputatie over den Catechismus,* fol. cccclixD.

[84]Ibid. After this letter, another (undated) letter from Coornhert to the *vroedschap* of Haarlem is printed, with a similar request: ibid., fols. cccclxD–cccclxiB.

[85]Cornelisz and Donteclock, *Wederlegginghe eens boecxkens ghenaemt Proeve* [*Refutation of a Booklet Named Examination*] (Delft: Aelbrecht Hendricxz, 1585).

[86]Cornelisz and Donteclock, *Wederlegginghe,* 7–8, 13.

[87]Coornhert, *Dolingen des Catechismi...* [*Errors of the Catechism*] (1586), *Wercken,* vol. 2, fols. cclviii–cccxxxvi. According to Nijenhuis, "Coornhert and the Heidelberg Catechism," 200, *Dolingen* contains the fullest explanation of Coornhert's rejection of the Catechism.

ing "church" usurp the magistrate's power.[88] The tide was, however, increasingly turning against toleration. After Orange's death and under the English Lord Leicester, the center of gravity in the Dutch Republic for a while shifted in favor of the Reformed. Coornhert had been Orange's protégé,[89] and now that the Prince was dead, Coornhert felt the noose being tightened. He refers to rumors that were afoot about plans to have him jailed should he write anything else against the ministers, and he foresees that his response to the ministers' *Refutation* may not be published during his lifetime.[90]

Until his death, Coornhert kept hoping for a resumption of the debate. One can only surmise why it was never resumed, but I suspect that the *communis opinio* among the Reformed ministers was that this debating was a wasted effort, for the more they debated the "gainsayer," the more they fanned the flames of his opposition. Debate only served the purpose, they felt, of feeding Coornhert's already considerable ego[91] and of creating interest for his heterodox ideas. It would thus be counterproductive in two ways. With regard to the authorities, it may well be that they lost interest and no longer regarded such debating as very fruitful, or even wise, under the pressing war conditions.

The link between the debates held in the late 1570s and 1580s and Coornhert's struggle to protect and promote freedom of conscience is evident. The very fact that these religious issues, so important to Coornhert, were publicly debated at all was a practical expression of Coornhert's concept of toleration. The perceived unfairness and partisanship attendant to the debates, especially to the one in Leiden, 1578, reflected the new position of the Reformed church as a favored religion and illustrated the points Coornhert made so eloquently in his 1582 *Synod on the Freedom of Conscience.* A casual reference in this last-named book also reveals that in Coornhert's mind there was no clear distinction between his theological disputes and writings and his struggle for toleration. In the dedication of the *Synod* (1582), he remarks that his struggle against the constraint of conscience had started ten years ago.[92] This must

---

[88]Coornhert, *Dolingen*, fol. cclxxR.

[89]*Het leven van D. V. Coornhert*, fol. 4C: "Coornhert...was generally, for the good of the nation, given Prince William's protection."

[90]Coornhert, *Dolingen*, fol. cclxxiiV; a bit later (fol. cclxxiiiv) he asserts that, if a law were to be passed holding punishable what Coornhert feels obliged to do (under the Golden Rule), he is ready to brave imprisonment and death.

[91]In their *Wederlegginghe*, 9, the Delft ministers speak of Coornhert's "thirst for glory" [*roemgiericheyt*].

[92]Coornhert, *Synod,* fol. A2v (unpaginated).

refer to his *Van de Toelatinge ende Decrete Godts* (1572) [*On What God Permits and What He Decrees*],[93] a work in which he attacks Calvin and Beza on the doctrine of predestination and which we would therefore be inclined to see as purely "theological." But the root of Coornhert's concerns is religious, and his belief in man's freedom of choice, perfectibility, and educability fundamental. The dedication of *Van de Toelatinghe* decries the Reformed dogmatic errors, which Coornhert sees as the substitution of human invention for the pure teachings contained in what should be the only, unpolluted wellspring of people's beliefs, the Bible. He warns his readers that they should not accept his words at face value either, but must test all the "pretenders" to truth.[94]

Coornhert's own reflections on all his debating reveal that he was not too modest about the impact he thought he could make. In a letter dating from the time of the debate with Saravia, Coornhert relates how some of his well wishers had expressed their doubts about the usefulness of disputations, but he disagrees.[95] Had Luther not "disputed," he writes, then his Reform would not have taken place.[96] If Luther was able, as a simple little monk, to take on the Catholic Church and even the emperor, then Coornhert could certainly take on Saravia, despite his own lack of learning.[97] Coornhert highlights the heroism of his lone struggle. He takes on the ministers and their assistants single-handed, with all the cards stacked against him, and he does so for the good of the nation, without any remuneration except in the form of the slander and vituperation hurled at him from the pulpits and in the writings of the ministers.[98] Disputations, he assures his readers, are free of

[93]Coornhert, "Van de Toelatinge ende Decrete Godts. Bedenckinghe of de H. Schrift ook inhoudt, sulcks als Mr. Johan Calvijn ende T. Beza daer van leeren," *Wercken,* vol. 2, fols. 526–534.

[94]See the poem quoted above, p. 73. In the 1580s his name becomes a liability, and his works published anonymously, e.g. his "Ware beschrijvinghe der Conscientien" ["True Description of Conscience"], *Wercken,* vol. 2, 209–22, or his *Zedekunst dat is Wellevenskunste* [*Ethics*], both written or finished during his 1585 stay in Emden. Elsewhere, Coornhert admonishes his readers not to be distracted from the wholesome message of a tract just because his name is attached to it, as with his *Toetzsteen der Ware Leeraren* [*Touchstone of True Teachers*], *Wercken,* vol. 1, fol. 46R.

[95]Coornhert, *Brieven-boeck,* Letter 74, undated (must be 1583; it speaks of an impending disputation and mentions Neeltje is mortally ill), fols. cxxviD–"cxxxiB" (must be cxxviiB). This letter is translated into modern Dutch in Coornhert, *Weet of rust,* 102–5.

[96]Coornhert, *Wercken,* vol. 3, fol."cxxxiAB" (must be cxxviiB); the same analogy in *Disputatie over den Catechismus,* fol. ccccxxxiV.

[97]Coornhert, *Disputatie,* fol. ccccxxxiV; see also *Hemel-werck ofte Quay-Toe-Verlaet,* in *Wercken,* vol. 2, fol. cccxlvA; and *Theriakel,* fol. ccxlviiiD.

risk. If he, the challenger, has truth on his side, then the others should be grateful to him for pointing out their error, and if the others turn out to be right, then they have nothing to fear, for their truth will shine all the more brilliantly.[99] The conditional nature of the preceding sentence probably reveals an essential difference between Coornhert and his opponents, for even to conceive of the theoretical possibility that they might be wrong was beyond them.

COORNHERT VS. JUSTUS LIPSIUS

The clash between Justus Lipsius, renowned humanist scholar and the pride of the newly founded University of Leiden, and Coornhert, self-styled critic and gadfly, in the end pitted two men against each other who both cherished humanist ideals and interests. The clash came about because they each harbored a very different agenda.[100] In his analysis of the debate between Coornhert and Saravia in The Hague, Nijenhuis characterized that confrontation as a "moment in the struggle between Humanism and the Reformation."[101] But such a characterization must necessarily be refined if we want to understand the confrontation between the humanist notary from Haarlem, and that other, famous, humanist scholar in Leiden. Their initial contacts, elicited by disagreements over fate and human freedom, set the tone. Their exchanges in connection with Lipsius's acclaimed manual for princes, published in 1589, resulted in a total rift between the two men.

Thus the debate signalled a parting of ways between, on one side, the humanist who regards the well-being of the state as his chief priority, and on the other side the humanist-Spiritualist who clings to the individual's right to follow the guiding light of his conscience. Both positions become understandable when placed in the context of developments of their era and the two men's very different value systems and mind-set.

---

[98]Coornhert, *Disputatie*, fol. cccclxivC: first he gives an account of Reformed slander against him, then follows question no. 112 of the Catechism on the ninth Commandment against backbiting.

[99]Coornhert, Letter 24, *Brieven-boeck*, foi. "cxxxiAB" (must be cxxviiAB).

[100]An earlier version of the following account is Gerrit Voogt, "Primacy of Individual Conscience or Primacy of the State? The Clash between Dirck Volckertsz. Coornhert and Justus Lipsius," *Sixteenth Century Journal* 28 (1997): 1231–49.

[101]Nijenhuis, "Coornhert and the Heidelberg Catechism"; cf. H. A. Enno van Gelder, *The Two Reformations in the 16th Century: A Study of the Religious Aspects and Consequences of the Renaissance and Humanism* (The Hague: Martinus Nijhoff, 1961), 309, who fits Coornhert into his category of the "major" [i.e. humanist] Reformation, together with Cassander and Lipsius.

Chapter 8

The precocious Lipsius entered the University of Louvain at age 16. At 24 he secured a position at the Protestant University of Jena, where he conformed to Lutheranism and accepted the Confession of Augsburg (a fact which he would later deny).[102] In 1576 he became Doctor of Law, and three years later he accepted a chair in History and Law at the fledgling University of Leiden. Corresponding with a general shift of gravity in the field of humanism and classical learning to the northern Netherlands, Leiden quickly became an important center of learning. At Leiden, Lipsius was seen as a spokesman of international Christian humanism.[103] His approach to history, using historical exempla as mirrors for one's behavior in the contemporary world, held great appeal.[104]

Lipsius became the great exponent and leading light of Neostoicism. Neostoicism represented a revival of Stoic philosophy. It aimed at harmonizing this outlook on life with Christianity. In this philosophy, constancy is the greatest virtue, a constancy that brings inner peace and is based on the rationality pervading everything and proceeding from the Λόγος that is equated with God's providence.

One of the attractions of Neostoicism was that it appeared to be able to transcend the religious divisions which were causing such misery at the time.[105] Humanist attention to the Roman Stoa, in trying to design a system of ethics containing a minimal amount of theology and an optimum of classical philosophical content,[106] was attractive to people seeking to steer clear of the endless doctrinal bickering and religious polarization with which Lipsius's age was so rife. Lipsius was conscious of his role at the vanguard of this Neostoic movement. He was sensitive to the needs of his time and thought he could be a

[102]Jason Lewis Saunders, *Justus Lipsius: The Philosophy of Renaissance Stoicism* (New York: Liberal Arts 1955), 1; on Lipsius's biography, see also Gerhard Oestreich, "Justus Lipsius in sua re," in *Formen der Selbstdarstellung: Analekten zu einer Geschichte des literarischen Selbstportraits.* Festgabe für Fritz Neubert (Berlin: Duncker und Humblot, 1956), 291–311; also M. E. H. N. Mout, "In het schip: Justus Lipsius en de Nederlandse Opstand tot 1591," in Groenveld et al., eds., *Bestuurders en Geleerden.* Festschrift for Prof. Dr. J. J. Woltjer (Amsterdam: De Bataafsche Leeuw, 1985), 56–57.

[103]Gerhard Oestreich, *Neostoicism and the Early Modern State*, ed. Brigitta Oestreich and H. G. Koenigsberger, trans. David McLintock (Cambridge: Cambridge University Press, 1982), 66.

[104]Gerhard Oestreich, "Justus Lipsius als Universal-gelehrter zwischen Renaissance und Barok," in Th. H. Lunsingh Scheurleer and G. H. M. Posthumus Meyjes, eds., *Leiden University in the Seventeenth Century: An Exchange of Learning* (Leiden: Universitaire Pers/E.J. Brill, 1975), 177–201. See also, for Lipsius' approach to history, David Halsted, "Distance, Dissolution and Neostoic Ideals: History and Self-Definition in Lipsius," *Humanistica Lovaniensia* 40 (1991): 262–74.

[105]Oestreich, *Neostoicism,* introduction, 8.

[106]M. E. H. N. Mout, "Heilige Lipsius, bid voor ons," *Tijdschrift voor Geschiedenis* 97, no. 1 (1984): 199.

guide. As one bent on transcending divisions by linking Christianity once again with Antiquity, he can perhaps be seen as the middle link between Erasmus and Grotius.[107] Lipsius and his kindred spirit, Michel de Montaigne, in their focus on Tacitus, combined skepticism with Stoicism. But Lipsius did not want to be considered a moral relativist. He saw Tacitus's description of court intrigue and vice as an analogy with what was wrong in his own age.[108]

Lipsius scored an immediate success with *De Constantia*,[109] published in 1584. This book was hailed as a font of Neostoic, confessionally neutral[110] exhortations and advice. At the time of publication, the fortunes of the new Dutch state seemed to be at an all-time low, with the prince assassinated in Delft, Parma's seemingly unstoppable conquests proceeding inexorably, and the constitutional muddle—revolving around the search for a sovereign for the rebellious provinces—far from over. In *De Constantia*, Lipsius refers to these tragic circumstances and offers the Stoic way to transcend and rise above the misery.

At the time relations between Lipsius and Coornhert—inasmuch as these existed—were still good. To be sure, Lipsius had been wary of Coornhert during the Coolhaes affair, but in a letter to Marnix of St. Aldegonde, he had also expressed veiled admiration.[111] Coornhert, who expressed his appreciation of *De Constantia*, announced that he planned on translating it. Plantin—who had recently become friends with the Haarlem notary—said he would imme-

[107] Oestreich, "Justus Lipsius als Universalgelehrter," 185.

[108] Halsted, "Distance, Dissolution and Neo-Stoic Ideals," 268. See also Richard Tuck, *Philosophy and Government 1572–1651*. Ideas in Context (Cambridge: Cambridge University Press, 1993), 40; Martin van Gelderen, "Holland und das Preussentum: Justus Lipsius zwischen Niederländischem Aufstand und Brandenburg-Preussischem Absolutismus," *Zeitschrift für historische Forschung* 23, no. 1(1996): 34.

[109] The full title is: *De Constantia libri duo, Qui alloquium praecipue continent in Publicis malis*. I used the "Ultima editio," (Antwerp: Plantin, 1615); translated into English as *Two Bookes of Constancie*, by Sir John Stradling, 1594, ed. and intro. Rudolf Kirk, notes by Clayton Morris Hall (New Brunswick, N.J.: Rutgers University Press, 1939).

[110] See Gerhard Oestreich, *Antiker Geist und Moderner Staat bei Justus Lipsius (1547–1606): Der Neustoizismus als politische Bewegung*, ed. and introd. Nicolette Mout (Göttingen: Vandenhoeck & Ruprecht, 1989), 54.

[111] *Iusti Lipsi Epistolae* (hereafter *ILE*) (Brussels: Koninklijke Academie voor Wetenschappen, Letteren en Schone Kunsten van België), vol. 1(1564–1583), 1978, ed. A. Gerlo, M. A. Nauwelaerts, Hendrik D. L. Vervliet, 82 03 17, 17 March 1582: "Miscent se huic negotio quos nollem, atque in caeteros Harlemensis quidam tibi notus: mihi hactenus, ut sciam illum nec patriae nec religioni e[ss]e aequum, Cornhartium dico."

diately publish the translation. But Coornhert soon discovered an objectionable passage in *De Constantia* on fate and free will.

This passage was not central to Lipsius's book. In *De Constantia*, Lipsius,
wanting to escape the troubles in the Netherlands, is instructed in wisdom
and constancy by a friend (Charles Langius), who assures him that flight cannot be a remedy for the inner maladies of the mind. The public evils that sur-
round them come from God, the originator of everything, except sin.[112] He
should not fret against God's providence and necessity, born of providence,
but should keep in mind that all things change and eventually perish. It is in
this context that he discusses fate as distinct from providence, though proceeding from it: providence is God's power to see, know, and govern all things,
but fate is in the things themselves.[113] However, when Lipsius accuses Langius
of thus introducing pagan Stoic notions through the back door, Langius sets
forth an elaborate defense in which he presents four differences between his
understanding of Fate, and what "they," i.e. the pagan-Stoic thinkers, have to
say about it.[114]

In the context sketched above, the passage on sinning occurs to which
Coornhert took exception. The question is whether, because God foresees all,
man therefore sins necessarily. Yes, Langius asserts, you sin necessarily, and yet
of your own free will, since God foresaw that man should sin freely.[115] God,
Langius explains, helps us with the good in us, but he is not the author of evil,
and Langius compares this situation with the playing of an instrument which
is out of tune: the fault is not in the player, but in the instrument.

This passage gave rise to an exchange of letters between the two.[116] Lipsius,
not wanting to meet personally with Coornhert, professed a lack of time and
preference for the clarity of written communication in such weighty matters. It
seems obvious, though, that he is quite aware of Coornhert's reputation as a
debater—indeed, how could he not be, after the great public debate of the previous year—and chooses to avoid confrontation and expected contentiousness.[117]

---

[112]"peccatum excipio": Lipsius, *De Constantia*, chap. 14, p. 23 [C4-r]; on the emphasis, in
Neostoicism, on the *vita activa*, see Thomas M. Conley, *Rhetoric in the European Tradition* (New
York: Longman, 1990), 113–14.

[113]"Fatum ad res ipsas magis descendere videtur, in iisque singulis spectari." Lipsius, *De
Constantia*, 33 [E1-r]

[114]Lipsius, *De Constantia*, 36 [E2-v].

[115]"Nempe hoc providit, ut eo modo pecces quo providit: providit autem ut libere: *igitur
necessario libere peccas.*" Ibid. (my emphasis).

[116]These letters can be found in *ILE*, vol. 2 (1584–87).

In his initial response to Coornhert's queries, Lipsius tries to shrug him off by assuring him that his intentions are good. He is even willing to meet him halfway by allowing him to leave out the sentence to which he objected.[118] This response does not satisfy Coornhert, who sees an insurmountable contradiction between the idea of free will and God's goodness on the one hand, and the posited necessity of man's sinning on the other. Again, in dealing with a seemingly abstruse theological question such as this one, Coornhert is especially adamant because he sees a direct link with the defense of the freedom of conscience. This is evident in a letter to Lipsius dated 12 April 1584, in which Coornhert states that he regards himself as God's "crowbar" (*breekijzer*), used to break open the prison of men's consciences.[119] He explains that in his view to sin implies that one does wrong voluntarily, a wrong that could be avoided. The element of choice in sinning leads Coornhert directly to his perfectibilist beliefs.

In his response, Lipsius reiterates that God created man with free will. Providence, an attribute of God, does not imply causation, but "necessity is found in the fact that God has foreseen that you shall do these things. There is necessity...in the outcome."[120]

This response did not satisfy Coornhert either; he would, one feels, take nothing short of complete surrender, that is, a formal withdrawal of the passage, or a rewriting in the Coornhertian spirit. Saravia, who had heard of Coornhert's correspondence with the Leiden scholar, privately alerted his colleagues in Delft that Coornhert was trying to ensnare Lipsius into a debate with him because he just could not get enough.[121] Their viewpoints are not very far apart, but Coornhert is not easily satisfied. Coornhert saw only three options in the matter:[122] (a) God is the originator of sin, humanity remaining

[117]See Bonger, *Leven en werk*, 141, who suggests that Coornhert also saw this refusal to meet as an excuse on Lipsius' part. Perhaps this perceived shyness and evasiveness on the part of Lipsius made Coornhert all the more persistent.

[118]*ILE*, vol. 2, letters of 18 March and 9 1584 (84 03 18 and 84 04 09).

[119]*ILE*, vol. 2, 84 04 12 (12 April 1584); cf. Brandt, *History of the Reformation*, 2:436, where Coornhert is described, in a final assessment, as, among other things, "a voluntary demolisher of the murthering prison of consciences."

[120]"necessitas t[ame]n hoc ipso est q[uod] De[us] p[rae]vidit id te facturum. Necessitas...in eventu." *ILE*, vol. 2, 84 04 15 (15 April 1584)

[121]Nijenhuis, *Adrianus Saravia*, 275, "Documents," no. 7, Saravia to Arent Cornelisz, Leiden, 23 April 1584:"Interea...Cornhertius...querit aliam antagonistam. Scis quem? Lipsium nostrum iam literis velitatur et in harenam pertrahere conatur hominem ei dissimulum."

[122]*ILE*, vol. 2, 84 04 24 C (24 April 1584).

passive; (b) sinning is done conjointly, by humanity and God; or (c) humanity sins without any action or will on God's part. Only the last of these options is acceptable, he writes, and neither fate nor predestination has a place here. Humanity sins, God witnesses his sinning and is hurt by it. If we allow, he writes, for necessity in this matter, then God would be unjustified in punishing humanity for its sins, and humanity, given such necessity, would have little incentive to better its wicked ways since it is God who wills the sinning. Such a sentiment was anathema to Reformed and Lutherans, for God's actions cannot be circumscribed by, or be subjected to, the laws of our logic. Still, Coornhert felt strongly that any view that implies involvement of God with humanity's sinning insults God's majesty and deprives humanity of its dignity and freedom. Sinning, Coornhert explains, occurs outside God's will: God did not want humanity to sin, but he did want humankind to have the power to sin in order to make itself free. What, otherwise, is the source of evil? Was not Satan himself a fallen angel?[123] This position reveals clearly the extent of Coornhert's faith in the power of humanity's reason. In the Augustinian, the Lutheran, or Reformed tradition, the mere thought that something could possibly be outside God's will, or that humans can determine or judge what God can or cannot do, is blatantly heretical. The difference between Coornhert's position and the criticized passage of De Constantia, on the other hand, seems minimal. Yet, no agreement is reached.

The outcome of the exchange was thus inconclusive: their correspondence simply ceased, and Moretus, not Coornhert, translated Lipsius's book. Relations between the two men had soured, and the encounter, in which Lipsius demonstrated his eagerness to avoid confrontation and Coornhert confirmed his intransigence in matters that he saw as vital to his notion of freedom of conscience, set the stage for the later, sometimes vitriolic, exchange elicited by Lipsius's book on politics.[124]

In the five years that passed after the publication of the De Constantia, the need for stability, consolation, and guidance in the war-torn Netherlands only increased. First Anjou died. A month later Orange died, at a time when moves were made that might have led to the conferring on him of the title of "count of Holland and Zeeland," and of sovereignty over these two provinces. The

[123]Ibid. Dekker, in "Wilsvrijheid volgens Coornhert," 107–19, points out that Coornhert's theological explanation was not new (as Bonger assumed), but can be found in the scholastic tradition of Thomas Aquinas and Duns Scotus.
[124]Bonger, Leven en werk, 143.

nation remained in constitutional limbo.[125] The greatest shock came in 1585 with the loss of Antwerp, which created an atmosphere of crisis in the rebellious provinces.[126] This momentous event shook the Republic's self-confidence and may have contributed to the willingness to grant extensive powers to Lord Robert Dudley, earl of Leicester, hailed as "governor general" of the United Provinces when he arrived from England as a result of the Treaty of Nonsuch. He was expected to exert authority in conjunction with the States General, but soon took on the airs of a sovereign overlord, established the government in Utrecht, and aligned himself with the militant, populist Calvinist faction. During this interlude (1586–87) chaos reigned and the rebellious provinces teetered on the brink of civil war.[127] Elizabeth's peace overtures to Spain were deliberately made public by Oldenbarnevelt,[128] to discredit Leicester. This move fatally undermined the earl's position, for it turned even the Calvinist faction against him. When Leicester left the Netherlands for good, the matter of sovereignty was left unresolved and fell, by default, into the lap of the States General—a most unfortunate thing, in Lipsius's view.[129]

The failed Armada (1588), that Spanish project of an invasion of England gone awry, proved a turning point in the Revolt. It also marked the beginning of the end of Parma's string of successes. After that date, Spain's distraction by its intervention in the French wars of religion, the military success of Maurice and Willem Lodewijk, and the political genius of Oldenbarnevelt would turn the tide of war in favor of the Dutch Republic.

Lipsius remained in Leiden during this period. True to his inclination not to involve himself in politics, he had remained aloof from the factional strife during the Leicester era and gave even his friend Saravia, who had become implicated in a pro-Leicester conspiracy, only lukewarm support.[130]

Coornhert's life after 1584 seems to have become rather unsettled. After the death of his wife in that year,[131] he left Haarlem and tried to settle in Leiden and to begin studying at the university. He was not admitted, despite

---

[125]See Parker, *Dutch Revolt*, 201, 205–7; Israel, *Dutch Republic*, 214–15.

[126]See A. M. van der Woude, "De crisis in de Opstand na de val van Antwerpen," in *Bijdragen voor de geschiedenis der Nederlanden* 14 (1959–60): 38–56.

[127]See Tjaden, "De reconquista mislukt," 255–57.

[128]Holland's *Advocaat*, i.e. dominant figure in the States of Holland and their spokesman in the States General, and champion of Holland's particularism.

[129]See Mout, "In het schip," 61.

[130]Nijenhuis, *Adrianus Saravia*, 105.

[131]See Becker, *Bronnen*, no. 145 (6 November 1584), p. 91.

the fact that he promised, in his request for admission, not to write about religion unless he were forced by published writings of his opponents.[132] In August 1585, he went to Emden in east Friesland, just across the border, a place traditionally harboring many Dutch religious refugees.[133] During this exile, which lasted about a year, he finished his *Ethics, or the Art of Living Well* (*Zedekunst dat is Wellevenskunste*), probably his best known book, and the first book on ethics to appear in a vernacular. It was Spieghel, not Coornhert, who sent a copy of the *Zedekunst* to Lipsius, a sign of the cooled relations between the professor and the debater.[134]

In 1586, Coornhert came back to Haarlem and sold his house.[135] In 1588, he planned to move to Delft to spend a quiet year there, during which he intended to complete and organize his *loci communes,* the concordance he had been working on for some thirty years.[136] He would stay with his friend, Cornelis Boomgaert. But things did not turn out as planned. First, when he was about to leave, Boomgaert let him know, in April, that the bailiff (*schout*) had notified him, on behalf of the mayors, that they would not allow Coornhert to reside in Delft. Coornhert by this time had already rented out his house, so now he had to find room and board in Haarlem.[137] Later, in June, he went to Delft anyway, and sent a petition to the Delft mayors that emphasized his unblemished name, commemorated his service to the country, having warned against the Enkhuizen conspiracy, and reiterated that he was not there to cause trouble but only wanted peace and quiet so he could work. He wrote that he

---

[132]Becker, *Bronnen*, no. 147 (March 1585) p. 92. Saravia was rector of the university at this time; see also Nijenhuis, *Adrianus Saravia*, Documents no. 11, Saravia to Arent Cornelisz, Leiden, 15 March 1585, p. 279.

[133]Becker, *Bronnen*, no. 152 (12 August 1585), p. 95: record of Coornhert's announcement that he was leaving Haarlem due to some "ill-wishers" (*quaetwilligen*). He wanted to remain on the books as a citizen of Haarlem. In January there were apparently rumors that Coornhert may have died abroad: see ibid., no. 153, p. 96.

[134]Bonger, *Leven en werk*, 143; see also Güldner, *Toleranz-Problem*, 90–91.

[135]Becker, *Bronnen*, pp. 96–97: from no. 154 (22 July 1586), we see that by then he is back; he sells his house in December: no. 155 (4 December 1586).

[136]Coornhert, *Naem-scherm D. V. Coornherts Tegen de ondaedt tot Delft aen hem betoont…,* in *Wercken*, vol. 3, fol. ccxciiiiAB. In 1583, in his request to the States of Holland after the suspension of the debate in The Hague, Coornhert had asked permission to go abroad—if he is not granted freedom of speech—so he can finish this monumental task: see *Het leven van D. V. Coornhart* fol. 4B (where the request is cited).

[137]This must be the correct meaning of Coornhert's statement; *Naem-scherm* fol. ccxciiiiB, that he had to "buy my table (my residence having been rented out)…" ["kocht mijn tafel (mijn woonplaats was verheurt)…"]. Bonger, *Leven en werk*, 134, implausibly takes this to mean that he had to buy back his own writing table.

hoped the magistrate would not, like the Spanish Inquisition, act against someone based on anonymous accusations only.[138] On behalf of the mayors, the pensionary of Delft came and personally explained to Coornhert that the refusal to let him stay in Delft had been caused by their desire to avoid religious commotion. His disputations had earlier caused quite a stir among the townsfolk, and they wanted to prevent further polarization.[139] However, he assured Coornhert that he could stay, so the latter had his belongings sent over from Haarlem and worked and lived quietly in Delft until October. Then, suddenly, on October 3, he was told to pack up and leave town within 24 hours. The only explanation given was that he was not a citizen. Coornhert naturally saw this unceremonious expulsion, without due process, as a practical example of intolerance, and clearly suspected his Reformed enemies in Delft as forces behind this deed. The tract that resulted from this event, *Naem-scherm*, bitterly denounces what had happened, and typically stresses that he is not seditious nor a traitor (reasons for expulsion under town laws). On the contrary, he asserts, it is the efforts of the Reformed to impose their straitjacket on consciences that has stirred up unrest. "Thus," he concludes, "my necessary denunciation of the Reformed religion with truth, and forced by my conscience, is also the reason of my expulsion."[140] However, had Coornhert not alerted the authorities to his presence in Delft through his petition, he might have been able to stay on in Delft indefinitely.[141]

Coornhert next settled in Gouda, which had a reputation of tolerance.[142] It was the residence of his regular printer (Tournay), and its liberal minister Herbertsz was quite popular.[143] With a typical pun, Coornhert expresses his appreciation for the hospitality accorded him by the "Goudenaars" by stating that "by 'delving' one reaches the 'gold,' and I found the people of Gouda via those of Delft."[144] In Gouda he would spend the rest of his days, planning to finish his concordance. This did not happen, due to his perusal of Justus Lip-

---

[138]Abels and Wouters, *Nieuw en ongezien* 2:161; Coornhert, *Naem-scherm*, fol. ccxciiiiD.

[139]Abels and Wouters, *Nieuw en ongezien* 2: 64, 243; Coornhert, *Naem-scherm*, fol. ccxciiiiD.

[140]Coornhert, *Naem-scherm*, fol. ccxcvB; fol. ccxcvC.

[141]Bonger, *Leven en werk*, 135.

[142]See Hibben, *Gouda in Revolt*. Coornhert, in his account of the 1583 debate in The Hague, *Disputatie over den Catechismus, Wercken*, vol. 3, fol. ccccxlixA, writes that Gouda was not represented at the disputation, adding: "(for, as I see it, they are impartial)."

[143]Hibben, *Gouda in Revolt*, 123–24.

[144]Becker, *Bronnen*, p. 292, Letter no. 49: "Door 't delven comt men aen 't gout, door de Delvenaars come ick by de Gouwenaers." Delft contains the root word *delven* ("to delve"), and *goud* is Dutch for gold.

sius's new book, in 1590, entitled *Politicorum sive civilis doctrinae libri sex*,[145] (from now on referred to as the *Politica*). This book delineated the features of an ideal political structure and was conceived, more or less, as a manual for princes and rulers. Lipsius saw the *Politica* as the political component of the personal Neostoic precepts he had earlier set forth in *De Constantia*.[146]

The discussion, in the *Politica*, of the problem of the role of the state and the prince vis-à-vis religion touched the core of Coornhert's beliefs. Aware of the passage of time and the imminent end of his life,[147] and apprehensive of the perils facing the cause of toleration, he geared up once more for battle. Coornhert by now was nationally known through his publications and debates. He had advised the late prince. His marriage, like that of Lipsius (who was about 25 years his junior), had remained childless, so his thoughts and deeds in a cause that was dear to him were his only heritage. Lipsius, on the other hand, who cultivated a public image of Stoic aloofness of the vicissitudes and tumult of contemporary life, dreaded and braced himself for the controversy that might be stirred by the portion of his book on the sensitive issue of church-state relations.[148]

As stated, the *Politica*, as a Neo-Stoic manual for rulers, was meant especially for the perusal of princes and the top echelons of society.[149] It distinguishes between the two main guides of political life, prudence and virtue. The latter embraces piety, which can be divided into belief and worship. It is striking that also in discussing belief and God, Lipsius only quotes the Classics, not Scripture. Also apparent, in his discussion of religion, is Lipsius's conservative bent. It is his conviction—and that, it should be added, of most of his contemporaries—that traditions ought not to be changed lightly.

---

[145]Justus Lipsius, *Politicorum sive civilis doctrinae libri sex*, 1589 (Antwerp: Moretus, 1610); this edition includes *De Una Religione adversus Dialogistam*, Lipsius's reaction to Coornhert's *Proces vant Ketterdoden*. There is a 1594 English translation: Justus Lipsius, *Sixe Bookes of Politickes or Civil Doctrine*, trans. William Jones (London: Richard Field, 1594; facsimile repr., Amsterdam: Da Capo Press, 1970).

[146]Halsted, "Distance, Dissolution and Neo-Stoic Ideals," 262 n. 2.

[147]See e.g. the letter to a friend, written sometime after 1582, where he speaks of his "old age, leading me to expect death's arrival at any hour," in Becker, *Bronnen*, Letter 48, p. 291. As we have seen, during the debate in Leiden (1578) he already brought up his advanced age (and contrasted this with the youthfulness of his Reformed interlocutors).

[148]Bonger, *Leven en werk*, 144; Güldner, *Toleranz-Problem*, 94.

[149]This is obvious in the full title: *Politicorum sive Civilis Doctrinae libri sex: Qui ad Principatum maxime spectant*. An extensive summary of the book in Oestreich, *Antiker Geist*, 106–47.

With regard to conscience, another aspect of piety, Lipsius states that a good man will cling to a sound conscience, even if it leads to his death. However, virtue in general remains subordinate to prudence, which is defined as "the awareness of or the love for the things that one ought, publicly or privately, to eschew or to strive for."[150] In the following pages Lipsius discusses the organization of government, the desirable features of a prince, the system of justice, and the need for and nature of good advisers. He subdivides civil prudence into human and "divine" affairs. In only three brief chapters Lipsius discusses the *res divinae* (religious matters), and then spins out the *res humanae* (secular matters) over the rest of book 4 (chapters 5–14).

Consistent with the audience he aims to reach, and the general purpose of his book, Lipsius restricts his treatment of religious policy in the three aforementioned chapters to the role of the state.[151] The prince does not have the right to determine dogma. His function with regard to dogma is to exercise "a certain supervision, and this more for the sake of protection than for the sake of knowing it [i.e. its contents]."[152] The care for religion is vital to the prince and for the realm's protection—since religious subjects are less likely to rebel and be disloyal—as well as for its expansion (Ad augmentum etiam Imperii).[153] Religion is the cement that holds society together,[154] and it is therefore vital that it remain pure and unmixed, for "where it is one, it is the source of unity, but where mixed, you always find turmoil."[155] He cites the warning given to Augustus against people who introduce new gods, because they will be the source of all sorts of disturbances. That prince is prudent who maintains "the religion of the one God" according to the old rites and customs. In the third chapter, after reiterating that there should only be one religion in a state, Lipsius utters an impassioned cry of dismay over the misery caused by religious dissension.[156] He advocates a nuanced policy with regard to religious

[150]"intellectum et dilectum rerum, quae publice privatimque fugiendae aut appetendae." Lipsius, *Politica*, bk. 1, chap. 7, p. 31.

[151]Güldner, *Toleranz-Problem*, 95; Güldner, 91–99, gives an excellent analysis of the chapters of the *Politica* that pertain to religion.

[152]"inspectio quaedam, idque tuendi magis quam cognoscendi caussa": Lipsius, *Politica*, bk. 4, chap. 2, p. 78.

[153]Ibid.

[154]Lipsius, *Politica: Religio, & timor dei solus est, qui cus odit hominum inter se societatem* [in the margin: Lactantius].

[155]"Unionis auctor illa una: & a confusa ea, semper turbe; ibid., 79.

[156]"O melior mundi pars, quas dissidiorum faces religio tibi accendit! Colliduntur inter se Christianae reipub. capita,& milleni aliquot homines perierunt ac pereunt per speciem Pietatis"; ibid., 80.

dissidents. Those who dissent in public and try to sway others to their cause, ought to be punished, "most of all if they are provocative,"[157] advice that is followed by the ominous sentence that would stir up much controversy: "This is not the place for clemency. Burn, cut, so that rather some parts perish than the entire body [in the margin: Seneca]."[158] But in handling religious dissidents the prince must take into consideration the timeliness of his actions. If the state should suffer from immediate intervention he should bide his time. Again, he uses the medical analogy (as, Lipsius would explain later, had been intended in Seneca's *ure, seca* ("burn, cut"), the phrase to which Coornhert would take such exception), for he states that a prudent physician, bent on healing, will also refrain from untimely intervention with his patient.

Those, on the other hand, who "sin" in private, Lipsius continues, should be left alone.[159] Forcing people's personal consciences will turn them into hypocrites. The arguments invoked in this connection are traditional arguments for toleration (some of which would be expurgated from later editions, after Lipsius's return to Louvain, because of the Index): that God is the ruler of people's minds, that nothing is more free than religion, that the only right approach is to teach and instruct,[160] for when an instrument is out of tune, you do not destroy it, but you tune it.[161]

Before Coornhert's critique is discussed, mention must be made of the wide acclaim with which this book was received in all of Europe as attested by the many reprints and translations. People admired the, by now famous, Lipsian-Tacitan style (concise, lucid), and appreciated his almost encyclopedic summary of the wisdom of the ancient world. Many contemporaries shared Lipsius's belief in the "similitudo temporum," the Polybian notion that certain ages are similar. A close parallel was seen between the troubled sixteenth-

[157]"Maxime si turbant": ibid.

[158]"Clementiae non hic locus. *Ure, seca, ut membrorum potius aliquod, quam totum corpus intereat* [in the margin: Seneca]"; Lipsius, *Politica*.

[159]Güldner, *Toleranz-Problem*, 98, emphasizes that Lipsius, in describing those who "privatim peccant," employs the first person, which seems to imply personal involvement (because of his sympathy for, or adherence to, the Family of Love, which is discussed later).

[160]Lipsius, *Politica*, 82.

[161]"In fidibus siquid discrepat, non abrumpis statim, sed paulatim reducis ad concentum: in Fide cur non idem fit?" Lipsius, *Politica*, 82. In the original edition (1589), the text read: "In fidibus siquid discrepat, non abrumpis per iracundiam, sed paullatim reducis ad concentum: in Fide cur non idem fit?": Güldner, *Toleranz-Problem*, 174 (Güldner, 169–74, juxtaposes the different versions of the chapters on religion in the *Politica*, to show the differences).

century world and the imperial Rome described by Tacitus.[162] The time seemed right for the resurrection of a Stoic philosophy incorporating and embracing a Christianity unencumbered by doctrinal factionalism.[163] In all of the *Politica*, there is "no word of faith in Christ,"[164] and the book could theoretically have just as well been published in a pre- or non-Christian society, that is, in the contemporary Ottoman Empire. Yes, Lipsius was convinced that it was best if a state recognize only one official religion. But in his polarized world of religious strife, and in the situation where he found himself as a Leiden professor, he himself was fully aware of the risks attached to a positive identification of the "one religion" that he wanted maintained in a state.

The tone of the correspondence which developed between Coornhert and Lipsius regarding the chapters of the *Politica* devoted to religion soon became acerbic, until Lipsius broke it off and wrote to their mutual friend, Spieghel, that he expected nothing from further communication with Coornhert, whom he labeled "savage, obstinate, and full of venom."[165]

In his first letter to Lipsius, Coornhert merely asks for clarification, giving Lipsius the option of either an oral or written clarification. From the onset Coornhert sounds peremptory, challenging, and somewhat threatening, promising that if Lipsius does not respond, "this person feels compelled by his conscience openly to publish his feelings, and to sprinkle water on your holy fire."[166] In response, Lipsius repeats his position. He is for one state religion, but punishment in his putative state is only meant for seditious and obstinate heretics. He beseeches his critic to refrain from personal attacks.[167] In his long and fundamental reply, Coornhert reiterates the view that also permeated his

---

[162]Oestreich, *Neostoicism*, 59–60; Halsted, "Distance, Dissolution and Neo-Stoic Ideals," 268.

[163]Oestreich, *Antiker Geist*, 68. See also J. Kluyskens, "Justus Lipsius's levenskeuze: Het irenisme," *Bijdragen en mededelingen betreffende de geschiedenis der Nederlanden* 88, no. 1 (1973): 19–37, esp. 20, 36.

[164]Oestreich, *Neostoicism*, 42; yet, Oestreich claims elsewhere that, nevertheless, the work is permeated by an "urchristlicher Geist": Oestreich, "Justus Lipsius als Universalgelehrter," 185. The same would be said of Coornhert's *Zedekunst*; e.g. Conrad Busken Huet, *Land van Rembrandt: Studiën over de Noord-Nederlandse beschaving in de zeventiende eeuw*, 5th ed. (Haarlem: H.D. Tjeenk Willink & Zoon, n.d.), 2:62, in reference to the *Zedekunst*: "Eene moraal dus, zonder geloof; een toegepast christendom zonder Christus...."

[165]"ferox, asperum et cum multa mixtione fellis." *ILE*, vol. 3, 90 04 17, Lipsius to Spieghel, 17 April 1590. Again, Güldner, *Toleranz-Problem*, 99–104, gives a thorough analysis of the correspondence.

[166]*ILE* vol. 3, Coornhert to Lipsius, 90 03 19 (19 March 1590).

[167]*ILE*, 90 03 23, Lipsius to Coornhert (23 March 1590). Contrary to his custom, Lipsius wrote this letter in Dutch.

Synod of the Freedom of Conscience. For a state to have but one religion would be beautiful, but there is no impartial judge to determine which of the competing sects of Christianity should be awarded that position.[168] His letter is wrathful and sharp, but does not contain invective. It sounds the familiar theme, namely that with fire and sword one can kill heretics, but not the heresy, that the truth kills heresy, leaves alive the heretic, and allows the latter the time in which he can still receive the gift of faith. For Coornhert, as our exploration of his ideas on the topic has amply demonstrated, the individual's conscience is the measure of all things, and it is the prerogative of no man, not even the prince, to judge. Thus he wants a separation of church and state, with the state as the neutral arbiter, standing above the sects and making sure that there is a level playing field and that law and order are maintained. Here lies the fundamental misunderstanding between the two men, for Lipsius also wants the separation of church and state and does not give theologians any role in politics, nor does he allow the state to interfere in doctrinal matters. He speaks from the vantage point of the prince, and this prince merely accepts the one official religion that he finds. Lipsius was indifferent to the theological coloring of the state's religion,[169] and in fact ultimately even the question about whether the state religion was Catholic or Protestant was meaningless to him.[170] Yet, in a polarized world in which so much hinged on religious allegiances, and in which Lipsius himself served at a Protestant university, it was difficult for him to come out and say this openly, and furthermore, such forwardness would have been incongruous with Lipsius's cautious nature. As a result, he became rather vulnerable to Coornhert's challenges and attacks.

From this point on (the end of March 1590), there is no longer any real communication between the two men: Lipsius does not send the brief, civil original of his response to Coornhert,[171] but rather sends a longer, bitter epistle crafted with an eye to publication. Lipsius reiterates his position, corrects the "misreading" of his *ure, seca* (by demonstrating that it had been intended as a surgical allegory), and emphasizes that there is simply no precedent for Coornhert's proposed unbridled freedom of religion, and that "all good men

---

[168]*ILE*, vol. 3, 90 03 29, Coornhert to Lipsius (29 March 1590).

[169]See Güldner, *Toleranz-Problem*, 114.

[170]"Nam omnis religio et nulla religio sunt mihi unum et idem. Et apud me lutherana et calvinistarum doctrina pari passu ambulant." Quoted in Oestreich, *Antiker Geist*, 55 n. 18. This indifference to the particular "label" of Christianity must of course be seen in connection with his sympathy for the Family of Love, to be discussed later.

[171]*ILE*, vol. 3, 90 03 31, Lipsius to Coornhert (31 March 1590).

and those who possess a mere spark of intelligence abhor excessive license...."[172]

It is worth noting that Lipsius's use of the verb *vincere* ("to defeat") in the passage cited above indicates that the exchange had by now turned into a battle. And Coornhert, also, in a letter to Spieghel, uses martial terms to describe the dispute, calling it "a mortal struggle to prevent the new murdering and burning...." And probably in response to his friend's advice to take it easy at his age and not rush headlong into a new unpleasant confrontation, he comments that "if I die in harness at a time that I [actually] ought to rest, then at least no one will accuse me of a lack of will."[173] In general it seems, as observed earlier in connection with the debate in The Hague, that pugnacity, honor, a lack of openness generally mark disputations and colloquies of the sixteenth century.

In his response, which remained unanswered, Coornhert gives full rein to his anger. He states that if Lipsius grants the prince the right to judge in religious matters—something Lipsius did not actually do, as has been shown—"then you make all the Reformed here...rebels guilty of a capital crime...."[174] The underlying suggestion is that Lipsius is a covert supporter of the Spanish king, certainly a grave accusation at a critical period in the struggle between the rebel provinces and King Philip! He challenges Lipsius to show his true colors and identify what "public" religion he embraces.[175] He defuses Lipsius's argument-by-precedent, for the latter had to show "not that it [i.e. enforcement of one religion] has been done, but that it has been rightly done. Or does antiquity turn injustice into justice?"[176]

This argument cuts to the core of Lipsius's entire approach to Antiquity and its models, based as it is on authoritative precedent.[177] Coornhert appears to recognize the primacy the state has for his opponent, but rejects it, asserting that "states exist for the sake of the people, not the people for the sake of the state."[178]

---

[172]"omnes boni viri abhorrent et quibus exiguum aliquod lumen mentis...." Ibid., 90 04 01, Lipsius to Coornhert (1 April 1590). This letter was incorporated in Lipsius's *De Una Religione*.

[173]Coornhert, *Wercken*, vol. 3, fol. 147r (Letter 97).

[174]*ILE*, vol. 3, 90 04 07, Coornhert to Lipsius (7 April 1590).

[175]Ibid.

[176]*ILE*. In this context, he also implies pedantry on Lipsius's part, speaking of the latter's pleasure in the artful sayings of the pagans.

[177]Halsted, "Distance, Dissolution and Neo-Stoic Ideals," 263, 270–71.

[178]*ILE*, vol. 3, 90 04 07, Coornhert to Lipsius (7 April 1590). This passage is also quoted in Bonger, *Leven en werk*, 146.

When communication ceases, and Spieghel's efforts at mediation remain fruitless, Coornhert publishes his last great work, the *Trial of the Killing of Heretics and the Constraint of Conscience* (*Proces van 't Ketter-dooden,* from now on referred to as *Trial*).[179] It is long, rambling in places, and overall rather uneven and repetitious.[180] Especially for one familiar with Coornhert's *Synod on the Freedom of Conscience,* the *Trial* would contain few surprises. Yet, it includes very effective and moving passages, sometimes crafted in inimitable Coornhertian poetic prose.[181]

A greater contrast in styles is difficult to imagine than that between Coornhert's florid, elaborate prose and the terse, Tacitan succinctness of Lipsius, who considered *brevitas* as the most important feature of style and as "an attribute of a mature writer."[182] On the other hand, Coornhert repeatedly criticizes Lipsius's pedantry,[183] and complains that his excessive brevity makes him unclear, as in his unfortunate use of the *ure, seca,* which Lipsius later tried to explain away.[184]

Generally, the themes running through the *Trial* had already been discussed in the correspondence preceding its publication. Most of them derive from the central issue for Coornhert: the absolute separation of church and state, which he felt Lipsius had violated by making the ruler the defender of the one religion.[185] Güldner, in *Toleranz-Problem,* states correctly, that the domi-

---

[179]Coornhert, *Proces* (1590), *Wercken,* vol. 2, fols. 43–170, followed by a second volume of the *Trial,* directed against Theodore Beza. A shortened Latin translation of the *Proces* was published posthumously: *Epitome processus de occidendis haereticis et vi conscientiis inferenda inter Justum Lipsium Politicorum auctorem anno 1589 ea asserentem et Theod. Coornhertium eadem refringentem* (Gouda: Zas-Hoensz., 1592).

[180]Lipsius's criticism of Coornhert's style, where he saw "flumen verborum ubique video, mentis vix guttam." (*ILE,* vol. 3, 90 10 00, Lipsius to the States of Holland, early October 1590), was partially inspired by rancor, but with regard to the "stream of words" his criticism hit the mark. Cf. Güldner, *Toleranz-Problem,* 105, on the difference in style.

[181]To give one example: In connection with the question whether one ought to take personal risks, he states: "Wie pericule bemint, die sal daer inne vergaen. Eyghen pericule *wijslijck* aen te gaen tot anderluyden nut is *prijslijck*: ende zo te *verderven* is het ware leven te *verwerven*." [my emphasis]: "Whoever loves danger [for the sake of it], will perish by it. Prudently to accept danger for the benefit of others is laudable: and to die in this way means to attain eternal life."; *Proces,* fol. lxxviiiC.

[182]Mark Morford, *Stoics and Neostoics: Rubens and the Circle of Lipsius* (Princeton, N.J.: Princeton University Press, 1991), 72.

[183]Coornhert, *Proces,* fol. lxxiB, where he calls Lipsius a "word-juggler"; and fol. lxxiiB, where he attacks Lipsius's "boastful pagan Latinizing."

[184]Ibid., fol. lxxvCD.

[185]The crucial statement is made at the beginning of chap. 2, bk. 4 of Lipsius's *Politica,* where the prince is given the "inspectio" of religion, although limited.

nant themes of the *Trial*—how a prince should know that the religion he selects is indeed true in content, and so on—in fact have nothing to do with the political "agenda" of Lipsius's *Politica*.[186] Still, Lipsius's apparent (though never explicitly stated) premise, namely, that the prince just defends whatever religion happens to be the dominant one in a state, was one that Coornhert just could not accept.

The *Trial*, as the title indicates, has the format of court procedure, with Lipsius acting as the state's prosecutor and Coornhert as the defender of the people. In accordance with Coornhert's familiar modus operandi, the relevant chapters from the *Politica* are quoted in Dutch translation, in small segments followed by copious commentary and criticism. To liven up the performance, both sides have an assistant: *Byemondt* (implied meaning: "added mouth") for Lipsius, and *Vryemondt* (meaning: "who dares to say everything," or literally "free mouth") for Coornhert. The sources quoted—and listed at the beginning—are current political and theological documents and, of course, the Bible (not included in the aforementioned listing). The absence in Coornhert's bibliography of any classical authors is telling.

As the motive for writing the *Trial,* Coornhert again states the defense of the common good by trying to combat the recurrence of persecution and religious intolerance. In doing this, he claims to be defending the essence of what the revolt against Spanish oppression was all about.[187] He defends publishing this critique in the vernacular, for thus the people themselves may "judge in this matter—because it is of importance to each and every compatriot, no less than to the government itself."[188] His objective, he assures the reader, is not to attack ad hominem, but to defend the truth.[189] There are in the *Trial* some crass accusations against Lipsius, at times certainly undeserved, but these all occur in a rational context, never as mere name-calling.

As stated, Coornhert regards the perceived mixture of civil and ecclesiastical affairs as Lipsius's crucial error. This theme of the separateness of the two realms, "as different as heaven and earth," was inspired by Coornhert's spiritualist proclivities.[190] Those who think that the secular arm needs to defend reli-

[186]Güldner, *Toleranz-Problem*, 106.
[187]Coornhert, *Proces*, fol. liiiA; elsewhere (ibid., fol. livA) he invokes the Golden Rule and public interest.
[188]Ibid., fol. liiiB.
[189]Ibid., fol. xcviiD.
[190]Ibid., fol. livD.

gion belittle or underestimate the power of Christ and of the all-powerful truth.[191] Truth needs no crutches.

Coornhert outlines the tasks of a well-functioning government as including the protection of good citizens, of its widows and orphans, the maintenance of law and order, and the meting out of correct justice and punishment for the doers of evil, but never the punishment of those who err in religious matters.[192] Since Lipsius wants to put such enormous power into the hands of princes, Coornhert repeatedly makes the point that most princes so far have been unwise, unjust, or cruel;[193] here he misunderstands the ideal or prescriptive (rather than descriptive) nature of Lipsius's manual for princes.[194]

In Coornhert's view, the limitations Lipsius wants to impose on the power of the prince with regard to religion are of little significance, because, the controversialist argues, with God and in godly matters it is all or nothing: God gave to no one beside himself power in his realm—not even to the prince.[195]

What must have really stung Lipsius and added to his feelings of discomfort in Leiden, was the barely veiled charge—already made in Coornhert's last letter to him, but now repeated several times with force—that he was on the side of the enemy (Spain), or at least that the drift of his arguments logically placed him there. The pressure on Lipsius to come out and show his true colors permeates the *Trial*.[196] In his exhortations to Lipsius to name the "one true religion" that he intends, Coornhert often cannot hide his irritation.[197] So far, he reminds his readers, the States General have not officially forbidden other faiths, but Lipsius's advice could sway them to do so.[198] With this argument, Coornhert presents a distortion of the de facto reality possibly inspired by wishful thinking. After all, Catholic and other non-Reformed public worship

---

[191]Ibid., fols. lxxiiC; cf. ibid., fol. lviB, with regard to Christ; similar passages: ibid., fols. lviD; lviiD, lviiiB, and lixB.

[192]Ibid., fols. lxD and lxviiiD. With regard to the position of the government, Coornhert emphasizes popular sovereignty: ibid., fol. lvC, and the right to rise up against an unjust ruler: ibid., fol. lxB, also fol. lxviiC. This right of the people, though not immediately relevant to the topic at hand, was, however, a sensitive issue, and it is clear that in all of Lipsius's writings on politics there is not much room for popular participation.

[193]Ibid., fols. lvCD and lixCD.

[194]See Bonger, *Leven en werk*, 147–48.

[195]Coornhert, *Proces*, fol. lviB.

[196]Cf. Güldner, *Toleranz-Problem*, 107.

[197]E.g.: "Dear man, tell us which is the one?" [i.e. the true religion]: Coornhert, "Proces," fol. lxix-a. Also: "What he [i.e. Lipsius] is God may know, perhaps he himself knows it, but I don't know": Coornhert, *Proces*, fol. lxxxivA.

[198]Coornhert, *Proces*, fol. lxxxA.

in the Dutch Republic had been forbidden for quite a few years already. Perhaps Coornhert felt that, as long as the other faiths had not been outlawed, there was still hope.

Contrary to what Lipsius wants to suggest, he continues, Inquisition and persecution are the natural consequences of his teachings.[199] The States, the Reformed, and sincere compatriots, he writes, are one and all against the king of Spain, "whose ideas in this matter [that is, of not allowing religious dissent] are identical to those of Lipsius."[200] This accusation must have been an important incentive for Lipsius to write his venomous response. His situation was extremely vulnerable. Perhaps we may compare it with that of a leading intellectual who, occupying a politically sensitive position at the height of the Cold War, comes out with a statement that it really is best that a state recognize only one ideology, but when pressed, refuses to identify which one. And Coornhert was a debater who had proven his mettle and was quite skilled at driving an opponent into a corner, especially an opponent whom he suspected of pusillanimity.

The same thinly veiled attack on Lipsius's patriotism can be seen more indirectly in the accusation that the latter "machiavellizes" in allowing princes to break pledges and to perjure themselves, and even to commit murder if the situation requires this; or when Lipsius states that, if the maintenance of one religion would plunge the state into disorder, the prince should temporarily tolerate deviants, until he feels strong enough. Coornhert states that lies and deceit are never acceptable, and is quick to draw the parallel with the duke of Alva, always presented as the Machiavellian par excellence (due to the generally accepted image of Alva's extreme cruelty and his continual breach of promises).[201] Although Lipsius has his reservations with regard to some aspects of Machiavelli's teachings, he clearly admires the Florentine's realism.[202]

---

[199]Ibid., fol. lxxviiB. Cf. Coornhert, *Brieven-boeck,* Letter no. 100, fol. cliiiiC.

[200]Ibid., fol. lxiiiiA. A sampling of similar passages: fol.s lviD, lxiiA, lxvB, lxviiD, lxviiiA, lxixB, lxxxviiiC, and lxxxixA.

[201]Ibid., fol. lxviii; fols. lxxxixB; fol. lxxiiiiC gives the example of the deceit of Don John. Cf. Oestreich, *Neostoicism,* 48.

[202]Oestreich, *Antiker Geist,* 167–68; I disagree with Oestreich, when he calls Coornhert's accusation that Lipsius "machiavellizes" and brings his princes to lie, murder, and perjure themselves, a "false slander" (167); Coornhert, *Trial,* fol. lxviiiB, cites Lipsius, where the latter approvingly paraphrases Machiavelli's contention that in times of great peril, princes may lie, murder, and deceive. The passages on Machiavelli are from bk. 4, chap. 13 and 14 of Lipsius's *Politica;* cf. also Tuck, *Philosophy and Government,* 57; Van Gelderen, "Holland und das Preussentum," 34–35.

Chapter 8

In the context of one of the many passages urging Lipsius to define "the one religion," Coornhert shows more clearly that he realizes the primacy that the state has for Lipsius, and that thus the *content* of the state religion might not really matter to him, but at the same time he states that such a position is abhorrent to him, for it would mean "that one religion is not any better than another one, and that one can attain salvation in any religion, no matter how false or idolatrous it might be. And this would be complete Libertinism, and a shoe that is made to fit any foot.[203]

Such a position implies an admission of the relativity of religious truth, and we have seen before that Coornhert rejects this position. To him, a more weighty matter than the preservation of a strong state is man's salvation and freedom of conscience. If everyone, he argues, had always obeyed the state's laws, Christianity would not have emerged. Was not Christ himself persecuted and crucified as a "disturber of the public peace" of a state?[204] Lipsius, he claims, just does not take religion seriously enough. Unity at the cost of freedom and with the risk of supporting a false religion is unacceptable.[205] In using religion as a crutch for a powerful state, Lipsius wants to abuse "the very best" [i.e. religion] to achieve the most base, namely the grandeur of earthly power.[206]

Coornhert rejects Lipsius's reliance on pagan, classical sources in an area where only scriptural evidence counts. He accuses Lipsius of using the (classical) past as a fetish. Customs are not good just because they are old, he asserts.[207] In his response, Lipsius ridicules the sources Coornhert relies upon, e.g. Albada.[208] The self-made man, who had only taken on the study of Latin relatively late in life to read patristic sources, had locked horns with the erudite scholar to whom the classics were a goal and an ideal in themselves.

As stated in the previous chapter, Coornhert overall did not regard plurality of faiths as a nuisance that had to be tolerated, but as an opportunity and challenge.[209] Using positive and negative examples from the past, Coornhert

[203]Coornhert, *Proces*, fol. lxD.
[204]Ibid., fol. lxiiiiB; fol. lxvB; fol. lxvC.
[205]Ibid., fol. lxiiC; fol. lxxC.
[206]Ibid., fol. lxiD; also fol. lxviiBC.
[207]Ibid., fols. lxiiiB, lxixA, lxixD, lxxB, and lxxxiiB. Elsewhere he accuses Lipsius of throwing together a "hodgepodge" of quotes, together forming a lethal brew: fol. lxxxB.
[208]"Nobis Albada non nisi Albada est: nec viro cedimus aut credimus, rationibus tamen si quas adfert": Lipsius, *De Una Religione*, 81.
[209]This point is somewhat overlooked by Güldner in his otherwise very thorough and complete analysis: he merely states that Coornhert did not see the presence of various religions in a country as a threat to the peace and unity of that country; see Güldner, *Toleranz-Problem*, 107.

maintains a position that is radically different from Lipsius's, since in his view it is the forcing of consciences which leads to sedition and upheavals, not the toleration of the coexistence of different sects.[210]

Coornhert's criticism of the Lipsian advice to the princes to allow the public existence of deviating creeds for a while (until peace and stability have returned), contains a revealing illustration of his positive appreciation of plurality of faiths in a state. First, he reasons, you *make* the state sick by introducing compulsion, and then you look for an appropriate medicine (i.e. toleration "for the time being"). Is it not better not to make the state sick in the first place? After all, if a postponement of persecution helps to stabilize the situation in a country, then why persecute at all?[211]

In the months succeeding the appearance of the *Trial,* Lipsius tried to resist the pressure to respond to Coornhert's public criticism. In his correspondence, he tries to portray himself in the customary way, as aloof from all the strife, a rock of constancy, unchanged by the onrushing waves of criticism, above responding in kind to the angry barbs contained in the *Trial.*[212] Although he professes, in several letters, not to desire or need a ban on Coornhert's book,[213] it becomes clear that he actually counts on such a prohibition, but he advises caution, lest people interpret this as confirmation of Coornhert's warnings of a "new Inquisition."[214]

Upon inspection, it quickly becomes clear that Lipsius's response to the *Trial,* entitled *De Una Religione adversus Dialogistam liber,*[215] which he sent to his friend Janus Dousa (first curator of Leiden University) and others on 12 October 1590, is not the promised dispassionate, cool rebuttal. Several historians have commented on this, generally denouncing the vituperations, but usually adding that Lipsius just paid Coornhert back in kind.[216] Although Coornhert comes up with some extreme accusations in the *Trial,* that is when

---

[210]Coornhert, *Proces,* fol. lviC; on fol. lxixC he states specifically that toleration must also be extended to all law-abiding Jews and Muslims, on the basis of the Golden Rule, ever-present in Coornhert's thinking; examples from history: see fols. lxiiiAB, lxiiiD, and lxxxviiiA.

[211]Ibid., fol. lxxxviiiA; fol. lxxxixD.

[212]See *ILE,* vol. 3, 90 10 00, Lipsius to the States of Holland (early October 1590: this is the letter that was printed in the *De Una Religione*); ibid., 90 10 12 D, Lipsius to Janus Dousa, Sr. (12 October 1590); ibid., 90 10 30, Lipsius to Adrianus Blijenburch (30 October 1590).

[213]Ibid., 90 09 03, Lipsius to Aerssens (secretary of the States of Holland) (3 September 1590).

[214]Ibid., 90 09 03, Lipsius to Aerssens (3 September1590).

[215]Lipsius, *De Una Religione.*

[216]Saunders, *Justus Lipsius,* 32; Oestreich, *Antiker Geist,* 178, states that Lipsius, in *De Una Religione,* is not quite convincing; Güldner, *Toleranz-Problem,* 108.

he implicitly equates Lipsius with Nero,[217] I found no instances in which he descends to the level of outright name-calling. In Lipsius's *De Una Religione,* however, Coornhert is called a loudmouth, an inept man without shame, an amateur, a pig's head, and a jackass.[218] These rather coarse, at times almost puerile-sounding, attacks seem somehow out of character for Lipsius and indicate his extreme annoyance. Perhaps Coornhert's misreading him, and his accusations that Lipsius wanted to introduce a new Inquisition, truly upset him. What must have irritated Lipsius in equal manner, however, is the way in which Coornhert had proceeded: writing his sharp critique of the *Politica* in the vernacular and thus opening the arena to the general public. Lipsius's book was meant for princes and "those who rule," and the common people should be kept out of these things.[219] It is clear that in his dispute with Coornhert, Lipsius considers himself terribly mismatched. In one outburst, provoked by the bourgeois Coornhert's questioning of his credentials, he even proudly lists his degrees and his (partially) noble and prominent lineage.[220] In connection with Coornhert's criticism of princes in general, Lipsius asks, incredulously, if then "we should subject everything to [the will of] the people?"[221] In this conviction that the "rabble" should be kept out of affairs of state, Lipsius was supported by the authorities. Thus, the magistrates of Leiden wrote, in their letter denouncing the *Trial,* that "uneducated people" *[ongeleerde mensen]* should not just feel free to criticize and slander learned people and the clergy at will.[222]

---

[217]Coornhert, *Proces*, fol. lxxxviiiC.

[218]Lipsius, *De Una Religione*, 81, 83, 88, 89. Other examples: Coornhert suffers from "amentiam": 91; he hints at Coornhert's age and possible senility: ibid.; calls him a "camelum saltantem": ibid.;"oleum perdit & impensas ... qui bovem mittit ad ceroma" (with Coornhert, of course, as the "bovem"): 94; and finally, on p. 94, he addresses Coornhert as "senior bulla dignissime"; in his letter to Aerssens, *ILE*, vol. 3, 90 09 03, he called Coornhert a tramp (*scurra*); Coornhert himself gives a more complete listing in his unfinished response: see his *Verantwoordinghe van 't Proces vanden Ketteren te dooden,* in *Wercken,* vol. 3, fol. ccclxxxCD.

[219]*ILE*, vol. 3, 90 09 03, Lipsius to Aerssens (3 September 1590); also in Lipsius, *De Una Religione,* 97.

[220]Lipsius, *De Una Religione*, 88. Oestreich, "Justus Lipsius in sua re," 297–98.

[221]"ex tua sententia subiicimus omnia plebi?" Lipsius, *De Una Religione,* 76; elsewhere, he speaks about "tuam plebeculam": ibid., 88.

[222]Becker, *Bronnen,* 101, no. 162,"Veroordeeling van Coornhert's *Proces,*" 18 October1590. In Delft, the assertiveness and temerity of a simple weaver (Joost Jacobsz) was attributed to Coornhert's influence: see Abels and Wouters, *Nieuw en ongezien,* 2:160.

In Lipsius's defense of the *Politica,* the central notion is that the prince has no rights over the church, but must prevent disorders (*turbas*).[223] Lipsius, affirming the necessity of maintaining only one religion, claims that virtually all sources agree with him on this point and that Coornhert stands alone.[224] Lipsius just cannot imagine the kind of freedom—he calls it *licentia*—that Coornhert wants to allow in a state. It has never been done before, or if it has—and in this context he tries to defuse the historical examples given by Coornhert—it was only a temporary and undesirable situation.[225] Too much freedom in religion will destroy, Lipsius asserts, the foundations of the church and confuse the people. Furthermore, public dissenters and innovators generally cannot be trusted. He gives some examples of such innovators and pseudoprophets and the harm they wrought (e.g. John of Leiden and the tragedy of Münster).[226]

In the post–1591 editions of *De Una Religione*—when Coornhert, who had pressed him, was dead, and Lipsius had safely returned to Louvain and the Mother Church—Lipsius states unequivocally that the "one Church" he had written about was the Roman Catholic Church, that great "fount of truth."[227]

In his comments on the *ure, seca,* and the punishment of deviants, Lipsius specifies the levels of punishment, showing his reasonable moderation. Only in the worst of cases, he states, should capital punishment be imposed.[228]

In the final two weeks of his life, while he was lying sick in bed, Coornhert still managed to write a partial response to *De Una Religione,* entitled *Verantwoordinghe van 't Proces van den ketteren niet te dooden* (*Defense of the Trial of Not Killing Heretics,* from now on referred to as *Defense*).[229] This document

[223]Lipsius, *De Una Religione,* 76.

[224]Ibid., 81.

[225]See Lipsius's letter to Aemilius Rosendalius, *ILE,* vol. 3 (12 July 1590). For the interpretation of current and past events/ situations in accordance with the principles of the *Politica* see Lipsius, *De Una Religione,* 80, 82–83. Lipsius's view of history is also colored by his focus on the state, using a "top-down model": Halsted, "Distance, Dissolution and Neo-Stoic Ideals," 264. A view such as Coornhert's of the Peasant War, placing responsibility for that tragedy squarely with the oppressive landlord class, is not likely to be shared by Lipsius.

[226]Lipsius, *De Una Religione,* 81.

[227]"fons veritatis," ibid., 87; at the beginning of *De Una Religione,* the censor (Henricus Cuyckius) had also made sure to state expressly that the "one religion" mentioned was the Catholic church: p. 70.

[228]Lipsius, *De Una Religione,* 93–95.

[229]Coornhert, *Verantwoordinghe van 't Proces van den ketteren niet te dooden, tegen de drie hoofdstucken des vierden boecx Iusti Lipsii, vande Politie of Burgerlijcke Regheeringhe,* in *Wercken,*

bears the mark of haste and repeats many arguments found in the *Trial*,[230] but I consider it significant for its directness—there simply was no time for the lengthy quotations and frequent tangents that reduced the effectiveness of the *Trial*—and for the emotions expressed.[231]

Coornhert, whose *Defense* shows his expectation of imminent death, cannot hide his hurt at the accusations and vituperations directed against him in Lipsius's *De Una Religione* and the defamation of his character, complaining that "certainly, love has not taught you that."[232] He sees, as the main reason why so few people dare or wish to speak out against Lipsius, the latter's position and reputation as the humanist luminary of Leiden University,[233] that bastion of knowledge that earlier Coornhert himself had stormed in vain. He assails Lipsius's perceived vanity, self-importance and elitism. Book learning, Coornhert argues, is not everything, and "learning" does not equal "wisdom": he points to the fact that Jesus and his apostles were also common, uneducated folk.[234] Coornhert regards himself as a champion of these simple people, unlearned, but endowed with common sense. He describes the Leiden scholar as a hypocrite, although he does not use the term (in this retort he still refrains from the kind of invective Lipsius had employed against him). He gives several examples of this hypocrisy, e.g. Lipsius's claim to be the most peace-loving man of Holland, whereas the advice he gives in the *Politica,* if applied, would

---

vol. 3, fols. 478–89; the title page, introduction, and epilogue describe the dire circumstances under which the response was written; shortly after Coornhert's death, in 1591, a Latin translation of the *Verantwoordinghe* was published: *Defensio processus de non occidendis haereticis, contra tria capita libri IIII Politicorum J. Lipsii: Eiusque libri adversus Dialogistam confutatio* (Gouda: Peter Simonsz. Kies, 1591; *Bibliotheca Belgica,* C 49, 704–5).

[230]Therefore, Güldner, *Toleranz-Problem*, 111, does not go into it; Bonger, *Leven en werk,* 153, calls it "repetitive" and "wordy," but also convincing and dignified.

[231]Thus, I agree with the judgment by Francine de Nave, who considers the *Defense* very important because of its brevity and lucidity: Francine de Nave, "De polemiek tussen Justus Lipsius en Dirck Volckertsz. Coornhert (1590): Hoofdoorzaak van Lipsius' vertrek uit Leiden (1591)," *De Gulden Passer* 48 (1970): 28.

[232]Coornhert, *Defense,* fol. cccclxxxA.

[233]E.g. ibid., fol. cccclxxxiB, where Coornhert refers to Leiden's condemnation of the "Trial" on 18 October 1590.

[234]Ibid., fol. cccclxxxB; also fol. cccclxxxviC. Indirectly, this concern for the fate of common people is expressed when Coornhert discusses the grades of punishment that Lipsius proposed: the first and presumably mildest punishment consists of fines; but how, Coornhert objects, can you pay when you have no money? In that case, he assumes, physical punishment will be applied anyway: fol. cccclxxxviiC.

certainly, Coornhert asserts, cause a critic like himself to be "burnt and sawn asunder."[235] Similarly, he calls Lipsius dishonest or even shallow, for hiding behind his quotations and disavowing their message, for "if you have a different opinion [i.e. than what can be found in your quotations], then why don't you write it? or do you lack the learning, artifice, and words to state your opinion in a straightforward manner?"[236]

The *Defense* also mentions efforts at mediation that had taken place. They had remained fruitless, Coornhert writes, because in Lipsius's definition "sedition" remained coupled with the introduction of changes in religion. Defined in such wise, he asks again, were not all the Dutch who had rebelled against Spain punishable?[237] This question Lipsius never answered directly until he answered it with his feet, by leaving Leiden and the rebellious Netherlands.[238] The question was of extreme importance to Coornhert, who feared that as a result of Lipsius's teachings and the zealous striving of the Reformed ministers, all that had so far been achieved during the Revolt would come to naught.[239]

The authorities in Holland overwhelmingly supported Lipsius in the months after the appearance of the "Trial." The magistrates of Delft and Dordrecht sent the *Trial* back to its author, and, as stated earlier, Leiden publicly denounced it. Finally, on 31 January 1591, the States of Holland prohibited publication of the *Trial* or other writings against Lipsius by Coornhert's supporters.[240] The chief motivation for this support for Lipsius was undoubtedly the wish to avert the humanist's feared departure from Leiden.[241] Another motive may have been that the ruling class of town magistrates—the *regenten*—understood, better perhaps than Coornhert, the emancipation, under Lipsius's scheme, of the state from any interference by theologians, and, inversely, the noninterference of the state in people's personal beliefs, as long as they showed a public acquiescence in the dominance of the Reformed religion. Finally, there is once more, as a reason for their support, the matter of personalities: on the one side was the "eminently learned and widely famous ...

---

[235]Ibid., fol. cccclxxxi.

[236]Ibid., fol. cccclxxxvD.

[237]Ibid., fols. cccclxxxii and cccclxxxviiB.

[238]Cf. Simone Zurawski, "Reflections on the Pitti Friendship Portrait of Rubens: In Praise of Lipsius and in Remembrance of Erasmus," *Sixteenth Century Journal* 23 (1992): 730.

[239]Coornhert, *Defense*, fol. cccclxxxviD.

[240]Cf. Bonger, *Leven en werk*, 150, 152.

[241]Bonger, *Leven en werk*, 150; see also Güldner, *Toleranz-Problem*, 114.

Lipsius,"[242] and on the other side Coornhert with his reputation as an argumentative, pugnacious critic. Lipsius describes his opponent as a restless man, who only wants to quarrel, and states that he is like "certain dogs that bark without any reason."[243]

Despite the support received, Lipsius left Leiden in 1591 and returned to the Catholic fold during his stay in Mainz; he finally made his triumphant reentry in Louvain on 9 August 1592.[244] The dispute with Coornhert and his supporters appears to have furnished the decisive reason for his departure,[245] but other factors played a role as well: displeasure with what he considered the lukewarm rallying to his cause by certain authorities,[246] his dislike of the ubiquitous Reformed theologians,[247] and especially, the fear (or calculation) that the North was losing the struggle with Spain.[248] In Louvain he tried his best to remove any lingering doubts the authorities might have as to his Catholicity and to accommodate the wishes of the Roman Catholic censor when Lipsius found his Politica (and other works) placed on the Index. The changes he had to make in the text of especially chapter 4 of book 4 of the *Politica* all tended to undermine what toleration had been extended to those who "sinned in private."[249] As stated earlier, Lipsius now unequivocally identified the "one religion" as the Roman Catholic faith, and claimed that, also during his Leiden years, he had always remained a loyal Catholic.

[242]The magistrates of Leiden, in their condemnation of the *Trial*, 18 October 590, in Becker, *Bronnen*, 101; cf. Saravia's description of the chasm separating the unlearned Coornhert from his illustrious opponent.

[243]*ILE*, vol. 3, 90 10 00, Lipsius to the States of Holland (early October 1590) [also in *De Una religione*]. For a similar description by one of his correspondents, see ibid., 90 10 17, Adriaan Cooper to Lipsius (17 October 1590).

[244]For his departure see Mout, "In het schip," 54–64; Saunders, *Justus Lipsius*, 34 ff., and Güldner, *Toleranz-Problem*, 115–18.

[245]See De Nave, "De Polemiek," 1–36; Van Gelderen, "Holland und das Preussentum," 52, denies this, but provides no evidence.

[246]See Bonger, *Leven en werk*, 154; even prince Maurice (Lipsius's student) bought copies of the *Trial*: see Becker, *Bronnen*, 102, n. 1; cf. *ILE*, vol. 3, 90 10 19, Lipsius to Cornelius Aerssens (October 19, 1590), stating that Maurice was for publication of the *Trial*.

[247]*ILE*, vol. 3, 90 10 31 A, Lipsius to Cornelius Aerssens (31 October 1590). It is interesting to hear this from the mouth of someone who would be forced, by Catholic censorship, to modify substantially parts of the chapters on religion in the *Politica*!

[248]Letter from Franciscus Raphelengius to Abraham Ortelius, quoted in Güldner, *Toleranz Problem*, 117; cf. Brandt, *History of the Reformation* 1, 435.

[249]Güldner, *Toleranz-Problem*, 124–25.

All these actions and claims, and his uncritical embrace of Catholic ortho-doxy (as manifested in his treatises on purported Marian miracles)[250] tar-nished Lipsius's reputation in the Dutch Republic and seemed rather spectacularly to confirm some of Coornhert's criticisms. As a result, we find very few references to Lipsius in the "pamphlet war" that accompanied the struggle between the Arminians and Gomarists during the Truce in the Dutch Republic's war with Spain (1609–19) since by appealing to Lipsius one would immediately be prone to the accusation of harboring sympathy for Rome.[251] Yet if Coornhert's criticism had been entirely correct, then it must surprise us that Lipsius's work was placed on the Index in the Southern Netherlands, where the Counter-Reformation held sway.

A final evaluation of this entire episode should probe beneath the surface of polarized and bitter debate and the assigning of blame.

In the confrontation described in the preceding pages, our two antago-nists mostly seemed to be operating on different wavelengths. Superficially, one is struck by the points that Lipsius and Coornhert seem to have had in common: insistence on a separation of church and state, avoidance of the clergy's interference with politics, the claim that the ruler was not permitted to judge religion, rejection of the Inquisition (although Coornhert questioned Lipsius's sincerity in this regard), the obligation of the government to maintain law and order, also when disorders are caused by religious quarrels.[252] Both men have been presented as carrying on the Erasmian tradition of toleration and moderation in religious matters. "It is … tempting to see Coornhert as the successor of Erasmus," writes Martin van Gelderen in *The Political Thought of the Dutch Revolt,* adding that "Coornhert fitted the pattern of Christian

---

[250]The *Diva Virgo Hallensis* (1604) and the *Diva Sichemiensis sive Aspricollis* (1605): see Kluyskens, "Justus Lipsius' levenskeuze," 35 n. 140. These uncritical accounts were mercilessly attacked by Protestants, e.g. in a 1612 broadside entitled *History of the wondrous Miracles, that happened in droves and are still happening daily within the famous Merchants' Town of Amsterdam, in a place called the House of Corrections.…* This pamphlet claims that true miracle healings occur in Amsterdam's Rasphuis, a correctional facility where the inmates were put to work, where saints "Raspinus" and "Labor" cured the afflictions of beggars and thieves through work: see Bonger, *Leven en werk,* 155. The treatment accorded to criminals in the Rasphuis was based in part on Coornhert's tract entitled *Boeventucht,* which had appeared in 1587.

[251]Cf. Güldner, *Toleranz-Problem,* 138–47; Zurawski, "Reflections," 729, 731, emphasizes the apologetic nature of the portrait and of the efforts to glorify Lipsius.

[252]See Bonger, *Leven en werk,* 147; superficially one could see a similarity *in religiosis,* since Lipsius also claimed that man had the freedom to choose the good and the ability to "fully achieve true virtuousness": see Enno van Gelder, *Two Reformations,* 319. (Van Gelder does not, however, compare Lipsius and Coornhert on this point).

humanism very well...."[253] On the other hand the circle of Lipsius also tried to create an image of their idol as a worthy and natural successor of Erasmus.[254] Yet in the heat of confrontation, these apparent similarities did not help to bring the two any closer. Lipsius left the Republic, Coornhert's *loci communes* were left unfinished, his last intellectual activity being the penning down of yet another critical tract in another bitter dispute. Why?

Primarily, we see a fundamental difference in the mental preoccupations of the two opponents. A powerful, authoritarian state was at the core of Lipsius's thinking, and his work was essentially political.[255] Lipsius wanted to place himself above the parties and factions of his day, and felt that his Neostoic philosophy and precepts based on the wisdom of the classics allowed him to do so.[256] As stated earlier, Lipsius's preoccupations did not include the particular theological coloring of his state. Unity of religion was for him merely something that the Staatsraison required.[257] Coornhert, on the other hand, reasoned from a primarily Spiritualist perspective. This perspective, to be sure, did not exclude a strong admixture of rationalism and a humanist emphasis on choice and freedom of the will, but the first foundation and bedrock of his activity was his deep-seated religious conviction, revolving around perfectibilism and the Golden Rule, and a keen awareness of the misery recently and currently wrought by compulsion in religious matters. It is important to note, once again, that during Coornhert's later years there seems to be a shift away from any preoccupation with the state side of the religious question, a side that he had still focused on in the *Justification* written for the Leiden magistrate during the Coolhaes affair. This shift, which may have been a reaction against the restrictions imposed by the authorities on his freedom of expression in religious matters, is perhaps not fundamental since the kind of state that Coornhert had envisaged all along was one that would act, first of all, as a keeper of law and order, not imposing a choice between the competing creeds nor designating one of these faiths as the official religion. But it does seem that

---

[253]Van Gelderen, *Political Thought*, 256; he qualifies this assessment by claiming that Coornhert "did not hold Erasmus in great esteem"; I doubt this: in his "Defense," Coornhert warmly praises the prince of the humanists, whose *Paraphrasis* he had recently translated. Coornhert assured his readers that Lipsius comes nowhere near Erasmus: Coornhert, "Defense," fol. ccclxxxD, where he calls Erasmus "a miracle of all of Europe ... in whose footsteps you are not able to tread."

[254]See Zurawski, "Reflections on the Pitti Friendship Portrait," 745–52.

[255]Oestreich, *Antiker Staat*, 41,128.

[256]Ibid., 147, 150; Van Gelderen, *Political Thought*, 186.

[257]Güldner, *Toleranz-Problem*, 113.

when, in 1579, he took up his pen in defense of the Leiden magistrate, and made liberal use of the argument that it was the state that had decided, back in 1572, to adopt the Reformed religion, and not vice versa, and that therefore the state should have control over church appointments, that at that time Coornhert had been much closer to Lipsius's position than he himself would probably have liked to admit.

It is, therefore, insufficient just to contrast a "very modern" Coornhert with a "conservative and traditional" Lipsius,[258] or merely to characterize Coornhert as a humanist, pure and simple: a characterization that might work in a discussion of Coornhert's interaction with the Reformed ministers and dogmas,[259] but that seems of little use in understanding his confrontation with Lipsius.

At the time, the authorities in the northern Netherlands supported Lipsius, as we have seen, in part because his statist approach suited them well. They were not too interested in the theological aspect of the question. In this regard, Lipsius, as the trailblazer of seventeenth-century absolutism, is more "immediately modern" than Coornhert. Coornhert's abhorrence of Lipsius's scheme was based, in part, on his analysis of the immediate past, a time riven by religious strife and warfare. This fear of a recurrence of Inquisition and stake in the newly liberated Netherlands—the "never again" that we for instance can also hear each year as the liberation from Nazism is commemorated—led Coornhert greatly to exaggerate the cruelties associated with Lipsius's scheme.[260] We cannot expect Coornhert to have foreseen that the situation in the Dutch Republic with regard to dissenters would in many respects be similar to the one that had existed before the Revolt, when the local authorities had often turned a blind eye to illicit religious activities (sometimes after having pocketed a bribe).[261]

Whereas Lipsius presaged seventeenth-century absolutism, Coornhert's basic premise of the absolute sanctity of the individual conscience (as long as this did not result in antisocial behavior) and his positive appreciation of

[258]As does De Nave, "De Polemiek," 2.

[259]As does Nijenhuis in his treatment of the 1582 debate between Coornhert and Saravia: Nijenhuis, "Coornhert and the Heidelberg Catechism: Moment in the Struggle between Humanism and the Reformation."

[260]This exaggeration can already be seen in the title of his refutation of Lipsius's *Politica*: "Trial of the Killing of Heretics," suggesting a severity that was certainly alien to Lipsius.

[261]See Jones, "Reformed Church," 119; on p. 122 Jones explains how the local town government would sometimes accommodate Anabaptists.

several faiths living and competing together peacefully made the latter more "modern" in the long run, even though the root of his toleration was a deeply felt religious concern that has little to do with the indifferentism and "scientific" rationalism so much more prevalent today.[262] Coornhert was not entirely blind to the priority Lipsius gave to the state, but he rejected the conformism, which he paints as severe persecution, required by the *Politica*. Thus, though it is true that both men wanted a separation of church and state,[263] only Coornhert took the most radical step and rejected, against the prevailing consensus among the elite of his day, the notion of the existence of a state-sanctified religion or a religiously sanctified state.

With regard to their personal convictions and temperament, the two men again show marked similarities, but also telling differences. Coornhert adhered to an optimistic, self-styled, Christian philosophy of man's actual, not imagined or forensic, perfectibility. He had shown affinity with, but ultimately rejected, the Family of Love, unable to accept the claims of its leaders, whom he regarded as self-appointed, false prophets.[264] Lipsius was a member of this same sect,[265] a fact which sheds further light on his attitude toward religion. The Family of Love, founded by Henry Niclaes, was indifferent to the outward forms of Christianity and allowed its members to dissimulate and conform to the dominant religion. This made it difficult for the authorities to persecute the sect, and for the same reason made it attractive to humanists, faced with the uncertainties of a fast-changing religio-political situation.[266] When Niclaes tried to set up a Familist hierarchy modeled after the Roman Catholic one, and made what some members thought were exaggerated claims regarding his own status, Barrefelt broke ranks with Niclaes. Barrefelt (alias Hiel) presented himself to his followers as no more than an example and guide.[267] Its public con-

---

[262]An interesting point, in this connection, is one made by Tuck, *Philosophy and Government*, 59, that of the two men, Lipsius was the one close to skepticism, not caring which denomination ruled, and Coornhert, the defender of toleration and so-called "Libertine," acted from his absolute religious conviction "that Christ requires toleration among his followers." On the extent and nature of Dutch "Libertinism," see Kaplan, "Remnants of the Papal Yoke." Cf. the quotation above, where Coornhert accuses Lipsius of Libertinism.

[263]Cf. Oestreich, *Neostoicism*, 63.

[264]See Bonger, *Leven en werk*, 264–70.

[265]See Mout, "Heilige Lipsius," 202; this fact was not known until 1950: see Güldner, *Toleranz-Problem*, 129 n. 462. The evidence consists of a 1608 letter from Saravia to Richard Bancroft, Archbishop of Canterbury. In his letter, Saravia draws an analogy between Hielism—as the Familist branch that followed Barrefelt was called—and Stoicism: see Hamilton, *Family of Love*, 97–98.

[266]Hamilton, *Family of Love*, 2–3.

[267]Ibid., 39, 62–63, 83ff.

formism with the prevailing cult placed Familism in the very category that Lipsius had singled out in the *Politica* as those who "sinned in private" and should be left alone by the authorities. Furthermore, the Family of Love already combined eschatological spiritualism with Neostoicism well before the publication of *De Constantia*.[268] It is understandable that Lipsius should have felt at home in this sect, as did quite a few other prominent contemporaries, such as Ortelius, Benito Arias Montano, Franciscus Raphelengius, Carolus Clusius, Andreas Masius, and Plantin, who generally sided with Barrefelt after the split.[269]

Finally, beneath the cerebral surface of this bitter exchange, we soon find a more visceral clash of personalities that should not be overlooked. Lipsius was ever-cautious, ever-fearful, vacillating, wanting to please and to accommodate as much as possible. He was evasive, preferring to come up with pretexts and obfuscations in order not to have to tell the truth, as in 1591, when he gave his health as the reason for requesting a leave of absence from Leiden University to travel to Germany.[270] A greater contrast of personalities is hardly imaginable since Coornhert was a man of strong principles and proved himself generally unwilling to compromise on them. He was far from afraid of stirring up controversy; indeed, one gets the strong impression that he enjoyed it, and although Lipsius, in *De Una Religione,* far outdid Coornhert in the use of invective, yet it was also Lipsius who had tried to meet his opponent halfway by modifying (although not substantially altering) some of his statements.[271] One can sense the desperation of Coornhert's friends, who tried to keep him from going public with his *Trial* but hit a brick wall of unwavering determination on the part of Coornhert to follow the promptings of his conscience.

·   ·   ·

[268]See Mout, "Heilige Lipsius," 203.

[269]Plantin's adherence to the sect was questioned by Paul Valkema Blouw, who maintains there simply is not enough proof: idem, "Was Plantin a member of the Family of Love? Notes on his dealings with Hendrik Niclaes," *Quaerendo* 23, no. 1 (1993): 3–23.

[270]Cf. Saunders, *Justus Lipsius*, 28; Oestreich, *Antiker Geist*, 60, states that the main flaws in his character were, that he always tried to avoid strife, that he harbored "übertriebene Menschenfurcht" and quickly submitted to the powers that be, and he notes the paradox that such a person should have been the herald of an ethics of heroism, perseverance, and constancy.

[271]Cf. Güldner, *Toleranz-Problem*, 170–72; I. Schöffer, "Coornhert," in Bonger et al., eds., *Dirck Volckertszoon Coornhert*, 15, who describes Coornhert as "sometimes aggressive in an intolerant way on behalf of toleration."

Coornhert did die "in the harness," for he was feisty and ready to enter the battlefield until the end. He addressed the ministers assembled in Gouda for the 1589 synodal meeting and challenged them to resume the debate that had been suspended in 1583. He told them that he needed to satisfy his conscience in speaking out against their errors, as much, he adds provocatively (plausibly already expecting a negative response), as they wanted to force others' conscience in order to convenience themselves.[272] He assured them of his willingness to dispute with them anyplace, anytime, with all of them together, as assembled there, or with just one person that they would designate.[273] But he warned them that if they ignored his plea, he would issue yet another publication against their errors.[274]

The biography that precedes the *Wercken* describes the end of Coornhert's long life of action as follows: "[A]fter having almost completed his translation of Erasmus's *Paraphrasis* from Latin into Dutch, he fell ill, and this illness finally resulted in his passing on 29 October 1590, at the age of sixty-eight. He was very patient during his illness, of clear mind and with solid trust in God."[275] The introduction to the *Defense,* his refutation of Lipsius's *De Una Religione,* shows that this was the last document he worked on.[276] Several people who looked after him or visited him during his final days—including Spieghel, and Cornelis Boomgaert who took care of Coornhert's literary legacy—attested to his fortitude and lucidity in order to dispel later rumors that during his illness he had fallen short of the quiet confidence in God he had described so well in his *Ethics.* One of the last people to see Coornhert, two days before his death, said that he found him seated "in his clothes at the foot of his bed, next to the hearth, supported by pillows,"[277] and reported that Coornhert said to him (despite his difficulty in speaking):

> I received my soul from God. It belongs to him. If I possessed it as if it were my own, I would be doing wrong, but if I keep it as if it is God's, I do what is right.... It is not my property, he may reject or save it as he pleases, it is not mine to complain. But God is good,

---

[272]Coornhert, *Remonstrantie D. V. Coornhert aen de Synodale vergaderinghe binnen der Goude Anno 1589,* in *Wercken,* vol. 2, fol. cccxxxviiC.

[273]Ibid., fol. cccxxxviiBC.

[274]A reference to his forthcoming *On Predestination* [*Vande Predestinatie*], *Wercken,* vol. 3, fols. clxxi–cclxxxvii.

[275]*Het leven van D. V. Coornhart,* fol. 6AB.

[276]Preface to Coornhert, *Verantwoordinghe,* fol. cccclxxxR.

[277]*Het leven van D. V. Coornhart,* fol. 6B.

He only does what is good, and He will therefore not doom his good creatures.[278]

No priest was called in to his bedside in his final hour. He was buried in the St. Janskerk in Gouda. His tombstone was recently (during the restoration of the church, 1964–80) placed under the church's stained glass window that gives an allegorical depiction of the freedom of conscience.[279] Coornhert's friend, Spieghel, composed the epitaph, which invokes Coornhert's ceaseless quest for virtue and truth.[280]

[278]Ibid.

[279]See H. A. van Dolder-de Wit, *Dirck Volkertsz. Coornhert in Gouda* (Gouda: Stichting Fonds Goudse Glazen, 1989), 5, 10.

[280]Freely translated, the epitaph reads: "Here rests/ he whose quest's/ supreme pleasure/ finest treasure/ was to pursue/ truth, virtue/ whatever toll/ taken, his pen/ still frees men/ from chains/ his remains/ here will lie/ God on high/ owns the soul." *Het leven van D. V. Coornhart,* fol. 6v.

9

EPILOGUE

I N HER HISTORICAL NOVEL on the years 1585–86 of the Dutch Revolt, Truitje Toussaint writes:

> The one [who entered] ... was a grizzled old man of a conspicuous appearance. If you had only looked at the sight of that classical head and that heavy, silvery-white beard, you could have considered his appearance patriarchal; but the distinct features of his pale and somewhat wan face did not give an impression of the supreme calm and dignified tranquillity that correspond with one's mental image of a respectable Abraham. They spoke more of sharpness and of cunning than of pious earnestness, and the thin lips of his broad mouth ... looked like they could easily turn white with anger and rage; but especially the eyes, those small, deep, lively eyes, revealed yet other things besides intelligence and acuity: It seemed as if they were sparkling with a restless pugnacity. When people of an irenic disposition discern this flame in a person's eye, they carefully stay out of his way.[1]

In the description, it is not difficult to recognize the person she portrays, even if one has not seen the portrait that she clearly had before her mind's eye as she wrote the above passage. It is a good example of how, in the appraisal of the Haarlem notary, admiration is often mixed with reservation.[2] A recent

---

[1]A. L. G. Toussaint, *De graaf van Leycester in Nederland*, 2 vols. (Amsterdam: G. T. A. Beijerinck, 1845), 2:57–58 [my translation].

[2]Another example from the older literature is Busken Huet, *Land van Rembrandt*, vol. 2, who first (53 ff.) gives a laudatory survey of Coornhert's life and works, but then (59–60) speaks in critical tones of Coornhert's ability and eagerness to antagonize everyone around him: Catholics, the followers of Joris or Niclaes, Mennonites, and of course the Reformed.

example of the same ambivalence towards this highly gifted but difficult individual can be seen in an article on Coornhert's struggle for freedom of conscience, which concludes rather disparagingly, and in my view unfairly, that Coornhert was no more than a utopian dreamer, whose anti-Reformed prejudice made him focus exclusively on what he perceived as fanatical Reformed zealots.[3] As stated in the introduction, more than with other topics, in the case of an evaluation of the mercurial Coornhert it seems difficult to approach the topic *sine ira et studio.*

Classification of the controversialist has also presented historians with problems. Through Coornhert course the collective thoughts of many previous thinkers. Israel, in his panoramic history of the Dutch Republic, repeatedly connects Coornhert with his illustrious predecessor, Erasmus.[4] He was prepared for the secretaryship of Haarlem by Erasmus's former secretary, Quirinus Talesius. He admired Erasmus's artful penmanship and put it far above his own.[5] Bonger concludes, after describing Coornhert's criticism of Erasmus's obedience to the Catholic Church, that Coornhert was not an Erasmian.[6] But Coornhert called Erasmus "the only Phoenix of all of Europe."[7] One of the last projects on which Coornhert worked was a translation of Erasmus's *Paraphrasis,* and in his dispute with Lipsius he emphatically denies Lipsius the honor of being compared with the prince of the humanists.[8] Perhaps, then, we need to

---

[3]Bergsma, "Godt alleen mach die ziele dooden': Coornhert en de godsdienstpolitiek," in Bonger et al., eds., *Dirck Volckertszoon Coornhert,* 41–43. Bergsma in fact blames Coornhert for not having foreseen that the Dutch Republic would turn out much more tolerant than he expected. This is, I feel, an objectionable application of hindsight. Arguably, the efforts of men like Orange and Coornhert strongly contributed to the tolerance that became a reality in the Republic. That tolerance was not as predictable as Bergsma assumes. In his statement on Coornhert's anti-Reformed "myopia," Bergsma overlooks that some of Coornhert's works, e.g. the "Synod," also feature moderate and pro-toleration representatives of the Reform (e.g. Duplessis-Mornay), and that all along, Coornhert had good friends who were Reformed (Boomgaert, Van der Laen), Catholic (Spieghel), etc. Cf. E. K. Grootes, "Dwars maar recht" [review of Bonger et al., eds., *Dirck Volckertszoon Coornhert*], *Literatuur* 7 (1990): 318–20, esp. p. 319].

[4]Israel, *Dutch Republic,* 97–99.

[5]Becker, *Bronnen,* 339. This was in response to a friend's complaint about the sharpness of Coornhert's pen; but Coornhert immediately adds, that truth always bites the hypocrite.

[6]Bonger, *Leven en werk,* 261. Yet, in a brief article on Coornhert's "identity," Bonger concludes that Coornhert was primarily a Christian humanist upholding a rationally based morality: Bonger, "De identiteit van D. V. Coornhert," *Rekenschap,* v 15/2 (1968): 64. How can Coornhert be such, and at the same time *not* be an Erasmian?

[7]Coornhert, *Wercken,* fol. cccclxxxviiiB.

[8]On his translation of the *Paraphrasis* (unfinished due to his controversy with Lipsius), see Becker, *Bronnen,* 247, 252. His remark to Lipsius in Coornhert, *Verantwoordingh,* in *Wercken,* vol.

qualify, and say that, sometimes, Coornhert could be an "Erasmian." But if a choice had to be made as to who was, ultimately, "more" of an Erasmian, Lipsius or Coornhert, my choice would more likely be Lipsius, whose linguistic pursuits, learning, scholarly achievements, and whose cautiousness and longing for quietude seem much more reminiscent of Erasmus than Coornhert's restless activism and self-made background.

Nijenhuis defines Coornhert as a humanist, Enno van Gelder, in *Two Reformations*, calls him a "Christian-Stoic." Benjamin Kaplan, in *Calvinists and Libertines*, ranks Coornhert with the Libertines.[9] But Coornhert himself always emphatically rejected that label and loathed Libertinism as he defined it.[10] Because Coornhert was, in essence, an individualist, any brief characterization is going to be partially off the mark.

Hans Guggisberg distinguishes, with regard to advocates of toleration, between the early-sixteenth-century type, men predominantly prompted by religious motives, and the late-sixteenth-century type, men who increasingly employed political, economic, and pragmatic arguments. Coornhert clearly belongs to the earlier type of toleration advocates.[11] Coornhert's deepest motivation is firmly rooted in his spiritualist-Christian convictions. The other elements all play a role as well: his rationalism, the influence of the classics, the tumultuous circumstances in the surfacing new state, his personality traits, even his partaking in what foreigners see as a general Dutch trait of stubborn independence.[12] But all these other elements are embedded in the gainsayer's religious preoccupations: these are so prevalent that they inevitably spill over

---

3, fol. cccclxxxD, where he speaks of "Erasmo die een wonder van gantsch Europa gheweest is, *wiens voetstappen ghy niet en vermoght te volghen…*" [my emphasis].

[9]Nijenhuis, "Coornhert and the Heidelberg Catechism"; he also characterizes him as a rationalist: ibid., 190; Enno van Gelder, *Two Reformations*, 312, sees a logical progression from Cassander, through Coornhert, to Lipsius; Kaplan, *Calvinists and Libertines*, passim; see also Petrus Johannes Blok, *History of the People of the Netherlands*, vol. 3: *The War with Spain* (1898–1912; reprinted New York: AMS Press, 1970), 191, where Blok distinguishes between the "simon pure" Calvinists (*preciezen*) and the latitudinarian Libertines, and places Coornhert with the latter.

[10]See Coornhert, *Verscheyden t' samen-spraken* no. 4, "Van't Godtwesen der Libertijnen," *Wercken*, vol. 1, fol. 442A; *Consistorie, Wercken*, vol. 1, fols. 353–65.

[11]Hans R. Guggisberg, "Wandel der Argumente für religiöse Toleranz und Glaubensfreiheit im 16. und 17. Jahrhundert," in *Zur Geschichte der Toleranz und Religionsfreiheit* (Darmstadt: Wissenschaftliche Buchgesellschaft, 1977), 466–67.

[12]Van Gelderen, "Holland und das Preussentum," 50, feels that Coornhert perfectly illustrates "das Bild des eigensinnigen Holländers.…"

from one of the longest chapters in this study, devoted to his theologico-philosophical arguments (chapter 6), into the next chapter, intended to examine his political ideas on toleration separately. Coornhert himself had difficulty separating these aspects in his thought: he calls part 1 of his *Proces,* written against Lipsius's *Politica,* "political," and calls part 2, chiefly a refutation of Beza's defense of compulsion, "ecclesiastical," but the reader does not notice much of a difference between these two parts, either with regard to subject matter, or arguments used.

Thus, Coornhert's ideas on toleration bear the unmistakable marks of the influence of earlier mystical-Spiritualist thinkers, especially Sebastian Franck. This Spiritualism can be seen in Coornhert's negative appraisal of what he calls "ceremonialism." We see it in his refusal to join any new church unless someone can prove to have received a divine calling to erect one, and in his consistent refusal to start a sect of his own or a claim to objective validity for his writings and criticisms. We even see it in his occasional use of a term such as *stilstand,* or the definition of self-proclaimed religious leaders as "teachers who run at their own initiative." But Coornhert never became an epigone. In connection with Coornhert's indebtedness to Franck, a recent article concludes that, although at times Franck undoubtedly speaks through Coornhert, the latter's personality is too strong for it to hand over its reins to anyone. And of course the subjectivity and individualism of the Franckian spirit are by their very nature incompatible with slavish imitation.[13]

This solid Spiritualist-Christian foundation also circumscribed, to an extent, Coornhert's rationalism. The rational element, often in the form of plain common sense, features frequently in his works and debates. Nijenhuis, in an assessment of Coornhert's dispute with the Reformed ministers over the Heidelberg catechism, emphasizes this rationalism on Coornhert's part. It is difficult for anyone to engage in a meaningful debate without having recourse to rational arguments: Coornhert's Reformed interlocutors were, in this respect, no different from Coornhert. In fact, one may wonder if the Reformers' realistic assessment of man's sinful nature was not *more* rational than Coornhert's optimistic belief in man's perfectibility. Similarly, in the eyes of the majority of his contemporaries, Coornhert's belief in religious pluralism— let alone his insistence that even the nonbeliever be tolerated—seemed

[13]Augustijn and Parmentier, "Sebastian Franck," 309

irrational and dangerously naive.[14] We do well to realize that Coornhert's ethical rationalism, and his moralistic concerns, were ultimately inspired by this same perfectibilism, which most of his contemporaries, and later observers, regarded as an illusion.[15]

Coornhert shared his optimism with that other optimist-against-all-odds, William of Orange, the controversialist's Reformed protector.[16] According to A. Th. van Deursen, it is mainly due to Orange's presence that his Calvinist allies were prevented from turning the Dutch Republic into a theocracy.[17] The citizens of the Dutch Republic gloried in their newly acquired freedom, and to many, Dutchmen as well as outsiders, "this celebrated 'freedom' of the Dutch Republic was based on freedom of conscience."[18] In his way, Coornhert contributed to this outcome. He pointed out inner contradictions in the viewpoints of his opponents. He was, in his day, admired for the strength of his courage, feared for the sharpness of his tongue, reviled for his relentless criticism. And, it is, in my eyes, remarkable and highly significant that he was given a platform. The authorities went out of their way to enable the gainsayer to mount his soapbox, and overall, despite intermittent censorship, he did not encounter insurmountable difficulties in having his ideas, regarded in his day as radical in the extreme, published.

•   •   •

So far, no exhaustive investigation has been attempted of Coornhert's posthumous influence.[19] The Rijnsburger Collegiants were chiefly influenced by his ideas, and perhaps he exerted indirect influence on Wesley and Methodism.[20]

---

[14]Cf. Hibben, *Gouda in Revolt*, 103, who explains the support that the liberal *vroedschap* of Gouda gave to the monopoly position of the Reformed church in the young Republic, by pointing out that the general feeling, at the time, was that to allow more than one religion in the state meant to invite chaos and anarchy.

[15]Cf. Becker, "Coornhert de 16de eeuwsche apostel," 79–81.

[16]For Orange's optimism as a central character trait, see Van Deursen, "Willem van Oranje," 127; cf. Swart, *Willem van Oranje*, 37.

[17]Van Deursen, "Willem van Oranje," 134–35.

[18]Israel, *Dutch Republic*, 3.

[19]An extensive exploration, similar to what Guggisberg did for Castellio, would be welcome: cf. Guggisberg, *Sebastian Castellio im Urteil seiner Nachwelt*.

[20]Becker, "Coornhert de 16de eeuwsche apostel," 83–84. A recent, thorough history of the Reformed church in Delft mentions Coornhert's popularity among a number of congregants: Wouters and Abels, *Nieuw en ongezien*, 1:119, 149, 242–45; 2:64;, 159–162, 166. See also, Bonger, *Leven en werk*, 199.

His influence on the Remonstrants is assumed, for he is widely seen as their forerunner.[21] Perhaps the account, given in the biography of Coornhert that precedes the *Wercken,* of how Arminius was given the task of refuting Coornhert's writings but was won over to Coornhert's viewpoint instead, is apocryphal.[22] However, the perfectibilism in Arminius's theology is unmistakable,[23] and that seems to point to Coornhert's influence. The Gomarist opponents of the Arminians seemed only too well aware of the connection, as is attested by a well-known satirical pamphlet, entitled *The Arminian Dung Cart* [*Den Arminiaenschen Dreck-waghen*]. The following lines, accompanying a drawing of the dung cart, were dedicated to Coornhert:

…There we have Volckertszoon, Secretary of the States
One of whom not many tell the tragic tale
Of how for Arminius' teachings he blazed the trail,
so that, as we call the poets Homerists
we may justly call Arminians Coornhertists.
Like a baby sucks all it needs from mother's breast
likewise from him suck they, Arminius and the rest.
…You who twist the truth, your own teaching to convey
—that of one's own free power, one may perfectly obey
God's law entire—all your quarrels shall, at best,
have as much effect as did your popish request.…[24]

[21]The first, unfinished, edition of Coornhert's *Wercken* appeared in 1612, in the midst of the Arminian conflict (*Bibliotheca Belgica*, C 148, p. 749). See also, e.g., the posthumous dedication "To the Christian reader of good will," of Coornhert's *Dolingen des Catechismi*, in *Wercken*, vol. 2, fol. cclxxiVº. The author of this dedication claims that "Gomarus accuses and casts suspicion on his fellow brethren [by saying] that they want to put their feet in Coornhert's shoes.…"

[22]*Het Leven van D.V. Coornhart*, in Wercken, vol. 1, fol. 4D.

[23]See Carl Bangs, *Arminius: A Study in the Dutch Reformation* (Nashville: Abingdon Press, 1971), 345–47.

[24]For Coornhert's request on behalf of the Catholics of Haarlem, see above, chapter 5. The above text—translated somewhat freely in order to preserve the rhyme—is my translation of part of the pamphlet, quoted in Bonger, *Leven en werk*, 200.

The Arminian Dung Cart (1618). Engraving (Museum Catharijneconvent, Utrecht, SPKK g210). Eight Remonstrants and kindred spirits are riding on a cart, including Jacobus Arminius (B), David Joris (F), and Dirk Volckertsz Coornhert (H). The cart's driver is Johannes Wtenbogaert (A). Two Jesuits (K) show him where to go. On the right are three men: the middle one represents a Reformed minister refusing to take a seat on the cart. Reprinted by permission of Museum Catharijneconvent, Utrecht.

Appendix

Dirck Volckertsz Coornhert
Spiritualist and Controversialist

1522	Birth in the Warmoesstraat, Amsterdam; son of a prosperous bourgeois family.
1539	Marries Cornelia Symonsdr (Neeltje), against parental wishes. Settles in Haarlem.
1541	Steward for the Brederodes at Vianen. Access to many heterodox works.
1546	Back in Haarlem. Earns a living as an etcher and engraver, especially collaborating with Maarten van Heemskerck.
1560	Starts a printing office with three others.
1562	Sworn in as secretary of Haarlem's town government.
1564	Appointed secretary of Haarlem's mayors. In this and following years, travels much on behalf of the town. Dutch Revolt begins, with Brederode's Petition to the regent, and the iconoclastic upheaval. Travels intensively, has frequent meetings with Orange.
1567	With Alva on his way to the Netherlands, Coornhert takes brief refuge in Cologne, Germany. Arrested after his return. Imprisoned in The Hague (September).
1568	Trial; when his case takes a turn for the worse, he once more flees to Germany. Banished at Alva's command.
1568-72	During his exile, is in touch with William of Orange, and helps raise money for the Revolt.
1572	Returns to the Netherlands and becomes secretary to the Free States Assembly of Holland. Put on death list by Beggar leader Lumey,

whose outrages against Catholics Coornhert's report, on behalf of the States, threatens to expose. Flight to Germany.

1572–76 Third German exile. He is excluded from Requesens' General Pardon. The Pacification of Ghent makes it possible to return to Haarlem.

1577 Beginning of the disputations with Reformed ministers.

1578 After an abortive debate in Delft on what constitutes a true church, in April first public debate on same topic in Academy Building in Leiden. Coornhert forbidden to write or speak out against the Reformed church.

1579 In the Coolhaes affair in Leiden, on the relationship between magistrate and Reformed church, Coornhert voices magistrate's objections in the Justification. Debate in Haarlem on original sin (February). States of Holland will treat him as "disturber of the public peace" if he should publish anything else on religion. The Unions of Utrecht and of Arras signal the breaking apart of the "seventeen Netherlands provinces."

1581 Draws up Request to Orange on behalf of a number of prominent Roman Catholics in Haarlem, asking for maintenance of their freedom of worship; destroys Request. The rebellious Netherlands issue their proclamation of independence from Spain, the Act of Abjuration. The Reformed hold a synod in Middelburg.

1582 Publishes the *Synod on the Freedom of Conscience,* his most eloquent and most cogent defense of toleration.

1583 Public disputation in The Hague on Heidelberg Catechism with professor Saravia. Interruption due to his wife's illness. Debate suspended indefinitely.

1584 Assassination of Orange in Delft. Death of Neeltje, his wife.

1585 Lacking Orange's protection, takes temporary refuge in Emden. Finishes the *Ethics, or the Art of Living Well (Zedekunst dat is Wellevenskunste).* Fall of Antwerp to Parma. Tumultuous period of Leicester's overlordship (1585-86) begins.

1588 Stays in Delft, until forced out in October. Moves to Gouda. Spanish armada destroyed.

1589 Writes his most voluminous work, *On Predestination.*

1590 Confrontation with renowned humanist scholar, Justus Lipsius, over latter's *Politica,* eliciting Coornhert's refutation, *Trial of the Killing of Heretics.* Dies on 29 October.

BIBLIOGRAPHY

Abels, P. H. A. M., and A. Ph. F. Wouters. *Nieuw en ongezien: Kerk en samenleving in de classis Delft en Delfland 1572–1621.* 2 vols. Delft: Eburon, 1994.

Acontio, Jacopo. *Satan's Stratagems.* 2 vols. Trans. Walter T. Curtis. Introd. Charles D. O'Malley. Occasional Papers, English Series no. 5, parts 1 and 2. San Francisco: California State Library, 1940.

Algemene Geschiedenis der Nederlanden. Bussum: Unieboek, 1980. Vols. 5, 6, 7.

Andel, C. P. van. *Jodenhaat & Jodenangst over meer dan twintig eeuwen antisemitisme,* 2d ed. Amersfoort: De Horstink, 1984.

Arnold, Gottfried. *Unpartheyische Kirchen- und Ketzer-historie vom Anfang des Neuen Testaments bis auf das Jahr Christi 1688.* 2 vols. Frankfurt am Main: Thomas Fritschens, 1729; repr., Hildesheim: Georg Olm Verlagsbuchhandlung, 1967. Coornhert in 2:60–66.

Augustijn, C. "Erasmus und die Juden," *Nederlands Archief voor Kerkgeschiedenis.* 60, no. 1 (1989): 22–38.

———. *Erasmus van Rotterdam.* Toronto: University of Toronto Press, 1991.

Augustijn, Cornelis, and Theo Parmentier. "Sebastian Franck in den nördlichen Niederlanden 1550 bis 1600." In Müller, ed., *Sebastian Franck (1499–1542).* Wiesbaden: Harrassowitz Verlag, 1993, 303–18.

Bainton, Roland H. *Hunted Heretic: The Life and Death of Michael Servetus 1511–1553.* Boston: Beacon Press, 1953.

———. "The Parable of the Tares as the Proof Text for Religious Liberty to the End of the Sixteenth Century." In *Church History,* vol. 1 (1932), 67–89.

———. *The Reformation of the Sixteenth Century,* 14th ed. Boston: Beacon Press, 1966.

———. "The Struggle for Religious Liberty." *Church History*: 10 (1941), 95–124.

———. *The Travail of Religious Liberty.* New York: Harper & Brothers, 1958.

Bakhuizen van den Brink, J. N., and W. F. Dankbaar. *Handboek der kerkgeschiedenis,* vol. 3: "Reformatie en Contra-reformatie." Leeuwarden: De Tille B.V., 1980.

Bangs, Carl. *Arminius: A Study in the Dutch Reformation.* Nashville: Abingdon Press, 1971.

Bayle, Pierre. *Dictionnaire historique et critique.* Geneva: Slatkine Reprints, 1969, repr. of the Paris edition of 1820–24.

Becker, Bruno, ed. *Bronnen tot de kennis van het leven en de werken van D. V. Coornhert.* Rijks geschiedkundige publicaties, Kleine Serie, 25. The Hague: Nijhoff, 1928.

Becker, Bruno. "Coornhert de 16de eeuwsche apostel der volmaakbaarheid." *Nederlandsch Archief voor Kerkgeschiedenis,* vol. 19 (1926), 59–84.

———. "'Het leven van D. V. Coornhert' und seine Verfasser: Eine Quellenkritische Untersuchung." *Bijdragen voor Vaderlandsche Geschiedenis en Oudheidkunde,* 6e reeks, vol. 2 (1925), 1–18.

Bibliography

———. "Nicolai's Inlassching over de Franckisten." *Nederlands Archief voor de Kerkgeschiedenis* 18 (1925): 286–96.

———. "De 'Theologia Deutsch' in de Nederlanden der 16e eeuw." *Nederlands Archief voor de Kerkgeschiedenis* 21 (1928): 161–90.

———, ed. *Autour de Michel Servet et de Sebastien Castellion.* Haarlem: Tjeenk Willink & Zoon, 1953.

Beemon, F. E. "The Myth of the Spanish Inquisition and the Preconditions for the Dutch Revolt." *Archiv für Reformationsgeschichte* 85 (1994): 246–64.

Bergsma, Wiebe. *Aggaeus van Albada (c. 1525–1587), schwenckfeldiaan, staatsman en strijder voor verdraagzaamheid.* Meppel: Kripps Repro, 1983.

———. "'Godt alleen mach die ziele dooden': Coornhert en de godsdienstpolitiek." In Bonger et al., eds., *Dirck Volckertszoon Coornhert,* 32–43.

Berkel, K. van. "Aggaeus de Albada en de crisis in de Opstand (1579–1587)." *Bijdragen en mededelingen betreffende de geschiedenis der Nederlanden* 96, no. 1 (1981): 1–25.

Berkvens-Stevelinck, Christiane. "Coornhert, een eigenzinnig theoloog," in Bonger et al., eds., *Dirck Volckertszoon Coornhert,* 18–31.

Bibliotheca Belgica: Bibliographie générale des Pays-Bas. Ed. Marie-Thérèse Lenger, vol. 1 (A–C). Brussels: Culture et Civilisation, 1964.

Bläschke, Lotte. "Der Toleranzgedanke bei Sebastian Franck," *Blätter für deutsche Philosophie: Zeitschrift der Deutschen Philosophischen Gesellschaft* 2, no. 1 (1928–29): 40–56.

Blok, Petrus Johannes. *History of the People of the Netherlands* 3: "The War with Spain." New York: AMS Press, 1970.

Blouw, Paul Valkema. "Was Plantin a member of the Family of Love? Notes on His Dealings with Hendrik Niclaes." *Quaerendo* 23, no. 1 (1993): 3–23.

Bodin, Jean. *Colloquium of the Seven about the Secrets of the Sublime.* Trans. and ed. M. L. D. Kuntz. Princeton, N.J.: Princeton University Press, 1975.

Bonger, Henk. *Dirck Volkertszoon Coornhert: Studie over een nuchter en vroom Nederlander.* Lochem: "De Tijdstroom," 1941.

———. "De identiteit van D. V. Coornhert." *Rekenschap* 15, no. 2 (1968): 58–66.

———. *Leven en werk van D. V. Coornhert.* Amsterdam: G. A. van Oorschot, 1978.

———. *De motivering van de godsdiensvrijheid bij Dirck Volckertszoon Coornhert.* Arnhem: Van Loghum Slaterus, 1954.

———. "Prins Willem van Oranje en Coornhert." In Bonger et al., eds., *Dirck Volckertszoon Coornhert,* 54–59.

——— et al., eds. *Dirck Volckertszoon Coornhert: Dwars maar recht.* Zutphen: De Walburg Pers, 1989.

Bonger, Henk, and A. J. Gelderblom. "Coornhert en Sebastian Franck." *De zeventiende eeuw* 12, no. 2 (1996): 321–39.

Bor, Pieter. *Oorsprongk, begin, en vervolgh der Nederlandscheoorlogen* 3. Amsterdam: 1679–84.

Bots, Hans. "Tolerantie of gecultiveerde tweedracht. Het beeld van de Nederlandse tolerantie bij buitenlanders in de zeventiende en achttiende eeuw." *Bijdragen en mededelingen betreffende de geschiedenis der Nederlanden* 107 (1992): 657–69.

Bouwsma, William J. *John Calvin: A Sixteenth Century Portrait.* Oxford: Oxford University Press, 1988.

Brands, M. C. "Het verkeerde verleden." *Bijdragen en mededelingen betreffende de geschiedenis der Nederlanden* 90, no. 2 (1975).

Brandt, Geeraert. *Historie der reformatie en andere kerkelyke geschiedenissen in en omtrent de Nederlanden* 1. Amsterdam: Jan Rieuwertsz, Hendrik en Dirk Boom, 1671–74.

———. *The History of the Reformation and Other Ecclesiastical Transactions in and about the Low-Countries* 1. London: T. Wood, 1720.

Brink, Jan ten. *Specimen historico-ethico-theologicum de Diderico Volckertsen Coornhert, Scriptore ethico.* Dissertation, Utrecht, 1860.

———. *Dirck Volckertsen Coornhert en zijn Wellevenskunst: Historisch-ethische studie.* Amsterdam, 1860.

Buisson, Ferdinand. *Sébastien Castellio, sa vie et son oeuvre (1515–1563): Étude sur les origines du protestantisme libéral français,* 2 vols. Paris, 1892.

Busken Huet, Conrad. *Het land van Rembrandt: Studiën over de Noord-Nederlandse beschaving in de zeventiende eeuw.* 5th ed. (2 vols. in 1), Haarlem: H.D. Tjeenk Willink & Zoon, n.d.

Calvin, John. *Defensio Orthodoxae Fidei (1554), Corpus Reformatorum, Ioannis Calvini Opera quae supersunt Omnia.* G. Baum, E. Cunitz, and E. Reuss, eds. 59 vols. Brunswick, 1893–1900 (from here on referred to as CR with the *Opera Calvini* volume and page numbers) 8: 453–644.

———. *Epistolae duae de rebus hoc saeculo cognitu necessariis* (1537), CR 5: 239–78.

———. *Excuse de Iehan Calvin a messieurs les Nicodemites sur la complaincte qu'ilz font de sa trop grand' rigueur* (1544), CR 6: 591–614.

———. *Institutes of the Christian Religion,* 2 vols. Ed. John T. McNeill. Trans. Ford Lewis Battles. Library of Christian Classics, vols. 20 and 21. Philadelphia: Westminster Press, 1960.

———. *Petit traicté monstrant que c'est que doit faire un homme fidèle...quand il est entre les papistes* (1543), CR 6: 540–88.

———. *Quatre sermons de M. Iehan Calvin, traictans des matieres fort utiles pour nostre temps* (1552), CR 8: 374–440.

———. *Response a un certain Holandois, lequel sous ombre de faire les Chrestiens tout spirituels, leur permet de polluer leurs corps en toutes idolatries* (1562). CR 9: 584–628.

Cameron, Euan. *The European Reformation.* Oxford: Clarendon Press, 1991.

Castellio, Sebastian. *Advice to a Desolate France.* Trans. Wouter Valkhoff. Ed. Marius F. Valkhoff. Shepherdstown, W. Va.: Patmos Press, 1975.

———. *Concerning Heretics.* Trans. R. H. Bainton. New York: Octagon, 1965.

Conley, Thomas M. *Rhetoric in the European Tradition.* New York: Longman, 1990.

Coornhert, Dirck Volckertszoon [Thierry]. *A l'Aurore des Libertés Modernes: Synode sur la Liberté de Conscience (1582).* Ed., trans., and introd. Joseph Lecler and Marius-François Valkhoff, pref. Pierre Brachin. Paris: Les Editions du Cerf, 1979.

———. *Boeventucht.* Ed. Arie-Jan Gelderblom et al. Muiderberg: Dick Coutinho, 1985.

———. "About the Constraints upon Conscience Practised in Holland. A Conversation between D. V. C. and N. V. L., 7 November 1579." *Texts concerning the Revolt of the Netherlands* 43: 191–96.

———. *De Dolinge van Ulysse: Homerus' Odysseia 1–8 in Nederlandse verzen van Dierick Volckertsz. Coornhert.* Ed. Th. Weevers. Bibliotheek der Nederlandse Letteren. Amsterdam: Elsevier, 1939.

————. *Het Roerspel en de comedies van Coornhert.* Ed. P. van der Meulen. Leidse drukken en herdrukken uitgegeven vanwege de Maatschappij der Nederlandse Letterkunde te Leiden, Kleine Reeks, 4. Leiden: E.J. Brill, 1955.

————. *Weet of rust: Proza van Coornhert,* 2d ed. Ed. H. Bonger and A. J. Gelderblom. Amsterdam: Em. Querido's Uitgeverij, 1993.

————. *Wercken,* 3 folio volumes. Amsterdam: Colom, "1630"; Becker, "'Het leven van D. V. Coornhert," p. 2 n. 1, proves that the actual date of publication was 1633.

————. *Zedekunst, dat is Wellevenskunste: vermids waarheyds kennisse vanden mensche, vande zonden ende vande dueghden, nu alder eerst beschreven int Neerlandsch.* Ed. B. Becker. Leiden: Brill, 1942.

————. *Op zoek naar het hoogste goed.* Ed. and introd. H. Bonger. Geschiedenis van de wijsbegeerte in Nederland. Baarn: Uitgeverij Ambo B.V., 1987.

Cornelisz and Donteclock. *Wederlegginghe eens boecxkens ghenaemt Proeve.* Delft: Aelbrecht Hendricxz, 1585.

Dekker, E. "Wilsvrijheid volgens Coornhert in het traditiehistorisch licht van de scholastiek: Een kleine dieptepeiling." *Nederlands Theologisch Tijdschrift* 45 (1991): 107–19.

Deursen, A. Th. van. "Staatsinstellingen in de Noordelijke Nederlanden 1579–1780." *Algemene Geschiedenis der Nederlanden* 5: 350–87.

————. Bavianen en Slijkgeuzen. *Kerk en kerkvolk ten tijde van Maurits en Oldenbarnevelt.* Assen: Van Gorcum & Comp., 1974; repr., Franeker: Van Wijnen, 1991.

————. "Willem van Oranje." In A. Th. van Deursen and H. de Schepper, *Willem van Oranje: Een strijd voor vrijheid en verdraagzaamheid.* Weesp: Fibula-Van Dishoeck, Tielt: Lannoo, 1984.

Dilthey, W. *Weltanschauung und Analyse des Menschen seit Renaissance und Reformation.* Vol. 2 of id., *Gesammelte Schriften,* 5th ed. Stuttgart: B. G. Teubner Verlagsgesellschaft; Göttingen: Vandenhoeck & Ruprecht, 1957. Coornhert on pp. 95–100.

Dolder-de Wit, H. A. van. *Dirck Volkertsz. Coornhert in Gouda.* Gouda: Stichting Fonds Goudse Glazen, 1989.

Doumergue, E. *Jean Calvin: Les Hommes et les Choses de son Temps* 6. Neuilly-sur-Seine: Editions de "la Cause," 1926.

Dufour, Alain. "La notion de liberté de conscience chez les Réformateurs." In Guggisberg et al., eds., *La liberté de conscience,* 15–20.

Duke, Alastair. "The Ambivalent Face of Calvinism in the Netherlands, 1561–1618." In *International Calvinism: 1541–1715,* ed. Menna Prestwich. Oxford: Clarendon Press, 1985, 109–34. This article was incorporated in Duke, *Reformation and Revolt,* 269–95.

————. *Reformation and Revolt in the Low Countries.* London: The Hambledon Press, 1990.

Duke, Alastair, and Rosemary L. Jones. "Towards a Reformed Polity in Holland, 1572–78," in Alastair Duke, *Reformation and Revolt,* 199–227.

Duke, A. C., and D. H. A. Kolff. "The Time of Troubles in the County of Holland, 1566–1567." *Tijdschrift voor Geschiedenis* 82 (1969): 316–37.

Eire, Carlos M. N., "Calvin and Nicodemism: A Reappraisal." *Sixteenth Century Journal* 10, no. 1 (1979): 45–69.

————. "Prelude to Sedition? Calvin's Attack on Nicodemism and Religious Compromise," in *Archiv für Reformationsgeschichte* 76 (1985): 120–45.

———. *War against the Idols: The Reformation of Worship from Erasmus to Calvin.* Cambridge: Cambridge University Press, 1986.

Erasmus. *The Colloquies of Erasmus.* Trans. Craig R. Thompson. Chicago: University of Chicago Press, 1965.

Fatio, Olivier. *Nihil Pulchrius Ordine: Contribution à l'étude de l'établissement de la discipline ecclésiastique aux Pays-Bas, ou Lambert Daneau aux Pays Bas (1581–1583).* Leiden: E.J. Brill, 1971.

Fleurkens, Anneke. "Leren met lust: Coornherts toneelspelen." In Bonger et al., eds., *Dirck Volckertszoon Coornhert,* 80–97.

———. *Stichtelijke lust: De toneelspelen van D. V. Coornhert (1522–1590) als middel tot het geven van morele instructie.* Dissertation, University of Amsterdam: Hilversum: Verloren, 1994.

Franck, Sebastian. *280 Paradoxes or Wondrous Sayings.* Trans. and introd. E.J. Furcha. Texts and Studies in Religion, vol. 26. Lewiston: Edwin Mellen Press, 1986.

———. "A Letter to John Campanus." In Williams, ed. *Spiritual and Anabaptist Writers,* 145–60.

Friedman, Jerome. *Michael Servetus: A Case Study in Total Heresy.* Travaux d'Humanisme et Renaissance 163. Geneva: Librairie Droz S.A., 1978.

———. "The Reformation Merry-Go-Round: The Servetian Glossary of Heresy," *Sixteenth Century Journal* 7 (1976): 73–80.

Fruin, R. *Tien jaren uit den Tachtigjarigen Oorlog 1588–1598.* 5th ed. The Hague: Martinus Nijhoff, 1899.

Geeraerts, D. "De dialogen van D. V. Coornhert: Een vergelijkend onderzoek." *Spiegel der Letteren* 2, no. 4 (1958): 241–55.

———. "D. V. Coornhert: Zijn comedies en samenspraken in het licht van de XVIde Eeuwse, Westeuropese Toneel- en Dialoogliteratuur." Dissertation, Gent, 1962.

Geisendorf, Paul F. *Théodore de Bèze.* Geneva: Alexandre Julien, 1967.

Gelder, H. A. Enno van. *The Two Reformations in the Sixteenth Century: A Study of the Religious Aspects and Consequences of the Renaissance and Humanism.* The Hague: Martinus Nijhoff, 1961.

Gelderen, Martin van, *The Political Thought of the Dutch Revolt 1555–1590.* Ideas in Context. Cambridge: Cambridge University Press, 1992.

———. "Holland und das Preussentum: Justus Lipsius zwischen Niederländischem Aufstand und Brandenburg-Preussischem Absolutismus." *Zeitschrift für historische Forschung* 23, no. 1, (1996): 29–56.

Geyl, Pieter. *The Revolt of the Netherlands (1555–1609).* New York: Barnes & Noble, 1958.

Gijswijt-Hofstra, Marijke, ed. *Een schijn van verdraagzaamheid: Afwijking en tolerantie in Nederland van de zestiende eeuw tot heden.* Hilversum: Verloren, 1989.

Gilson, Etienne. *Dogmatism and Tolerance.* Address to Students and Faculty at Rutgers University. Rutgers University Press, 1952, 1–14.

Goldammer, Kurt. "Friedensidee und Toleranzgedanke bei Paracelsus und den Spiritualisten: II. Franck und Weigel." *Archiv für Reformationsgeschichte* 47 (1956): 180–200.

Groenveld, S., M. E. H. N. Mout, I. Schöffer, eds. *Bestuurders en geleerden.* Festschrift for Prof. Dr. J. J. Woltjer. Amsterdam and Dieren: De Bataafsche Leeuw, 1985.

Grootes, E. K. "Dwars maar recht" (review of Bonger et al., eds., *Dirck Volckertszoon Coornhert: Dwars maar recht*), *Literatuur* 7 (1990): 318–20

Guggisberg, Hans R. "Castellio auf dem Index (1551–1596)." *Archiv für Reformationsgeschichte* 83 (1992): 112–29.

———. "The Defence of Religious Toleration and Religious Liberty in Early Modern Europe: Arguments, Pressures, and Some Consequences." *History of European Ideas* 4, no. 1 (1983), 35–50.

———. "'Ich hasse die Ketzer': Der Ketzerbegriff Sebastian Castellios und seine Situation im Basler Exil." In Silvana Seidel Menchi, ed., *Ketzerverfolgung im 16. und 17. Jahrhundert.* Wiesbaden: Otto Harrassowitz, 1992, 249–65.

———. *Sebastian Castellio im Urteil seiner Nachwelt vom Späthumanismus bis zur Aufklärung.* Basler Beiträge zur Geschichtwissenschaft 57. Basel & Stuttgart: Verlag von Helbing & Lichtenhahn, 1956.

———. " Sebastian Franck und Sebastian Castellio: Ein Diskussionsbeitrag," in Müller, ed., *Sebastian Franck (1499–1542),* 293–302.

———. "Wandel der Argumente für religiöse Toleranz und Glaubensfreiheit im 16. und 17. Jahrhundert." In *Zur Geschichte der Toleranz und Religionsfreiheit.* Darmstadt: Wissenschaftliche Buchgesellschaft, 1977, 455–81.

———, ed. *Religiöse Toleranz: Dokumente zur Geschichte einer Forderung.* Neuzeit im Aufbau: Darstellung und Dokumentation 4. Stuttgart-Bad Cannstatt, 1984.

——— et al., eds. *La liberté de conscience (XVIe–XVIIe siècles): Actes du Colloque de Mulhouse et Bâle (1989).* Geneva: Librairie Droz, 1991.

Güldner, Gerhard. *Das Toleranz-Problem in den Niederlanden im Ausgang des 16. Jahrhunderts.* Historische Studien 403. Lübeck and Hamburg: Matthiesen, 1968.

Haitsma Mulier, E. O. G. "Coornhert in de geschiedschrijving." In Bonger et al., eds., *Dirck Volckertszoon Coornhert,* 154–70.

Halsted, David. "Distance, Dissolution and Neo-Stoic Ideals: History and Self-Definition in Lipsius." In *Humanistica Lovaniensia* 40 (1991): 262–74.

Hamilton, Alastair. *The Family of Love.* Cambridge: James Clarke & Co, 1981.

Hibben, C. C. *Gouda in Revolt: Particularism and Pacifism in the Revolt of the Netherlands 1572–1588.* Utrecht: HES Publishers, 1983.

Huizinga, Johan. *Erasmus and the Age of Reformation.* Trans. G. N. Clark. Princeton, N.J.: Princeton University Press, 1984.

———. *Herfsttij der Middeleeuwen: Studie over levens- en gedachtenvormen der veertiende en vijftiende eeuw in Frankrijk en de Nederlanden,* 13th ed. Groningen: H.D. Tjeenk Willink, 1975. Transl. as: id., *The Waning of the Middle Ages: A Study of the Forms of Life, Thought, and Art in France and the Netherlands in the Fourteenth and Fifteenth Centuries.* Trans. F. Hopman (Harmondsworth: Penguin, 1990).

Israel, Jonathan I. *The Dutch Republic: Its Rise, Greatness, and Fall 1477–1806.* Oxford History of Early Modern Europe. Oxford: Clarendon Press, 1995.

Jaanus, H. J. *Hervormd Delft ten tijde van Arent Cornelisz, 1573–1605.* Amsterdam, 1950.

Jansen, H. P. H. *Middeleeuwse geschiedenis der Nederlanden,* 4th ed. Utrecht, Antwerp: Uitgeverij Het Spectrum, 1974.

Janssens, G. "Van de komst van Alva tot de Unies 1567–1579." *Algemene Geschiedenis der Nederlanden* 6: 215–43.

Jones, Rosemary. "Reformed Church and Civil authorities in the United Provinces in the late 16th and early 17th centuries, as reflected in Dutch state and municipal archives." *Journal of the Society of Archivists* 4 (1970–73): 109–23.

Jones, Rufus M. *Spiritual Reformers in the 16th and 17th Centuries.* London: MacMillan and Co., 1928.

Jong, Otto de. "Les idées du Taciturne sur la religion et la tolérance." *Réflexions sur Guillaume le Taciturne,* 87–102.

Kamen, Henry. *The Iron Century: Social Change in Europe 1550–1660.* New York: Praeger Publishers, 1972.

———. *The Rise of Toleration.* New York: McGraw-Hill, 1967.

Kaplan, Benjamin J. *Calvinists and Libertines: Confession and Community in Utrecht 1578–1620.* Oxford: Clarendon Press, 1995.

———. "'Remnants of the Papal Yoke': Apathy and Opposition in the Dutch Reformation." *Sixteenth Century Journal* 25, no. 3 (1994): 653–69.

Kluyskens, J. "Justus Lipsius' levenskeuze: Het irenisme." *Bijdragen en mededelingen betreffende de geschiedenis der Nederlanden* 88, no. 1 (1973): 19–37.

Kolakowski, Leszek. *Chrétiens sans église: La conscience religieuse et le lieu confessionnel au xviie siècle,* 2d ed. Trans. Anna Posner. Paris: Editions Gallimard, 1987.

Kooi, Christine. "Popish Impudence: The Perseverance of the Roman Catholic Faithful in Calvinist Holland, 1572–1620." *Sixteenth Century Journal* 26, no. 1 (1995): 75–86.

Kossman, E. H., and A. F. Mellink, eds., *Texts concerning the Revolt of the Netherlands.* London: Cambridge University Press, 1974.

Krahn, Cornelius. *Dutch Anabaptism: Origin, Spread, Life, and Thought.* Scottdale, Pennsylvania: Herald Press, 1981.

Kristeller, Paul Oskar. *Renaissance Thought II: Papers on Humanism and the Arts.* New York: Harper Torchbooks, 1961.

Kühn, Johannes. "Das Geschichtsproblem der Toleranz." In *Autour de Michel Servet et de Sebastien Castellion.* Ed. B. Becker. Haarlem: H. D. Tjeenk Willink, 1953, 1–28.

———. *Toleranz und Offenbarung: Eine Untersuchung der Motive und Motivformen der Toleranz im offenbarungsgläubigen Protestantismus: zugleich ein Versuch zur neueren Religion- und Geistesgeschichte.* Leipzig: Meiner, 1923.

Land, J. P. N. *De wijsbegeerte in de Nederlanden.* Ed. and trans. by C. van Vollenhoven. The Hague: Martinus Nijhoff, 1899.

Lecler, Joseph. *Toleration and the Reformation,* 2 vols. Trans. T. L. Westow. New York: Association Press; London: Longmans, 1960.

Lefebvre, Joel. "Sebastian Franck et l'idée de tolérance." *Etudes Germaniques* 14 (1959): 227–35.

Les premiers défenseurs de la liberté religieuse, 2 vols. Ed. Joseph Lecler and Marius-François Valkhoff. Paris: Les Editions du Cerf, 1969. The selections from Coornhert's writings are in vol. 2, chap. 6, 63–90.

Linde, S. van der. "Calvijn en Coornhert." *Theologia reformata* 2 (1959): 176–87.

Lindeboom, J. *Stiefkinderen van het Christendom.* The Hague, 1929. Reprint, Arnhem: Gijsbers & Van Loon, 1973.

Lipsius, Justus. *De Constantia libri duo, Qui alloquium praecipue continent in Publicis malis.* Ultima editio. Antwerp: Plantin, 1615. New Brunswick, N.J: Rutgers University Press, 1939.

Bibliography

————. *Iusti Lipsi Epistolae (ILE)*. Brussels: Koninklijke Academie voor Wetenschappen, Letteren en Schone Kunsten van België 1 (1564–83), 1978 ed. A. Gerlo, M. A. Nauwelaerts, Hendrik D. L. Vervliet; id., vol. 2 (1584–87), 1983, ed. M. A. Nauwelaerts, S[ylvia] Sué; id., vol. 3 (1588–90), 1987, ed. Sylvette Sué and Hugo Peeters.

————. *Iusti Lipsi Politicorum sive Civilis Doctrinae libri sex, 1589*. I made use of the modified 1610 edition. Antwerp: Moretus, part of the *Opera Omnia*.

————. *Six Bookes of Politickes or Civil Doctrine*. Trans. William Jones. The English Experience: its Record in Early Printed Books published in facsimile vol. 287. London: Richard Field, 1594; facsimile reprint, Amsterdam, New York: Da Capo Press, 1970.

————. *Two Bookes of Constancie*. Trans. Sir John Stradling, 1594. Repr. ed. and introd. Rudolf Kirk, notes Clayton Morris Hall.

————. *De Una Religione adversus Dialogistam liber: In quo tria Capita Libri quarti Politicorum explicantur (1590)*. Antwerp: Moretum, 1610.

Locke, John. *A Letter concerning Toleration*. Ed. and introd. James H. Tully. Indianapolis, Ind.: Hackett Publishing, 1983.

Lorentzen, Carl. *Dieryck Volkertszoon Coornhert, der Vorläufer der Remonstranten, ein Vorkämpfer der Gewissensfreiheit: Versuch einer Biographie*. Jena: Frommansche Buchdruckerei, 1886.

McGee, Julie L. *Cornelis Corneliszoon van Haarlem (1562–1638): Patrons, Friends and Dutch Humanists*. Bibliotheca Humanistica et Reformatorica, vol. 48. Nieuwkoop: De Graaf Publishers, 1991.

McLaughlin, Robert Emmet. *Caspar Schwenckfeld, Reluctant Radical: His Life to 1540*. New Haven: Yale University Press, 1986.

————. "Sebastian Franck and Caspar Schwenckfeld: Two Spiritualist Viae." In Müller, ed., *Sebastian Franck*, 71–86.

Meer, Suffridus van der. *Bijdrage tot het onderzoek naar klassieke elementen in Coornhert's Wellevenskunste*. Amsterdam: Huisman en Hanenburg, 1934.

Mellink, A. F. "Prereformatie en vroege reformatie 1517–1568." *Algemene Geschiedenis der Nederlanden* 6: 146–65.

Moorrees, F. D. J. *Dirk Volkertszoon Coornhert: Notaris te Haarlem, de Libertijn, bestrijder der Gereformeerde predikanten ten tijde van Prins Willem I: Levens- en karakterschets*. Schoonhoven: S.& W.N. van Nooten, 1887.

Morford, Mark. *Stoics and Neostoics: Rubens and the Circle of Lipsius*. Princeton, N. J.: Princeton University Press, 1991.

Mout, M. E. H. N. "Van arm vaderland tot eendrachtige republiek: De rol van politieke theorieën in de Nederlandse Opstand." *Bijdragen en mededelingen betreffende de geschiedenis der Nederlanden* 101, no. 3 (1986): 345–65.

————. "Heilige Lipsius, bid voor ons." *Tijdschrift voor Geschiedenis* 97, no. 1 (1984): 55–64.

————. "In het schip: Justus Lipsius en de Nederlandse Opstand tot 1591." In Groenveld et al., *Bestuurders en Geleerden*, 195–206.

————. "Het intellectuele milieu van Willem van Oranje." *Bijdragen en mededelingen betreffende de geschiedenis der Nederlanden* 99, no. 4 (1984): 596–625.

Mulier, E. O. G. Haitsma. "Coornhert in de geschiedschrijving." In Bonger et al., eds., *Dirck Volckertszoon Coornhert*, 154–70.

Müller, Jan-Dirk, ed. *Sebastian Franck (1499–1542)*. Wolfenbütteler Forschungen, vol. 56. Wiesbaden: Harrassowitz Verlag, 1993.

Nauta, D. "Religieuze situatie bij het begin van de strijd,1568–1579." *Algemene Geschiedenis der Nederlanden* 6: 202–14.

Nave, Francine de. "De polemiek tussen Justus Lipsius en Dirck Volckertsz. Coornhert (1590): Hoofdoorzaak van Lipsius' vertrek uit Leiden (1591)." *De Gulden Passer* 48 (1970): 1–36.

Newman, Jay. *Foundations of Religious Tolerance*. Toronto: University of Toronto Press, 1982.

Nierop, H. F. K. van. "Coornherts huwelijk: Een bijdrage tot zijn biografie." *Bijdragen en Mededelingen van het Historisch Genootschap* 106, no. 1 (1991): 33–44.

Nijenhuis, W. *Adrianus Saravia (1532–1613): Dutch Calvinist, first Reformed Defender of the English Episcopal Church Order on the Basis of the ius divinum*. Leiden: E.J. Brill, 1980.

———. "Coornhert and the Heidelberg Catechism: Moment in the Struggle between Humanism and Reformation," in id., *Ecclesia Reformata: Studies on the Reformation*, vol. 1. Kerkhistorische Bijdragen, vol. 3. Leiden: E.J. Brill, 1972, 188–206.

———. *Ecclesia Reformata: Studies on the Reformation* 2. Kerkhistorische Bijdragen 14. Leiden: E.J. Brill, 1994.

———. "Een monoloog van Dirk Volckertsz. Coornhert." *Nederlands Archief voor Kerkgeschiedenis* 60 (1980): 90–106 [critique of Bonger, *Leven en werk*].

———. "De publieke kerk veelkleurig en verdeeld, bevoorrecht en onvrij." *Algemene Geschiedenis der Nederlanden* 6: 325–43.

———. "Variations within Dutch Calvinism in the Sixteenth Century." In id., *Ecclesia Reformata*, vol. 2, 163–82.

Nugent, Donald. *Ecumenism in the Age of the Reformation: The Colloquy of Poissy*. Harvard Historical Studies, vol. 89. Cambridge: Harvard University Press, 1974.

Oestreich, Gerhard. *Antiker Geist und Moderner Staat bei Justus Lipsius (1547–1606): der Neustoizismus als politische Bewegung*. Ed. and introd. Nicolette Mout. Göttingen: Vanderhoeck & Ruprecht, 1989.

———. "Justus Lipsius in sua re." *Formen der Selbstdarstellung: Analekten zu einer Geschichte des literarischen Selbstportraits*. Festgabe für Fritz Neubert. Berlin: Duncker and Humblot, 1956, 291–311.

———. "Justus Lipsius als Universalgelehrter zwischen Renaissance und Barok." In Scheurleer and Posthumus Meyjes, eds., *Leiden University in the Seventeenth Century*, 177–201.

———. *Neostoicism and the Early Modern State*. Ed. Brigitta Oestreich and H. G. Koenigsberger. Trans. David McLintock. Cambridge: Cambridge University Press, 1982.

Overdiep, G. S. *Geschiedenis van de letterkunde der Nederlanden*, vol. 3: *De letterkunde van de Renaissance tot Roemer Visscher en zijn dochters*. Ed. F. Baur et al. Antwerp, Brussels: N. V. Standaard Boekhandel; 's-Hertogenbosch: Teulings' Uitgevers-mij., N. V., n.d. [1944], chap. 8, "D. V. Coornhert," 351–87.

Oxford Encyclopedia of the Reformation, ed. Hans J. Hillerbrand. New York: Oxford University Press, 1996.

Ozment, Steven E. *Mysticism and Dissent: Religious Ideology and Social Protest in the Sixteenth Century*. New Haven: Yale University Press, 1973.

Parker, Geoffrey. *The Dutch Revolt*. Harmondsworth: Penguin Books, 1977.

Bibliography

Pettegree, Andrew. *Emden and the Dutch Revolt: Exile and the Development of Reformed Protestantism.* Oxford: Clarendon Press, 1992.

———. "Michael Servetus and the Limits of Tolerance," in *History Today* 40 (Feb. 1990): 40–45.

Prims, Fl., ed. *Register der Commissie tot onderhoud van de Religionsvrede te Antwerpen (1579–1581).* Brussels: Paleis der Academiën, 1954.

Popkin, Richard. *The History of Scepticism: From Erasmus to Descartes.* Rev. ed. New York: Harper and Row, 1968.

Posthumus Meyjes, G. H. M. "Protestants irenisme in de 16e en eerste helft van de 17e eeuw." *Nederlands Theologisch Tijdschrift* 36 (1982): 205–22.

Réflexions sur Guillaume le Taciturne. Une série de conférences à l'Institut Néerlandais de Paris, mars 1984. The Hague: Ministerie van Onderwijs en Wetenschappen, 1984.

Rinck-Wagner, Olga. *D. V. Coornhert 1522–1572 mit besonderer Berücksichtigung seiner politischen Tätigkeit.* Ed. E. Ebering. Historische Studien, Heft 138. Berlin, 1919. Repr., Vaduz: Kraus Reprint Ltd., 1965.

Rogge, H. C. *Caspar Janszoon Coolhaes, de voorlooper van Arminius en der Remonstranten,* 2 vols. Amsterdam, 1856–58.

Rogier, L. J. *Eenheid en scheiding: Geschiedenis der Nederlanden 1477–1813.* 5th ed. Utrecht: Uitgeverij Het Spectrum, 1976.

Romein, Jan and Annie. *De lage landen bij de zee: Een geschiedenis van het Nederlandse volk.* Amsterdam: Em. Querido's Uitgeverij B. V., 1973.

Rompaey, J. van. "De Bourgondische Periode." In *De Lage Landen van prehistorie tot 1500.* Ed. R.C. van Caenegem and H. P. H. Jansen. Amsterdam/Brussels: Elsevier, 1978, 343–424.

Rutgers, F. L. *Calvijns invloed op de reformatie in de Nederlanden voor zooveel die door hemzelven is uitgeoefend.* Leiden: Donner, 1901.

Salmon, J. H. M. *Society in Crisis: France in the Sixteenth Century.* New York: St. Martin's Press, 1975.

Saunders, Eleanor. "Old Testament Subjects in the Prints of Maarten van Heemskerck: 'Als een Claere Spiegele der Tegenwoordige Tijden.'" Ph.D. diss., Yale, 1978.

Saunders, Jason Lewis. *Justus Lipsius: The Philosophy of Renaissance Stoicism.* New York: Liberal Arts Press, 1955.

Schelven, A. A. van. "De opkomst van de idee der politieke tolerantie in de 16e eeuwsche Nederlanden." In id., *Uit de strijd der geesten: Historische nasporingen.* Amsterdam: Ten Have, 1944, 9–71.

Schepper, Hugo de. *"Belgium Nostrum" 1500–1650: Over Integratie en Desintegratie van het Nederland.* Antwerp: De Orde van den Prince, 1987.

Scheurleer, Th. H. Lunsingh, and G. H. M. Posthumus Meyjes, eds. *Leiden University in the Seventeenth Century: An Exchange of Learning.* Leiden: Universitaire Pers/E.J. Brill, 1975.

Schöffer, I. "Coornhert." In Bonger et al., eds. *Dirck Volckertszoon Coornhert,* 9–17.

Schutte, G. J. "Nederland: Een calvinistische natie?" *Bijdragen en mededelingen betreffende de geschiedenis der Nederlanden* 107, no. 4 (1992): 690–702.

Scribner, Bob, et al., eds., *The Reformation in National Context.* Cambridge: Cambridge University Press, 1994.

Seeberg, D. Erich. *Gottfried Arnold: Die Wissenschaft und die Mystik seiner Zeit.* Studien zur Historiographie und zur Mystik. Meerane i/Sa: Verlag von E. R. Herzog, 1923.

Siegenbeek, Matthijs. "Over de verdiensten van Dirk Volkertszoon Coornhert als zede-schrijver." *Museum of verzameling van fraaije kunsten en wetenschappen,* vol. 2 (1813), 1–52.

Spaans, Joke. *Haarlem na de Reformatie: Stedelijke cultuur en kerkelijk leven, 1577–1620.* Hollandse Historische Reeks 11. The Hague: Stichting Hollandse Historische Reeks, 1989.

Steinmetz, David. *Calvin in Context.* Oxford: Oxford University Press, 1995.

Swart, K. W. *Willem van Oranje en de Nederlandse Opstand 1572–1584.* Ed. R. P. Fagel et al. Introduction by Alastair Duke and Jonathan I. Israel. The Hague: Sdu Uitgeverij, 1994.

Tazbir, Janusz. "Poland." In Bob Scribner et al., eds., *The Reformation in National Context.* Cambridge: Cambridge University Press, 1994, 168–80.

Tjaden, A. J. "De reconquista mislukt. De opstandige gewesten 1579–1588." In *Algemene Geschiedenis der Nederlanden* 6: 244–57.

Toussaint, A. L. G. *De graaf van Leycester in Nederland,* 2 vols. Amsterdam: G.T.A. Beijerinck, 1845.

Tracy, James D. *Holland under Habsburg Rule, 1506–1566: the Formation of a Body Politic.* Berkeley: University of California Press, 1990.

———. "Magistracy: Germany and the Low Countries," *Oxford Encyclopedia of the Reformation,* ed. Hans J. Hillerbrand. Oxford: Oxford University Press, 1996, vol. 2, 487–93.

Troeltsch, Ernst. *Die Soziallehren der christlichen Kirchen und Gruppen.* Tübingen, 1923, first ed. 1912.

———. *The Social Teaching of the Christian Churches,* 2 vols. Trans. Olive Wyon. Introd. H. Richard Niebuhr. Chicago: University of Chicago Press, 1981.

Tuck, Richard. *Philosophy and Government 1572–1651.* Ideas in Context. Cambridge: Cambridge University Press, 1993.

Veldman, Ilja M. "Coornhert en de prentkunst." In Bonger et al., eds., *Dirck Volckertszoon Coornhert,* 115–43.

———. *Leerrijke reeksen van Maarten van Heemskerck.* The Hague: Staatsuitgeverij, 1986.

———. *Maarten van Heemskerck and Dutch Humanism in the Sixteenth Century.* Trans. Michael Hoyle. Maarssen: Gary Schwartz, 1977.

———. *De Wereld tussen Goed en Kwaad: Late prenten van Coornhert.* The Hague: SDU Uitgeverij, 1990.

———, ed. *Dirck Volkertsz. Coornhert.* The Illustrated Bartsch, 55. Supplement. N. p.: Abaris Books, 1991.

Voogt, Gerrit. "Primacy of Individual Conscience or Primacy of the State? The Clash between Dirck Volckertsz. Coornhert and Justus Lipsius." *Sixteenth Century Journal* 28, no. 4 (1997): 1231–49.

Weigelt, Hans. "Sebastian Franck und die lutherische Reformation: Die Reformation im Spiegel des Werkes Sebastian Francks." In Müller, ed., *Sebastian Franck,* 39–54.

White, Robert. "Castellio against Calvin: The Turk in the Toleration Controversy of the Sixteenth Century." *Bibliothèque d'Humanisme et Renaissance* 46, no. 3 (1984): 573–86.

Wijnaendts Francken, C. J. *Vier Moralisten: Confucius–Plutarchus–Montaigne–Coornhert.* Amsterdam: Wereld bibliotheek N.V., 1946.

Bibliography

Williams, George Huntston. *The Radical Reformation,* 3d ed., Sixteenth Century Essays & Studies 15. Reprint, Kirksville, Mo.: Truman State University Press, 2000.

Williams, George Huntston, ed. *Spiritual and Anabaptist Writers: Documents Illustrative of the Radical Reformation.* Library of Christian Classics 25. Philadelphia: Westminster Press, 1957.

Woltjer, J. J. *Tussen vrijheidsstrijd en burgeroorlog: Over de Nederlandse Opstand 1555–1580.* N.p.: Uitgeverij Balans, 1994.

Woude, A. M. van der. "De crisis in de Opstand na de val van Antwerpen." *Bijdragen voor de geschiedenis der Nederlanden* 14 (1959–60): 38–56.

Wouters, A. Ph. F., and P. H. A. M. Abels. *Nieuw en ongezien: Kerk en samenleving in de classis Delft en Delfland 1572–1621,* 2 vols. Werken van de Vereniging voor Nederlandse Kerkgeschiedenis nrs. 1 and 2. Delft: Eburon, 1994.

Zijderveld, A. "Het laatste werk van prof. Kalff." *Tijdschrift voor geschiedenis* 41 (1926): 261–84.

―――. "Verwaarloosde 'Renaissance'-literatuur: Een bijdrage tot nader verstand van Coornhert en Spieghel." *Nieuw theologisch tijdschrift* 16 (1927): 125–64.

Zijlstra, Samme. "'Tgeloove is vrij': De tolerantiediscussie in de Noordelijke Nederlanden tussen 1520 en 1795." In Gijswijt-Hofstra, ed., *Een schijn van verdraagzaamheid,* 41–67.

Zurawski, Simone. "Reflections on the Pitti Friendship Portrait of Rubens: In Praise of Lipsius and in Remembrance of Erasmus." *Sixteenth Century Journal* 23, no. 4 (1992): 727–53.

INDEX

Index

Index

Index